BUYING RETAIL IS STUPID!

CHICAGO

The Discount Guide to Buying Everything at up to 80% Off Retail

TRISHA KING, DEBORAH NEWMARK,
AND BARBARA JACOBS

CB
CONTEMPORARY BOOKS

Library of Congress Cataloging-in-Publication Data

King, Trisha.
Buying retail is stupid! Chicago : the national discount guide to buying everything at up to 80% off retail / Trisha King, Deborah Newmark, and Barbara Jacobs.
p. cm.
ISBN 0-8092-3134-4
1. Shopping—Illinois—Chicago—Guidebooks. 2. Chicago (Ill.)—Guidebooks.
I. Newmark, Deborah. II. Jacobs, Barbara. III. Title.
TX336.I32C585 1998
380.1'45'0002577311—dc21 97-43829
CIP

Important notice: The authors have taken great care and made all reasonable efforts to ensure the accuracy of the information in this book. Nevertheless, there is the chance that an error may have occurred, or circumstances may have changed. Please check the information with the listed businesses before visiting them and making purchases. Advice, tips, and strategies presented in this book should be used as a guide and not be relied upon as a substitute for the reader's own experience, judgment, and common sense in buying goods and services and in making decisions. The authors, publisher, distributors, and other entities connected with this book do not assume any responsibility or liability in connection with the information contained herein or the use to which it is put.

Cover design by Scott Rattray
Interior design by Mary Lockwood

Published by Contemporary Books
A division of NTC/Contemporary Publishing Group, Inc.
4255 West Touhy Avenue, Lincolnwood (Chicago), Illinois 60646-1975 U.S.A.

Printed in the United States of America
International Standard Book Number: 0-8092-3134-4
18 17 16 15 14 13 12 11 10 9 8 7 6 5 4 3 2 1

Contents

Overview

Acknowledgments

With five editions of our bestselling book *Buying Retail Is Stupid!—Southern California* on the market, we were seeking new challenges and considering expanding to new cities. So, when Contemporary Books offered us the opportunity to do a discount shopping guide for the great city of Chicago, we were ready and eager. However, it was clear that we would need a coauthor who is a Chicago resident, a good writer, and an expert discount shopper—someone who knows the ins and outs of Chicago's discount outlets.

When we first contacted Barbara Jacobs, we knew we had found the right person for the right job at the right time. Much appreciation goes to Barbara for a job well done.

Many thanks also to Kara Leverte of Contemporary Books, who first saw the possibilities of the project and got us off to a good start; and to Susan Schwartz, also of Contemporary Books, who put all the pieces together and guided the project to a successful conclusion.

Special thanks to our agent, Stan Corwin, whose confidence in our vision brought the project to fruition and also for his ongoing advice and encouragement.

And finally, a special thanks to all of the individuals mentioned by Barbara Jacobs who were important to the completion of the Chicago edition.

Trisha King
Deborah Newmark

Innocence is bliss.

That's the way we felt when approached by Susan Schwartz, senior editor of Contemporary Books, about coauthoring the Chicago version of *Buying Retail Is Stupid!* "A piece of cake," we reasoned. "First, we write professionally as part of our day job. And second, retailing coupled with bargain shopping is in our blood. No problem!"

Boy, were we wrong!

On the other hand, we learned to rely very heavily on the kindnesses of both friends and strangers. Herewith, our list of thanks, in no particular order:

- To Susan Schwartz, for putting up beautifully with first-author willies;
- To Gerilee Hundt and the other folks at NTC/Contemporary for not wincing about our stupid-computer-trick calls;
- To Trisha, Deborah, and Jerry Newmark, none of whom questioned our "deal worthy" knowledge of Chicago;
- To Mary Carroll, who cheerfully designed and explained the workings of a relational database just for a technodolt—and then translated it all into word processing again;
- To Jean Cardwell, aka Gloria Levinson, who eagerly accompanied us on our forays in the little-known highways and byways of the city and beyond;
- To Lisa Zaroogian and Stephanie Anderson, for inputting and outputting, dialing and recording, and reading our mind with the most positive of attitudes and gung-ho enthusiasm;
- To Randi Killian, Melitta Budler, and other friends who never tired of providing psychic (and other) support;
- To the countless local retailers who actually got excited about the book concept—and participated;
- And to innumerable clients, colleagues, and friends who always queried with a smile, "Well, you're almost done, aren't you?!"

Finally, to my help- and heart-mate, Rick Robins, who endured months of "book chats" while providing the absolute best store information and emotional backup a budding author could ask for.

And if we've inadvertently omitted any retailer, or missed saying thanks to all who helped, our apologies.

Barbara Jacobs

Preface

It is with great pleasure that we present to the shopping public of Chicago this first edition of *Buying Retail Is Stupid!—Chicago*. Just as our Los Angeles version, a bestseller since 1987 and now in its fifth edition, has proved to be a valuable resource to economy-minded Southern Californians, we know the Chicago guide will fulfill the same high expectations.

Bargain hunting has always been one of America's favorite pastimes; however, in the '90s, it has become a way of life. Just look at the tremendous increase nationwide of discount businesses! Since consumers throughout the United States are seeking ways to stretch their hard-earned dollars and get the best value for everything they buy, we decided it was time to expand to other cities.

As we questioned shoppers, it became clear that Chicago consumers are eager for a tool that can help them spend less and get more value for their money. We trust that this book will be a welcome and valuable resource for the cost-conscious, value-seeking Chicago public. Savings on one purchase alone could more than pay for the price of the book, and when it's used consistently as a regular shopping companion, the consumer can save hundreds of dollars each year. The discount coupon section is a bonus for saving additional hundreds of dollars.

Buying Retail Is Stupid!—Chicago is the most complete guide of its kind on where and how to buy everything at up to 80% off retail. Years of discount shopping and research have enabled us to locate new and exciting discount opportunities, enriched by descriptions and stories from individuals about their favorite discount outlets.

As a purchaser of *Buying Retail Is Stupid!*, you now have an excellent tool to save time, money, and energy—adding fun, pleasure, and convenience to your shopping experience.

We welcome your comments and suggestions that will help us improve and continue to serve all consumers who want to find the right product, at the right price, with the greatest ease. Thank you for supporting our efforts.

We wish you happy shopping and happy savings!

Trisha King
Deborah Newmark
Barbara Jacobs

Introduction

How to Get the Most Out of This Book

Welcome to *Buying Retail Is Stupid!—Chicago*, the tristate area's discount shopping guide. In these pages, we've compiled the most comprehensive resources available for educating yourself to become a smart shopper and for identifying the most cost-effective places to shop. We describe where and how to buy everything and anything—from A to Z—at up to 80% off the retail price. This is not a book that you are going to read in large segments, like a novel. It is a reference book, a manual, a guide—one that you will refer to frequently. Since everyone shops for something—daily, weekly, monthly, throughout the year—the more you use the book, the more money you will save, and the more efficient and pleasurable your shopping experience will be. The following information should make it easier for you to use this book to best advantage.

First Steps

Given the wealth of information in this book, initially you will want to familiarize yourself with its contents. We suggest you proceed as follows:

- Review the Contents. This will give you a feel for the overall book.
- Skim Chapter 1, "Smart Shopping," for a quick overview of some of the basic principles, strategies, and approaches to value-oriented, economy-minded shopping.

- Skim Chapter 2, "Grassroots Bargain Outlets," for an overview of how to get great buys and avoid pitfalls when shopping for bargains at garage sales, resale stores, thrift shops, and flea markets.
- Read the brief introduction to Chapter 3, "Directory of Discount Stores and Outlets," to learn what's in each of the four sections and when and how best to use each one.

  Chapter 3 describes more than 500 stores in Chicagoland that offer big shopping savings you can enjoy. Every entry includes names, addresses, telephone numbers, products sold, and amount of discounts offered. Also discussed are tips on how to apply the information in the chapter.
- Review Chapter 4, "Directory of Consumer Resources," which introduces you to over 35 publications that can serve as your personal adviser on buying any item on the market with confidence regarding price and value. The chapter includes publications that specialize in items such as automobiles, appliances, homes, clothing, and much more. Many of these publications are free.
- Review briefly the Indexes at the back of the book to get an idea of how to locate anything you want quickly and easily.
- Skim through the Glossary of Discount Terms on page xviii to familiarize yourself with discount terminology used throughout this book.

Ongoing Actions

After completing the initial steps just mentioned, you'll have a good idea of the contents of this book. The following are ways to use it on an ongoing basis, at your own speed, and within your own time schedule and needs:

- Write or call for the free publications in Chapter 4 and start your own bargain hunter's reference library.
- Before purchasing a high-priced product, check Chapter 4 for publications that might help you become more knowledgeable. You can consult the publication in a public library. In some cases you may want to purchase it—especially if the cost is very low and/or you expect to get much use out of it.
- Reread Chapter 1 on smart shopping. This time, make notes on

the most important strategies, ideas, and tips that you will want to incorporate into your daily, weekly, monthly, or yearly shopping routine. Keep them on 3 × 5 cards or use any other system that makes them easily accessible at the appropriate time. This may include reviewing them from time to time.

- Before buying from any of the major discount alternatives—especially when you expect to make a substantial dollar expenditure—reread the introduction to the appropriate chapter to increase the probability of getting the most for your money.
- Things change—some stores may have changed locations or gone out of business. Always call and check on availability of products and location of stores before your shopping trip.

Bonus Discount Coupons

The last section of *Buying Retail Is Stupid!—Chicago* contains more than a hundred discount coupons. These coupons represent, for the most part, additional percentage or dollar discounts on the products sold by participating stores and outlets described in Chapter 3, "Directory of Discount Stores and Outlets." Using these extra-bonus coupons—available exclusively to *Buying Retail Is Stupid!—Chicago* purchasers—can save you a considerable amount of additional money yearly. Before making a purchase, check the Index listing all companies offering these discount coupons and the store descriptions in Chapter 3. Remember to take the coupon with you when visiting the store.

Senior Discounts

More than 50 discount stores and outlets in Chapter 3 offer special senior discounts. These discounts are obtained merely by showing proof of age. The specific age differs for each store and is indicated in the description. Some stores accept the bonus discount coupon in addition to the senior discount; others do not. The store description indicates how to use the discount(s).

Glossary of Discount Terms

The following are some of the terms most commonly used in connection with discount shopping:

Auction: A public sale where goods are sold to the highest bidders.

Auctioneer: A person who conducts sales by means of an auction.

Bankrupt Stock: When a business goes bankrupt, the stock on hand is sold in lots at lower than wholesale or manufacturer's prices to pay off creditors.

Closeouts: Usually odds and ends or last season's merchandise sold at discounted prices to make room for new inventory.

Cost: Either the price incurred manufacturing an item or the wholesale price a business pays for items to be resold.

Cost Plus: The cost of an item to the dealer plus his or her percentage of profit. When calculating cost, a dealer is likely to include operating expenses—shipping, rent, advertising, and so forth—and then add an override.

Coupons: Specified discounts or rebates on forms redeemable in person or by mail.

Department Store Outlet (also called clearance center or off-price outlet): Merchandise from all company stores brought together in one location (in either a separate facility or a designated area of one of the company's larger stores) to be sold at reduced prices. Includes nonselling items, seconds, slightly damaged goods, returns, floor models, previous seasons' merchandise, demonstration models, and mismatched goods.

Discontinued or Manufacturer's Closeout: A product that has been discontinued and is sold at a discount to make room for current goods. Quality of the merchandise is not affected.

Discount: A percentage or dollar amount reduced from the manufacturer's suggested retail price.

Discount Business: One that sells merchandise regularly at a percentage or dollar amount below the manufacturer's suggested retail price.

Discount Clearance Center (also called outlet or off-price outlet): A special center or outlet that sells products from retail chain stores at discounted prices (see Department Store Outlet).

Discount Mail-Order Company: A company that sells products at discount prices to customers who order through catalogs by mail, telephone, or fax.

Discount Retail Chain Store (also called off-price store): A discount store that sells directly to consumers and has multiple locations—sometimes throughout a city, but also statewide or nationally; includes general-merchandise and specialty stores.

Flea Market: Groups of vendors in individually rented areas. Low overhead usually means lower markups or below-retail prices on new and used merchandise. Sellers will often negotiate price.

Floor Sample: A model used for display in a store.

Freight Damage: Items that are broken, burned, chipped, marred, or otherwise affected during shipment. The merchandise may be noticeably damaged, but often it is in top condition.

Garage Sale: Accumulated unwanted "stuff" people sell at very low prices either individually or through organized neighborhood groups in residential areas. Sometimes excellent buys are available.

In-Season Buying: Most retailers buy merchandise months in advance (e.g., summer items are purchased in winter). Discounters often purchase goods during the season (e.g., winter items are bought in winter), relieving the manufacturer of goods from canceled orders or overruns.

Inventory Reduction: A big sale to improve cash flow rapidly and make room for new merchandise. Also, reduced stock means fewer person-hours will be needed to take inventory.

Irregular: Merchandise with minor imperfections that are often barely discernible.

Job Lot: Miscellaneous goods gathered for sale as one quantity.

Jobber: A person who buys or imports quantity goods from manufacturers and then sells the merchandise to dealers.

Liquidated Stock: Stock sold by the lot at less than wholesale prices to convert assets into quick cash.

Loss Leader: An item purposely priced low to attract customers into the store.

Manufacturer's Outlet: A store containing a single manufacturer's products at discounted prices. The merchandise may include discontinued lines, unsold merchandise, overruns, irregulars, seconds, and sometimes new lines made specifically for the outlet.

Manufacturer's Outlet Center: A number of outlet stores together in one location.

Megastore: Generic term used to describe warehouse stores, superstores, and membership clubs similar in their extremely large facility size and the quantity and variety of name-brand and private-label products offered at substantially discounted prices—either within a special product category (office supplies, home building) or in a general merchandise store offering just about everything.

Membership Club: Warehouse stores, superstores, and other businesses that require a small annual membership fee (sometimes for a specific category of customers—e.g., government employees, teachers, businesses).

Odd Lot: A small quantity of unsold merchandise that remains after orders have been filled at the wholesale level.

Off-Price Chain Store: A store that sells name-brand and other products at discounted prices and has multiple locations on a national, state, or city level.

Overrun: An excess of quantity over the actual amount the manufacturer wanted to produce.

Past-Season or Last-Season Goods: Items left over from a previous season.

Rebate: A refund, usually a certain dollar amount, offered from the manufacturer when you purchase one of its products.

Resale Store: Generally, a store that sells used clothing. Some also sell used furniture, decorative accessories, and miscellaneous items. Quality varies from store to store. Some stores carry only certain brands; others carry anything and everything. Goods in most stores are sold on consignment. Some items may be brand-name products that are like new—that is, used once or not at all.

Retail: The selling of goods directly to the customer or end user, generally at or close to the manufacturer's suggested price.

Sample: An item used by a salesperson or manufacturer to show to prospective buyers, but not for sale itself.

Second: An item with either cosmetic or functional flaws.

Suggested Retail Price: The price the manufacturer recommends the retailer charge the consumer.

Surplus or Overstock: A quantity in excess of what is needed by a dealer or manufacturer.

Thrift Store: A store that carries secondhand items that are resold at very low prices.

Warehouse Store: A very large—50,000-to-100,000-square-foot range—department store–type business selling almost every product on the market, in a no-frills, self-service atmosphere, including name-brand and private-label items, frequently in quantity packages at discount prices.

Wholesale Price: The actual cost of an item to the retailer.

Wanted: Feedback from Readers

We want to hear from *you*! If you know of any great discount businesses not already included in this book, please send us names, addresses, and telephone numbers. We'd like to include them in future editions of *Buying Retail Is Stupid!—Chicago*. If you have any comments about any of the businesses listed in this book, we'd like to hear those too. This book is for *you*. Please write to us at *Buying Retail Is Stupid!—Chicago*, P.O. Box 872, Tarzana, CA 91357.

How to Be Included in the Next Edition

All businesses are included in this book at the sole discretion of the authors. No fees are required or accepted. If you operate a discount or off-price business within the Chicago area and wish to be included in the next edition, either write to us for a questionnaire or send us the details of your business following the format in this edition. Address correspondence to: *Buying Retail Is Stupid!—Chicago*, P.O. Box 872, Tarzana, CA 91357.

Legend: Symbols Used in This Book

ADDITIONAL LOCATIONS

Whenever any of the listed stores has from one to five other locations in the Chicago area, the towns/cities, addresses, and telephone numbers have been included following the store's description. When any store has six or more additional locations, only the number of locations is indicated. In such cases, please consult your local telephone directory for a store located near you. Note that store hours may vary from location to location, so be sure to check for hours open.

CREDIT CARD ABBREVIATIONS

AE = American Express

DIN = Diners Club

DISC = Discover

MC = MasterCard

NOV = Novus

OPT = Optima

V = Visa

Other forms of payment are also listed if a vendor doesn't accept credit cards.

STORES ACCEPTING COUPONS

Stores that accept *Buying Retail Is Stupid!—Chicago* discount coupons are designated by a star [★] placed at the end of the store name in the store directory chapter, and in the Index.

STORES OFFERING SENIOR DISCOUNTS

Stores offering senior discounts are designated by a diamond [◆] in the text and Index.

1

Smart Shopping

Strategies for Saving Money and Time

Smart shopping enables a consumer to make wise decisions, spend less, and buy more with greater ease, convenience, and confidence in having received true value for every dollar spent. It involves formulating an approach to shopping and following it. The information in this book is designed to help all consumers become smart shoppers.

Goals

The goals of a smart shopper include the following:

- Saving money. Getting good buys by obtaining merchandise or services at the most favorable prices—below full retail.
- Conserving time and energy. Locating discount opportunities close to home; traveling only for multiple purchases, higher-ticket items, or special products.
- Getting value for your money. The quality of a product must be consistent with, or even better than, what might be expected for the price you are paying. Cheaper is not a better value if the lower-priced "bargain" product lasts only half as long as it should or doesn't work well. Buying for value includes avoiding rip-offs by knowing what you are getting.

Misconceptions About Discount Shopping

You might wonder how discounters can compete with the buying power of large retail operations such as department stores or supermarket chains. The answer involves a combination of factors: high sales volume, which makes up for low profit margins; low overhead achieved by the absence of large corporate staffs and executive salaries; limited or no advertising; fewer personnel; less expensive locations; and no-frills offices. The buying approach of a discount operation is also different; it is flexible and unrestricted by established procedures, formulas, or traditions. This allows discounters to take advantage of opportunities to buy any product at any time of year. Finally, management is often closer to the operation and can keep expenses down by paying closer attention to details.

Here are some of the truths behind misconceptions surrounding discount shopping.

ISSUE 1: QUANTITY AND LOCATION

Myth: Discount stores are few in number and are usually located in out-of-the-way, hard-to-find locations.

Truth: In larger cities such as Chicago, the opposite is true. There is an incredibly large number of discount entities, and they are *everywhere*—downtown areas, suburbs, main streets, back streets, exclusive areas, industrial parks, malls, small shopping centers, and manufacturer outlet parks.

ISSUE 2: SIZE AND TYPE

Myth: Discount stores are generally mom-and-pop operations.

Truth: On the contrary, a tremendous variety exists in the discount field, including small single-owner, one-item specialty stores; large specialty stores (of almost every kind—books, plants, clothes, food); small and large department stores selling just about everything; local and national chain stores; resale stores; manufacturer's outlets;

membership warehouse companies; plus hundreds of mail-order discount catalog businesses throughout the country.

ISSUE 3: QUALITY

Myth: Discount stores carry products of inferior quality—seconds or "knockoffs" of name-brand goods.

Truth: Almost every top-quality and name-brand product can be purchased at discounts from 20% to 80%. Some stores do carry seconds or slightly damaged goods, but these are usually marked. The buyer does, however, have to be careful of the occasional unscrupulous discounter who would attempt to pass these items off as first quality.

ISSUE 4: SERVICE AND ATMOSPHERE

Myth: When buying discount, you have to give up service as well as atmosphere.

Truth: In many of the larger operations, such as membership warehouse stores, staffs are smaller, and you'll do more waiting on yourself. But take a moment to consider just how much attention you get in the typical retail department store these days. The decor in discount stores is often simple or barren. On the other hand, there are numerous discount stores where you will be waited on by the owners themselves or some dedicated employees. And, many of them will be in beautiful settings where coffee, soft drinks, and snacks are served.

ISSUE 5: SELECTION

Myth: Limited selection is available when buying discount.

Truth: Almost everything produced, from A to Z, can be bought at a discount. The same is true for a considerable number of services. In large specialty stores that carry a wide selection in a single product category, you are more likely to find the size, color, and style you want than you would at a typical department store.

Issue 6: Convenience

Myth: To buy discount, you have to give up convenience and travel long distances to seek out stores that don't advertise.

Truth: With books such as *Buying Retail Is Stupid!—Chicago* and weekly bargain columns such as the one King and Newmark write for the *Daily News* in Los Angeles, the work has been done for you. They make it easy for you to find what you want at the right price. And frequently you can find discount stores in the vicinity of your home or workplace. In addition, given the large number of discount mail-order companies, sometimes you don't even have to leave home to get a bargain.

Issue 7: Bargain Integrity

Myth: All merchandise marked "sale," "reduced," "regularly $250 now $62.50," or "savings up to" constitutes a true bargain.

Truth: "Savings up to 80%" may refer to only one item in the store, with the rest at 5% or 10% off retail. "Reduced" may refer to a price excessively marked up originally and then discounted. "Regularly" may mean a price that is listed for only a brief period of time; otherwise, it's always on sale. These are the practices of some less-than-honest merchants. By knowing what items are selling for at other stores, you can avoid being fooled.

The Elements of Smart Shopping

Remember That Time Is Money

Do you ever find yourself wishing that there were more hours in the day? The old adage "time is money" has never been more important. Let's review some simple ways to save time and money when it comes to shopping:

- Call ahead. After you've decided on a particular model of any given product, call the store to make certain they have it in stock. If they do, ask the clerk to put it on hold for you. The few minutes it takes to call can save you the round-trip drive to the store, including gas and wear and tear on your car—as well as your psyche—when you find out the item is not there.

- Check out the merchandise before you purchase it. Regardless of what you are buying, look it over, plug it in, try it out. Don't wait until you get home. Returning items is not only a waste of travel time but also includes the red tape of the store's return or exchange policy.

Start Your Own Gift Shop

Every year millions of Americans are faced with the problem or pleasure (depending on your point of view) of spending their hard-earned dollars on gifts for all sorts of occasions: birthdays; anniversaries; graduations; confirmations and bar mitzvahs; and holidays such as Christmas and Hanukkah, Mother's Day, Father's Day, Valentine's Day, and Secretary's Day.

Many people frequently find themselves looking for a present at the last minute. Usually they feel rushed and wind up paying more than they had planned and sometimes not being especially satisfied with their choices. There is a way to deal with this that saves both money and time, and actually is a lot of fun. At any time during the year, if you find a great bargain that could possibly be a gift for someone, buy it—even if you don't have any particular person in mind at the time. In other words, create your own gift shop. When an occasion arises for which you need a gift, the first place you'll look will be in your own shop.

- Having your own gift shop is really a lot of fun. You would be amazed at the great gifts you can get for $5, $10, and $20. And you'll almost never find yourself rushing around at the last minute looking for a present.
- Buy greeting cards and wrapping paper at one time. When you make a special trip to the store to buy a card and/or wrapping paper, you probably are using an average of about one hour per occasion. Since you generally celebrate birthdays and anniversaries with the same friends and relatives every year, why not buy these items all at once? The savings in both time and gas can really add up.

Take Advantage of Free Advice

In decision making it's important to distinguish between low-risk and high-risk decisions. In shopping it's important to do the same for low-priced and high-priced purchases. Low-priced items do not require or merit as much thought and consideration as high-ticket items. For these more important purchases, it is worthwhile to consult one or more of the resource books listed in Chapter 4, "Directory of Consumer Resources." You might also consult a friend who may know something about the item, or check the phone book to locate a specialist. One or two calls may enable you to shop for your bargain with confidence.

Research Items

- Check your local library for the *Consumer Reports* rating of high-priced products in which you are interested.
- Use books such as the Better Business Bureau's *A to Z Buying Guide,* by Ralph Nader, and *The Frugal Shopper*, by Wesley J. Smith, to check for features to look for and pitfalls to avoid. These books and others are described in Chapter 4.

Comparison Shop for Availability and Price

- Call retail stores to find out their prices; also consult newspaper ads.
- Check the Yellow Pages for the nearest locations of discount stores that are likely to carry the item.
- Check the Contents of this book for possible sources for the item.
- Call discount stores to check on availability of items and prices. Some discount stores will not give a price over the phone; however, if you specify a price, they will usually tell you if they can beat it.
- Compare the store's price with the prices of discount mail-order companies.

COMPARISON SHOP FOR FAVORABLE STORE POLICIES

- Ask if the store guarantees the lowest price and what proof is required to verify the offer you've received.
- Check on the return policy.
- Check on whether the item is in stock and the quantity available before going to the store.
- If the item is in short supply, ask to have it held for you.

ESTABLISH PERSONAL RELATIONSHIPS

- Select your favorite store(s) and shop there regularly.
- Establish a relationship with a particular salesperson and/or manager. That person will level with you and give you useful information, advice, and personal attention.
- Have the store notify you when it has a special sale and when items or brands of interest to you arrive.

PLAN YOUR BUYS

- Identify discount stores that are located near each other, such as a cluster of stores or an outlet mall; this way you can visit several on one trip.
- Find out the best time to buy certain items—for example, the January white sales that are mentioned in the "Seasonal Shopping" section later in this chapter. Unless there is an urgent need, wait for the best time to buy.
- Buy only what you need—avoid buying a bargain item if you don't need it, unless it is for your own gift shop, as mentioned earlier.

TALK SHOPPING

Talk smart shopping with your friends and acquaintances. At one time it was considered tasteless to mention prices or bargains, but in the '90s—called the "Bargain Hunting" decade by *USA Today*—it is very "in" to talk about a terrific buy or a discount store you discovered. You'll be pleasantly surprised at how many good ideas you can get from talking with others. There's a wealth of information within yourself and your circle of friends. Something you take for granted might be unknown to someone else and vice versa. When you share an idea, a lead, or your latest bargain with someone, you'll probably get one or more back. Make smart shopping a habit; begin by making it a topic of conversation. And last but not least, have fun in the process.

Seasonal Shopping

Retailers make their money on the wants and needs of their customers. Have you ever noticed how many different kinds of fans are for sale during hot weather? Go to the same store in the dead of winter and there is a much smaller selection, but that's the time to buy if you want bargain prices. During the sweltering summer heat, a company that specializes in air conditioning is going to be in demand and therefore, in most cases, has no problem getting full retail for an air-conditioning unit.

All retailers have months when they can sell at full retail and months when they must drop their prices to make sales. Sometimes common sense tells us when certain goods are likely to go on sale. It's no surprise that Christmas cards, wrapping paper, and ribbons go on sale after Christmas and continue on sale during the month of January. But why appliances and linens go on sale during that month is not clear. Fortunately, we do not have to understand the underlying reasons to take advantage of these off-season sales.

According to major retailers, shopping for in-season clothing (bathing suits in July) means you are actually buying off-season clothing because in July retailers are featuring fall clothes. We know this doesn't seem to make sense, but this is the formula for shopping in retail stores, because production schedules require retailers to buy two seasons in advance. In August, stores are ordering goods for January.

A retailer must clear the shelves of goods toward the end of every season to make room for the coming season. The closer the next season is, the better the sale prices become on the current merchandise. You can save money by planning ahead and buying certain products off-season. Here are some things to keep in mind:

- Best buys when the weather starts to warm up: winter clothing, winter sporting goods such as skis and ice skates, heating systems, beds, and toys. People tend to spend more time outside during warm weather, so household goods such as china and furniture generally go on sale at this time.
- Best buys when the weather starts to cool down: warm-weather clothing, bicycles, gardening tools, and outdoor sporting goods. At the end of the outdoor entertaining season, Labor Day sales feature outdoor grills and patio furniture. Wait until after the holiday to make your purchases—that is the time when prices will hit rock bottom.
- Retailers usually drop their prices 50% the day after a holiday. That is the best time to pick up next year's holiday items. While retailers may have big ads in the newspaper featuring special holiday sales (President's Day, Memorial Day, Valentine's Day), the "sale" prices frequently offer minimal savings and are used to entice you into the store to buy other goods at full retail.

Grocery Store Shopping

Since most of us eat every day, grocery shopping is an area where expenses or savings can add up. Here's how you can save money when grocery shopping:

- Try to limit yourself to one day a week for shopping. The more times you enter the market, the more likely you are to purchase items on impulse.

- Shop from a list. This will also cut down on impulse buying.
- Watch food-section newspaper ads once or twice a week. You'll save money planning your menus around specials. It's also an easy way to comparison shop.
- Enroll in "preferred customer" programs that offer reduced prices only for cardholders (no charge for cards) and give special coupons with purchases.
- Coupons can save you money; however, unless you can really use a new item, stick to clipping coupons on products and brands you normally use. (See the following section.)
- Take your calculator with you. Sometimes breaking prices down to individual units is the only way to tell which of two differently sized items is the better buy. We are led to believe that the bigger the container, the better the price, but sometimes that's not true. A small container of dishwashing liquid may run several cents an ounce higher than a larger one; but then again, it may not. Using your calculator removes the guessing.
- We all have our favorite brand names, but a lot of money can be saved by buying the store brands. The following are just a few items of which the store brand is usually of similar quality but priced lower: ammonia, all-purpose enriched white flour, bleach, distilled white vinegar, granulated sugar, and iodized table salt.
- There are a few places in the market to avoid. One of these is the end-of-the-aisle product displays. Manufacturers pay a premium to feature their products in these displays, which are away from similar products, making price comparison difficult. They also want their products at eye-level on the shelves, so for lower prices, take a look at the top and bottom shelves. Supermarkets and other retailers with checkout lines also make money on the impulse buys you make while waiting your turn in line.
- Finally, recognize that supermarket scanners are not always correct. Pay attention both to prices displayed on shelves and those that come up at the cash register. Prices change often, and many times the scanner has not been corrected. It's up to you, the consumer, to be observant. Some stores will even give you the item free if you've been incorrectly charged. Ask!

Couponing

With prices continuing to go up, we suggest using coupons as another way to put extra money in your pocket. Today we see more and more people sifting through their coupons at the grocery store. We've also been pleased to see many more men using coupons.

So, what's the big deal about coupons? The big deal is saving money on food and sundry items that all families need. Some people think it's a waste of time to cut, sort, and use a coupon just to save 25¢ on a jar of mustard. Of course, 25¢ doesn't sound like a lot of money, but if you save 25¢ here and 50¢ there, it adds up. If you save a total of $12 a week using coupons, it doesn't seem like much money. But if you save $12 every week, in one year you'll have an extra $624. Saving $30 a week adds up to $1,560 in a year. That's not too bad.

WHERE DO YOU GET DISCOUNT COUPONS?

Coupons are very easy to find. Just about every newspaper in the country has glossy coupon inserts in the Sunday issue. In addition to offering cents-off, or even dollar-off coupons, these publications may contain forms you can fill out to request coupons through the mail. Most newspapers also have a special food section once a week, which contains recipes, supermarket ads, and coupons. These special food sections usually come out on Wednesdays or Thursdays, depending on the newspaper.

Magazines geared toward women and families are another good source for coupons. *Family Circle*, *Good Housekeeping*, *Ladies Home Journal*, and many other similar publications have brand-name coupons scattered throughout their pages.

Friends and family are also good resources for coupons. After going through our coupons and cutting out the ones we can use, we trade coupons with friends and relatives. This leads us to the number-one rule in clipping coupons: only clip coupons for things you normally use. Saving $1 on a $3 item that will never be eaten or used is a waste of money. One exception to the rule is clipping a coupon for an item you know someone else uses. For example, one of our sisters used a particular brand of disposable diapers, and another frequented a certain restaurant that was geared toward children. Whenever we saw a coupon for this particular brand of diapers, or a coupon for extra game tokens at the restaurant, we clipped it and gave it to our sister.

To get more deeply involved in saving money with coupons, you can join a coupon club. Usually information about these clubs is posted on the community bulletin boards located in many local grocery stores.

What Do I Do with My Coupons?

There are many ways to file and sort coupons. Some people organize their coupons by date, brand name, or subject while others lump them all together in a box. While we don't recommend the latter method, do whatever you are comfortable with. We have found that arranging our coupons by subject works best for us.

To store your coupons, you might purchase an accordion file at a stationery store and label the sections, or order a coupon holder through the mail that has everything needed to organize coupons to your specific needs. In addition to sections such as canned goods, dairy and deli products, snacks, frozen goods, soft drinks, and sundries, we have a section specifically for coupons that expire within the current month.

This brings us to another coupon rule: on any designated day toward the end of the month, it's a good idea to go through your coupons and pull out those that will expire in the coming month. On some coupons it is nearly impossible to find the expiration notice, while on others it is printed quite clearly. In order to make things easier, we highlight the expiration notice on each coupon with a fluorescent marker.

Shopping with Your Coupons

Once you have the coupons organized, you're ready to put them to good use. Always make a shopping list before going to the market.

If you usually go to the same market, save time by making out your list in the order the products are arranged in the store. To the necessities on your list, add any items you can use that are on special at the market. You can find out what is on special by consulting the Sunday newspaper or the special food sections on Wednesdays or Thursdays. Next, go through your coupons and pull those that match items on your list. We have found it helpful to mark an asterisk next to each item on our list for which we have a discount coupon. Combining special sales with discount coupons can result in big savings.

Now that your list and coupons are ready, you're poised to hit the market. Be sure to take all your coupons with you, not just the ones for items on your shopping list. You may find unadvertised specials at the store, and you'll be glad you have your coupons available. And remember, don't go grocery shopping on an empty stomach, or you'll be tempted to buy unnecessary food.

Coupons and Loss Leaders

Although you aren't supposed to buy anything you don't really need, there is an exception to this rule—loss leaders. These are items sold at or below cost to entice you into the store. If your favorite grocery store is running a special loss leader and you have a coupon for the item, go for it.

This is a great way to get things for free. The supermarket we frequent doubles the face value of coupons, and we do our best to take advantage of loss leaders. Recently, a shaving gel was on special for $1.99 and we had several $1-off discount coupons for this product. Doubling the face value of the coupon meant a $2 discount, and although this market doesn't give money back when a doubled coupon exceeds the price of an item, we did walk away with several free cans of shaving gel.

Taking advantage of loss leaders works best with sundry items. After all, a container of shaving cream or body lotion has a very long shelf life. Unless you have a big family that can eat everything before the expiration dates, you should stick to stocking up on nonperishable goods.

WHAT ABOUT REBATES?

Many manufacturers provide rebate application blanks that you can send in along with a required proof of purchase and cash register receipt to receive cash, coupons, or gifts through the mail. There are people who have furnished their entire homes simply by saving money from rebates or gifts received from rebates. If you are interested in how to make extra money with rebates, here is some basic information:

- Proofs of purchase: Any part of the packaging from box top to can label can be designated by its manufacturer as a proof of purchase; the one most commonly required is the bar code—the rectangle of black vertical lines on a package that is used by cashiers to scan prices.
- Organizing proofs of purchase: The best way to organize proofs of purchase is alphabetically by brand name. Because there is no brand name on the bar code, it helps to cut the brand name off the package of the product and staple it to the bar code before filing.
- Cash register receipts: Keep your cash register receipts accessible, as they will most likely be required in addition to the proof of purchase and rebate form.

Using coupons is a great way to add extra dollars to your savings account, your child's college education fund, next year's vacation, or whatever it is you never seem to have enough money for. In the long run, the few hours a month that it takes to clip, sort, and utilize coupons pay off. Rebates can add considerably to your savings too, if you are willing to take the time required to pursue the process.

Shopping for Clothing

Clothing can take a chunk out of the individual or family budget. Since few of us can afford to buy an entirely new set of clothes every season, building a wardrobe of basics and staying away from fads are good strategies for saving money. To ensure that you will have the necessary clothes for all occasions, make a list of what constitutes a minimum basic wardrobe for you. Consider the types of clothing, quantity of each, quality, and fabric as well as colors and seasonal wear. Obviously, this list will differ for each person according to work requirements, lifestyle, personal taste, and income.

When shopping with your basic list in hand, you will be less likely to buy something you don't need or won't wear often or at prices you can't afford. You'll be able to scan the newspaper ads and use *Buying Retail Is Stupid!—Chicago* with greater focus to get the best buys on your entire basic wardrobe. Once you have completed your basic wardrobe, ask yourself the following questions before making each new purchase:

- Will it go with anything else in my closet?
- Will I actually wear it more than once?
- Will it wear well?
- Will it resist soiling?
- Does it need special maintenance or dry cleaning?
- Is it within my planned price range for this type of item?

When you shop for clothes, make sure you are not only saving money but also buying well-made items. If a shirt falls apart the first time you put it through a wash cycle, you have wasted your money. Here's a checklist to consult when purchasing clothing:

- Tug gently on the seam and zipper areas to make sure they've been completely sewn.
- All seams should be flat and even, with no puckering.
- Stitching should be even, and the smaller the better.
- Shoulders and armholes of jackets should be wrinkle-free.
- Jacket lapels should spring back into shape when you crumple them.
- Zippers should zip, lie flat, and be sewn in straight.
- Buttons should fit easily.
- Try on skirts or pants and make sure you can sit comfortably in them.

It takes only a minute or two to go over a garment while you're at the store, and it sure beats finding out there's something wrong with your new outfit five minutes before leaving for work. Remember, a little checking can save you a lot of money!

Shoes

When you buy shoes, make sure they are comfortable at the time of purchase. If the idea that they'll stretch out a bit and then they'll be perfect crosses your mind, go up a half size. Unless they are made of extremely soft leather, shoes should be comfortable right at the start. Also, buy your shoes toward the end of the day, when your feet will be a bit larger. Many of us, especially women, wear our shoes too small. If you haven't had your feet measured since high school, we recommend you have it done the next time you shop for shoes.

Return Strategies

Have you ever bought something and decided to return it because you changed your mind, someone at home didn't like it, or it didn't fit or work exactly as you thought it would? Perhaps you decided it had been too expensive, or the next day or week you saw it advertised for much less than you paid. If so, join the club. Millions of dollars' worth of merchandise is returned every year for many reasons, including buyer's remorse.

Save yourself some headaches by knowing the return policies of the stores you buy from. Remember, they vary greatly. Some of the differences are:

- Time limit: Seven days to six months
- Conditions: From full refund, to in-store credit only, to no refunds or exchanges
- Customer satisfaction: Satisfaction guaranteed—no questions asked, to must show damage or malfunction
- Receipt: Absolutely necessary to not necessary at all or credit card slip acceptable

Here are suggestions for dealing with returns effectively:

- Return policies usually are posted or can be found in the small print of your receipt. If not, ask about the return policy. Wherever possible, get it in writing. Salespeople and managers change. You don't want to be faced with the words "Who told you that? That's not our policy."

- Keep receipts, and file each by date so that it will be easy to locate when needed.
- If you've purchased an item with a warranty, complete and return the warranty card immediately after purchase. If you put it aside to complete later, you may never get to it and probably won't be able to find it when you need it. Staple your sales receipt to each warranty card you keep. File all warranty cards in one place.
- When returning something that is somewhat outside the store policy, don't take no for an answer from the first salesperson you talk to. Ask to talk to the manager. In today's competitive market, with the emphasis on customer service, they will frequently go along with your request.
- Another option is to call the customer service department of the manufacturer. Many have 800 numbers. The company often will accept the return that the store won't.

Finally, all other things being equal, shop more often at the discount stores that have the most flexible return policies.

Reminders for the Smart Shopper

Learn all you can about the high-priced products you wish to buy—features, models, and brands. This information can be obtained from consumer guides (see Chapter 4, "Directory of Consumer Resources"), sales representatives, and people you know. Consider the various places from which you could possibly buy the item. Compare availability, price, reputation, convenience, and company policies. Don't forget to consider using money-saving coupons, off-season buying, and renting rather than purchasing if the situation warrants it.

Challenge yourself to find or create the best deal you can. Shopping will soon seem like a game with all the fun of competing skillfully and the rewards of saving money, conserving time and energy, and getting more value for your dollar.

And don't forget to use your *Buying Retail Is Stupid!—Chicago* coupons for extra discounts.

2

Grassroots Bargain Outlets

Everything and Anything for Sale at Low and Negotiable Prices

(Garage Sales, Resale Stores, Thrift Shops, and Flea Markets)

Economic conditions of the '80s and '90s have energized a multitude of grassroots, money-saving opportunities for the bargain-seeking consumer. Among the most popular are garage sales, resale stores, thrift shops, and flea markets. The buyer is attracted by the generally low prices and the possibility of finding a terrific buy. For the seller, it is a way to clear out the clutter, make some money, and participate in recycling rather than just contributing to the city dump. We call them grassroots bargain outlets because, for the most part, the merchandise sold is provided by private individuals, from their own homes and possessions. Prices are uniquely flexible and open to negotiation.

Shopping at flea markets and garage sales can be a real treasure hunt. Sometimes you can uncover incredible buys, such as a necklace of Victorian glass beads bought for $6 and found, after appraisal, to be valued at $300, or a beautiful walnut fruit bowl purchased for 50¢ that turned out to be worth several hundred dollars. Several times, we've been impressed with a unique or interesting piece of furniture in someone's home only to be told, "Oh, I found it at a garage sale—you should have seen it before I got it cleaned up!" Some special items to look for at these sales include art and paintings, antique jewelry, costume jewelry, Oriental rugs, children's clothing and furniture, appliances, dishes, silver, glassware and crystal, pottery and vases, collectibles, and sporting gear. Thrift shops and resale stores offer the same possibility for great buys in the area of clothing.

Getting What You Want at the Right Price

General Tips

- The earlier you arrive, the better. You'll skip the crowds, have greater choice, and frequently receive better prices from owners eager to get cash early.
- Don't be afraid to negotiate price.
- If you feel an item is overpriced, give the seller reasons.
- Once the owner seems firm about an article you really want, don't hem and haw too long, or someone will buy the item out from under you.
- If you are not totally sold on an item, make a final offer and then be willing to walk. Frequently, you'll get it at your price.
- Ask questions. The more you know, the better you'll be able to spot bargains.
- Be prepared for rejection. Sellers are not all equally flexible. If it's something you want, but only at your own price, come back another time if you can; the longer the item is there, the more likely it is that the price will come down.
- Don't be penny-wise and dollar-foolish. If it's being sold at a bargain price and you really want it, don't get into an ego battle with the seller and lose out on the purchase because of a few dollars.

Garage Sales

Garage sales have become big business in recent years, generating millions of dollars in income. Many people are turning their front lawns, garages, alleys, and driveways into virtual showrooms of castoffs and hand-me-downs. Some have created a garage sale business and hold regular weekly or monthly sales. For others, it's a one-shot deal or perhaps once or twice annually, like spring cleaning. Making money on a continuing basis with garage sales takes an eye for value and knowing how to repair things. Repeat garage sellers collect merchandise over several weeks, generally at other yard sales (sometimes buying a seller's entire lot in preparation for their own sale). They take home the items, clean them up or repair them, then double or triple the value at resale. Whether you are holding a one-time cleanup or going into the garage sale business, certain strategies can increase your likelihood of success.

Why Have a Garage Sale?

You might have a garage sale because you have too many possessions, a lot of clutter, and not enough storage space; or maybe you're tired of holding on to things you never use. Perhaps you just need a little cash, or you think it will be a good family project—educational for the kids. A garage sale can be a great way to mix fun and profit. Once you've held one, you are likely to find it an interesting and profitable experience.

Choosing What to Sell

Involve all members of the family. Without consulting with the others, each person makes a list of things to sell by answering the following questions:

- What things of my own do I know I want to get rid of?
- What are some things in the house I don't like?
- What are some things nobody seems to use?
- What are some things I haven't used or worn in over a year?
- What are some things I question whether to keep?

After making the lists, have every family member go through the house looking for anything else that might be added. Have one person combine all the lists, eliminating duplication. Then hold a meeting to review the combined list as follows:

- Quickly check off each item for which there is no disagreement.
- Discuss the remaining items, and seek a consensus.
- Decide on a final sale list.
- Include everything you want to get rid of. Don't assume no one will want to buy a particular item.

Pricing—How Much to Charge

What to charge depends on your main purpose. Is the amount of profit important, or are you mainly looking to get rid of clutter and simplify your life? Some people price things higher because they assume shoppers will want to haggle and won't feel anything is a bargain unless they can knock the price down. However, absolutely not wanting to put anything back in their house, some people will price on the low side. You may want to set up tables on which all the items are one price—for example, $1, $2, or $5. Mark prices on everything. In pricing clothing, mail-order catalogs might help you remember what you originally paid. The condition of each item should influence the price. Asking too much for items that are hardly usable will make you look foolish and will send the potential customer away quickly.

Length of the Sale

The length of the sale depends on how many items you have to sell. Typically, a garage sale will run from one to three days. If you have lots of merchandise, a two- or three-day sale gives you ample time to sell most of your goods. Word of mouth can increase your clientele substantially after the first day. You can expect to be visited by professional shoppers such as antique dealers and others who regularly scour the newspapers for weekend sales and plan their shopping itineraries accordingly. You will also have amateurs, browsers, and people who were just driving by and noticed your sign. At the end of each day, mark down any items you want to move faster. With one-day sales, you will do this in the afternoon. Near the end of the day of a one-day sale or on the last day of a longer sale, all prices should be slashed to giveaway levels. Sometimes you can simply ask people to make you an offer.

Advertising—Letting People Know About the Sale

Probably the easiest and cheapest advertising is simple word of mouth. Talk it up as much as possible. Send postcards to your friends and tell them to mention it to others. Post index cards, signs, and posters wherever you can—in the local laundromat, grocery store, or school.

The most effective form of advertising is the classified section of the newspaper. These little ads are read religiously by bargain hunters everywhere. One small, well-worded ad is worth a thousand well-placed signs. It's a good idea to list special items such as furniture—a draw for antiques dealers—and yard equipment, bicycles, and children's items.

You should begin your ad with an attention-grabbing phrase. Then list some of the most appealing items. Be sure to include your address and easy-to-follow directions. Here's an example:

WORLD'S BEST GARAGE SALE!

RIDING TRACTOR MOWER, ANTIQUE BEDROOM SUITE OF BIRD'S-EYE MAPLE, CAST-IRON STOVE, PLUS ORIGINAL OIL PAINTINGS, FUR COAT, AND PERIOD CLOTHES. MANY ADDITIONAL WONDERFUL ITEMS. SAT. & SUN. JUNE 4 & 5 FROM 10 A.M. TO 4 P.M. FOLLOW EXETER DRIVE WEST, TURN RIGHT ON GLENHAVEN, THEN LEFT ON GLENOIT TO 2517.

Run your classified ad two or three days in advance of the sale and during the sale. Newspapers often have a staff person who can help you write the ad. Take advantage of this assistance.

PREPARING FOR YOUR SALE

- Get a permit. The need for a permit varies among communities and types of sales. Check with your city or town clerk to learn which ordinances apply.
- Use signs. Stake out signs on a pole planted in your lawn. String balloons to attract attention and direct shoppers to your sale.
- Locate for accessibility. Locate the sale in an area that's easily accessible and has safe parking. If weather permits, rope off your cement driveway to increase your display space and save wear and tear on your lawn. If you live in a condominium or apartment, see if you can use the complex recreation room or yard.
- Get ready early. If you're planning to start at 9:00 A.M., be ready at 7:00 A.M. Dealers of antiques and secondhand goods may visit

sales the night before or first thing in the morning; regular shoppers also come early. If this will disturb you, include in your advertisement "no early birds."

Organizing for Convenience and Efficiency

- Have plenty of small bills and change. A small adding machine will come in handy and help keep your sales straight. Set up a head table that is convenient for your customers where you can keep an eye on the entire sale. Never leave the sale unattended. Keep your change in a box and your adding machine, paper, pencils, tags, and sacks all at the head table.
- Place sale items in aislelike rows so everything is easily accessible. Leave plenty of walking room to minimize accidents and breakage. Hang clothes on a rack or line for easy access, and provide a mirror for people trying on hats and outerwear. Keep string and rope on hand to help in packing furniture and bicycles into car trunks. Providing old grocery bags will keep shoppers from standing around juggling items.
- Have enough help. There should be at least two people working the sale at all times—one to field questions and another to handle cash exchanges. It also helps to wear an apron with pockets to hold bills and change.
- Keep your house locked. Don't assume that some people won't take advantage of an unlocked front or side door.
- Plan what to do with unsold items. Donate leftover goods to places such as charity thrift shops, homeless shelters, soup kitchens, churches, or the Salvation Army.

Joint Sales

A one-home yard sale may work fine if you live in the city or on a main street. But in Chicago neighborhoods and suburbs, multifamily or neighborhood sales offer a better draw. Many people don't want to venture out for one sale. A neighborhood sale attracts people because they can shop at half a dozen places at once.

Whether in the city or suburbs, if you have gathered a fair amount of goods but not enough to make a sale worthwhile, check with a neighbor or friend and see if you can conduct a joint sale. There are many advantages besides the companionship and the sharing of ideas. You can split the cost of advertising and have help on pricing and moving of goods. Plus you'll have two people for more word-of-mouth advertising. Separate inventories for double sales can easily be kept straight by color coding the price tags or marking off items on the inventory sheet.

Resale Stores

Resale stores are another fun way to save money, and they are starting to appear everywhere. Resale stores generally take in clothes on consignment from individuals and keep a percentage of the sale price. Even though these stores deal mainly in used clothes, some garments have been worn only once or sometimes not at all. Many offer high-end clothing, unlike thrift stores, which deal with low-end used clothes.

If you've never been in a resale store, you are in for a treat. It's a great way to get expensive clothing at rock-bottom prices. For example, you can pick up a Jones New York skirt for $12 instead of the $50 it would cost you at retail. Or you might find a cocktail dress for $195—one made of French lace by Caroline Herrera that originally retailed for more than $2,500. Usually, resale stores are for women, but stores geared strictly for children, men, and families are growing in number.

Most clothing in resale stores is secondhand, but you'll also find brand-new merchandise with tags still attached. We picked up a gorgeous wool suit, with the $300 Nordstrom tags still attached, for $95. Many resale stores also carry manufacturer samples, overruns, and last season's clothing from retail stores.

Shopping resale for children's clothing is a fabulous way to save money. Kids outgrow their clothes long before they wear them out. The best buys for children are play clothes and party clothes. A frilly girl's party dress that was probably worn on only one occasion is a much better buy at $18 than at $80.

How to Shop in a Resale Store

- Usually, the better organized the resale store is, the better the merchandise is.
- Almost always, clothes for sale have been laundered or dry cleaned, but ask anyway.
- Pay special attention to cuffs, collars, pockets, armpits, and crotches for stains and wear and tear.
- Make sure the garment has all necessary parts—buttons, working zippers, and so forth.
- If the item is made of a natural fabric such as wool, look it over to make sure there are no moth holes.
- When you find a resale store that carries brands you prefer, ask the owner or manager to give you a call when items of interest arrive.
- Since new merchandise is always coming in, find stores conveniently located so that you can stop by periodically.

You can find a variety of resale stores for men, women, and children in your local Yellow Pages.

Thrift Shops

Saving money and doing a good deed go hand in hand when you shop at thrift shops. Most thrift shops are affiliated with charitable organizations and are staffed by volunteers. Whether you're buying or donating, it's all for a worthy cause.

In addition to clothing, thrift stores feature all manner of other merchandise—housewares, books, toys—in short, anything that people want to clean out of their cluttered garages, attics, and closets. You never know what you will encounter at a thrift store. Most of the merchandise is visibly used, but sifting through everything from clothing to housewares can be rewarding. One of our best finds at a retirement-home thrift shop was a huge fruit bowl made of bird's-eye walnut for 50¢. Sometimes you will be lucky enough to find clothing that has been worn only once or not at all—possibly even a high-end, designer item.

Even though everything is wonderfully priced, be sure to examine the items closely to make sure that, no matter how low the cost, you don't end up with something that you will regret having purchased.

Flea Markets

Flea markets are made up of groups of vendors in individually rented booths, under one roof or in one large area. A flea market is like one big yard sale where you can find new and recycled items alike, all at bargain-basement prices. Since overhead is quite low, prices usually are too; best of all, you will be dealing directly with the "store owner," and haggling is part of the experience.

Vendors are frequently local people selling their own handcrafted products, or they may be dealers from surrounding areas—sometimes specializing in antiques and collectibles or just selling anything they have. In addition to the regulars and semiprofessionals, you'll spot the occasional and one-time customers and vendors. Prices for merchandise range from a few dollars to hundreds, and stories regarding incredible bargains abound. You may also hear about the occasional rip-off because someone overvalued an item.

Flea markets are enjoying ever-increasing popularity and have turned into a big business. There are thousands of them covering just about every state in the country. They exist in and around urban areas and in rural locations. Some have only a handful of vendors; others have hundreds. Outdoor markets are held at drive-in theaters, county fairgrounds, sports arenas, vacant lots, and other locations. Though fewer in number in the Midwest, indoor markets—many heated or air-conditioned—are insurance against bad weather and are more likely to function throughout the year.

Most flea markets offer a tremendous variety of merchandise ranging from valuable antiques to backyard junk—almost everything and anything can be found at these events, even new merchandise. By adding restaurants, entertainment, music, games, and children's play areas, many flea markets have created a down-home, country amusement park–type atmosphere, where the whole family can enjoy a day together.

For specific information about buying and selling effectively at flea markets and for the locations and descriptions of some of the most popular in the Chicago area, see Chapter 3.

Common Aspects of Grassroots Outlets

Grassroots bargain outlets are very accessible and are growing in number. They are in our front yards, just down the block, or almost anywhere you look. They are the most down-home example of the free-market system and have several things in common:

- You can participate as a buyer or a seller and can profit in either role.
- You can engage in them occasionally as an amateur, or regularly, taking a more businesslike approach.
- You can negotiate the price for which you are willing to buy or sell.
- They provide a terrific recycling program—"one person's trash is another person's treasure!"
- They give you the opportunity to clear out your excess possessions for fun, profit, or charity.
- You can obtain something you want for much less than it would cost new. Being aware of the item's value helps you bargain intelligently. Checking the condition of your prospective purchase prevents buyer's remorse.

3

Directory of Discount Stores and Outlets

Where to Find Giant $$$ Savings in Your Local Area

In this chapter we provide you access to hundreds of discount stores and outlets of every type, shape, kind, and variety imaginable—from the Kane County Flea Market with its hundreds of different vendors to the small mom-and-pop shop in your neighborhood, and everything in between. You'll find almost every product from A to Z (antiques to zippers)—and also an incredible variety of generic and name-brand items. You can locate them by product category in the Contents or by company name in the Indexes. We describe the stores in enough detail to give you a good feel for what they offer—products, services, atmosphere, price range, discounts, credit cards, brand names, and more; also, we tell you where they are located and how to contact them. Before going to a store, call to verify store hours and address, to make sure it is still in business, and to check that what you want is in stock.

Plus, we've tried to make this directory as reader-friendly as possible. To avoid long stretches of pages featuring store after store, we've divided the hundreds of entries into four categories of discounters. The four sections are:

A. **Local discount stores.** Strictly, only stores located in the tri-state area and nowhere else—from Kenosha/Milwaukee, Wisconsin, to Merrilville, Indiana, and parts of Michigan.

B. **Local stores of regional and/or national discounters.** Covered here are the names you know coast to coast (sometimes, state to state), from JCPenney Outlet to Sears Retail Outlet Stores. Yes, we're fortunate enough to have these representatives in our backyards.

C. **Factory mall outlets.** They're appearing everywhere—these collections of (usually) one-store-high shopping centers with every consumer product under the sun. And we single out the unusual, the unique.

D. **Antiques and collectibles.** Whatever happened before the age of the collectible object, whether Elvis paraphernalia or Pez dispenser? Many avid nonshoppers swear by flea markets. Other passionate bargain hunters avoid "recycled stuff" like the plague. To each his or her own: our motto is "There's no such animal as an ex-consumer."

Telephone Numbers

Dialing a telephone in Chicago and its burbs used to rely on seven digits—no prefixes, no area codes, no fancy fingerwork.

Not anymore. We call it "catch 312." Beginning in the early 1990s, Ameritech (our local telecommunications provider from the old Ma Bell system) began to subdivide the old area codes: 312 (city), 847 (north and northwest), 708 (west and south). Now 773 has been added as a Chicago code (outside the central city), and 630, for the western areas beyond Oak Park and Brookfield. So, someone living in Old Town must dial the 773 prefix to reach a friend less than a mile away. And believe us, it'll get worse. The media has just reported that the now-prestigious 847 area code will probably split in the not-too-distant future.

Why bother with this? Simply to alert you in advance to check area codes very carefully. Otherwise, that bargain you're seeking could end in a wrong number.

☒ Bonus Discount Coupons

More than 100 stores offer bonus discount coupons representing, for the most part, additional percentage or dollar savings off their already discounted prices. Using these bonus coupons—available exclusively to *Buying Retail Is Stupid!—Chicago* purchasers—can save you a considerable amount of extra money yearly. Take the clipped coupon, page, or entire book with you to the store for additional savings. (The store will initial the coupon and return the page or book to you.) A ☒ next to its name indicates that the store offers a discount coupon, and the amount is indicated in the description.

◆ Senior Discounts

More than 50 discount stores and outlets in this chapter offer special senior discounts. A ◆ next to its name indicates that the store offers a discount to seniors. These discounts are obtained merely by showing proof of age. The specific age requirement and amount of discount differ for each store and are indicated in the description of the store. Some of the stores accept the bonus discount coupon in addition to the senior discount. Others do not. The store description indicates when the bonus discount is not valid in addition to the senior discount.

A

Local Discount Stores

Appliances

Major & Small Appliances

Douglas the TV Giant
4027 N. Lincoln Ave.
Chicago, IL 60618
(773) 281-7600
Hours: Mon–Thurs: 9:30–9; Fri–Sat: 9:30–5:30; Sun: 11–5
AE, MC, V

Used to be, Douglas sold appliances in addition to TVs and stereos. Now the emphasis is strictly on "big-kid" toys, apparent from the minute you glide into stores arranged like mini home theaters (with cushy black leather Natuzzi sofas and sectionals). Every name in the electronics industry is on the floor, from Admiral and JVC to Mitsubishi and Zenith. And though, from the posted prices, it's difficult to tell the range of discounts, a salesman assured us they'll meet/beat any advertised price. A confirmation: some of our couch-potato buddies buy from Douglas. Think high-end for the most part: an 80-inch Mitsubishi TV for $8,998; a 35-inch Zenith for $1,198; and an in-store special offering a 13-inch JVC for $198.

Chicago—7243 W. Touhy Ave., (773) 763-4300
Deerfield—350 Lake Cook Rd., (847) 945-9000
Mt. Prospect—621 Main St., (847) 259-2600
Orland Park—9520 W. 159th St., (708) 873-9300

GRAND APPLIANCE ✪

2915 Grand Ave.
Waukegan, IL 60048
(847) 549-9807
Hours: Mon–Fri: 10–8; Sat: 9–5
DISC, MC, V
◆ **Senior Discount:** 5% **Age:** 65+

In a large metropolitan area littered with deals on majaps (the industry term for major appliances) and bedding, it can be difficult for an independent chain to peddle similar wares. This four-store retailer, claims executive Tom Van Dyck, attracts customers because of its personal service and brand-name merchandise—such as Amana, Creda, KitchenAid, Sealy, Thermador, and Whirlpool. Discounts run about 20% off suggested list prices—with an extra $20 subtracted from any $350+ purchase of *Buying Retail Is Stupid!* readers.

Libertyville—216 Peterson Rd., (847) 549-9807
Skokie—4001 W. Golf Rd., (847) 677-7569
Kenosha, WI—3601 Roosevelt Rd., (414) 656-1661

PLASS APPLIANCE OUTLET STORE ✪

22W011 Army Trail Rd.
Addison, IL 60101
(630) 351-4020
Hours: Mon–Thurs: 10–8; Fri & Sat: 10–5:30; Sun: 11–4
DISC, MC, V

This warehouse for the last one-of-a-kind appliances from Plass's seven regular retail stores means that sharp-eyed shoppers will benefit from some good prices. A lot of the merchandise is first quality; from the high-end brands such as Jenn-Air, KitchenAid, and Sub-Zero; and all tags reflect a 2% discount for cash or checks. Typical examples of dollars to be saved: Mitsubishi 50-inch TV at $1,999.99 (from $3,099.99); a bottom-freezer refrigerator, here $759.99 (was $1,099.99); and a Maytag washer at $559.99 (once $609.99). There's a reason why ABC News rated Plass number one in the United States . . . and *Buying Retail Is Stupid!* readers will benefit even more—from free delivery and installation.

Trage Brothers

7439 W. Madison St.
Forest Park, IL 60130
(708) 366-4200
Hours: Mon: 9–2; Tues, Wed, Fri: 7–5:30; Thurs: 9–8; Sat: 9–5
MC, V

It's hard to argue with 54 years in business and the third generation of one family in control. At the one-store Trage Brothers in Forest Park, appliances and electronics are the specialties—selling regularly at about a 15%–18% discount. Amana, KitchenAid, Mitsubishi, and other similarly upscale brands represent their stock; a Mitsubishi 50-inch stereo TV with tons of special features, for instance, was tagged at $1,799.99, regularly $1,999. The best bet: check prices carefully and then, armed with competitive ads, march in. They'll match any printed or quoted-on-paper prices.

Sewing Machines & Vacuums

Singer Factory Distributor ★

4914 W. Irving Park Rd.
Chicago, IL 60641
(773) 545-6834
Hours: Mon, Thurs: 10–8; Tues, Wed, Fri, Sat: 10–5; Sun: 12–5
AE, DISC, MC, OPT, V

Yes, for the experienced home stitcher (and even high-school home ec students), the name "Singer" means machines and accessories worth sewing about. Four factory distributors—two standalone and two located in JoAnn Fabrics stores—offer discounts on new and used sewing machines, cabinets and tables, and pressing equipment as well as industrial machines. Free extended warranties and free lessons with purchase will ease novice owners' qualms; watch for the best deals at warehouse warranties and truckload sales events. Plus, it'll be easier for *Buying Retail Is Stupid!* sewers to lug that machine home—with this outlet's free-carrying-case coupon offer.

Chicago—3906 N. Harlem Ave., (773) 625-1515
Niles—8245 W. Golf Rd., (847) 966-0298 (in JoAnn Fabrics)
Oak Lawn—8734 S. Cicero Ave., (847) 422-5300 (in JoAnn Fabrics)

USED APPLIANCES

PAYLESS APPLIANCE WAREHOUSE, INC. ✪

1549 W. Cortland St.
Chicago, IL 60622
(773) 384-9136
Hours: Mon–Fri: 8–5; Sat: 8–2
MC, V

It really is a warehouse, hidden off a little-used street near Armitage (and if you have a predilection toward asthma, or must avoid dust, then wear a mask or take along an inhaler). But, if used appliances wearing a few dents, dings, or scratches don't bother you, then brave the bare-bones look—and save some big bucks. Large and small, branded or no-name, refrigerators and stoves and rebuilt and reconditioned washers and dryers are arranged in rows—and at prices starting from $99 (washers and dryers), $125 (stoves), and $145 (refrigerators). Every once in a while a new factory-defect machine walks onto (and quickly off of) the floor. Otherwise, all appliances are accompanied by at least a 3-month guarantee—and for *Buying Retail Is Stupid!* readers an additional 10% off with any purchase of $275 or more with coupon.

Art

Frames & Framing Services

Frame Factory ✪

1909 W. Diversey Pkwy.
Chicago, IL 60614
(773) 929-1010
Hours: Mon–Wed: 9–7; Thurs: 9–8; Fri & Sat: 9–5:30; Sun: 12–5
AE, DISC, MC, V

Is it a frame maker or an art gallery? We decided to ask our expert, who gave us a "thumbs-up" review of the Frame Factory. No do-it-yourself work here, this one-and-only store delivers on its quality promise—and offers some excellent picture buys, whether matted and framed or straight posters. A few of the reasonable art prices, all ready to be hung (in metal): $111.95 for Keith Haring's *Fire Dancers*; and a large McKnight *Carnival in Venice* for $178.50. And any *Buying Retail Is Stupid!* reader with barren walls might find the extra-10% coupon for the Frame Factory a welcome piece of art, indeed.

Picture Us Galleries

2828 N. Clark Street
Chicago, IL 60657
(312) 281-5558
Hours: Mon–Fri: 10–9; Sat: 10–7; Sun: 11–6
MC, V

Wow! Every year, 50,000 pictures of all shapes and sizes and values waltz through the doors of 12 Picture Us Galleries stores here. (A stumper for the math wizards: How many pictures sold each hour at one store?) Most of the artworks are poster-type and rather traditional, such as Edward Hopper's *Nighthawks* framed at $275; Monet's *Irises* at $68.99; or a Dennis Rodman photo (gotta love dem Bulls) for $59.99 in frame. But other options exist—open and limited editions, paper sculptures, and custom framing—all at good, below-retail prices. We especially appreciate the "buy one and the second's half off" sale, since we tend to gang up our posters to frame a deal.

Chicago—2 N. LaSalle St., (312) 726-6334

Arts & Crafts

Art Supplies

Baraka/Genesis Artist's Village
2417 N. Western Ave.
Chicago, IL 60647
(773) 292-2992
Hours: Mon–Fri: 7–9; Sat & Sun: 9–6
AE, DISC, MC, V

Inside, it looks like rooms from three to four different homes. And human assistance to locate specific wares always seems to be needed. But, when you find the right oils, acrylics, brushes, or canvases, all are accompanied by some of the lowest prices in town—usually a 40%+ discount. (And sometimes more, if you're a member of their club at $5 each year.) In no way does the selection equal Pearl's; in fact, at times it can be downright difficult to find a tube of cadmium yellow, for instance, since Baraka's stock is not instantly replenished. Still, Art Institute students do shop here for good deals on brand names such as Winsor & Newton, Arches, and Graham.

Fletch's the Artists Bargain Store

786 Rand Rd.
Arlington Heights, IL 60004
(847) 392-7000
Hours: Mon–Fri: 9:30–7; Sat: 10–5; Sun: 11–5
MC, V

◆ **Senior Discount:** 10% on Wed **Age:** 60+

One of the mysteries of retailing (in our minds) is why so many

great discount stores rarely promote their wares. Are the owners satisfied with the customer base? Is it a tax write-off? Or are advertising and related marketing vehicles simply too expensive for most locals? Whatever the case, we were fortunate enough to discover 25-year-old Fletch's while meandering through the countryside. Strictly for artists (and primarily the painters and watercolorists of the world), Fletch's features deep discounts on both materials and equipment (books, too). Our day's outing showed these prices: 19¢ artist brushes; Shiva acrylic tubes for $1.99; $12.95 easel art lamps; a huge Bieffe table for $699 (originally $1,200).
Elk Grove Village—Fletcher Lee, 1681 Elmhurst Rd., (847) 758-0100

IRCO ART PRODUCTS CO., LTD. ☆

3229 S. Ashland Ave.
Chicago, IL 60608
(773) 847-4700
Hours: Mon–Fri: 8:30–5
MC, V
◆ **Senior Discount:** 10% **Age:** 60+

It's a challenge, says president Chip Freeman, to find his South Side artist supplies store. Once you're in that neck of the woods, though, this retailer housed in a converted factory is worth the search. In business for nearly 40 years, IRCO is best not only for budding Picassos, but also for the business worlds of engineers, graphic designers, and other similar professionals. Check out, for example, any one of the rainbow range of Pantone markers for 99¢ (rather than $2.85). Or doodle creative thoughts and floor plans on Bienfang newsprint pads for $17.95 (listed at $25.95). Usual discounts are 25%–40%. The last few pages in IRCO's catalog offer even deeper savings on closeout items. And no matter when the school term or semester starts (or stops), *Buying Retail Is Stupid!* readers now have no excuse not to save another 10% on IRCO-nian items with our discount coupon.

CRAFT & FLORAL SUPPLIES

CRAFTS FOR LESS
3314 Ridge Rd.
Lansing, IL 60438
(708) 474-1214
Hours: Mon–Fri: 9–9; Sat: 9–5
AE, MC, V

Busy fingers make little mischief—or so our forefathers thought. Yet, crafting today takes on new dimensions as handmade traditions are being rediscovered and resurrected. And there's a real choice of activities at Crafts for Less, with its 29,000 items (we dare you to count them!) for making jewelry, wedding supplies, invitations, and other do-it-yourself ideas. In fact, there are a lot of bucks to be saved by arranging your own celebrations as well as crafting your own gifts. Gather together a 100-foot aisle runner ($19.95), bunches of white silk roses (at $7.89 a dozen), gold floral baskets (99¢ to $4.99), and bags of confetti (from $1.99 to $2.49). Voila! The streamlined wedding. Even more melodious to our ears are the extra discounts: another 10% on $100 purchase; 20% for $200; 30% for $300.

FIBRE CRAFT OUTLET STORE
6310 W. Touhy Ave.
Niles, IL 60714
(847) 647-1144
Hours: Mon–Fri: 9–5; Sat: 9–3
MC, V
◆ **Senior Discount:** 10% **Age:** 60+

There's a phenomenon common to all crafters known as the "back room" where half-finished projects of all kinds languish for weeks, months, even years, until someone decides to complete them. So, there's a pull-push quality to the news of Fibre Craft Outlet Store; after all, how many spools of yarn and containers of beads can one individual accumulate? Yet the prices are certainly alluring: 20%–75% off retail, a 10% seniors' discount every day—even phone orders on volume purchases! More specifically, our fingers started twitching at these tags: $2.69 each for decorating stencils; $1.50 for a 150-yard ball of crochet cotton; and $2.20 for a 2-ounce package of FIMO modeling clay. Fingers, don't fail us now!

Fabrics & Notions

Fishman's Fabrics
1101 S. Desplaines St.
Chicago, IL 60607
(312) 922-7250
Hours: Mon–Sat: 9–5:30; Sun: 9:30–5
AE, DISC, MC, V

At a par with the prices of Vogue Fabrics (almost directly across Roosevelt Road), 90+-year-old Fishman's differs in some important ways. One, extremely fine fabrics come straight from the workrooms of European couturiers; Fishman's buys the remaining bolts at a substantial discount. (We fingered a buttery soft, black-and-white Chanel houndstooth for $125 a yard.) Two, their recent emphasis on upholstery, with simply scads of ornate and contemporary fabrics to select. Three, the not-so-well-known bridal department, with better-than-average prices on a variety of top-quality headpieces and veils (from $24 to $99). Plus, there's an on-site dressmaker as well as lists of professional sewers; ask for Virginia.

Fraerman's Fabric Co.

314 W. Adams St.
Chicago, IL 60606
(312) 236-6886
Hours: Mon–Fri: 8–5:45; Sat: 8:30–4:30
DISC, MC, V

Only one firm is left in the district that once housed a very bustling garment center, now in the shadow of the Sears Tower. From the outside, Fraerman's Fabric, founded in 1927, is indistinguishable from rows of dusty Loop storefronts. Inside, the difference is apparent as we run our hands longingly over sumptuous elegant fabrics, all substantially discounted: a 100% Czech damask blue-and-white buffalo cotton plaid for $19.98 a yard; Dolce + Gabbana yardage; black merino textured wool at $28.95 (once $59.95). It is a literal treasure hunt, with bolts of luxurious pima cottons, notions, and patterns all vying for attention. Even boxes of collector buttons, from $5 to $20, are appealing.

ROOSEVELT FABRIC
555 W. Roosevelt Rd., #3
Chicago, IL 60607
(312) 733-7370
Hours: Mon–Sat: 9:30–6
AE

This storefront's a bit dingy and drab, but home sewers just might discover their field of dream supplies come true in this fabric and notions shop. Displays are limited to rows of tables, haphazard shelving, and boxes on the floor. Digging a bit yields the following: three spools of thread for $1; denim at $4.98 a yard; remnants at 99¢ each. Few if any fabrics climb beyond the $9 price point.

VOGUE FABRICS
718 Main St.
Evanston, IL 60202
(847) 864-9600
Hours: Mon, Thurs: 9–9; Tues, Wed, Fri, Sat: 9–5:30; Sun: 12–5
DISC, MC, OPT, V

Dedicated home sewers here don't lift a needle without consulting the choices available in Vogue—including not only fine fabrics but also all the accoutrements thereof, such as buttons, thread, and other necessities. The selection is vast and runs the gamut from 50¢ cotton print remnants to fine pricey wools, velvets, and silks from the likes of DKNY, Calvin Klein, and Ungaro. The staff is extremely knowledgeable and generally helpful, except on crowded weekends. Even the $5 swatch set of 54 coordinated fabrics isn't adequate preparation for viewing Vogue up close and personal.
Chicago—Water Tower Place, (312) 787-2521, Mon–Fri: 10–7; Sat: 10–6; Sun: 12–6

Chicago—623-627 W. Roosevelt Rd., (312) 829-2505,
Mon–Wed, Fri, Sat: 9:30–6; Thurs: 9:30–8; Sun: 12–5
Lansing—P.O. Box 5224, (708) 474-4200, Mon, Thurs: 9:30–9;
Tues, Wed, Fri, Sat: 9:30–6; Sun: 12–5

NEEDLEWORK

MIDWEST DISCOUNT YARNS ✪

3157 W. Irving Park Rd.
Chicago, IL 60618
(773) 588-3120
Hours: Mon–Sat: 9:30–4:30
Cash, check

Don't let the jumble in the front windows dissuade you from entering; owner Lynette Opolka—in business for more than 25 years—offers yarns, booklets, and needles for good prices. Although it is a bit difficult to sift through the cones and skeins in the open bins (and even more so with two-plus people in one aisle), Lynette and her helpers spin extra threads out of the back room to match dye lots and your needs. Best buys are cones of wools, chenilles, cottons, and synthetics obtained from apparel manufacturers (up to a 75% discount); discriminating eyes will also find both high- and lower-cost brand names—Bernat, Cascade, Red Heart, Spinrite. And discriminating purses will like the 10% extra savings from the *Buying Retail Is Stupid!* coupon.

Automobile Needs

Parts & Accessories

ABC Auto Parts & Sales, Inc. ✪

13741 S. Ashland Ave.
Blue Island, IL 60406
(708) 389-1456
Hours: Mon, Tues, Thurs–Sat: 8–5; Wed: 9–5
AE, DISC, MC, OPT, V

Two large recycling complexes might prove to be treasure troves for auto buffs fixing older cars. Established in 1936, Blue Island–headquartered ABC Auto Parts—and its younger sister, Circus—specialize in both U.S. and foreign manufacturers, from Chrysler models to Toyotas. Everything from alternators to steering columns is priced right (according to our auto experts); there's a 101-day warranty; and, yes, installation is available. Before ordering, though, here's good advice: be sure of the exact part needed; know the vehicle's year, make, and model (failing that, obtain the VIN); provide the following data: engine size, front/rear-wheel drive, and two- or four-door; and specify driver's or passenger's side (not left or right). Another piece of good advice: make sure you're using the 10%-extra-discount coupon from *Buying Retail Is Stupid!*.

Blue Island—Circus Auto Parts, 13701 S. Ashland Ave.,
(708) 389-5121

Julio's Auto Parts

3000 W. Diversey Ave.
Chicago, IL 60647
(773) 292-1643
Hours: Mon–Sat: 9–7; Sun: 9–2
AE, DISC, MC, V

If you're an under-the-hood tinkerer who can quickly distinguish rack and pinions from brake shoes (plus install either or both), Julio's Auto Parts is worth more than a drive-by. Most of the merchandise is discounted 30%–50%. Depending on budgets, there's a range of items to select. Some of their 11th-anniversary sale prices: halogen headlamp replacement bulbs starting at $5.95; oil filters from $2.50 up; shock absorbers (including major brands) beginning at $11.95.

Beauty Supplies

COSMETICS, FRAGRANCES & SUPPLIES

BEAUTY WAREHOUSE

2065 N. Clybourn Ave.
Chicago, IL 60614
(773) 880-5700
Hours: Mon–Fri: 9:30–8; Sat: 9:30–6; Sun: 10–6
MC, V

Health and beauty aids, with an emphasis on the latter, fill the shelves of these two outlets. And it's the hair salon labels that predominate: Paul Mitchell, Redken, KMS, Nexxus. Look also for tanning lotions and brushes, usually reduced about 20%.
Darien—2141 W. 75th St., (630) 963-3331

MARLENA'S

127 W. Huron St.
Chicago, IL 60610
(312) 266-4600
Hours: Tues–Fri: 11–5:30; Sat: 10–5
AE, MC, V

A Chicago cosmetics legend with a glamorous Oak Street boutique, Marilyn Miglin quietly and without any fanfare opened a mini-outlet—named after daughter Marlena—in November 1996 after an August experiment during the Gold Coast art fair. Savings are, in a word, phenomenal, though it's catch as catch can to find exactly what you want. Examples from a spring scenting: $3 lipsticks (retail is $13.50); $5 mascara ($15 retail); $15 Destiny eau de parfum ($40 originally).

SAV-A-LOT
1953 N. Clybourn Ave.
Chicago, IL 60614
(773) 472-4177
Hours: Mon–Fri: 8:30–8; Sat: 8:30–6; Sun: 8:30–5:30
Cash, check

Originally located in a high-traffic section of Chicago's Clark Street, Sav-A-Lot now has a store in the busy Clybourn area. Savings remain the same on household items, cosmetics, perfume, and other beauty aids. Suggested list price for Rogaine twin-size, for example, is $59.95; here it's $42.99. Expensive fragrances flaunt even better discounts, close to 50%. Other brand-name items don't feature such deep cost-cutting, but rather a more modest 10%–20% savings.

Park Ridge—110 Euclid St., (847) 823-1105

VALENTINE & SON, INC. ✪
34 W. Van Buren
Chicago, IL 60604
(312) 939-3221
Hours: Mon–Fri: 9:30–6; Sat: 10–3:30
DISC, MC, V

It's a Sally's, for men, although the Valentines have not neglected women's needs in their merchandise selection. Sure, you'll find everything in the shampoo, coloring, setting, and cutting lines as in the big chains, plus products that only a barber (er, hairstylist) would love, such as Egyptian henna powder and some distinctly unfamiliar-looking "tonsorial" supplies. Other names provide a consumer comfort level—Andis, Oster, Revlon, Wahl—and a decent discount, about 20%. Snip your way to even greater savings with the 10% *Buying Retail Is Stupid!* coupon.

HAIRSTYLING

IVANNOEL

12 W. Maple St.
Chicago, IL 60610
(312) 266-4247
Hours: Mon: 10–5; Tues, Fri, Sat: 8–6; Wed: 8–7
MC, V

Big hair or cropped, pageboy or pixie, this unisex hair salon holds weekly classes on Tuesday evenings from April to December for its assistants, which means consumers can find un-haired-about savings, with haircuts and color beginning at $10 (usually priced at $50–$100). Appointments must be scheduled in advance depending on the hairstyle presented that week. Our newfound motto: "Help your local stylist maintain accreditation" week.

PASCAL POUR ELLE

507 N. Wells St.
Chicago, IL 60610
(312) 670-7007
Hours: Tues: 9–5; Wed: 9–5:30; Thurs: 11–7; Fri: 8:30–5;
Sat: 9–4:30
MC, V

Chichi and cheap, to boot: at Pascal Pour Elle, stylists and apprentices undergo a series of workshops every Tuesday evening at 5:00 from June through September. During this time, haircuts cost $5; a change of hair color can range anywhere from $5 to $10. Interested? Call at least 2 weeks in advance to ensure a spot. Workshops are held only downtown (i.e., no Winnetka calls, please!).
Winnetka—75 Glencoe Rd., (847) 501-3100

VIDAL SASSOON
835 N. Michigan Ave.
Water Tower Place, 3rd floor
Chicago, IL 60611
(312) 337-9497
Hours: Mon–Fri: 9–6 (for apprentice hairstylists)
AE, MC, V

"If you don't look good, we don't look good": Vidal Sassoon's slogan could well extend to the beauty salon's apprentices who, after a 14-month course, are elevated to stylists. Before that promotion, though, take advantage of the student rate for haircuts, color, and perms. On Tuesdays and Wednesdays, step in for $16 haircuts (we advise a call ahead). On Fridays, apprentices apply color (starting at $16).

Books

NEW & USED

BOOKSELLERS ROW
408 S. Michigan Ave.
Chicago, IL 60605
(312) 427-4242
Hours: "7 days a week, early 'til late"
AE, DISC, MC, OPT, V

A fixture in the South Loop for eons, Booksellers Row's "open early, stay late" policy has benefited night-owl bookworms of all ages. It's completely possible, for instance, to rub shoulders, unknowingly, with major local authors and book critics who are in the browsing mode. The selection is iconoclastic: sample new review copies, modern first editions, antiquarian books, and general reference material that someone, somewhere, needed to retire. Spotted on a recent visit: $4.95 or less for children's books, $6.50 or less for mysteries, $1.50 to $4.95 for proofs and galleys, and 40%–60% off retail every day.

BOOKWORKS

3444 N. Clark St.
Chicago, IL 60657
(773) 871-5318
Hours: Mon–Thurs: 12–10; Fri & Sat: 12–11; Sun: 12–6
MC, V

The smell of a bookstore can be rather seductive; erudition seems to infiltrate your brain almost immediately upon entrance. "What's one more?" you mutter as yet another tome finds its way to your bookshelf. And Bookworks, in the heart of Wrigleyville, the land of the ever-losing Cubs, feels like home, a personal library. It's a well-arranged general collection of about 40,000 tomes, a mix of hardcover, paperback, and various audio formats. Browse here for a while—and save a good 50% off cover prices.

USED

ASPIDISTRA BOOKSHOP

2630 N. Clark St.
Chicago, IL 60614
(773) 549-3129
Hours: Mon–Fri: 12:30–9; Sat: 11:30–9:30; Sun: 12:30–7
DIN, DISC, MC, V

An Asiatic lily, says Webster's. A fun used bookstore to browse in, we retort. Though ambiance and parking leave something to be desired, this Clark Street fixture offers a broad mix of paperback, hardcover, and remaindered books—some well loved, others hardly touched—at a minimum 40% off original cover price. The store is heavily trafficked and usually populated with aisle readers. But it is also entirely possible to locate a rare, vintage, or hard-to-find edition.

KEP'S PAPERBACK EXCHANGE
61 N. Williams
Crystal Lake, IL 60014
815/459-4343
Hours: Mon–Sat: 10–5
AE, DISC, MC, OPT, V

Paperback junkies alert: an inexpensive way to feed your habit. This cluttered little bookstore in downtown Crystal Lake isn't much to look at, but it's a great place to stock up on a summer's worth of trashy novels. Gently used books are sold at half price. Customers can also bring in paperbacks and receive store credit. Heavy on romance, with most popular writers represented. A selection better than the local public library, our scouts report, plus you get to own the books you really love.

O'GARA & WILSON BOOKSELLERS, LTD.
1448 E. 57th St.
Chicago, IL 60637
(773) 363-0993
Hours: Mon–Sat: 9–10; Sun: 12–10
DISC, MC, V

It is, quite possibly, one of the oldest and most selective used bookstores in greater Chicago. (We recall that our business and cookbook review copies were oh-so-politely rejected for sale there many, many years ago.) Judging from its proximity to the University of Chicago campus in Hyde Park and its age (founded in 1882), this bookseller's stock of 200,000+ volumes is geared to its scholarly audience—mainly art, history, the humanities, and religion. Check here for the unusual, the academic.

Powell's
2850 N. Lincoln Ave.
Chicago, IL 60657
(773) 248-1444
Hours: Sun–Fri: 11–9; Sat: 10–10
MC, V

Myth number one: this three-store chain is owned by someone on the West Coast. Myth number two: expect only used books at any of the three outlets. Actually, Powell's is a real study in fiction busting: their stores are well laid out, and the merchandise is chock-full of used books, remainders, and rarer or out-of-print editions. (We looked longingly at a $450 Picasso *Guernica* compilation.) Other titles pressing: $6.95 for Bebe Moore Campbell's *Brothers and Sisters* (once $22.95); $17.95 for Ansel Adams's National Park Service photographs. We absolutely adored their first-of-any-month, dress-up promotion: wear any Powell-insignia item (T-shirt, sweatshirt, bag) and get 20% off your entire purchase that day.
Chicago—828 S. Wabash St., (312) 341-0748, Mon–Fri: 10:30–6; Sat: 10–6; Sun: 12–5
Chicago—1501 E. 57th St., (773) 955-7780, Sun–Sat: 9–11

Building & Remodeling

Cabinets, Closets & Countertops

Cabinet World, Inc.
1401 W. North Ave.
Chicago, IL 60622
(773) 772-9900
Hours: Mon, Thurs: 10–8; Tues, Wed, Fri, Sat: 10–5; Sun: 12–4
AE, DISC, MC, V

High noon must mean contractor time: when we popped into Ron Turkin's brand-new 30,000-square-foot Cabinet World (previously housed at 3311 N. Halsted) at 12:00, we found a dozen or so professionals wandering around with gauges, calculators, and the like.

Which is a great signal for good deals. We weren't wrong: because he buys components from other manufacturers and then assembles all cabinets and vanities, there are no brand names. But, there are substantial discounts—an average 30% savings over any other retailer. (We're not naming names.) Over 100 different kitchens and 30 vanities are on display, in a choice of contemporary or traditional frameless (i.e., no post in the middle of the shelf) wood cabinets. Factory direct, explains Ron, equals major savings; as proof, he cites one North Shore couple who spent $4,000 on his cabinets. Their architect quoted triple that price.

CONSUMERS SUPPLY CO.
1110 W. Lake St.
Chicago, IL 60607
(847) 666-6080
Hours: Mon–Fri: 8–5; Sat: 8–1:30
DISC, MC, V

The low-slung exterior of Consumers Supply sprawls out under the el tracks near Chicago's wholesale food markets. Inside is a whole 'nother story: some pretty impressive displays of shower, kitchen, bathroom, and miscellaneous fixtures. In business since 1938, this Lake Street family-owned store is well trod by contractors and do-it-yourselfers; its 20%–65% discounts extend to names such as Braun, Kohler, Newport, Porcher, and Schrock, among many others. On our walk through the showroom: an old-fashioned white porcelain pedestal sink for $250; a "low-rise" Kohler San Raphael toilet for $367; and a good-looking honey-colored Schrock Harmony kitchen display for $1,995 (originally $3,600).

Windy City Kitchens & Baths

2719 N. Maplewood Ave.
Chicago, IL 60647
(773) 227-7027
Hours: Mon: 10–8; Tues–Fri: 10–5; Sat: 10–3
MC, V
◆ **Senior Discount:** 10% **Age:** 60+

Across a dead-end street from Frederick Cooper Lamps (which very occasionally opens its warehouse to the public), under the din of the Diversey ramp to the Kennedy Expressway is Windy City Kitchens. Many of their cabinets are no- or low-name, but if status brands are not an issue, then styles and savings are yours. Woods are cherry, hickory, maple, and oak; countertops include granite, Swanstone (a Corian competitor), and laminate. Multiply those options by the 50+ cabinet designs and hundreds of finishes—and the selection of the right kitchen for your home could take a dangerously long time. Nonetheless, we persevered: the Hatteras oaklike cabinet set with stainless sink for an apartment (read: small) kitchen ran about $548; a bathroom two-mirrored and ledged medicine cabinet chest was $69.95. Installation is extra.

Ceramic & Stone Tile

King of Tile, Inc. ✪

4401 N. Pulaski Ave.
Chicago, IL 60630
(773) 463-1771
Hours: Mon–Thurs: 9–8:30; Fri & Sat: 9–5:30; Sun: 10–3:30
AE, DISC, MC, V

The sign attracted us as we drove to Midway Airport: "King of Tile: We are carload buyers." Naturally, we had to investigate—after the conclusion of our trip. Current owner Joel Taustein informed us that his great-grandfather started the business in 1916 on Maxwell Street, the first floor-covering store in Chicago. Today, his two stores sell all kinds of parquet, ceramic, mosaic, and quarry tile for decent discounts, usually a 40% savings. But, don't expect installation. Instead, the prices might be seductive enough to hire it out yourself:

closeout ceramic mosaics at 99¢ a square foot (regularly $2.99) and Italian quarry tile from $1.79 to $1.99 a square foot. And it does get even cheaper by the square foot with the 10%-off *Buying Retail Is Stupid!* coupon in hand.
Chicago—5360 S. Archer Ave., (773) 581-0334

TILE OUTLET LTD.
2434 W. Fullerton Ave.
Chicago, IL 60647
(773) 276-2662
Hours: Mon–Fri: 9–9; Sat: 9–6; Sun: 10–6
DISC, MC, V

Any type of square for the floor—be it made of rubber, mosaic, ceramic, vinyl, linoleum, or marble—is more than fairly priced at the appropriately named Tile Outlet. Samples, broken lots, discontinueds, and irregulars find a home here before being whisked away quickly by do-it-yourselfers, contractors, interior designers, and architects. Great names, great tags infiltrate the store: Congoleum's Majestic vinyl at $1.20 to $1.75 a square foot; marble from $2.50 to $4.05; granite from $8 to $10. Loose samples (for the newly fashionable mosaic work) are even cheaper.

FLOOR COVERINGS

CARPET STYLES CO. ✪
1099 W. Lake St.
Addison, IL 60101
(630) 628-6188
Hours: Mon–Fri: 9–9; Sat: 9–5; Sun: 11–5
DISC, MC, V

Like furniture, floor coverings are almost always sold at discount—say, about 30% and sometimes more. Carpet Styles, in its two suburban Chicago stores, offers further savings (20%–30% less than national discounters) by buying its carpeting in full rolls. Though other coverings are available (even the trendy laminate flooring), best buys here are of the wall-to-wall fabric kind, with a good selection from many major manufacturers. Plus, *Buying Retail Is Stupid!*

readers could possibly be floored by the extra $3.00-off-per-square-yard discount coupon.
Wheeling—52 S. Milwaukee Ave., (847) 537-9070

CARPET WAREHOUSE CENTER

1640-52 N. Milwaukee Ave.
Chicago, IL 60647
(773) 384-2600
Hours: Mon, Thurs, Fri: 10–8; Tues & Wed: 10–6; Sat: 10–4; Sun: 11–4
DISC, MC, V
◆ **Senior Discount:** 10% **Age:** 60+

An unprepossessing strip mall at the beginning of Bucktown houses a flooring discounter proffering great unbiased advice and a famous name (the manager is a cousin of guitarist/soul singer Jose Feliciano). Any category of flooring product can be found here at a decent discount; examples range from Lee's Stainmaster Extra Life carpet at $19.99 per square yard installed (elsewhere, $32.99) to more than 100 carpet remnants starting at $89 for a 9 × 12 stretch. Ask for guarantees, service, and installation; Carpet Warehouse stands behind its tile, carpet, ceramic, vinyl, and wood laminate.

CENTURY TILE

300 Townline Rd.
Mundelein, IL 60060
(847) 566-3200
Hours: Mon–Sat: 8–9
AE, MC, V

Watch for demonstrations by Pete, the Century Tile pro. Even if the closest thing you do to do-it-yourself is dialing the telephone for assistance, seminars help smart consumers figure out what their hired contractors should (and should not) be doing. Along with this educational bent, the 10 stores of this 50-year-old local chain carry both branded and private-label floor coverings—ceramic, wood, vinyl, and laminate. Some of their recent "celebrate our new store" prices: Armstrong no-wax tile from 99¢ to $1.18 per square foot,

and Century's own wood laminate at a very good tag of $2.99+ per square foot.
Nine locations; 1-800-CENTURY
Corporate headquarters is at 747 E. Roosevelt Rd., Lombard, IL 60148, (630) 889-0800.

EXPOSITION CARPET CO., INC. ✪

5718 N. Broadway
Chicago, IL 60660
(773) 784-5600
Hours: Mon–Fri: 10–9; Sat: 10–5; Sun: 12–5
AE, DISC, MC, OPT, V
◆ **Senior Discount:** 10% **Age:** 60+

The differences among floor-coverings stores are subtle but still noticeable—and are usually pegged to service, not necessarily price, such as the ability to take home swatches or samples. Or the offer to measure and estimate on-site . . . free! Twenty-five-year-old Exposition Carpet offers that—and more, including a goodly selection of remnants, rolls, area rugs, and, soon, wood laminate (Pergo, specifically). They'll also match or beat competitors' prices; a sample of recent sales: carpeting beginning at $13.95 per square yard (yes, with delivery, padding, and installation); 9 × 12 remnants from $99. And our favorite: an 8-ounce bottle of Tech (a little-known and highly underrated "everything" cleaner) for $3.95. Cover yourself and your floors with an extra 10% savings from your *Buying Retail Is Stupid!* coupon.

JEFFERSON INDUSTRIES OUTLET STORE

2100 S. Marshall Blvd.
Chicago, IL 60623
(773) 277-6100
Hours: Mon–Sat: 9–4:30
MC, V

It's hard to tell from the words "Jefferson Industries" just what the manufacturing results are. Once you're inside, the merchandise is unmistakable: rugs, carpets, mats, remnants—anything to do with flooring of the fibrous or plastic kind—all at major discounts. In this land of lower-end carpeting, most are protected against all types of spots and spills, stains, and general dirt. So, for the proverbial rumpus room, den, or guest quarters, its flooring is a natural: doormats for 99¢; a 6 × 9 carpet at $36; and $7.95 small denim accent rugs (once $15).

OLYMPIC CARPET CENTER

2719 N. California Ave.
Chicago, IL 60647
(773) 276-1212
Hours: Mon–Fri: 9–9; Sat: 9–7; Sun: 10–6
AE, DISC, MC, V

Consider this flooring outlet as a source for rental apartments and student housing, because Olympic is essentially a remnant warehouse. Which is why prices are about as low as we've seen anywhere. Who else could offer a typical room-size leftover carpet for $39? Or seamless vinyl flooring from Congoleum at $5.99+ per roll? Also seen: those heavy-duty commercial mats, from $24.99 (a 3 × 5 footer), perfect for mudrooms, home offices, and well-trafficked areas.

Chicago—2614 N. California Ave., (773) 276-0384
Chicago—3017 N. Central Ave., (773) 736-3390

WHOLESALE CARPET DESIGNS, INC. ★

1470 S. Milwaukee Ave.
Libertyville, IL 60048
(847) 549-9500
Hours: Mon–Fri: 9–5; Sat: 9–5; Sun: 11–5
DISC, MC, V

◆ **Senior Discount:** 15% **Age:** 60+

Don't let the name fool you: family-owned-and-operated Wholesale Carpet Designs also carries wood laminate, hardwood, vinyl, ceramic, and marble flooring for a 35% savings. The reason they're able to pass on good dollar discounts is their membership in a co-op buying group. Other reasons to shop there are personalized service and shop-at-home appointments, in addition, of course, to the

Buying Retail Is Stupid! coupon: $3 off per yard if you buy a yard or more of floor covering. Look for brand names such as Bruce, Lees, and Masland; and ask for Winston, the family dog.
Arlington Heights—349 E. Rand Rd., (847) 398-9900

PLUMBING & ELECTRICAL

AMERICAN KITCHEN AND BATH OUTLET ✪

2211 N. Elston Ave.
Chicago, IL 60614
(773) 395-3500
Hours: Mon, Tues, Thurs: 10–8; Wed, Fri: 10–5; Sat: 10–5
MC, V

Ask owner James Lange about his merchandise, and he'll spout poetry about 800 possible combinations of kitchen and bath designs. Some big names stock their floors, including Kohler, Cabinet, Triangle, and Ventaca, for about a 60% discount. A set of raised, oak-panel kitchen cabinets—seven top, six base, five drawers—sells here for about 25% off retail. Fed by Lange's six Chicago-area retail stores, this outlet's stock and prices will fluctuate, depending on availability. What will not fluctuate is the additional 10% off that *Buying Retail Is Stupid!* readers can enjoy with the coupon in this book.

J & D WHIRLPOOL AND BATH OUTLET

2730 N. Elston Ave.
Chicago, IL 60647
(773) 252-6886
Hours: Mon–Fri: 9–5; Sat: 9–4
AE, DISC, V
◆ **Senior Discount:** 5% **Age:** 65+

What's the difference between a whirlpool, a hot tub, and a spa? Except for the materials and finish, the last two pieces of plumbing are synonymous, says manager Doug Denning. Sold here at a discount are all types of fixtures: bathroom vanities starting at $50, whirlpool baths at $499. Names, too, stand out, such as American

Standard, Kohler, and Jacuzzi; the specialties here are closeouts and B-grades.
Chicago—2745 N. Harlem Ave., (773) 622-5420

Max Gerber ✪

2293 N. Milwaukee Ave.
Chicago, IL 60647
(773) 342-7600
Hours: Mon, Thurs: 8–8; Tues, Wed, Fri: 8–6; Sat: 9–5
DISC, MC, V

The kinds of names you associate with those oh-so-chic bathrooms and kitchens, including Corian, Grohe, Kohler, and Rubern, can be found here in abundance—and at a 10%–50% discount. Calling itself a "whotailer," a cross between retail and wholesale, at least to the consumer, Gerber displays its plumbing wares (everything but the cabinets) in its 8,000-square-foot showroom, a fixture for more than 75 years. Some examples of savings: a Grohe faucet listed at $449, sells for $359.10; Euroview shower enclosures once $75 per square foot, now $49.95 per square foot; and an Astracast sink retailing at $443, now $376.55. Another example of savings is the 10% additional discount that *Buying Retail Is Stupid!* readers can plumb to its depths.

Wall & Window Treatments

Glover Shade Company

406 N. Wells St.
Chicago, IL 60610
(312) 245-5353
Hours: Mon–Fri: 9–5
AE, DISC, MC, V

OK, so Chicago is ripe with discount window-coverings stores. And the savvy bargain shopper already knows that the best deals are to be found from those stores with their own factories. Go to 60-something-year-old Glover Shade, then, for savings on unusual vertical blinds, shades, and shutters. Need to protect your furniture with shades for 18-foot wall-to-wall windows? No problem (and

Glover figures out how to squeeze them into your high-rise elevator). How about remote-controlled motorized coverings for way-too-tall apertures? All in a day's work. No matter what the job, the Glover name (not the nationally advertised brand) will be priced substantially lower.

HABITAT WALLPAPER & BLINDS

2070 N. Clybourn Ave.
Chicago, IL 60614
(773) 404-8500
Hours: Mon–Fri: 9:30–9; Sat: 9:30–6; Sun: 11–5
AE, DISC, Habitat, MC, V

No blind purchases possible: 10-year-old local chain Habitat vies with the Eddie Z's and Glovers of this area to outfit Chicago's windows—and does a good job of discounting as well. Included in its merchandise mix are shades, blinds, and wallpaper too at a 20%–70% reduction. Spec the store's private label (Habitat Preferred) for top savings. A birthday celebration ad featured some good plummeting prices: $8.99 per roll of in-stock wallpaper and borders; 60%–70% off on Honeycomb Duette pleated shades.
Nine locations; see the Yellow Pages

VERTICAL BLINDS FACTORY ★

2191 N. Clybourn Ave.
Chicago, IL 60614
(773) 525-1800
Hours: Mon–Sat: 9–6; Sun: 11–4
AE, DISC, MC, OPT, V
◆ **Senior Discount:** 10% **Age:** 65+

Heed well the name of this four-store chain: executive Brian Pinsky says they offer the best discounts on vertical, not horizontal, blinds. In fact, because it is a factory, Vertical Blinds manufactures while you wait—and will also train customers in the art of do-it-yourself installation (or, for an additional fee, you can hire one of its professionals). Warranties, a selection of more than 4,000 colors and styles, and a guarantee of best price, in sum, make this a suggested stop when window (covering) shopping. Highly recom-

mended as well is use of the 10% extra discount with your *Buying Retail Is Stupid!* coupon.
Burbank—8036 S. Cicero Ave., (708) 346-9993
Downers Grove—1630 Ogden Ave., (630) 971-3900
Niles—9161 N. Milwaukee Ave., (847) 470-8828

Clothing & Accessories

Sometimes, designer discounting just doesn't pay.

Consider, for instance, the case of The Backroom at 8 East Chestnut in Chicago. For years, this shop (and its owners) had peacefully coexisted with its Gold Coast neighbors, selling Armani, Escada, Laurel, Moschino, etc. duds for men and women at amazingly small fractions of their retail worth.

On April 24, 1997, that life abruptly ended. Chicago's finest charged The Backroom's two female employees (owner and clerk) with felony theft—and suspect that the operation might have deeper roots than just a high-class shoplifting ring stealing from the likes of Field's, Neiman Marcus, and Saks. Higher authorities on the federal side have joined the investigation. What's next? It takes a while for the wheels of justice to grind. But it's enough to warn all that if it's too good to be true, then it's probably not a bargain.

Bridal & Formal

Bride$mart

600 E. Roosevelt Rd.
Lombard, IL 60148
(630) 495-6600
Hours: Mon–Thurs: 12–9; Fri: 12–4; Sat: 10–5; Sun: 12–4
MC, V

There is a very good reason for the dollar sign in the name of this store: the monies saved on a wedding dress here could very well pay for a portion of a Hawaiian honeymoon. Reductions are from 50% to 80%, sizes from 6 to 44. New bridal gowns can sport smaller price tags than Filene's semiannual "I do" extravaganzas. Styles are as severe or as flouncy as desired; on our visit, a Demetrios gown carried a $295 tag ($1,099 retail). Special orders are discounted less. And expect to pay for alterations.

I DO, INC. ★

6742 W. Belmont Ave.
Chicago, IL 60634
(773) 205-1234
Hours: Tues–Fri: 12–8; Sat & Sun: 12–6
DISC, MC, V

Owner Kelly Hamilton, after looking in vain for a previously owned bridal gown for her 1993 remarriage, knew she had the germ of an entrepreneurial idea: a resale shop specializing in bridal and wedding finery. Today, a senior citizen mails in a dress worn in 1947. Tomorrow, another consignor, a gown purchased for a 1967 ceremony. Over 350 gowns and 100 veils and accessories constantly change in I Do, from Alfred Angelo to Vera Wang, all at 50% off retail (except for vintage finery). A wondrous touch is the addition (whenever available) of the original gown owner's wedding photograph, tacked discreetly next to the dress. Clean, spacious dressing rooms and accommodating management are Kelly's second gift to her customers—the third is $25 off the veil price to every *Buying Retail Is Stupid!* gown purchaser with the coupon from this book.

IRENA'S BRIDAL

244 E. Roosevelt Rd.
Lombard, IL 60148
(630) 932-8222
Hours: Mon–Thurs: 12–9; Fri: 11–5; Sat: 10–5
DISC, MC, V

There's a stretch of Roosevelt Road in Lombard that could easily be renamed Bridal Row: both discounters and retailers of wedding paraphernalia vie for attention along this commercial strip. Irena's stands out, since it provides one-stop shopping for brides-to-be; everything, from Aberdeen's wedding flowers to Edward Fox photography, is available. (Except, of course, for the groom.) But, the real focus is on a roomful of gowns . . . and some hard-to-beat prices on stock dresses. A recent visit revealed an entire section of new wedding wear for $199; rarely, if ever, did prices reach the four-figure zone.

LADY JOYCE CO. ★
2332 W. Logan Blvd.
Chicago, IL 60647
(773) 486-7993
Hours: Mon–Fri: 9–6; Sat: 9–4
AE, DISC, MC, V

The day job of Lady Joyce owner Christine Ree is imagining fanciful headdress creations for every female member of the wedding party, sold at well-known bridal shops across the country. But behind the desolate look of this warehouse building off busy Elston Avenue are some remarkable prices for clothing the whole bride. Bolts of elegant fabrics, realistic garlands, trims, accessories, and hat forms are all marked down and stacked on metal shelves. A series of doors and rooms lead to other sewing materials, an array of 50%-off gowns, and, best yet, seamstresses who will fabricate the gown of your dreams with free alterations at a $300–$800 total charge (or a substantial 40% discount). Ask to see Ree's scrapbook of customers' testimonials; it's pretty impressive. So is the extra 10% discount extended to *Buying Retail Is Stupid!* readers who present the coupon.

FAMILY APPAREL

MEYSTEL'S WAREHOUSE
1222 S. Wabash Ave.
Chicago, IL 60605
(312) 294-2270
Hours: Mon–Fri: 10–6:45; Sun: 10–5:45
AE, MC, V

Established in 1923, Meystel's Warehouse has been gentrified out of its longtime headquarters and thus is moving south (to the 47th and Halsted Street area). The 50%+ price reductions North Siders enjoyed for years will still be available . . . but a few miles farther away. Name brands proliferate: $28 Perry Ellis America men's jeans; $11 French Toast jean skirt for girls; $76 I.B. Diffusion silk/wool jacket. Handbags, shoes, and outerwear for the entire family are similarly discounted. By applying for a Meystel's card, shoppers can reap an extra 3% (with charge or check) or an additional 5% (cash) for a VIP discount.

BERRY-CUTLER HOSIERY ★

546 W. Harrison St.
Chicago, IL 60607
(312) 939-5777
Hours: Mon–Fri: 8–4:30; Sat: 10–2
MC, V

Don't let the word *hosiery* in the store name mislead you. Anything considered an accessory is the province of Berry-Cutler Hosiery. Their deep discounts, says president Ira Berry, are courtesy of private-label, sometimes irregular, goods produced by some of America's largest casual-wear manufacturers: Dockers, John Henry, Gitano, Spaulding, Wrangler. Near Joseph Cinofsky, and open since 1983, Berry-Cutler, we found, more than lives up to its promise of "saving on quality without sacrificing wearability": 89¢ a pair for pantyhose; $2.93 a pair for men's designer socks. And to the delight of *Buying Retail Is Stupid!* readers, the store is offering another 10% reduction with its book coupon.

FASHION ACCESSORIES

BILL THE HATTER/STAR HEADWEAR

2700 N. Elston Ave.
Chicago, IL 60622
(773) 384-2000
Hours: Mon–Fri: 10–5; Sat: 10–4
MC, V

Chapeaux, Stetsons, baseball caps, berets, toques, safaris, pith helmets—hats of virtually every size and shape are draped on walls or displayed in bins at Star Headwear Company. About 70 years young, this manufacturer's outlet also sells other accessories at closeout prices such as socks at $1.50 a pair, gloves for $6 to $12, and sportswear. But gear for heads is its specialty, at about a 30%–40% discount. Our absolute favorites? Cooler-than-cool black leather caps for a mere 12 to 18 bucks.

BURNHAM GLOVE ✪

1602 Tennessee St.
Michigan City, IN 46360
(219) 874-5205
Hours: Mon–Fri: 8–4; Sat: 9–5
AE, DISC, MC, V

Everything to fit the 10 fingers of man, woman, and child is on display at Burnham Glove—at headquarters and at its Lighthouse Mall outlet. The Stronghold brand name, says president Roger Frye, means over one thousand styles are available at a 20%–60% savings, along with hats, scarves, and safety glasses. Gear up for a winter, Midwest style, with the additional 10% off *Buying Retail Is Stupid!* coupon.

Michigan City, IN—Burnham Glove "The Works," Lighthouse Mall, (219) 878-0905, Mon–Sat: 9–8; Sun: 10–6

I. WEINBERG HOSIERY

632 W. Roosevelt Rd.
Chicago, IL 60607
(312) 922-3710
Hours: Mon–Fri: 8–4:30; Sat: 10–2
Cash, check

In a town hosting a baseball team called the White Sox, wouldn't you expect major bargains on hose? On Roosevelt Road, there are no disappointed Sox-ers; a cluster of shops offers low, lower, and lowest prices on socks and undergarments, and other clothing essentials. I. Weinberg at 632 West is one of those stores; prices here are hard to match. Examples are various colors and sizes of men's socks for 50¢–75¢ a pair; three pairs of women's socks for $1.50; and half a dozen pairs of ladies' briefs for $5.

Marlo Warehouse Outlet ✪
111 E. Marquardt Dr.
Wheeling, IL 60090
(847) 215-1400
Hours: Tues–Sat: 10–4
DISC, MC, V

Remember Imelda Marcos and her 2,000 pairs of shoes? Well, certain acquaintances of ours (a-hem!) could be said to enjoy a similar relationship with purses, shoulder bags, wallets, and other carryalls. Sound familiar? Marlo, then, is a godsend for leather-container addicts, with its astounding two rooms full of totes and carryalls and sunglasses and acrylic accessories. Its own labels as well as others (Nicole Miller, Perlina, Sharif) hang on hooks everywhere: a gold vinyl signature Sharif tote for $51.25 (once $77); an interwoven, black-leather, ergonomically designed shoulder bag at $112 (was $150); and an array of irregulars at $7.50 each or two for $12. Started about 4 years ago after owner Adrienne Faber's last kid entered high school, the Marlo Outlet now maintains a 12,000-customer mailing list. Hang 'em high for savings of at least 25% (add much, much more during major blowouts). Plus, save an additional $5 off a $25 purchase with the coupon exclusively for *Buying Retail Is Stupid!* readers.

That's Our Bag
50 E. Randolph St.
Chicago, IL 60601
(312) 984-2626
Hours: Mon–Sat: 9–6; Sun: 12–5
AE, DIN, DISC, MC, V

Randolph Street store employees were quick to point out that "That's Our Bag" referred only to their location and the 540 North Michigan Avenue outlet. (There is a same-name store at 230 North Michigan.) Regardless of probable strained relationships, this discounter has expanded beyond the "bag" in its 17+ years of existence. Now accessories mean brand-name shoes for both men and women—Bandolino, Kenneth Cole, Naturalizer—as well as a decent

selection of mid-priced luggage, at 20%–35% discount. (Clearance items are reduced 50% to 75%.) Their deals? An Impuls wheeled overnighter at $109.97 (once $250); a Latico leather duffel for $179.99 (was $240).
Chicago—540 N. Michigan Ave., (312) 984-3510

Wells Lamont Factory Glove Outlet

7525 N. Oak Park Ave.
Niles, IL 60714
(847) 647-8200, ext. 3399
Hours: Mon–Fri: 10–5; Sat: 10–3
AE, V

Hands of almost any shape and size will be protectively cloaked at a discount, thanks to the factory outlet of Wells Lamont. Choose from first-quality, irregulars, and closeouts fashioned of leather or goatskin, plus Thinsulate-lined gloves and mittens, at about 25%–40% less than retail. There's a smaller selection of accessories for other body parts—such as socks, ski jackets, belts, and wallets—all at reduced prices.

Infants' & Children's Apparel

The Baby's Room Clearance Center

3841 W. Columbus Ave.
Chicago, IL 60652
(773) 581-9700
Hours: Mon, Thurs, Fri: 10–9; Tues & Wed: 10–5:30; Sat: 10–6; Sun: 11–5
DISC, MC

If we ask enough questions, we discover that almost every national chain has an outlet or discount warehouse or dumping grounds. (After all, unsold merchandise doesn't necessarily travel directly into the arms of liquidators.) The trick is to find that outlet within our geographic limits. Here is one result of our ever-inquiring minds: the clearance center for The Baby's Room. Sometimes 20%, sometimes greater reductions on almost everything parents need

(except mattresses). For example: a Simmons pine crib for $179.99 (regularly $409.99); $55 for a 12-position rise-and-dine high chair; and a Graco swing-cradle tagged at about $90. Best for baby showers are the $5–$10 selection of discontinueds, such as canopies, wall hangings, and musical mobiles.
10 locations; see the Yellow Pages

Kids' Express
770 120th Ave.
Kenosha, WI 53142
(414) 857-6750
Hours: Mon–Fri: 10–9; Sat & Sun: 10–6
DISC, MC, V

An unprepossessing two-store discount clothier, Kids' Express can literally cover a child in fashion from newborn to size 16 (girls) and size 18 (boys). Grandparent-friendly, it showcases first-quality, designer-type merchandise at great prices. Its markdown rule of discounting? An immediate 30% upon arrival in store; 40% after 2 months; 50% after 4 months. Try these prices: a 100% silk party dress for $39 ($105 elsewhere); boys' Flapdoodle garments at $5 each or two for $7.
Gurnee—6170 W. Grand Ave., (847) 855-0880

One Step Ahead Outlet Store
120 S. Waukegan Rd.
Deerfield, IL 60015
(847) 714-1940
Hours: Mon–Fri: 10–7; Sat: 10–6; Sun: 11–5
AE, DIN, DISC, MC, OPT, V

A Lake Bluff–based kids catalog concern now sends its overstock and discontinueds straight to one store only—in Deerbrook Mall. With savings from 20% to 70%, One Step Ahead features wares for babies, toddlers, and parents, including such items as cotton terry tunics (cut from $29.95 to $22.46); a Plus Four stroller (from $109.95 to $96.46); and air-filtering machines ($89.95 reduced to $67.46). Famous brands (e.g., toys from Berchet) appear from time to time, but quantities are limited.

RUBENS BABY FACTORY STORE

2340 N. Racine Ave.
Chicago, IL 60614
(773) 348-6200
Hours: Mon–Fri: 8–4:30
Cash, check

Familiar to DePaul residents is a hulking brick building on West Fullerton with a nondescript sign announcing the "Rubens Baby Factory Store." Not so familiar are the factory's contents: seconds and first-quality, white infant and toddler undergarments and crib and bassinet sheets. These necessities of life for new parents are priced right: polyester kimonos at $2.49 (were $3.50); stretch diapers, $9 a dozen. A Chicago institution since 1890.

THE WEAR HOUSE

222 Merchandise Mart Plaza, Suite 216
Chicago, IL 60654
(312) 836-0612
Hours: Mon–Fri: 9–6; Sat: 10–5
DISC, MC, V

A shock of color greets every visitor to The Wear House outlet in Chicago's Merchandise Mart, selling samples, overruns, and past-season kids' apparel manufactured by Weather Tamer (with a few odds and ends from other labels). Through the showroom's glass fronts are seen racks and racks of snowsuits, rain suits, swimsuits, and casual togs for boys and girls; outer- and swimwear fit infant to 14, while sportswear is only to sizes 6X (girls) and 7 (boys). Our visit revealed major savings: $8 jeans; $6 striped cotton boy's shirt.

Larger Sizes for Women

Jean's Boutique, Inc.

555D W. Roosevelt Rd.
Chicago, IL 60607
(312) 226-3669
Hours: Mon–Sat: 10–5:30
AE, MC, V

Housed in the same shopping center as Morris & Sons is Jean's Boutique, featuring the Harvé Benard label and other suitable business attire for women. Sizes run 6 to 16+, with emphasis on BBW (Big Beautiful Women) and the traditional 30% discount; included in stock are dresses, pants, overcoats, and suits.

Leather Garments & Furs

American Fur Mart

5309 W. Touhy Ave.
Skokie, IL 60077
(847) 763-8000
Hours: Mon–Fri: 10–7; Sat: 10–5 (hours change seasonally)
AE, DISC, MC, V

Prices quoted at this Skokie establishment will jump-charge the fantasies of those shoppers with no aversion to wearing fur. Besides, in the last few years, American consumers have returned to buying coats made of animal pelts—since the activities of animal activists have died down. As to be expected at this combo manufacturer-wholesaler, there's a fur for every budget: full-length mink coats for $1,495 and up; raccoon outerwear starting at $995. Best bet we saw one day: a full-length red fox, regularly $8,985, usually on sale at $5,990 and recently reduced to $2,995. (Our furry adviser recommends shopping in August for the best selection.)

CHICAGO FUR OUTLET ☆

777 W. Diversey Ave.
Chicago, IL 60614
(773) 348-3877
Hours: Hours vary; call first
AE, DISC, MC, V

In the heart of Lakeview—and at one of the busiest intersections in Chicago—is a resale fur shop now celebrating its 10th anniversary. Proprietors Eve and Howard Bresnik do know their furs . . . and price their previously owned creations sensibly, whether for men or women. A few choices: a Galanos for Maximillian full-length blue iris mink at $3,500 ($10,000 new) and a men's coyote jacket at $500 ($2,000 new). The full services of this "home of the furry godmother" also include cleaning, storage, and a selection of new furs. However, the best deals are "used" . . . and the 5% off *Buying Retail Is Stupid!* coupon that applies to any $500+ purchase.

THE LEATHER OUTLET

222 Merchandise Mart Plaza, Suite 204
Chicago, IL 60654
(312) 329-9583
Hours: Mon–Fri: 9–6; Sat: 10–5
AE, DISC, MC, V

A name change (formerly Cary & Co.) and an across-the-street move (from the Apparel Center) might dissuade some bargain seekers from finding leather deals. Not so, our intrepid shoppers. Now housed on the second floor of the revamped retail Merchandise Mart, The Leather Outlet's new quarters still boast similar savings. Lots of Italian leathers (our personal preference) in lots of male and female sizes—up to 4X or 5X and by special order—provide a decent selection. Though the store is known for shearlings, leathers, and furs, owner Cary Feldman just might stock purses, great sweaters, and other apparel accoutrements. Present during our shop-in: $800 Walter DaVoucci brown shearling (compare to $1,899); $949 white leather Kadosh women's coat (originally $1,999).

LEATHER OUTLET ✪

205 Army Trail Rd.
Glendale Heights, IL 60139
(630) 307-0280
Hours: Tues, Thurs, Fri: 11–7; Wed, Sat: 11–6; Sun: 11–5
AE, DISC, MC, V
◆ **Senior Discount:** 10% on Wed **Age:** 65+

We have a recurring dream of a biker's life, dressed head to toe in black leather and metal. Such is the stuff that wishes (or is it nightmares?) are made of. We've found that we can fulfill our fantasies—at a discount—at the Leather Outlet (in no way related to the Mechandise Mart store of similar name). Though the stock is not designer, made-in-Italy (or Israel) quality, it's good, serviceable leather, great for wearing astride a motorcycle. What we modeled during our visit: Jeff Hamilton Bulls' leather coats for $300 each ($499 at the United Center) and long leather coats at $175 (regularly $350). And what we want to own permanently will be forever enhanced (in our eyes) by the extra-10% *Buying Retail Is Stupid!* coupon discount.

LINGERIE

CHICAGO HOSIERY AND UNDERWEAR

601 W. Roosevelt Rd.
Chicago, IL 60607
(312) 226-0055
Hours: Mon–Sat: 9–5; Sun: 9–4
MC, V

There is a plethora of options for clothing the feet inexpensively on Roosevelt Road. Such as Chicago Hosiery and Underwear, with both designer and no-name socks and pantyhose—and, of course, undergarments—at reasonable, below-department-store prices. Our foray netted the following: a buck a pair for hose; girls' socks, four pairs for $5; boys' socks, five for $5.

LORRAINE LINGERIE OUTLET
4220 W. Belmont Ave.
Chicago, IL 60641
(773) 283-3000, ext. 238
Hours: Mon–Sat: 9–6
MC, V

The exquisitely soft Cuddle Duds casual clothes and sleepwear, as seen on national retail floors, are probably better known than the parent—Lorraine Lingerie. Housed in a strip with other discounters, this particular factory outlet is strictly bare bones, with samples pinned to walls and a bunch of racks holding hanging apparel. Savings, though, can be substantial, ranging over 50% reductions on irregulars and discontinued merchandise.

MATERNITY CLOTHES

EXPECTATIONS OUTLET ✪
3926 W. Dempster St.
Skokie, IL 60076
(847) 677-0010
Hours: Mon–Wed, Fri & Sat: 10–5:30; Thurs: 10–8; Sun: 12–5
DISC, MC, V

Pregnancy, even in the healthiest of moms-to-be, can be an awkward time. What to wear for work . . . and home? What to expect after the birth? And so on. The Expectations Outlet in Skokie, however, has at least one of these questions covered: a wardrobe for the most important 9 months—at prices 20%–70% below retail. Here, an elegant black lace dress bedazzles at $39.99 (retail was $188), while getting suited was never easier with Expectations' 100% cotton style at $88 (was $126). Plus, bring a smile to that new parent with the 10% extra discount coupon from *Buying Retail Is Stupid!* (on a minimum $50 purchase).

MATERNITY WORKS

50 E. Washington St., 2nd floor, #210
Chicago, IL 60602
(312) 332-0022
Hours: Mon–Sat: 10–6
AE, MC, V

One-half retail, one-half discount: this second-floor, heart-of-the-Loop apparel store for moms-to-be is labeled for savings, so it's not difficult to distinguish discount from regular in this very cramped space. All the brands you know—A Pea in the Pod, Maternity Works, Mimi, Motherhood, Mothers Work, and Steena—are well represented. A regular $240 career dress marked $89; a navy blue work shirt marked from $88 down to $29; and as-is and samples are reduced even further. Usually located in outlet malls, this mom-to-be store, with soon-to-be companion in the Clybourn & Fullerton area, attracts downtowners and Lincoln Parkers.

Gurnee—Gurnee Mills, Maternity Works, (847) 855-9665
Michigan City—118 Lighthouse Place, (219) 873-9278
National chain, (215) 873-2200

MEN'S APPAREL & ACCESSORIES

BUY-A-TUX SUPERSTORE ✪

615 W. Roosevelt Rd.
Chicago, IL 60607
(312) 243-5465
Hours: Mon–Sat: 10–6; Sun: 10–5
AE, DISC, MC, OPT, V

For the times in life requiring the elegance of a tux, it really can be cheaper to buy than to rent. Especially when lower-than-retail prices are offered. At Buy-A-Tux, nestled in the Roosevelt Row of apparel discounters, owner Michael Shea offers new, first-quality evening suits for $139.95 to $719+, a marked savings compared with finer men's stores. Experienced staff also helps create a boutique atmosphere in the midst of a very busy street. Also enjoy a 10% additional savings through the *Buying Retail Is Stupid!* coupon.

CENTRAL DISCOUNT CLOTHING

3031 N. Central Ave.
Chicago, IL 60634
(773) 777-5556
Hours: Mon, Thurs, Fri: 10–7; Tues, Wed, Sat: 1–6; Sun: 10–5
AE, DISC, MC, V

The name's changed. But the location and savings remain the same: Central Discount Clothing on North Central Avenue, once known as Spencer's. It is strictly odds and ends, a little bit of this and that, so patience is definitely a virtue at this liquidator. In terms of clothing the man, however, it's hard to beat the prices: Giorgio Brutini or Stacy Adams shoes at $60 or two pair for $80; $10 ties (mostly silk); suits from $99 to $299. Great rummaging for all sizes, all shapes of males.

EISENSTEIN CLOTHING COMPANY

555 W. Roosevelt Rd., Store E
Chicago, IL 60607
(312) 738-0028
Hours: Mon–Sat: 9–4:30; Sun: 10–3
AE, DISC, MC, V

Vanity plates such as "RAGMAN" and "THREADS" stud the lot of this never-deserted Near South Side discount shopping center. And no wonder, because some of the better apparel deals in town are found along Roosevelt Road. Like its upstairs rival Morris & Sons, Eisenstein trades in upscale men's clothing—and some accessories, usually at 20%–50% off retail. But unlike with its famed competitor, labels are nowhere in sight; a salesman says all are European-styled, American-made . . . usually overruns, credit returns, hard-to-detect flaws, and one-of-a-kinds. Nonetheless, we spied a few brands: Hugo Boss, Pallesco, Tulliano. Sample prices: shirts $22.50–$37.50 (about a 25% reduction); a double-breasted wool gabardine suit for $220 (originally $425); and $75 silk ties for $50.

EURODIRECT INTERNATIONAL ★
606 E. Irving Park Rd.
Bensenville, IL 60106
(630) 766-3300
Hours: Fri: 11–9; Sat: 10–6; Sun: 11–5
AE, DISC, MC, V

"If you look good, we look good" might be a Vidal Sassoon trademark, but it applies just as well to the philosophy of Eurodirect. Near O'Hare Airport and open weekends only, this menswear distributor-discounter offers 40%–50% savings on designer suits and sports coats from Europe. (Suits ordinarily priced at $850, for instance, have recently been advertised for $199.50.) Once on the mailing list, customers will occasionally receive special-discount postcards. And those fortunate enough to have their own copy of *Buying Retail Is Stupid!* can redeem the Eurodirect coupon for a free tie with suit/coat/pants purchase.

FRANKLIN FRIEDMAN CLOTHING CO.
7219 W. Grand Ave.
Elmwood Park, IL 60635
(708) 453-2112
Hours: Mon–Fri: 9:30–8:30; Sat: 9:30–5:30; Sun: 10–5
AE, DISC, MC, V

No vents. Double-breasted jackets. Some old comfortable brands, such as Petrocelli and Yves Saint Laurent. The home of Franklin Friedman, then, caters to men preferring Euro-style tailoring of the classic variety. Except for specials, such as $250 sports coats for $149.90, the rule here is 20% discount on all tags, with suits individually priced. But, where the bargains truly might make a difference will be in the free-alterations offer, a potential savings of up to $75 or $80. Sizes from 36 short to 50 portly; a half century of operations (originally the Jack Robbins Clothing Company on Belmont Avenue).

GINGISS FORMALWEAR OUTLET

542 W. Roosevelt Rd.
Chicago, IL 60607
(312) 347-9911
Hours: Fri: 10–8; Sat: 9–5; Sun: 11–5
AE, DISC, MC, V

It's your choice at Gingiss: pick from generics, labels, used, or new tuxedos, reflecting, of course, a wide range of prices. Up to 60% is saved on this national rent-a-tux chain's wearables (most are seconds, closeouts, discontinueds, and samples). What we saw? Christian Dior at $207.50 (once $415); Bill Blass for $197.50 ($395 retail); and already-rented tuxes in top condition at $125. Stepping out on the town, Chicago-style.

HICKEY FREEMAN

6132 Broadway
Crossroads Shopping Center
Merrillville, IN 46410
(219) 884-8444
Hours: Mon–Sat: 9:30–5:30
AE, MC, V

The worst-kept secret in the Midwest, especially after a 1996 *Fortune* magazine article praised both prices and wares: the Hickey Freeman outlet in Merrillville, Indiana. In fact, it's not easy for non-Midwesterners to find, as it's tucked away in the Crossroads Shopping Center. The trek, however, is worth every toll paid; imagine $50 cotton suits, $660 for 100% cashmere topcoats, and wool suits ranging from $99.99 to $149.99—all with the impeccable tailoring and finger-soft textiles of Hickey Freeman. Selections, of course, are limited; occasional sales increase the average 40%–50% discount. And other brands from Hartmarx, such as Austin Reed, are also stocked.

IMPERIAL CLOTHIERS ☆

4560 W. Touhy Ave.
Lincolnwood, IL 60646
(847) 676-2020
Hours: Fri: 11–7; Sat & Sun: 10–5
MC, V

In sheer numbers alone, Imperial Clothiers astounds: 30,000+ men's suits; 10,000 sports coats; 1,500 tuxedos; 5,000 pairs of pants. Started in Northbrook and recently relocated to Lincolnwood, this combination manufacturer-wholesaler warehouse, all 22,000 feet of it, is open only on weekends. No matter, because prices do entice: 100% wool suits for $149; three pairs of slacks for $75; Albert Nipon dress shirts for $17 or $25 each (a limited offer). Of note are Imperial's near-the-door rack, where all proceeds are contributed to Lamb's Farm in Libertyville (e.g., ties for $4 each) and the "Oops Hall," a bevy of imperfect odds and ends for extremely low prices. And yes, there's a tailor on-site; alterations, natch, cost extra. On any weekend, saunter in with the 5% extra discount (on a $100+ purchase) from *Buying Retail Is Stupid!*.

IRV'S CLOTHING ☆

610 N. Milwaukee Ave.
Prospect Heights, IL 60070
(847) 459-8060
Hours: Mon–Fri: 10–9; Sat & Sun: 10–5
AE, DISC, MC, OPT, V

Longtime customers of the "inconveniently located" Irv's fondly remember $39 sports coats, cash or checks only. Though prices like that are history, and Irv's has since expanded to four locations, executive males in all professions (and a few women) still patronize Irv's. And why not? The merchandise is studded with trusted names (Bill Blass, Perry Ellis, Pancaldi, Nino Cerruti); the prices, enticing (e.g., $225 for a $395 Ralph Lauren Polo worsted wool two-piece suit). And certainly no inconvenience to *Buying Retail Is Stupid!* readers is the extra-10%-discount coupon.
Chicago—2841 N. Laramie Ave., (773) 286-7293
Chicago—431 N. Orleans St., (312) 832-9900
Darien—7511 Lemont Rd., (630) 910-1333

Joseph Cinofsky Inc.
560 W. Harrison St.
Chicago, IL 60607
(312) 922-5560
Hours: Mon–Fri: 9–4:30; Sat: 9–4
DISC, MC, V

Close to the Rush medical complex is a virtual Chicago institution: the middle-aged Joseph Cinofsky Inc., which specializes, according to president Mort Cinofsky, in the irregularities of menswear. Indeed, the prices are hard to match: $5.95 dress or sports shirts (up to $30 retail); $4 silk ties (up to $45 regularly); $25 all-wool slacks (up to $125 retail). So are the brand names: Arrow, Enro, Hanes, Palm Beach, and Superba, among others. Despite the "no fancy fixtures and off-the-beaten track location," Cinofsky does very well, thank you, on word-of-mouth advertising and satisfied regular customers.

M. Stuart's Ltd.
568 W. Roosevelt Rd.
Chicago, IL 60607
(312) 663-3125
Hours: Mon–Sat: 9–5
AE

Named for its owner, M. (for "Mark") Stuart, jockeys with the other men's clothing stores on Roosevelt Road for attention. Its merchandise certainly is different from the Euro-style fare featured by Eisenstein and Morris, et al. You'll find more knockoffs, "in the style of," and little-known labels that imitate, say, a Coogi sweater. Some spring '97 offerings: 100% rayon short-sleeve print shirts at $15; fisherman-like leather sandals at $30+; $150 all-wool suits (elsewhere $550); and a $175 full-length all-season Kenneth Barnard trench coat (regularly $550).

Manny's

Rte. 83 and St. Charles Rd.
Elmhurst, IL 60126
(630) 832-7630
Hours: Mon–Fri: 10–8:30; Sat: 9–5; Sun: 10–5
AE, DISC, MC, V

Manny's has been around Chicago since the word *discount* was added to Webster's. Originally associated with big and tall men's clothing only, Manny's has considerably expanded its wares to include "normal-sized" items as well. The store, now in a nondescript shopping mall, is jammed with merchandise (and people), so hovering salespeople are a necessity just to ferret out appropriate styles and sizes. Middle- and high-end labels nestle comfortably here for at least 20% off. A few examples: Newport Harbor raincoat at $200 (reduced from $300); Ballantyne cashmere sweater for $75; diSilva cashmere-blend topcoat tagged $300 (was $500).

Meyerson Associated Clothing

555 W. Roosevelt Rd., #4
Chicago, IL 60607
(312) 421-5580
Hours: Mon–Sat: 9–5; Sun: 10–3
AE, DISC, MC, V

The number-one key to success, according to most small shopkeepers, is the relationships they start and continue with their customers. Certainly, Meyerson's, founded in 1945 and owned by one family since its beginnings, attributes its longevity to generations of satisfied Chicagoland men. In the same Roosevelt Road complex as Morris & Sons, Meyerson's features lesser-known brands of European and American apparel than the standard Armani to Zegna—but the quality's still there. Suits usually start at $200 and reflect a 25%–30% discount; one very handsome Modesto Uoma suit, for instance, was priced $650. All prices include alterations, a real bonus for the hard-to-fit man.

Mort Cooper Ltd. ☆
161 N. State St.
Chicago, IL 60601
(312) 332-8410
Hours: Mon–Fri: 9–5:30; Sat: 9–5:15
AE, DISC, MC, V

For more than four decades, Mort Cooper has existed as an enigma to out-of-town shoppers in the Loop. Little attention to advertising. A rather nondescript storefront. Yet, the good buys on men's clothing are unmistakable—and have been communicated primarily by extremely satisfied customers over the years. Names such as Daniel Hechter, Peerless, Martin Wong, and Utex are regular brands here, with average discounts about 20%–30%. What's more, the store offers, within limits, free alterations; for suits, there's no charge for shortening or lengthening cuffs or sleeves and fixing waistlines. And it's gratis to fix the cuffs on dress pants. *Buying Retail Is Stupid!* customers realize another freebie: a $40-value silk tie with the purchase of a dress suit.

Sagrani Clothiers ☆
540 N. Michigan Ave.
Chicago, IL 60611
(312) 644-0604
Hours: Mon–Fri: 10–7; Sat: 10–6:30
AE, DIN, DISC, MC, OPT, V

Up on the second floor of the Michigan Avenue Marriott—take the escalators from the lobby—is a little gold mine of treasures for men: Sagrani Clothiers. (Sorry, ladies.) Global names that fill the closets of top executives are present and accounted for in sweaters, suits, jackets, and slacks, including France's Yves Saint Laurent, Germany's Konen, Italy's San Remo, and America's Perry Ellis, among many others. Owner K. Sagrani is quick to emphasize that her store, open since 1972, carries absolutely no seconds, irregulars, or damaged goods, yet the average discount is 30%. A case in point: one sunny April day, we drooled over a brilliantly colored Coogi sweater in the window, priced at $267. And *Buying Retail Is Stupid!* readers who prefer the international haut-monde styles will also appreciate the extra-10%-discount coupon in the back of our book.

SUITSMART ✪
115 N. Wabash Ave.
Chicago, IL 60602
(312) 236-6038
Hours: Mon & Tues: 10–7; Wed–Fri: 10–8; Sat: 10–5; Sun: 12–5
AE, ATM, DIN, DISC, MC, OPT, V
◆ **Senior Discount:** 10% **Age:** 60+

Better be prepared to buy something at Suitsmart because owners Dan Hoosen and Phil Cocomise could literally hawk the Eiffel Tower to Parisians . . . again. Though most perceive this menswear discounter as a resale store, Suitsmart's wearables do include substantial numbers of never-touched men's clothing. New Italian suits, for instance, sell for $299 (once $550); cotton dress shirts, $29.99 (originally $39.99). Obviously, best pickings are from the 2,000+ "gently worn" suits, from Armani to Zegna, beginning at $89. And either location will be glad to accept the 10%-additional-discount coupon found in the back of *Buying Retail Is Stupid!*.
Arlington Heights—388 E. Golf Rd., (847) 290-8008

MEN'S & WOMEN'S APPAREL

BELMONT ARMY/NAVY SURPLUS
945 W. Belmont Ave.
Chicago, IL 60657
(773) 975-0626
Hours: Mon–Sat: 11–8; Sun: 1–6
MC, V

The second floor of Belmont Army/Navy Surplus is the true focal point for bargains, with all things military sold at reduced prices. (Floor one features '90s punk and rad fashions; floor three, leather. Neither are discounted.) Find here the navys and olive drabs and camouflage colors of choice. European rucksacks go for $24.99; Doc Martens jackets, $29.99; and not-your-mother's used army boots,

$34.99. A few other recycled items, such as shirts, crop up at similarly attractive prices.

MARK SHALE OUTLET

2593 N. Elston Ave.
Chicago, IL 60647
(773) 772-9600
Hours: Mon–Sat: 10–6; Sun: 12–5
AE, DISC, MC, V

The fact that Mark Shale, a well-known upscale clothier, has just emerged from Chapter 11 is news for rejoicing. As is its sole outlet, filled with wares for both men and women (occasional accessories such as shoes, scarves, belts, and handbags wax and wane, according to available stock). Names are of the instant-recognition sort for intrepid high-fashion shoppers: an Eileen Fisher white linen blazer for $99 (was $144); Ann Freedberg mix-and-match separates ($259 for a $398 jacket; $99 for a $168 shirt); Cole-Haan men's shoes at $124 (were $200); and V-neck cotton summer sweaters at $39 (once $88). Regular private sales and advertised "blowouts" discount merchandise further.

MISTY HARBOR

410 S. First St./Piano Factory Outlet Mall
St. Charles, IL 60174
(630) 584-2099
Hours: Mon–Fri: 10–9; Sat: 10–6; Sun & holidays: 11–5
AE, DISC, MC, V

Trench coats or raincoats used to be the staple at Misty Harbor, a competitor to London Fog. Now, however, outer garb to protect us from downpours appears only in the fall, probably because neither of the two Chicago-area outlets is owned by the Misty Harbor manufacturer. Robbie Sport (or RS) seems to be the number-one label in the Piano Factory location, with the emphasis on women's sportswear at a 40%–60% savings. A few items to check out: $44.99 pantsuits (were $79.99); all-cotton patterned blouses for $19.99; and a large selection of separates from $16.99 to $59.99.
Aurora—42 W. New York St., (630) 892-1828; Mon–Sat: 9–5:30

Morris & Sons Co.

555 W. Roosevelt Rd.
Chicago, IL 60607
(312) 243-5635
Hours: Mon–Sat: 9–5:30; Sun: 9–4
AE, DISC, MC, OPT, V

It is difficult to beat Aaron Morris's claim that the best prices locally in designer clothing for men and women can be found on the second floor of a nondescript Near South Side shopping center. In business since 1953, the Morrises count many of the top local corporate, sports, and showbiz personalities among their clientele. And who could blame them? Names such as Armani, Escada, Genny, Versace, Yves Saint Laurent, a host of other Italian, French, and European designers, and a few American designers are regularly discounted 30%. Though the selection for men is much more extensive, good buys still prevail for both sexes—especially during the store's biennial, invitation-only sales.

Something Old, Something New

1056 W. Belmont Ave.
Chicago, IL 60657
(773) 271-1300
Hours: Mon–Fri: 9–9; Sat & Sun: 9–8
AE, DISC, MC, V

It's not a bridal shop. Nor, exactly, a consignment store. Rather, Something Old, Something New represents an original concept: a bargain treasure hunt featuring returned merchandise and odd lots from full-price retailers. (The exception: recycled jeans.) Our last visit revealed these deals: optical frames at $10 each (listed up to $200, minus prescription lenses, of course); women's shoes for $12 a pair (we spied some Joan & Davids); men's suits for $99.95. Worth rummaging around.

Resale Stores

There's a new profession to consider for all our *Buying Retail Is Stupid!* fans: resale consultant. Actually, it's the title held by Donna

Simon of Evanston, an independent businesswoman who, a few years ago, was casting about for another talent to add to her portfolio. Being a confirmed shopper in the consignment stores and a lifelong devotee of retailing, Simon conceived, first, of gathering together in one printed volume a directory of resalers. So, voilà! *Chicagoland's Directory of Resale Shops* was born about a year ago.

It focuses on advertisements only, divided into two sections: the traditional resale "contemporary" apparel and the antiques/collectibles/vintage variety. Best yet, it's free to consumers by sending a number 10 SASE (with 64¢ postage) to Simon aka The Resale Lady, Inc., P.O. Box 5166, Evanston, IL 60204.

Which generated Simon's second consignment business: for a fee, she will help stores coordinate special events (a bridal show, for instance) or lecture to a group of corporate women on the ins and outs of resale buying. In fact, we got a preview of her how-to-buy-resale tips:

- Go with an open mind; this is not Marshall Field's—so, the much coveted pair of black silk trousers may not be available yet.
- Don't plunk down money on apparel that needs a lot of alterations—more than a sleeve or a hem shortened, for example. Otherwise, you're negating one of the main purposes for having resale shops . . . to save dollars!
- Stains may not disappear. So, look over your intended purchases with great care.

Hmm, maybe we've got an idea . . . !

Infants' & Children's

CHILDREN'S ATTIC
703 Washington St.
Evanston, IL 60202
(847) 869-6222
Hours: Tues, Wed, Fri, Sat: 10–5:30; Thurs: 10–7
MC, V

The window display is appealing. As is its location, next to one of the two Crowded Closets in Evanston. Once inside this children's consignment shop, though, best ask owner Minna for how-to-find-what directions. Her cramped space doesn't always allow for casual browsing. Give it time, though, because the best resales eventually surface: a two-seater Emmaljunga baby carriage for $165; a $75 Peg Perego high chair. We saw linens, sheets, and top-name cribs (a Bellini for $125!) as the buys; also in evidence are toys, kids' clothes, and maternity wear. A plus service for busy moms and dads: pickup and delivery.

NINE MONTHS NEW ☒

1334 N. Halsted St.
Chicago, IL 60622
(312) 649-0043
Hours: Mon–Wed, Fri & Sat: 10–5; Thurs: 10–7
DISC, MC, V

Maternity resale boutiques are few and far between in Chicago—or anywhere, in fact, since moms-to-be tend to pass their child-in-waiting clothes on to friends and relatives. So, not only does Nine Months New president Holly Lane fill an expectant need, but she also has launched a first for any area consignment shop—a wish-list service for items not currently available in-store (once items arrive, she calls customers). Among her 50%–60%-off women's labels are Mama Mia, Olian, and Pea in the Pod; kids' apparel, furniture, nursing bras, and products are also represented. And a 15% *Buying Retail Is Stupid!* coupon (on specified items) stretches dollar amounts for expecting parents.

TINY TOTS TURNAROUND ☒

7224 W. College Dr.
Palos Heights, IL 60463
(708) 361-6628
Hours: Mon–Fri: 10–6; Sat: 10–5
MC, V

Upscale kids' clothing, says the *Wall Street Journal*, is the newest growth niche of the fashion industry today, with doting baby-boomer parents buying baby Armani, Moschino, Versace, and the like. So, instead of paying full price for such items (which can run up to $325 for a shirt-and-jacket set or $99 for a pair of jeans), we searched for an alternative. One choice: south suburban Tiny Tots Turnaround, featuring great-condition, gently used clothes for children at one-third off retail. In fact, owner Eileen McGonigal's known to refuse to buy or consign items not in perfect shape; names range from the Gap and OshKosh-type labels to Laura Ashley, Dior, and Polo. Sizes range from infant to size 14. There's also a selection of maternity wear as well as toddler equipment, furniture, and toys. With fitting and play rooms plus a 10%-extra-discount coupon on any one item for *Buying Retail Is Stupid!* readers, who wants to mess with Seventh Avenue?

TRENDY TOTS RESALE SHOP ✪

950 W. Army Trail Rd.
Carol Stream, IL 60188
(630) 483-8687
Hours: Mon, Thurs: 10–8; Tues, Wed, Fri, Sat: 10–5; Sun: 12–3
DISC, MC, V

Is it truly time for kids to have their own predriven-clothing stores? Yes, says Trendy Tots owner Jill Rudman, who finds clean and popular-name apparel, toys, equipment, and furniture for 10,000 area customers. Brands range from Gap and OshKosh to Fisher-Price and Little Tikes; recommended for additional savings is the store's frequent-buyer card, offering 20% off one "under $20" item each month for 1 year. Her best customers wait for seasonal by-invitation-only sales. *Buying Retail Is Stupid!* readers, however, can still benefit—with a $5-off coupon on purchases of $25 or more.

Family

See also Something Old, Something New on page 83

CROWDED CLOSET, INC.
701 Washington St.
Evanston, IL 60202
(847) 475-0355
Hours: Tues & Wed: 10–4; Thurs: 10–7; Fri & Sat: 10–5; Sun: 1–4
MC, V

Two resale stores, as different as night and day, from the same owner located in the same city. The Washington Street version of Crowded Closet truly lives up to its name: aisles are narrow, clothes overflow racks, and a basement full of bargains—for the family and for the home—a strong sense of balance is needed to navigate. In contrast, its Dempster Street sister is spacious and devoted to high-fashion women's consignment (e.g., Claude Montana, Sonia Rykiel). Deals, nonetheless, are great; $36 for a DKNY red jogging suit; $18 for a never-used Chantal teakettle (we see 'em for $50). Unique differences? One, they reduce all merchandise after 30 days for 3 consecutive months. And two, all unwanted consignment stuff eventually lands at Cathedral Shelter.
Evanston—824 Dempster St., (847) 475-1135

THE $5 STORE
2040 N. Milwaukee Ave.
Chicago, IL 60622
(773) 384-8831
Hours: Mon–Sat: 10–7; Sun: 10–6
AE, MC, V

Multiply the "Everything's $1.00" national chain by five. Seriously, the $5 Stores in the Bucktown and Pilsen neighborhoods adhere to their moniker—at least most of the time. In the same family as Something Old, Something New, these two stores gather both old and new merchandise to promote—mainly apparel for men, women, and kids. What we saw: all New Balance, Nike, and Reebok shoes for $19.95; ladies' jeans for $5.95; six pairs of socks for $4; oversized T-shirts for 99¢. Always on Sundays, too.
Chicago—1713 W. 18th St., (312) 666-9010

MY FAVORITE THINGS

120 S. Washington St.
Hinsdale, IL 60521
(630) 655-0054
Hours: Mon–Wed, Fri: 10–7; Thurs: 10–8; Sat: 10–5; Sun: 12–4
DISC, MC, OPT, V

Imagine: two thousand pieces of pre-owned (sometimes new) clothing arriving every week, says owner Linda Boley. Which supports her claim to being the largest resale store in the suburbs. No member of the family is forgotten. Resale merchandise is 70% off of retail, while new maternity apparel and new costume jewelry are priced at a 30%–50% discount.

VILLAGE DISCOUNT OUTLET

2855 N. Halsted St.
Chicago, IL 60657
(708) 388-4772
Hours: Mon–Fri: 9–9; Sat: 9–6; Sun: 11–5
Cash

To casual passersby, the neighborhood Village Discount Outlets (there are 11 in total) might resemble hospital thrift shops. Which is, we discovered, partially true; one of the few differences is that Village is operated as a for-profit business by the Salvation Army, we believe. Mostly located within the city limits (the Chicago Heights store is the only exception), the stores offer old, used merchandise—clothes and a few appliances—catered to the handyperson, the home sewer, the do-it-yourselfer. So, prices are scaled accordingly: as-is color TVs starting at $40; men's jeans for $3; a Laura Ashley print skirt at 90¢. A lot of digging, however, might net one or two finds: our discovery was a mint-condition two-piece John Weitz all-wool subtle plaid suit for $6. Strictly for those on limited budgets.

11 locations; see the Yellow Pages

Men's & Women's

BUY POPULAR DEMAND ★

2631 N. Halsted St.
Chicago, IL 60657
(773) 868-0404
Hours: Mon–Sat: 11–7; Sun: 11–5
MC, V

The sister store of Threads in Wicker Park, Buy Popular Demand is located in between two of Chicago's trendier neighborhoods—DePaul and Lakeview. Consequently, prices in this men's and women's recycled apparel shop run a bit higher than at its sibling. Deals we spotted on a winter visit: two-piece Christian Dior linen suit for $80; Jones linen plaid jacket at $30; and Neiman Marcus black suede 3-inch-heel shoes for $15. Mention *Buying Retail Is Stupid!* (and bring in the coupon) for another 15% reduction.

See Threads, Etc., on page 97

CACTUS TRADE

2040 N. Halsted St.
Chicago, IL 60614
(773) 471-7222
Hours: Mon–Fri: 11–7; Sat & Sun: 11–6
MC, V

◆ **Senior Discount:** 10% (hospital workers too) **Age:** 60+

Every Saturday, say resale store owners, there's a caravan of dedicated consignment shoppers who go from store to store seeking the best, the latest, and the newest. Most of that activity is confined to the Gold Coast, with occasional flurries in the Lincoln Park–DePaul–Lakeview area. Owner Jennifer Masseda of 5-year-old Cactus Trade gets some of those customers, mixed in with young professionals and college students. So, her men's and women's clothing collection caters to a rather wide swath of consumers; a Chanel suit is right next to a brown leather Diesel jacket. Men's apparel is 70% never-touched (primarily from reps), since, as she notes, "men do wear their clothes to rags." About 30% of the women's clothing is new; we spied an originally tagged $159 Max Studio black satin dress for $59. A second difference: she buys all clothes outright from their owners, instead of relegating them (and monies) to consignment. Catch her on Mondays from 11:00 A.M. to 1:00 P.M., or call for an appointment.

Cynthia's Consignments

2218 N. Clybourn Ave.
Chicago, IL 60614
(312) 248-7714
Hours: Tues–Sat: 11–6; Sun: 12–5
AE, MC, V

Model Cynthia Hodgkins is very busy these days. Since opening her shop in spring 1993, she's also continued her glamorous career—and managed to launch a male cousin (Duomo) to Cynthia's in fall 1996. What's different? Forty percent of her stock is never-worn new clothing in all sizes, tagged with computerized bar codes and grouped together. Once-worn and sample wedding gowns and headpieces hold court in the back of the store, along with bridal shoes, slips, and accessories. A few of the prices that entice customers to return again and again: a $2,500 Tomasina wedding gown for $1,250; black-and-white Hawaiian print Mary Jane Marcasiano pants for $46 (once $132); and a sky-blue linen Spirit of the Lake outfit for $79 ($225 retail). Duomo, in the heart of New Town, features similar merchandise, similar savings, for men only.
Chicago—Duomo, 2906 N. Broadway, (773) 325-2325

Disgraceland ✪

3330 N. Clark St.
Chicago, IL 60657
(773) 281-5875
Hours: Mon–Sat: 11–7; Sun: 12–6
AE, DISC, MC, OPT, V

Antiques dealers whisper to us that gently used blue jeans carry premium prices in Europe and Asia. If so, Disgraceland could be one of the major stomping grounds for buying and reselling these rugged pants, as well as a source for other pre-owned items of apparel. Owner Ann Cutler has issued pretty strict guidelines for store merchandise: no older than 2 years (a few vintage items have passed inspection); casual styles from the likes of J. Crew, Banana Republic, and The Limited; in season; clean and in good condition. And the savings in this heart-of-Wrigleyville store are often better than discount. Where else can Levi's be found for under $20? Applause, too, for her policy of donating to charity unsold items not reclaimed by their owners. And finally, a couple of "Encore!"s for the 10% *Buying Retail Is Stupid!* coupon to be used as noted.

ELLIOTT CONSIGNMENT

2465 N. Lincoln Ave.
Chicago, IL 60614
(773) 404-6080
Hours: Mon–Sun: 10–9 (will close early if not busy)
MC, V

Opened in May 1996, this mother-daughter consignment shop in the DePaul neighborhood already seems to have its share of loyal customers. Its pre-owned clothing sales are geared primarily to women, though there are a few men's suits, ties, and jackets. Resale prices are extremely competitive (e.g., yellow Fendi purse for $44; Baskin's coat for $98; Shamask suit for $128); however, collectibles and antiques tags are rather high. Find best savings on Elliott's markdowns (from 25% to 75% off) and in the notorious "Back Room" (no relation to Loehmann's).

STEVE AUSTIN ★

951 W. Grace St.
Chicago, IL 60613
(773) 296-2715
Hours: Wed & Thurs: 4–8; Fri & Sat: 12–6 (summer hours may vary)
AE, DIN, DISC, MC, OPT, V

It is very difficult, admit most resale store owners, to stock up on pre-owned top-quality men's apparel that hasn't seen better times. Unlike their feminine counterparts, men tend to wear and wear and wear out clothing, rather than replace every season, with every changing trend. So, it comes as a positive surprise that Steven Austin uncovers top-quality menswear in good condition with some great names—Hugo Boss, Giorgio Armani, Oxxford, Zegna, Ungaro, et al. Most suits have a savings of 60%–70% off the original retail price. There's a limited selection of tuxedos, top coats, and trenchcoats; sports coats, ties, and shirts are also stocked. A hefty 15%-extra-discount coupon for *Buying Retail Is Stupid!* readers . . . and, of course, a free tie with any suit purchase.

Women's

BELLA MODA
947 N. State St.
Chicago, IL 60610
(312) 642-0330
Hours: Mon–Fri: 10–6; Sat: 10–5
AE, MC, V

We call Bella Moda a new kind of trompe l'oeil: it's easy to be fooled into thinking that this shop, with its meticulous displays and Oak Street proximity, is a full-price retailer. It's not. A few years ago, co-owners Renee and Brenda moved their consignment business from the North Shore. They've never regretted it. Found here are women's high-end and couture clothing: a Sonia Rykiel scarf for $100; $60 DKNY navy print rayon skirt (the original tag reads $120); fur-lined Neiman Marcus Sorbara sports coat for $1,200. A bonus: ask about wardrobe appraisals and pickup service.

THE DAISY SHOP
67 E. Oak St.
Chicago, IL 60611
(312) 943-8880
Hours: Mon–Sat: 11–6; Sun: 12–5
DISC, MC, V

A gentle but elegantly named resale shop in the heart of Chicago's toniest shopping district reveals cared-for couture clothing that women just might die for. Names such as Armani, Chanel, Hermes, Thierry Mugler, Valentino, et al. cram every square foot of this shop; owner Barbara Abarbanell, though refusing to divulge her sources, collects both current and vintage classic apparel (and jewelry, too) that never become outmoded. Pristine condition; 80% off the original trunk show prices. What more could anyone ask?

DESIGNER RESALE OF CHICAGO, INC. ✪
6522 N. Lincoln Ave.
Lincolnwood, IL 60645
(847) 674-7989
Hours: Mon–Sat: 11–6; Sun: 12–5
AE, DISC, MC, V

It is sometimes puzzling to try to figure out how all these designer-only consignment stores can coexist peacefully. But in this age of reuse and recycle, Bonnie Barone's Designer Resale stores offer top names—and, sometimes, top prices for pre-owned clothing at 50%–80% off retail. Occasionally, a few new pieces do sneak in (local designer Peggy Martin is one example); most dresses, suits, slacks, and handbags and costume jewelry are labeled Escada, Louis Feraud, Gucci, Moschino, or Versace, among others. Frequent sales help ease sticker shock. So does the 10% *Buying Retail Is Stupid!* coupon for our dedicated smart shoppers.
Chicago—658 N. Dearborn St., (312) 587-3312, Mon–Sat: 11–6

ENTRE NOUS ✪
21 E. Delaware St.
Chicago, IL 60611
(312) 337-2919
Hours: Mon–Fri: 11–6; Sat: 11–5
Cash

Only the best in women's apparel, from Armani and Chanel to Ungaro, ever enters owner Duska Kuhlmann's consignment shop. No wonder, since she virtually launched the preworn-couture sales industry in 1960 from her Gold Coast perch. And while in Entre Nous, designs (plus time) seem to pass by in a refined European style, shopping is pursued in a leisurely manner—as are the savings. (Another 5% will be deducted from your Entre Nous purchase with the *Buying Retail Is Stupid!* coupon.)

McShane's Exchange

815 W. Armitage Ave.
Chicago, IL 60614
(773) 525-0282
Hours: Mon–Fri: 11–7; Sat: 10–6; Sun: 12–5
MC, V

The idea of buying resale clothing started to move into the mainstream in the 1980s, a bit before Denise McShane Caffrey opened her eponymous stores in the Old Town–DePaul neighborhood. Considered somewhat of a pioneer, she continues her innovations to this day, including a 24-hour information/hot line. It's a bit cramped in the stores, with women's wares and some decorative accessories carefully racked and stacked and displayed. But customers don't mind: Armani moss green silk pants at $128; a $10 charming Italian hand-painted pitcher; new leather-look tortoiselike handbags for $38 and up. A literal "back room" houses sale items, slashed to thrift-store prices.
Chicago—1141 W. Webster Ave., (773) 525-0211

My Mother's Closet ✪

2174 Ogden Ave.
Aurora, IL 60504
(630) 585-7131
Hours: Tues–Thurs: 10–6; Fri: 10–8; Sat: 10–4; Sun: 12–4
DISC, MC, V

A mother-daughter team (Randi Pickering and Lorraine Mackoy) offers some of the best consignment deals for women in the western suburbs. Higher demand results in slightly higher-than-average prices (only 30% off retail) on accessories and clothing from women's sizes 0 to 1X and on. But reduce your charges at the cash register with a 10% *Buying Retail Is Stupid!* coupon.

My Sister's Closet ✪
5419 W. Devon Ave.
Chicago, IL 60646
(773) 774-5050
Hours: Mon–Sat: 10–5
MC, V

"Nothing more than 2 years old," insists owner Joanne Nusbaum. And considering the vagaries of fashion, her resale boutique stocks everything from Levi jeans to a Stanley Korshak full-length lynx fur coat (at $350, it's a small fraction of its original price). Occasionally, new kids' clothing samples crop up, as do antique and costume jewelry, untouched perfumes, and bits and pieces of furniture. A true melting pot of wearables . . . at even better prices for *Buying Retail Is Stupid!* customers (don't forget to use the 10%-extra-discount coupon).

Second Vogue ✪
534 W. Dundee/Lynn Plaza
Wheeling, IL 60090
(847) 229-0355
Hours: Tues–Thurs: 10–7:30; Fri & Sat: 10–6; Sun: 11–4
AE, DISC, MC, V

There's a difference, says Second Vogue owner Jan Gunderson, between couture and upscale. And in her 2-year-old shop, the labels tell the rest of the story: 50% or more off the retail price of previously owned women's apparel, lingerie, furs, outerwear, and accessories from names such as Chaus, August Max, Pendleton, and Ralph Lauren. New wearables do creep in, at a savings of 33%–50%; Second Vogue also carries an incredibly broad range of sizes, from petite 2 through voluptuous 26. Which means that almost any woman, armed with our *Buying Retail Is Stupid!* 10% discount coupon, will make out like the proverbial bandit.

SELECTIONS
2152 N. Clybourn Ave.
Chicago, IL 60614
(773) 296-4014
Hours: Tues–Thurs: 11–7; Fri: 11–6; Sat: 10–6; Sun: 12–5
DISC, MC, V

Within Windy City neighborhoods, certain shops of a feather seem to stick together—in this case, consignment or resale stores. Less than a block north of Cynthia's Consignments is Alexa Winsberg's Selections, yet neither lacks for customers or bargains (here, typically, 70%–80% lower than retail). The apparel to be purchased is for women only, with a goodly mix of medium- and high-end designer clothing—such as Calvin Klein, Escada, and Ralph Lauren. Look for deals on accessories, too.

STYLE & SUBSTANCE ✪
2249 W. 111th St.
Chicago, IL 60643
(773) 881-8007
Hours: Tues–Sat: 11–6
AE, DISC, MC, OPT, V

Serving a spread of white- and blue-collar neighborhoods means that owner Shirley Hardiman gathers a wide mix of women's consignment apparel to suit her customers. So, South Beverly and Morgan Park residents (plus any visitor to these Chicago shores) reap the benefits; imagine a combination of Liz Claiborne and Calvin Klein, DKNY and Carole Little, all at 50%–75% off retail. Quarterly 10%-extra-discount sales—and, of course, a 10% additional savings from a *Buying Retail Is Stupid!* coupon—help ensure that women sizes 4 to 24 will find a feel-good wearable at a great price.

Threads, Etc. ★

1400 N. Milwaukee Ave.
Chicago, IL 60622
(773) 276-6411
Hours: Mon–Sat: 11–7; Sun: 11–5
MC, V

Like mother, like son: Buy Popular Demand is the parent, literally and figuratively, of Threads, Etc., a Wicker Park resale shop. Here, the prices are nothing short of cheap, cheap: quasi-designer women's shoes from the halls of Evan-Picone and Ferragamo, for instance, are priced at $5 (this is not a misprint). All in great condition. An Yves Saint Laurent men's wool suit was reduced from $30 to $15. And worn Levi's, on average, cost no more than $12. Look for even better savings (is that possible?) with the 15% *Buying Retail Is Stupid!* coupon.

See Buy Popular Demand on page 89

Services

Chicago's Discount Cleaner ★

1529 W. Howard St.
Chicago, IL 60626
(773) 274-1500
Hours: Mon–Fri: 7–7; Sat: 7–6; Sun: 10–5
MC, V

Living in south Evanston or Rogers Park, in addition to good apartment rents, nets another reward: the services of Chicago's Discount Cleaner on the Chicago side of Howard Street. There's a 20% savings when laundry or dry cleaning is prepaid. Plus, owner Ken Davis regularly offers prices much lower than those found in upscale or up-and-coming neighborhoods. Check out the other locations, and don't forget to use the extra-30% *Buying Retail Is Stupid!* discount coupon.

Eight locations; see the Yellow Pages

VOGUE CLEANERS
2701 W. Touhy Ave.
Chicago, IL 60645
(773) 262-2600
Hours: Mon–Fri: 7–7:30; Sat: 7–7
DISC, MC, V

It's bad enough living in a world where we spend hundreds of dollars on clothes or business attire alone. What is even more upsetting? The possibility that half these clothes would be ruined if we cleaned 'em ourselves. And the simple fact that most labels read "Dry clean only." So, then, we turn to one (or some) of the area's dry cleaners to perform the job—usually at tags we shrink from. Enter Vogue Cleaners, who believes in quality plus price. Some of the outstanding savings: tailored suits (both men's and women's), $4.50; men's dress shirts, 95¢ for 2-day service; and dresses, $4.25. Everything must be prepaid, and clothes are ready within days. Look for seasonal specials—and seasonal awards (a "free Thanksgiving gobbler" raffle with x amount of cleaning).

SHOES

Family

ALAMO SHOES ✪
5321 N. Clark St.
Chicago, IL 60640
(773) 784-8936
Hours: Mon–Fri: 9–8; Sat: 9–7; Sun: 10–6; hours vary at other locations
AE, DISC, MC, V
◆ **Senior Discount:** 10% **Age:** 55+

Andersonville residents and other patrons of this neighborhood shoe store with its occasionally high-pressure salespeople might be surprised to learn that four other clones exist—all owned by one firm. Each tailors its stock to the specific locale: the best known—Alamo—features high-end comfort for any family's feet, from Doc Martens to Rockport, usually at a 20%+ savings. (Only a few brands such as the French Mephisto walkers are exempt from any reductions, anywhere.) One recent sales special: an Ecco men's walking shoe for $99.99 (regularly $150). Walk into any of the Alamo relatives with a *Buying Retail Is Stupid!* coupon for another 10% reduction.

Chicago—Alamo Shoes, 4187 S. Archer Ave., (773) 890-1187
Chicago—Kay Shoes, 2957 N. Milwaukee Ave., (773) 384-7120
Chicago—Kay Shoes, 2839 N. Milwaukee Ave., (773) 489-4350
Chicago—Zemsky Shoe Department, 1700 W. 18th St., (312) 226-6230

CHERNIN'S SHOES, INC. ☒
606 W. Roosevelt Rd.
Chicago, IL 60607
(312) 922-4545 or 1-888-CHERNIN
Hours: Hours vary by store
AE, DISC, MC, OPT, V
◆ **Senior Discount:** Sales tax **Age:** 55+

It has been said that one out of every six pairs of shoes sold in the Chicago area hails from Chernin's . . . and that heavyweight champ Mike Tyson once bought 22 pairs of shoes there in 60 minutes. Yet, not as well known is the fact that Chernin's owns seven outlets in addition to its nine full-line stores, each offering different discounts. Like their Roosevelt Road flagship, now some 90+ years young, all full-line stores feature shoes at a 5%–15% discount; the outlets, from 30% to 70%. Almost every footwear name is here, from Allen-Edmonds and Bass, to Jumping Jacks and Little Capezios, to Nine West and Rockport. And an additional-10% coupon from *Buying Retail Is Stupid!* could just change that initial statistic to one in five Chicagoans "shoed here."

Seven outlet stores and nine full-line stores; see the Yellow Pages

CHICAGO SHOE MARKET SHOE BAZAAR ✪

1418 N. Milwaukee Ave.
Chicago, IL 60622
(773) 278-4100
Hours: Mon, Thurs, Fri: 10–7; Tues, Wed, Sat: 10–6; Sun: 11–5
AE, DISC, MC, V

Borrowing from Boston's best: Mehri Amrami of Shoe Bazaar in Wicker Park tags all newly arrived merchandise about 15% lower than retail. But, once footwear has rested in the store for 1 or 2 months, prices are slashed—just like the original Filene's Basement. Those generous discounts apply to both athletic and casual shoes, so with appropriate timing, a $19.99 pair of Stacy Adams sandals could be in your possession. Other deals we witnessed: $9.99 for your choice of boys' Adidas high-tops or girls' L.A. Gear suede boots; and $29.99 to take your pick from assorted Fila, Nike, and Reebok shoes. The final deal is the sweetest: a 10%-discount *Buying Retail Is Stupid!* coupon good on all wares except shorts or socks.
Chicago—3443 S. Halsted St., (773) 927-7779

CHICAGO SHOE OUTLET

3212 N. Lincoln Ave.
Chicago, IL 60657
(773) 528-4433
Hours: Mon, Thurs–Sat: 10–7; Wed: 10–6; Sun: 11:30–5:30
AE, DISC, MC, V

A few blocks from W&L (Wolinsky & Levy, for the non-shoe-conscious readers) is a competitor that emphasizes men's and kids' shoes, with only a few female representatives. Styles are casual, for the most part; discounts range from adequate (10%–25% off new merchandise) to the "gotta grab these before someone else does" prices. Converse, Fila, L.A. Gear, Keds, Nike, Reebok, et al. join in the offerings: a $9.90 your-choice-for-children includes L.A. Gear and Nike; 50% off on $99.50 Giorgio Brutini leather cowboy boots; a sweatshirt or two for $9.90.

ROGAN'S SHOES

147 N. Seymour
Mundelein, IL 60060
(847) 566-6077
Hours: Mon–Fri: 9–9; Sat: 9–6; Sun: 10–5
MC, V

Only two of these family-owned-and-operated shoe stores are within range of Chicagoland's smart shoppers—and both are quite a distance from the Loop. Nonetheless, with a typical savings of 20%+, a selection of 40,000 pairs, and an almost continual "buy one, get the second at half price" sale, it's worth putting miles on your odometer. Merchandise is casual, athletic, and dress shoes, such as Brooks, Capezio, Florsheim, Joan & David, Nike, Reebok, and Timberland. And though Rogan's practices self-service with shoes on display, you can usually find a helpful clerk or two. Look for their June tent sale, with up to 70% savings.
Kenosha, WI—11875 74th Pl., (414) 857-9086 (at Rte. 50 and I-94)

TOWNE SHOES

2414 W. Devon Ave.
Chicago, IL 60659
(773) 465-0330
Hours: Mon–Sat: 10–8; Sun: 11–6
AE, MC, V
◆ **Senior Discount:** 10% **Age:** 63+

Full disclosure time: a relative of ours owned Towne Shoes in the 1950s and '60s, but has since sold it. Nonetheless, it's one of the better places to find closeout and heavily discounted footwear for men, women, and children. The emphasis here is on women: a rack of $10 specials includes vinyl sandals, 3-inch Palovio heels, Pierre Dumas pumps. Other recognizable brands appear at savings: Reebok, Nike, Naturalizer, Giorgio Brutini. And other merchandise occasionally sneaks in, such as handbags, down coats, jeans, and sportswear.

Men's & Women's

Arrowsmith Shoes
30 N. State St.
Chicago, IL 60602
(312) 782-1320
Hours: Mon–Fri: 9:30–7; Sat: 10–6; Sun: 12–5
AE, DISC, MC, V

The original Loop outlets for Giorgio Brutini and Stacy Adams have disappeared—and through consolidation (or whatever) seem to have resurfaced as the Arrowsmith outlet on State Street. As a shop accepting the nonselling wares from its three South Side retail stores, Arrowsmith today carries more than these two brands—and more than just footwear. Inside this long, railroad-flat arranged store are leather jackets on the side walls, a few other racks of assorted men's apparel, and stacks and stacks of high-fashion shoes. Hanker for lizard, snake, and ostrich (of the footwear-covering kind)? It's here, in abundance, along with an upfront selection of ladies' western boots. A "buy one, get one free" shoe sale was in progress during our visit; the wares: brown lizard Brutini shoes for $129.95; a sheepskin-lined leather coat reduced to $399.95 (was $549.95). Expect about a 40% savings.

Loop Footwear
142 S. Wabash Ave.
Chicago, IL 60603
(312) 368-5010
Hours: Mon–Sat: 9:30–6:30
AE, DISC, MC, V

The prettiest four words in the English language (to us, at least): "We'll work with you." That sentence is very likely to be heard at Loop Footwear, especially in its newly established clearance room. Expect a wide variety of brand-name shoes for men, in the casual, sport, and business categories; old faithfuls are Stacy Adams, Carlo Morandi, Nunn Bush, and Giorgio Brutini, among others. Two-for-one deals are common; a few other bargains: $40 ICE boots; $20 GBX sandals.

SAVE ON SOLES

445 Palatine Rd.
Town & Country Mall
Arlington Heights, IL 60004
(847) 398-3002
Hours: Mon–Fri: 10–7; Sat: 10–6; Sun: 11–5
DISC, MC, V

Kitty-corner to the Lord & Taylor Clearance Center is Save on Soles, a self-styled liquidation shoe store with an abbreviation (SOS) that could spell relief to many feet—and many wallets (from 25% to 70% reductions). Most of the footwear is for women, a smaller selection for men; all are branded with well-known names: Nine West, Botany 500, Stacy Adams, Timberland. Narrow and wide widths occasionally appear; so do a few imperfects. Sort through the stack: men's shoes for $49.99, with the second pair at half that price; clearance-priced women's footwear at $19.95 for one pair, $29.95 for two, $45 for three. These boots were made for walking . . . and buying.

WOLINSKY & LEVY SHOE OUTLET

3259 N. Ashland Ave.
Chicago, IL 60657
(773) 880-5648
Hours: Mon–Fri: 10–9; Sat: 10–6; Sun: 11–5
DISC, MC, V

A full-service store it's not. And dedicated shoe bargain hunters may have to return again and again to find the right size, the right color, the right name brand. But, ah!, when it fits, even Cinderella couldn't do much better—33%–50% reductions and bargain racks for men and women that tag footwear at tiny fractions of the original retail price. Some examples: men's Johnston & Murphy dress shoes at $78.45 (values up to $200); Ann Taylor slippers at $19.83 (once, more than $70); and men's Rockport shoes at $29.83 (were $72.95).

Women's

LORI'S SHOES
808 W. Armitage Ave.
Chicago, IL 60614
(773) 281-5655
Hours: Mon–Thurs: 11–7; Fri: 11–6; Sat: 10–6; Sun: 12–5
AE, DISC, MC, V

Even early on a Saturday, when no self-respecting professional would be up and at 'em before 11:00 or 12:00, Lori's is jammed. Women trying on the latest business pump. Men waiting patiently. And kids giggling, bumping into stacked boxes of shoes and wearing Mom's new sandals. Lori's stock is as varied as her clientele; pick a cork-soled pair of Aerosoles slides for $44 (once $52) or an elegant Joan & David leather number for $136 (retail $195). Soles aside, there are simply too many choices: handbags, briefcases, hosiery, hair doodads, and silver and costume jewelry in addition to a well-stocked back corner, filled with shoes (and prices) ready to walk away. Modest reductions to start; best bargains at season's end.
Northfield—311 Happ Rd., (847) 446-3818

Work

ADAMS SHOE FACTORY OUTLET ★
3655-59 W. Irving Park Rd.
Chicago, IL 60641
(773) 539-4120
Hours: Mon–Sat: 9–6; Sun: 10–4:30
DISC, MC, V

Michael Jordan, we know, wears a size 16. So, who could claim feet that spread to a size 18? (Our mouths are sealed.) Regardless, Adams Shoe Factory Outlet can fit 'em large or small with footwear at a discount, whether the subject be man, woman, or kid. The basketball shoe does an occasional slam-dunk appearance here (Converse for $59 rather than $90), as do a few irregulars. The real concentration is on work shoes. A few of the 9:00-to-5:00 gear savings at up to 60% off: a nurse's white loafer for $39 (once $54); $99.99 for Red Wing leather work boots (regularly $142). In business since the 1950s. And work could be infinitely more comfortable, footwise, if you wield the 10% extra discount from *Buying Retail Is Stupid!*.

Uniforms

Chefwear

833 N. Orleans St., 4th floor
Chicago, IL 60610
(800) 568-2433
Hours: Mon–Fri: 9–4
AE, DIN, DISC, MC, V

Ever covet the well-deserved fame and recognition accorded such culinary stars as Chicago's own Charlie Trotter or Rick Bayless of Frontera Grill? Now there's a quick bypass to years and years of standing near the stove, whisking egg whites to their highest peaks of perfection. Chefwear, a mail-order catalog headquartered here, offers its restaurant-quality clothing—usually discontinueds and irregulars—for small percentages (50%–75% off) of the regular price. Sizes run from kids' stuff to supremely large (enough to fit a Paul Prudhomme); a few samples: denim bib apron for $6; trade-white cotton chef coats at $20; and toques for tots at $4.

Women's Apparel

Eileen Fisher Outlet ☆

228 E. Golf Rd.
Arlington Heights, IL 60005
(847) 290-1717
Hours: Mon–Thurs: 10–8; Fri: 10–7; Sat: 10–6; Sun: 11–5
DISC, MC, V

One of the best- (or worst-, depending on your view) kept bargain secrets in the northwest suburbs. Word is, women from either coast regularly fly in to select seasonal wardrobes from this manufacturer's outlet. And no wonder: the Eileen Fisher label, with its soft and comfortable unconstructed lines and colors and great fabrics (linen, silk, cotton, Tencil, and a few subtle stripes), appeals to females size small through 3X. As one of only two in the United States, this store is run by the designer's sisters. And for this major manufacturer represented in well-known department and upscale retailers throughout the country, advertising is strictly word of mouth. Typically lagging each season by 3 months, first-quality dresses, suit separates, pants, jackets, and sweaters are priced about 25% below retail; a rack or two is devoted to seconds, irregulars, and samples—and consequently tagged with lower prices. The first Fisher outlet, though limited in dressing rooms and stuffed to the gills with merchandise, featured lower prices than now. With the move to a larger, lighter space within the same almost-moribund shopping center, prices, unfortunately, increased a bit. Best bet one: get your name on the mailing list. Twice a year, a postcard arrives announcing a clearance sale with an extra 20% off everything by presenting the card. And best bet two: use your extra-10% *Buying Retail Is Stupid!* coupon.

FASHION FACTORY
570 W. Roosevelt Rd.
Chicago, IL 60607
(312) 913-0019
Hours: Mon–Sat: 10–5:30
DISC, MC, V

A newcomer to the Roosevelt Road crowd, Fashion Factory stands out for its attractive merchandising and its status as a women's-wear manufacturer outlet. Current-season, first-quality apparel is all on display: soft Italian napa leather handbags from $35 to $55 (easily three times that elsewhere); Alberta Makali wool pantsuits at $149 (compare to $400); and dress samples galore of the new Italian polyester (named polyomitica) for $39 (once $160). Watch this space; owner Michael Tajer has plans for expansion.

I.B. DIFFUSION: THE WAREHOUSE ★
5020 W. Roosevelt Rd.
Chicago, IL 60644
(773) 473-8048
Hours: Mon–Fri: 10–5; Sat: 10–3
AE, MC, V

No baubles or bangles, but sequins and beads do adorn the sweaters and blouses and tops in this manufacturer's warehouse clearance center. A designed-in-Chicago label for quite a few years, and former owner of retail stores, I.B. Diffusion is now carried by major department stores. Bright-colored silks, cottons, knits, and woolens in a dressy casual style usually sell for $36 (tops) to $400 (suits) and, here, are priced at least 30% lower. Frequent the mad racks at $9.99 and seasonal sales for the best discounts of all. (Our advice? Combine that with the 10% *Buying Retail Is Stupid!* coupon, and you'll emerge a shopping victor.)

Computers

CYBER EXCHANGE COMPUTER CENTERS ★
237 W. North Ave.
Chicago, IL 60610
(312) 337-4882
Hours: Mon–Fri: 10–9; Sat: 10–8; Sun: 11–5
DISC, MC, OPT, V

It had to happen sooner or later. The built-in obsolescence of the computer and its related merchandise prompted the idea of trade-ins on used software and hardware. So, entrepreneur and president Michael Mlsna started Cyber Exchange; one in-town and six suburban locations all buy, sell, or trade discounted new and used software and computers, offering full service and upgrades for all makes and models of computers, be they IBMs or Macintoshes. If no existing Cyber product meets your needs, the full-time technical department will modify, amend, or build a system from scratch. Some

best bets: the $9.99-or-less software blowout bin, and a "student special" system starting at $799.99. (A plus for nervous Internet-ees: all software sold is virus checked.) And a second PS for *Buying Retail Is Stupid!* readers: just saunter in, mention the book coupon, and a free piece of software is yours—no purchase required!
Seven locations; see the Yellow Pages

Department & Warehouse Stores

BENNETT BROTHERS, INC.
30 E. Adams St.
Chicago, IL 60603-5676
(312) 621-1600 or (800) 621-2626
Hours: Mon–Fri: 8:15–5 (special holiday hours)
AE, DISC, MC, V

It started with jewelry, way back in the 1900s. Today, Bennett Brothers, with showrooms in the Loop and in Mahwah, New Jersey, is the unsung precursor of the Service Merchandise concept: anything on display in cases or visualized in the catalog can be ordered and mailed within a certain amount of time. And leafing through the catalog or meandering through 30 East Adams helps keep a finger on the pulse of consumer tastes. A look-alike Cartier tank watch sells for $468 (retails at $725); a 40-piece place setting of Gorham stainless steel for $300 (list is $500); a Bionaire mother-of-all-humidifiers humidifier for $183.75 (was $294). Used by many corporations and businesses for employee and sales incentives and awards.

Goldblatt's

4711 N. Broadway
Chicago, IL 60610
(773) 989-3270
Hours: Mon–Sat: 9–9; Sun: 10–7
DISC, MC, V
◆ **Senior Discount:** 10% on Tues **Age:** 65+

A venerable Chicago retailing name for many years, Goldblatt's in the last few decades was forced to withdraw from certain neighborhoods, such as State Street and North Lincoln Avenue. Yet, what remains of this giant "incredible bargain store" is 11 Chicagoland sites offering good values for dollars spent in virtually every household category. Neat, unrummaged-through displays and courteous cashiers help make shopping easier in this somewhat jumbled arrangement of aisles. A sampling of branded and nonlabeled prices: 88¢ for a can of Glade air freshener; irregular pantyhose at 59¢ a pair; $2.99–$4.49 for beach towels; and a Daewoo VCR for $159. It's hard to beat Goldblatt's for city savings on health and beauty aids.
11 locations; see the Yellow Pages

Montgomery Ward "Outlet City"

701 W. North Ave.
Villa Park, IL 60181
(630) 834-9860
Hours: Mon–Fri: 10–8; Sat: 9–6; Sun: 11–6
AE, DISC, MC, V
◆ **Senior Discount:** 10% **Age:** 55+

"Outlet City"—in our minds—is a rallying phrase for dedicated shoppers to save big. And at the Villa Park site for Montgomery Ward (affectionately termed "Monkey Ward's" by natives), it's time to save money on larger items, such as appliances and furniture. The biggest discounts are posted on slightly bruised stuff, with some "we-can-live-with-them" dents and dings and scratches. Examples from our visit: a Whirlpool side-by-side for $859 (regularly $1,549); a Signature 2000 lawn mower at $139 (retail is $229.99).

The Sharper Image

6170 W. Grand Ave.
Gurnee, IL 60031
(847) 855-8917
Hours: Mon–Sat: 10–9; Sun: 1–6
AE, DISC, MC, V

"You never know what you'll find" used to be a sentence reserved for avid antiquers. Today, it also applies to discount shopping—and, in this case, to the outlet for direct merchant The Sharper Image. Obviously, inventory experiences a rapid turnover, so don't expect the same merchandise to be available next week, or even tomorrow. The gidgets and gadgets that piqued our interest? The Abflex, the perpetual sit-up machine (once $59.95) for $19.95. Or a water-slide pool, which is not recommended for high-rise dwellers, at $79.95 (regularly $169.95). Though we do tend to perceive this particular catalog as filled with toys for boys (and some women, too) still, there is merchandise for all—like The Great Escape foot and back massager from Panasonic at $149.95 (reduced from $269.95). Ah, now that's comfort after a long day of shopping!

Electronics

Entertainment & Communications

Abt Electronics & Appliances ✪

9000 Waukegan Rd.
Morton Grove, IL 60053
(847) 967-8830
Hours: Mon–Fri: 9–9; Sat: 9–5:30; Sun: 11–5:30
AE, DISC, MC, V
◆ **Senior Discount:** 5% **Age:** 65+

It is difficult not to wax rhapsodic about Abt, since almost every native and converted Chicagoan knows of the electronics and appliance store's tremendous reputation for great service and great prices. In its third generation of management, Abt continues to withstand the invasion of the monster stores by tending to business, hiring intelligent employees (over 350 now), and judicious expansion. Name brands proliferate, from high-end such as Gaggenau, Sub-Zero, and Thermador to mid-priced JVC, Kenwood, and Yamaha. Three private sales a year and guaranteed lowest prices make ABT a sure thing . . . and even surer with the extra 5% discount the *Buying Retail Is Stupid!* coupon offers.

DISCOUNT STEREO AND PHOTO

243 S. State St.
Chicago, IL 60604
(312) 786-0442
Hours: Mon–Fri: 8:30–6:30; Sat: 10–6
AE, DISC, MC, V

It is enlightening to find a local shop owner who admits that sometimes his prices just can't match the "best buys" advertised by national chains. On the other hand, Joe of 17-year-old Discount Stereo and Photo does offer the kind of service you can't buy; he'll switch headphones, for instance, from one type of stereo to another—and otherwise try to accommodate customer preferences. Price tags (when found) are mostly at parity with other retailers; Panasonic 900 mHz cordless phones, when available, sell for around $150. Best bargains are on the reconditioned portable stereos (aka boom boxes) and, at the time, on cellular phones: 3 months for $99, with no contract and no monthly fee (covering 60 minutes of talk).

ELITE AUDIO ★

2225 W. Roscoe St.
Chicago, IL 60618
(773) 327-5652
Hours: Mon–Fri: 12:30–8; Sat: 12:30–5
AE, DISC, MC, OPT, V

A limited selection of audio and stereo equipment, new and used, that will appeal to serious audiophiles and bargain hunters. More often than not, the used, reconditioned, and repaired speakers, amps, and turntables offer the best prices. A top-of-the-line 1975 vintage Marantz receiver blasts "great deal" at $250 ($675 when new). A once-$450 pair of Paradigm speakers with 8-inch woofers now sings at $100. Negotiations may be possible on used merchandise. And very acceptable to *Buying Retail Is Stupid!* readers is the additional 10% reduction (on minimum purchase of $100) with the book's coupon.

International Video & Electronics

2355 W. Devon Ave.
Chicago, IL 60659
(773) 338-9033
Hours: Mon–Sat: 10:30–7:30; Sun: 11–7
AE, DISC, MC, V

Concerns on West Devon jealously vie with each other for their share of foreign visitors' purchases. Since many tourists to the United States intend to lug or transport electronics back home, International Video caters to that market, offering all sizes of 220-volt electronic appliances as well as the standard 110 volt for use here. Prices are certainly less than retail (though better deals at national chains can be found); International Video's advantage is that they'll either handle shipping or recommend reliable overseas shippers—a definite plus when figuring out how to transport a washer, dryer, or refrigerator. A selection of spring selling prices: a 19-inch cable-ready Toshiba TV for $199; a Nikon 35mm lensed camera at $599.99 (retail is $699.99); and a $20 Sergio Valente canvas garment bag.

Saturday Audio Exchange ✪

2919 N. Clark St.
Chicago, IL 60657
(312) 935-8733
Hours: Thurs: 5:30–9; Sat: 10:30–5:30
AE, DISC, MC, OPT, V

Just north of the busy Clark-Diversey-Broadway intersection, Saturday Audio Exchange lives up to its name—operating for limited hours. But its discounts are not that limited. In fact, whether you choose to shop on Thursday or Saturday, in Evanston or Lincoln Park, savings on new and used stereo equipment can be consider-

able. Check the brands, from Bang & Olufsen to Harman-Kardon, as well as the choice of discounted, show sample, closeout, and factory-blemished merchandise. Rest assured that no one will apply pressure to buy. On the other hand, considering the free headphones with every stereo system purchased by *Buying Retail Is Stupid!* readers, maybe a little internal pressure isn't such a bad thing.
Evanston—520 W. Davis St., (847) 492-USED

20th Century TV & Stereo Center ☆
1611-15 W. Montrose Ave.
Chicago, IL 60613
(773) 528-1728
Hours: Mon–Sat: 10–9; Sun: 12–6
AE, DIN, DISC, MC, V

Twenty-seven years of service count for something. As does a love of the business of repairing and selling all things electronic. The Lewczuks are a real find—highly trained engineers who can diagnose problems with VCRs, TVs, stereos, and the like. About 50% of their time is devoted to service; the other half, to reconditioning used and selling new consumer and commercial-grade equipment, such as Jamo speakers and Bang & Olufsen stereos. All the recycled systems carry warranties and especially attractive prices: a $185 Onkyo stereo (originally $460); a commercial Panasonic VCR for $600, instead of $1,200. Tune up, *Buying Retail Is Stupid!* readers, for an extra 10% savings—no minimum purchase.

Flowers

Flower Bucket, Inc. ✪
1100 W. Belmont St.
Chicago, IL 60657
(773) 935-9773
Hours: Mon–Sat: 9–8; Sun: 9–6
AE, DISC, MC, OPT, V

A rose by any other name would probably not smell as sweet—given that the Flower Bucket, at all four locations, offers a dozen beauties for $8.99. (Valentine's Day and Mother's Day are, unfortunately, exempt.) Other cut stems, such as carnations, benefit from the cut rates, selling at close to wholesale. A blooming institution since 1979 that will smell even sweeter with the Bucket's six free carnations to *Buying Retail Is Stupid!* customers who purchase $10+ worth of blooms.

Chicago—1164 N. LaSalle St., (312) 943-9773
Chicago—158 W. Washington St., (312) 346-9773
Chicago—1375 E. 53rd St., (773) 955-9700

Food & Beverages

Bakeries

Eli's Cheesecake World ✪
6701 W. Forest Preserve Dr.
Chicago, IL 60634-1470
(773) 736-3417
Hours: Mon–Fri: 9–6; Sat: 9–5; Sun: 11–5
AE, MC, V

◆ **Senior Discount:** 10% on Mon, does not honor both simultaneously **Age:** 55+

Few things say Windy City as well as deep-dish pizza, Italian beef, Chicago-style hot dogs, and . . . Eli's cheesecake. Now in its second generation of family ownership, this store recently moved farther northwest from its longtime home on Dakin. No matter where they reside, "sweet imperfections" are found in quantity and taste as good as the full-priced versions—especially with a 50%+ reduction on original, chocolate chip, pumpkin, peppermint twist, and French silk cheesecakes. Selections do vary. And ensure an even sweeter result with Eli's extra-10%-discount offer on a $10 minimum purchase for *Buying Retail Is Stupid!* readers.

MAURICE LENELL/THE COOKIE JAR

4474 N. Harlem
Norridge, IL 60656
(708) 456-6500
Hours: Mon–Fri: 8–7; Sat: 8–6; Sun: 9–5
DISC, MC, V

A kitchen staple like sugar, flour, and, oh, Eli's cheesecake, Maurice Lenell has been rolling out the cookie dough since 1937. And next to the big picture window showing the baked goods being processed is the company's "seconds" outlet, with samples galore. (Our noses alone directed us to the right spot.) Even at midday, Chicagoans were loading up: 2 pounds of pinwheels for $2.99; 2 pounds of fancy chocolate chips for $4.65; and 6 pounds of assorted broken cookies for $5.29. Hey, they still taste the same!

MARKETS

Farmers markets sponsored by communities are certainly not exclusive to Chicago. The public's appetite for the freshest of the fresh has spawned a host of produce seller-entrepreneurs from Ann Arbor and Boston to San Francisco, operating either singly or en masse.

In Chicago and its burbs, the sight of tents and booths engorged with vegetables, fruits, and related foodstuffs is a sure sign of the approaching summer. Besides, the markets' prices for in-season produce are especially seductive (so much that we find ourselves cooking up bushel-fulls of applesauce or freezing huge quantities of pureed fruits for winter consumption).

Here, then, is the latest roundup of many city, village, and municipality-hosted markets. (Our advice: please place a call to the appropriate office or chamber of commerce to find out exact days and times—because with municipalities, everything's subject to change.)

Chicago Locations

- Austin—Iowa St. and Central Ave. in the parking lot of Byford School (Saturdays)
- East Edgewater—Winthrop and Thorndale Aves. (Saturdays)
- Englewood—63rd and Halsted Sts. at northeast corner (Saturdays)
- Far North—Pratt and Washtenaw Aves. (Sundays)
- Gately—103rd St. and Cottage Grove Ave. in the parking lot of Smith School (Saturdays)
- Hyde Park—52nd St. at the cul-de-sac at Harper Ct. (Thursdays)
- Jefferson Park—Ainslie St. east of Milwaukee Ave. (Wednesdays)
- Lawndale—11 S. Homan Ave. at Greenshaw St. in the parking lot of the Community Bank (Wednesdays)
- Lincoln Park—near the intersection of Armitage Ave. and Halsted St. in the Lincoln Park High School parking lot (Saturdays)
- Lincoln Square—at the intersection of Lincoln, Leland, and Western Aves. (Tuesdays)
- Logan Square—intersection of Milwaukee and Kedzie Aves. at the CTA station plaza (Tuesdays)
- Loyola University parking lot (monthly)
- Morgan Park/Beverly—95th St. and Ashland Ave. (Saturdays)
- Mount Greenwood—intersection of 111th St. and Christiana Ave. (Tuesdays)
- Navy Pier—Grand Ave. at Lake Michigan (Saturdays & Sundays)
- Near North—Division St. between Dearborn and State Sts. (Saturdays)
- Near South—29th St. and Martin Luther King Dr. in the parking lot of Dunbar Vocational High School (Saturdays)
- North Halsted—Broadway and Halsted Sts. in the Faith Tabernacle parking lot (Saturdays)
- Printer's Row—Polk and Federal Sts. (Saturdays)
- South Shore—71st St. and Jeffery Blvd. in the parking lot of the South Shore Bank (Wednesdays)

- Southeast Chicago—intersection of 90th St. and Commercial Ave. (Tuesdays)
- Wicker Park—Wabansia and Ashland Aves. (Saturdays)

Suburban Locations

- Aurora—233 N. Broadway (Saturdays)
- Barrington—308 W. Main St. (Saturdays)
- Batavia—100 N. Island Ave. (Saturdays)
- Deerfield—Northwestern Metra station parking lot, Deerfield Rd. and York Ave. (Saturdays)
- Des Plaines—River Rd. and Perry St. (Saturdays)
- Downers Grove—just east of Main St. in the train station parking lot (Saturdays)
- East Dundee—319 N. River St. (Saturdays)
- Elmhurst—536 S. York St. in the York State Bank parking lot (Wednesdays)
- Evanston—intersection of Maple and University Aves. (Saturdays)
- Glen Ellyn—Main St. parking lot (Fridays)
- Glencoe—675 Village Ct. (Saturdays)
- Glenview—Metra railway station parking lot, Lehigh and Glenview Rd. (Saturdays)
- Grayslake—Center St. between Whitney and Slusser (Wednesdays)
- Highland Park—Dean Ave. between St. Johns and Roger Williams Ave. (Wednesdays)
- Hinsdale—between Hinsdale Ave. and 1st St. (Mondays)
- Homewood—17951 Dixie Hwy. (Saturdays)
- Joliet—Joliet City Center, Van Buren and Chicago Sts. (Fridays)
- La Grange—parking lot next to Village Hall on La Grange Rd. (Thursdays)
- La Grange Park—400 N. La Grange Rd. (Tuesdays)
- Lake Bluff—on Village Green near Scranton and Center Aves. (Fridays)
- Lake Zurich—Rte. 22 east of Old Rand Rd. (Thursdays)
- Libertyville—Cook Park, Milwaukee Ave. and Church Street (Thursdays)

- Lisle—College Square Shopping Center, College Rd. and Green Trails Dr. (Saturdays)
- Mt. Prospect—Northwestern station parking lot on Northwest Hwy. (Sundays)
- Mundelein—Hawley and Seymour Aves. (Fridays)
- Naperville—Fifth Ave. Station (Saturdays)
- Northfield—New Trier West High School parking lot (Saturdays)
- Oak Lawn—9600 Yourell Dr. (Wednesdays)
- Oak Park—intersection of Lake and Elmwood Sts. (Saturdays)
- Palatine—Palatine Rd. municipal parking lot (Thursdays)
- Palos Park—12312 88th Ave. (Fridays)
- Park Ridge—Prairie and Garden Sts. (Saturdays)
- Schaumburg—208 E. Schaumburg Rd. (Fridays)
- Skokie—Oakton St., one block west of Lincoln Ave. in the parking lot between Skokie Public Library and Village Hall (Sundays)
- Wheaton—Main St. and Liberty Dr. (Saturdays)
- Wilmette—Metra railway station, Central Ave. parking facility (Saturdays)
- Winfield—Prairie Trail center on southwest corner of Country Farm and Geneva Rds. (Wednesdays)
- Worth—11139 S. Harlem Ave. (Wednesdays)
- Villa Park—St. Charles Rd. and Ardmore St. in the police parking lot (Tuesdays)

ANGELO CAPUTO'S

2560 N. Harlem Ave.
Elmwood Park, IL 60707
(708) 453-0155
Hours: Mon–Fri: 7–10; Sat: 6–8; Sun: 6–7
Cash, Food Stamps, MC, V

Go west (within the book's boundaries, that is) to find some real deals on fruits, vegetables, and Italian specialties (meats, in particular). Our alert to the savings found at family-owned-and-operated Angelo's is a Gold Coast resident who regularly drives to Elmwood Park for her fresh farm foods. A sampling of winter-green buys: broccoli at 49¢ a pound; strawberries for $6.49 per case; five varieties of Michigan apples at $1 for 3 pounds.

Addison—240 W. Lake St., (630) 543-0151
Hanover Park—1250 Lake St., (630) 372-2800

CHICAGO MEAT HOUSE

4750 S. California Ave.
Chicago, IL 60632
(773) 927-3200
Hours: Mon–Sat: 8–5:30
DISC, MC, V

Though the carnivorous population of the United States appears to be decreasing, according to health reports, ironically the number of steak houses and restaurants serving up meat and potatoes is on the upswing. (We strongly suspect that most folks, like us, say one thing and do another.) Even people who are assiduously monitoring their diets will admit to a craving—now and then, of course—for a juicy T-bone, porterhouse, or rib eye. Saving bucks on beef in a big way used to mean buying half a steer (or more). No need, since Chicago Meat House could supply the world—or the three million people located in Chicago—with meat at good prices: $3.99 for a pound of T-bone; 3 pounds of quarter-pounders (seasoned beef patties) at $2.97. For the quasi-vegetarian, there are other options: consider honeydew melons (99¢ each); $3.29 for a pound of turkey breast; and two Tombstone pizzas for $6.50. We're hungry now.

DELRAY FARMS, INC.

6150 N. Broadway
Chicago, IL 60640
(773) 381-0200
Hours: Mon–Sat: 7–9; Sun: 7–8
MC, V

Like a crop of spring asparagus after a big rain: the 16, soon-to-be-18 (if not more by the time of publication) local stores belonging to Delray Farms sprouted up almost overnight. All situated in Chicago neighborhoods of varying sizes and demographics, Delray stores bring the farm to you, often at prices good enough to eat. Try 20 limes for a buck, a 3-pound bag of carrots for $1.49, and top-round roast for $1.79 a pound. A limited selection of fish, poultry,

dairy, and grocery products makes Delray more than a quick-stop convenience.
18 locations; see the Yellow Pages

FAMILY FRUIT MARKET

4118 N. Cicero Ave.
Chicago, IL 60641
(773) 481-2500
Hours: Mon–Fri: 6–9; Sat: 6–7; Sun: 6–6
Cash, check

Same owners, different names, about a mile apart: out west and close to the city limits, the prices of produce sure do plummet, compared with downtown produce markets. Both Family and A&G offer shoppers much more than indicated, stocking meats, poultry, dairy, and nuts in addition to the USDA's recommended five to seven servings a day. Our gourmet nose picked up these scents: a variety of nuts (almonds, Brazil nuts, filberts, et al.) for $1.49 a pound; Braeburn apples at 39¢ a pound; and Aronias black currant juice costing $1.19 a liter.

Chicago—A&G Fruit Market, 3300 N. Cicero Ave., (773) 777-4480

L. ISAACSON & STEIN FISH CO.

800 W. Fulton St.
Chicago, IL 60607
(847) 421-2444
Hours: Mon–Fri: 7–4:15; Sat: 7–3
Cash only

Despite all the medical evidence, there are still a few of us (present company exempt, of course) who wrinkle up our noses when the main course has gills and fins. (And, believe us, the "it's good for you" line doesn't cut it with kids—and some adults.) Yet, whenever in the area, we find ourselves drawn to the Isaacson & Stein market—first simply to watch the bustle. Second, to partake of the swimmingly good prices. Everything's fresh that day unless otherwise marked; customers include some of the toniest eateries in town. In fact, when confronted with daily specials, we found it difficult to make up our minds: Should it be tilapia ($5/pound) or tuna loin ($6)? Do you prefer shucked oysters ($5) or scallops ($8) for appetizers? Few other fisheries can boast these kinds of straight-from-the-waters food—and good deals.

MOO & OINK ✪

7158 S. Stony Island Ave.
Chicago, IL 60649
(773) 493-2024
Hours: Mon–Fri: 9–7; Sat & Sun: 9–4
MC, V
◆ **Senior Discount:** 5% **Age:** 65+

Imagine these numbers: one million pounds of meat per day, with one store alone responsible for a 10,000-pound order of pork. But quantity is not the only reason for the success of three-store chain Moo & Oink. President Barry Levy pays attention to local needs (e.g., ham hocks, farm-raised catfish) and local pocketbooks, and even sends buses to nearby housing projects to pick up customers. Savings are typically better than those at grocery chains, thanks to a company-owned meat plant. Plus other brands and food star: Eckrich, Home Run Inn pizzas, Tennessee Pride, and southern frozen vegetables. Individuals will also star, thanks to the 5% additional discount on a minimum $10 purchase for *Buying Retail Is Stupid!* readers.

Chicago—8201 S. Racine Ave., (773) 962-8200
Chicago—4848 W. Madison St., (773) 473-4800

NORTHEASTERN FRUIT & GARDEN MARKET

6000 N. Lincoln Ave.
Chicago, IL 60659
(773) 338-0610
Hours: Mon–Fri: 8–8; Sat: 8–7:30; Sun: 8:30–5
Cash, check

Fruit and vegetable stands in Chicago and its suburbs in no way rival the area's summer farmers markets. Still, for a sampling of good in-season produce at hard-to-beat prices, these stores can save serious dollars. An institution for more than two decades, Northeastern offers pretty good deals: large Red Delicious apples for 69¢ per pound, onions at 10¢ per pound, and red leaf lettuce at 49¢ per pound.

OLYMPIC MEAT PACKERS
810 W. Randolph St.
Chicago, IL 60607
(312) 666-2222
Hours: Mon–Sat: 7:30–5:30; Sun: 8–1
Cash

It's one of those ever-changing neighborhoods in Chicago that never fails to fascinate: the west Fulton Street–area markets. Burly truck drivers and immigrant new-citizen shop owners work the proverbial cheek by jowl with high-toned lunch and dinner eating establishments. And nestled in those strips of wholesale food merchants, many of whom sell only to retailers, is Olympic Meat Packers. A sampling of packaged specials: 5 pounds of chicken legs for $2.95; an $8.90 tag on six T-bone steaks; and 4 pounds of Italian beef marked $9.50. And if Olympic doesn't have what the recipe demands, meander down the street and check the Columbus Meat Market (906 west) or Pepe's (853 west).

PEPE'S MEAT PACKING
853 Randolph St.
Chicago, IL 60607
(312) 421-2488
Hours: Mon–Fri: 6–5; Sat: 7–5; Sun: 7–1
DISC, MC, V

"Beef: it's what's for dinner." Notwithstanding the ad agency's deliberate misuse of the English language, more and more of us are clamoring for steaks, burgers, roasts, and loins from hoofed animals. Since satisfying meat-and-potatoes appetites can be a major financial drain, we frequently meander over to West Randolph, the site of Chicago's wholesale food market. (And also, not so coincidentally, the home of Oprah's studio, some extremely yupscale restaurants, and the land of soon-to-be lofts.) Pepe's is one of our stops. During our last stock-up of the freezer, we noted these per-pound prices: sirloin-tip steaks at $2.39; first-cut pork chops at $1.39; ducklings at $1.49; chicken nuggets at $8. Please, sir, can we have more?

RAN-DUN PRODUCE & DELI

1630 N. Rand Rd.
Palatine, IL 60067
(847) 776-2345
Hours: Mon–Sun: 8–7
AE, DIN, DISC, MC, V

It's usually cash on the barrel at farm stands. Not so with Ran-Dun Produce, which accepts—amazingly!—American Express and Diners Club in addition to the usual plastic. Prices on fresh in-season vegetables and fruits are competitive; compare, for instance, 10 kiwis, limes, or navel oranges for a buck during spring. Even better bargains lie in wait in the deli, where suburban shoppers could find such prices as $1.99 for a pound of turkey breast or $3.79 for a pound of roast beef.

STANLEY'S FRESH FRUIT AND VEGETABLES

1558 N. Elston Ave.
Chicago, IL 60622
(773) 276-8050
Hours: Mon–Sat: 6–10; Sun: 6–9
Cash, check

A block away from the foot of the North Avenue exit and entrance ramps to the Kennedy Expressway is Stanley's, a local stalwart and purveyor of fresh fruits and vegetables. Night or day, cars, vans, and trucks (even Chicago cabbies) fill the front and back parking lots to shop. Owned by the Stankers, Stanley's is known for some of the best local prices on seasonal produce. A sample spring selection: 98¢ each for honeydew melons, 39¢ a pound for fresh pickles, three heads of romaine lettuce for $1.49. Do pick your goods carefully; overly ripe produce crops up occasionally.

SUN HARVEST MARKET ★

1731 W. Golf Rd.
Mt. Prospect, IL 60056
(847) 718-9484
Hours: Mon–Sat: 8–10; Sun: 9–9
DISC, MC, V

All the green leafy things imaginable can be found in this three-location market billing itself as the grocery retailer "the competition doesn't want you to know about." Once known as the North Water Market in its Skokie location, Sun Harvest is more than just fruits and vegetables; typical savings range about 30% on "choice" meats and dairy products, too, from Dean's, Kraft, La Preferida, and other brands. A typical stop at what president Mark Braun calls the "best of fresh": California navel oranges at 39¢ a pound; cantaloupe, 49¢ a pound; and 10 pounds of Wisconsin russets for less than a buck. And for *Buying Retail Is Stupid!* readers whose kitchens and pantries need replenishing, the Sun Harvest 10%-extra-discount coupon on a $25 minimum purchase may indeed whet appetites.

Franklin Park—2745 N. Mannheim Rd., (847) 451-8440
Skokie—4949 W. Oakton, (847) 677-9330

SUPREME LOBSTER & SEAFOOD CO.

220 E. North Ave.
Villa Park, IL 60181
(630) 834-3474
Hours: Mon: 10–6; Tues–Fri: 9–6; Sat: 9–5
AE, DISC, MC, V

Thanks to the presence of O'Hare International Airport, Chicago-area shoppers have access to good-quality fresh and frozen seafood at a discount. At Supreme, fresh Chesapeake clams and bluepoint oysters run around $5.99 a dozen, while frozen lobster tails (Brazilian in origin) and king crab legs are priced at $11.99 a pound.

TED'S FRUIT MARKET

2840 W. Devon Ave.
Chicago, IL 60659
(773) 743-6739
Hours: Mon–Sun: 7–10
Cash, check

Certain neighborhoods in Chicago simply scream "discount"—like this stretch of Devon Avenue. Sandwiched between various ethnic restaurants and stores, secondhand shops, and appliance discounters are food mini-emporiums like Ted's. Prices on in-season fruits and vegetables are hard to match; a recent visit netted Costa Rican pineapples from $1.40 each, strawberries at 79¢ a pint, and cantaloupes at 98¢ each. And, yes, we have no bananas today . . . (bananas were marked at 3 pounds for $1 the day we shopped).

VALLI PRODUCE

450 E. Golf Rd.
Arlington Heights, IL 60005
(847) 439-9700
Hours: Mon–Fri: 7–9; Sat: 7–8; Sun: 7–7
Cash, check

Some produce markets specialize in just the farmer's reapings, while others expand to serve as a minigrocery as well. Arlington Heights–based Valli Produce is of the latter ilk . . . and though we won't vouch for their liquor prices, the fresh veggies and fruits—in-season, of course—represent some excellent buys. Our spring harvest of bargains: a dozen mangoes for $2.89; extra large eggs (12 of 'em) for 59¢; three heads of lettuce for a buck. No Valli girls here.

VIENNA BEEF OUTLET STORE

2501 N. Damen Ave.
Chicago, IL 60647
(773) 235-6652
Hours: Mon–Fri: 9–4:45; Sat: 9–3
MC, V

Yipes! No deli deals here, because this so-called outlet of Vienna Beef doesn't discount its take-out sandwiches. (A hot dog on a bun, during our visit, was tagged $1.99.) If you wanna buy in bulk and schlep the meats home, savings are adequate. Some of their per-poundage prices: New York–style pastrami for $5.49; corned beef or rare roast beef for $6.79. Hey, make mine with hot mustard and pickles on rye!

Nuts & Candy

Affy Tapple

7110 N. Clark St.
Chicago, IL 60626
(773) 338-1100
Hours: Mon–Fri: 7:30–4; Sat: 8–12
Cash

Halloween really isn't Halloween unless taffy apples appear. And to give little trick-or-treaters a thrill without Mom's melting all that caramel, sneak up to the Rogers Park headquarters of this candy manufacturer to buy caseloads of slightly "bruised" Affy Tapple goodies. "Bruised" is still first quality, but maybe the apple's missing a caramel corner or part of a stick, or features candy patchwork. Prices range from 40¢ to $1.90 each (oversized, humongous apples); purchase in cases of 24 to realize additional savings.

Blommer's Chocolate Factory

600 W. Kinzie St.
Chicago, IL 60610
(312) 226-7700
Hours: Mon–Fri: 9–5
DISC, MC, V

Ah: to the early-A.M. Lincoln Park joggers, the aroma can be somewhat cloying—especially before breakfast. But to the masses of us who say there's no such thing as too much chocolate, Blommer's West Loop factory produces a heavenly smell. Better yet are the free samples—raspberry chocolate chips when we dropped in. And lest those allergic to the beans of the cacao tree believe that abstinence is called for, Blommer's offers such delights as jelly beans ($4.50 a pound) and gourmet caramels ($3.99 a pound), among others.

Other sweet treats per pound: white chocolate discs ($2.33); English toffee turtles ($8.50); and for both of our ever-losing baseball teams, $1.25 for a chocolate mini-baseball glove. Better meander over at lunch; this Chicago factory is closed on weekends.

Evons Thrift Store

1717 Arthur Ave.
Elk Grove Village, IL 60007
(847) 593-2300, ext. 262
Hours: Mon–Fri: 8:30–5; Sat: 9–4
MC, V

We know it by another name: John B. Sanfillipo & Sons, the largest distributor of nuts in Chicago. You'll recognize it by the label—Evons, the packages hanging in grocery stores. And, we guarantee it, you'll snatch up the savings in this one and only outlet. Priced by the pound: peanuts at $2.26; cashews, $4.46 to $6.49; pecans, $5.96. (The reason for the range of costs? Your choice of pieces, halves, wholes, salted, or unsalted.)

Fannie May Candies

51 E. Randolph St.
Chicago, IL 60601
(800) 4CANDIES
Hours: Mon–Fri: 8–7; Sat: 9:30–7; Sun: 10–5:30
AE, DISC, MC, V
◆ **Senior Discount:** 15% on Wed **Age:** 60+

From the outside, it looks like a regular candy store of the Fannie May variety. But, one long section, with trays and white bags, is devoted to slight irregulars and imperfections—all at a 25% savings. Some of the tasty treats: hard candy at $3.19 per pound; assorted salted nuts for $10.46 per pound; mini truffles at $8.96 per pound. Note: Other Fannie May discount stores sell only irregular confections.

Chicago—4024 W. 79th St., (773) 582-7999
Chicago—1101 Jackson Blvd., (312) 243-2700
Chicago—1813 W. Montrose Ave., (773) 871-7186

Farley's Outlet Store

3025 N. Pulaski Rd.
Chicago, IL 60641
(773) 725-1661
Hours: Mon–Fri: 9–6; Sat: 9–5
Cash

It's a good thing we live many miles from Farley's. Because, when left to our standard eating habits (and no one's in sight), we're worse than most kids in candy stores. Herein is the allure at the two Farley's stores: candy, both hard and soft, good and not-so-great, at some toothy savings. If Mom OKs a healthy snack, there are fruit rolls at $1.25 a box or dried banana slices for 75¢ a bag. Calories also reign: minimarshmallows from Kraft for half a buck and peanut brittle for a quarter more.
Chicago—3057 W. 26th St., (773) 376-8105

Ferrara Pan Candy Co.

730 W. Harrison St.
Forest Park, IL 60130
(708) 366-0500
Hours: Mon–Fri: 7:30–4:45; Sat: 7:30–2:45
Cash, check

The exterior, shaded with a green-and-white-striped awning, resembles a Mediterranean storefront. Inside, the Ferrara Pan Candy outlet is doubly delightful: surrounded by a 1989 mural created by Charles Nitti, assorted candy and biscotti and Italian cookies parade under glass, ready for savoring. Established in 1908, Ferrara opened this tiny European-style store only 5 years ago—and it's probably one of River Forest's (and Chicago's) best-kept secrets. Along with rock-bottom prices on such classic sweets as Atomic Red Hots, Boston Baked Beans, and Lemonheads (a quarter for a small box, $7.50 for 200 pieces), the store stocks a relative's output—the twice-baked biscotti for $5 a pound and a mouth-watering variety of decorated Italian butter-rich cookies with the same tag. "Abondanza" applies here.

GOELITZ CONFECTIONERY (JELLY BELLY FACTORY CO. OUTLET)

1539 Morrow Ave.
North Chicago, IL 60064
(847) 689-8950
Hours: Mon–Fri: 10–4:30; Sat: 9–12
MC, V
◆ **Senior Discount:** 10% on Wed **Age:** 60+

President Ronald Reagan started it: a mass craze for an upscale gourmet candy made of sugar, corn syrup, cornstarch, and water. With 40 flavors, a tour of the fabrication process, and a price that's close to one-fourth retail ($3.75 for 2 pounds of Belly Flops), it's not such a bad idea to schlep the whole family to North Chicago's Goelitz Confectionery Co., home of the Jelly Belly. A 4-calorie strawberry daiquiri, anyone?

THE HOME ECONOMIST

9163 N. Grosse Point Rd.
Skokie, IL 60077
(847) 674-7252
Hours: Mon–Fri: 9:30–7; Sat: 10–6; Sun: 11–5
DISC, MC, V
◆ **Senior Discount:** 10% on Tues; not on cases **Age:** 60+

Even owners of boutique patisseries have been known to frequent The Home Economist, where buying candies, nuts, and spices in bulk can save some major bucks. Laid out in a help-yourself fashion, the store also offers even larger savings on by-the-case purchases—or what they claim is close-to-wholesale prices. A fall sales example: pecan halves for $2.99 a pound; imperial mix with macadamia nuts at $4.99 a pound; dried pineapple, $1.29 a pound.

Barrington—906 S. Northwest Hwy., (847) 382-4202
LaGrange Park—419 N. LaGrange Rd., (708) 352-1514
Oak Lawn—8759 S. Ridgeland Ave., (708) 598-5734
Westmont—6328 Cass Ave., (630) 852-0214

Long Grove Confectionery Co. Outlet ☐
333 Lexington Dr.
Buffalo Grove, IL 60089
(847) 459-0269
Hours: Mon–Sat: 9:30–5:30; Sun: 1–4
AE, DISC, MC, V
◆ **Senior Discount:** 10% on Wed **Age:** 60+

Five pounds later, we waddled out of the Long Grove Confectionery Outlet—fatter, but definitely in a sweeter disposition. Because manager Maureen Harrington absolutely insisted—OK, so she only suggested—that we sample a bunch of chocolate concoctions. Such as a 22-ounce myrtle—a melt-in-your-mouth mix of caramel, nuts, and chocolate—for $16, instead of $22.95. Or an amazingly scrumptious sugar-free bridge mix for $5.95 a pound. We gawked, too, at the solid-chocolate seven-piece tool set ($10 from an original $15.95); a 12-inch chocolate pizza for a mere $7 (was $12.95); and the $125 regulation-size chocolate basketball, the original of which says "Thank you Bulls for No. 5," presented to Michael Jordan's mom. It's obvious that Long Grove is of our mind (there is no such animal as too much chocolate!)—since they're generously offering *Buying Retail Is Stupid!* readers 10% off.

Superior Nut and Candy Bulk Stores
3046 W. 77th St.
Chicago, IL 60620
(773) 434-5500
Hours: Mon–Fri: 9–5
MC, V

Bulk is always a best buy—and even better at a factory outlet. What the West 77th Street site of Superior Nut and Candy is, well, superior at offering the Chicago public are some hard-to-crack prices on nuts and candies. Ready for eating and/or baking are red and natural pistachios ($2.99 a pound) and honey-roasted cashews at a buck more. And kids will argue over the bull's-eyes ($1.69 for those squooshy-soft caramel-and-white-fluff treats) plus the student mix for 10 additional cents. Cookies, too (Maurice Lenell et al.). There's no way not to buy.

Chicago—4038 N. Nashville Ave., (773) 282-3930
Chicago— 3102 N. Central Ave., (773) 237-4940

Specialty & Miscellaneous Foods

The Bagel Factory Outlet

9179 Grosse Point Rd.
Skokie, IL 60077
(847) 674-0488
Hours: Mon–Sat: 5–8; Sun: 6–6
AE, DISC, MC, V
◆ **Senior Discount:** 10% on Wed **Age:** 60+

This baked and boiled, but not fried, donut with a hole in the middle has captured the hearts of all Americans, not just those living in Manhattan. (Witness the product line of Sara Lee, which now features the bagel.) What a pleasure, then, to munch on one that costs less than those from the ovens of the Einstein or Bruegger's franchises. Actually, The Bagel Factory's best deals are after 6:00 P.M., when a baker's dozen costs $2.80 (before the discount hour, they're priced at $4.28). Weekday lunch specials at $2.99 feature a variety of sandwich fillings. And other foodstuffs, from Simon Brothers Bakery, for instance, are just as well priced.

Best's Kosher

1630 W. Deerfield Rd.
Highland Park, IL 60035
(847) 831-9435
Hours: Mon–Thurs: 10–7; Fri: 9:00 A.M.—call for closing time; Sun: 10–6
MC, V

The sign on the glass door clearly states that the store closes at 3:15 on summer Fridays. Coupled with the number of men wearing yarmulkes and occasionally wielding a foreign tongue, we know we're in Best's Kosher outlet territory. All foodstuffs are kashruth produced under strict rabbinical inspection. Partaking of their take-out deli saves some money ($3.75 for your choice of corned beef, pastrami, or seasoned brisket sandwich—with pickle); lunch spe-

cials offer a jumbo hot dog for a buck or a sandwich–small chips–soda combo at $4. But the largest number of pennies are saved with the packaged foods and frozen meats: stew meat for $3.49; shoulder tip, $4.29; and rib eye, $7.19. (If prices seem high, believe us, they represent a savings: kosher poultry and beef are expensive.) There's a second location in the city under the Sinai Kosher name.
Chicago—Sinai Kosher, 1000 W. Pershing Rd., (773) 650-6338

COFFEE & TEA EXCHANGE
3311 N. Broadway
Chicago, IL 60657
(773) 528-2241
Hours: Mon–Thurs: 9–8; Fri & Sat: 9–7; Sun: 10–6
AE, DISC, MC, V

In a sense, coffee imitates the stock market: up-and-down prices that change whimsically. The 20-something-year-old Coffee & Tea Exchange tries to moderate the ebb and flow of bean costs (tea and spices, too) via its own fresh-roasted warehouse. Too, it's known for its ability to emulate certain brewed tastes; they produce a Blue Mountain–style coffee, unique to this firm, that approximates the wonderful Jamaican taste but not the exorbitant price of $30 a pound and more.
Chicago—833 W. Armitage Ave., (773) 929-6730 (hours vary)

WINE & SPIRITS

BINNY'S BEVERAGE DEPOT
124 McHenry Rd.
Buffalo Grove, IL 60089
(847) 459-2200
Hours: Mon–Sat: 9–9; Sun: 10–6
DISC, MC, V

What's the discount division of a discounter called? In liquor sales, the name is Binny's Beverage Depot. In two suburban locations, Binny's, part of the Gold Standard liquor chain, routinely offers a 10%–20% savings on name and private labels. Particularly of note

is the large stock of craft beers from Celis, Pyramid, and Shipyard breweries, along with monikers such as Goat Island, Blue Fin, and Old Humper.
Des Plaines—767 W. Golf Rd., (847) 956-1000

CASEY'S LIQUORS ☆

1444 W. Chicago Ave.
Chicago, IL 60622
(312) 243-2850
Hours: Mon–Thurs: 11–9; Fri & Sat: 11–10:30; Sun: 12:30–9
AE, DISC, MC, V

What the Wine Discount Center and Zimmerman's are to the oenophile, Allen Kaleta, president of Casey's, would like to be to beer lovers. On the fringes of east Ukrainian Village, Casey's "The Beerstore" not only features unusual and exotic brands of brew at a 50% discount, but it also sells do-it-yourself supplies should customers be so inclined. Best brewing bargains are on cases of close-out beers, Kaleta's specialty. Or wield the additional 5% *Buying Retail Is Stupid!* coupon on any brewskis.

CROWN CUT-RATE LIQUORS

2821 N. Milwaukee Ave.
Chicago, IL 60622
(773) 772-9227
Hours: Mon–Thurs: 8–11; Fri & Sat: 8–11:30; Sun: 11–8
Cash

In the heart of the Polish community, Crown carries just about what you'd expect—a good variety of beers (though not a match for Casey's) and some interesting brands and varieties of spirits. Here, the emphasis is on saving with quantity buys: a half barrel of Bud is $39.95, while 30 cans of your-choice Miller, Old Style, High-Life cost $9.98.

FOREMOST LIQUOR STORES

3014 N. Ashland Ave.
Chicago, IL 60657
(773) 472-7471
Hours: Mon–Sat: 9–10; Sun: 11–8
MC, V

For standard selections of beers, wines, and liquor, it's hard to beat spirit supermarkets like Foremost with its 23 area stores. At any given time, depending on weekly specials, a four-pack of Bartles & Jaymes wine coolers could run $2.98 while a hefty bottle of Bailey's is $14.99. There's an adequate mix of imports and domestic beers—Bud, Coors, and Miller with Grolsch, Heineken, and Labatt's. But don't expect samples from small microbreweries or low-producing vineyards to be on the shelves.

23 stores; see flyers in Wednesday *Chicago Tribune* for additional locations

GOLD STANDARD/CHALET WINE SHOPS

40 E. Delaware Pl.
Chicago, IL 60611
(312) 787-8555
Hours: Mon–Sat: 10–8; Sun: 11–6
DISC, MC, NOV, V

"Liquor is quicker," the oft-besotted Dorothy Parker declared. But we venture to guess she was never confronted with as many choices in alcoholic beverages as today's consumer. It is obvious, too, that chains such as Gold Standard/Chalet have the buying clout to lower prices—and pass them along to shoppers. This several-store retailer promotes, almost weekly, a variety of wines, beers, and the hard stuff at decent prices. With newspaper coupons, the savings are even greater: 1.75 liters of Bacardi rum for $11.99, and a 25% reduction for a bottle of Robert Mondavi 1994 zinfandel. Foodstuffs from the in-store cheese, crackers, and gourmet noshables section are not as discounted as the imbibe-ables.

Nine locations; see the Yellow Pages

SAM'S WINES & SPIRITS
1720 N. Marcey St.
Chicago, IL 60614
(312) 664-4394
Hours: Mon–Sat: 8–9; Sun: 11–6
AE, DISC, MC, V

There is no denying that the owner of Sam's, Fred Rosen, is the most mediagenic of Chicago's wine and spirits merchants. And his recent move to 33,000-square-foot Marcey Street, adding a deli, bakery, coffee bar, and cigar shop to his offerings, completes his superstore status. Certainly, don't expect bargains on the comestibles; a grilled eggplant–roasted peppers–tomato sauce–goat cheese focaccia sandwich will run about the same as on Michigan Avenue. As always, though, the libations are aggressively priced; beers, wines, and liquors are of brand-name quality (Killian, Stags Leap, and Absolut, among many, many others) at discounts. Best buy the caseload.

WINE DISCOUNT CENTER ✪
1826½ N. Elston Ave.
Chicago, IL 60622
(773) 489-3454
Mon–Fri: 10–7; Sat: 9–5; Sun: 12–5
DISC, MC, V

Bud Schwarzbach, owner of Wine Discount Center, is a worthy competitor to Sam's. His concept? To seek out, taste, and select the best wines in all price categories. His searches lead him beyond France and California to Chile, Oregon, Australia, and points east, west, north, and south, with his two freestanding stores offering 75,000 bottles, 700 labels. (Two other Wine Discount Centers operate inside Famous Liquor stores in Forest Park and Lombard.) Other products: still and sparkling wines from all over the world as well as a small selection of fine spirits (Cognacs, single malt scotch, etc.). The only brands stocked, whether Beringer or Columbia Crest, Louis Jadot or Veuve Cliquot, are those passing the scrutiny of the Center's tasting panel. Every month, the staff samples 300 to 400 wines to select the 50 to 60 introduced in each monthly flyer. Bonus one:

free tastings of new wines every Saturday from noon to 5:00 P.M. Bonus two: sign up for the free monthly mailer. And bonus three: a free Vacu Vin vacuum wine-saver kit ($6.99 value) to every *Buying Retail Is Stupid!* reader who purchases $10 or more (one per family).
Highland Park—11350 Old Skokie Rd., (847) 831-1049
Two inside Famous Liquor stores:
Forest Park—7339 W. Madison St., (708) 366-2500
Lombard—105 E. Roosevelt Rd., (630) 629-3330 (hours vary)

Zimmerman's Warehouse Discount Liquor Store

213 W. Grand Ave.
Chicago, IL 60610
(312) 332-0012
Hours: Mon–Sat: 7:30–8; Sun: 11–5
MC, V

Believe it or not, the founder of Zimmerman's—Max with the ubiquitous hat—still works here 7 days a week, delivering the same kind of personal service as 60+ years ago. One store and one store only in River North caters to both city and suburban carriage trade—with great prices to boot. Though brand names do matter here (from Budweiser to Southern Comfort), of greater import to Max and son Marty are the wines. Any employee at the big Z's, when presented with a special-event description and menu, will recommend an equal and/or better substitute at a lesser price. The day's suggestion: San Andrea pino grigio at $6.99 versus the Santa Margarita, selling elsewhere for twice the price. Hats off to a super-warehouse discount party store.

Home Furnishings

CHINA, COOKWARE, CRYSTAL & SILVER

CHAR CREWS, INC.

670 N. Wells St.
Chicago, IL 60610
(312) 642-2202 or (800) 323-1972
Hours: Mon–Wed, Fri, Sat: 10–5; Thurs: 10–8; hours vary
DISC, MC, V

A bride's table perches in the center of many Char Crews stores, showing what to-be-marrieds have selected as their china, silver, and glass (along with cards indicating bride and groom names). Indeed, at all these carriage-tradelike stores, the bridal registry is alive and well—especially considering the everyday 10%–30% discounts offered by this 20-something-year-old Chicago institution. Almost every major producer is well represented, from Atlantis and Christian Dior to Villeroy & Boch and Wedgwood (though not all are discounted); semiannual sales and occasional promotions decrease prices further. Example: a five-piece place setting of Spode Christmas tree china for $42.95 (suggested at $75).

Barrington—Barrington Commons, (847) 382-5750
Hinsdale—8 Grant Sq., (630) 920-0190
Park Ridge—428 Touhy Ave., (847) 692-6360
Wilmette—Plaza del Lago, (847) 256-5910

CHEF'S CATALOG WAREHOUSE

3215 Commercial Ave.
Sky Harbor Industrial Park
Northbrook, IL 60062
(847) 480-9400
Hours: Mon–Wed: 1–7; Thurs & Fri: 11–8; Sat: 10–6; Sun: 11–6
AE, DISC, MC, V

Those in the know label it one of the best places around to buy kitchen instruments (and Calphalon anodized aluminum cookware). Twice a year and during their warehouse and store sales (in

March and September), Chef's Catalog outdoes even its mail-order prices. On our hit list for the holidays: $159.99 for a Cuisinart deluxe pasta machine ($400 list); a Weber Performer kettle grill at $399.99 (regularly $475); and a large butcher-block rolling cart for $599.99 ($900 originally). OK, we're asking for a lot—but, believe it or not, you'll save even more during sale time. Whistle while we cook.
Chicago—3009 N. Clark St., (773) 327-5210
Highland Park—Crossroads Shopping Center, (847) 831-1100

CHICAGO CUTLERY ETC.

11211 120th Ave.
Lakeside Mall
Kenosha, WI 53142
(414) 857-2509
Hours: Mon–Sat: 10–9; Sun: 11–6
DISC, MC, V

A little-known secret: the true and worthy competitor to Calphalon's anodized aluminum cookware—Magnalite Professional, with its cast, not stamped, aluminum lids—is in real danger of extinction. Once a fixture on houseware shelves, the line (and its new owners) is now valiantly trying for a comeback. And as part of the Chicago Cutlery Outlet in Lakeside Marketplace, Mag Pro (its nickname) re-debuts in style, with substantial savings (at least 25%) and promotions. Up to 60% discounts are offered on other essential home chef stuff: 11-slot wood knife block for $20.99 and a 3-inch parer for $3.99.

EDWARD DON OUTLET STORE ✪

2525 N. Elston Ave.
Chicago, IL 60647
(773) 489-7739
Hours: Mon–Fri: 10–6; Sat: 9–5; Sun: 11–4
DISC, MC, V
◆ **Senior Discount:** 10% **Age:** 55+

The only outlet for the Edward Don professional food-service equipment and supplies, this Elston Avenue location resembles a warehouse bulging with a hodgepodge of food-related merchandise. Yet, cooking demos with both well-known local and national chefs plus June and September sidewalk sales (10%–50% off all wares) can draw major crowds. Everything but the kitchen sink is featured: Rubbermaid two-piece janitor bucket for $71.99; any item in the Cuisinart professional line for 20% less than retail; Progressive five-piece Chinese wok set at $18.99. Always a sale and usually a 20% minimum discount—and even better savings with your 20% off *Buying Retail Is Stupid!* coupon.

Krasny & Company ★

2829 N. Clybourn Ave.
Chicago, IL 60618
(773) 477-5504
Hours: Mon–Fri: 10–6; Sat: 9–5
AE, DISC, MC, V

The Frugal Gourmet (aka Jeff Smith) shopped at Krasny's when he lived in Chicago. As do any number of home chefs who realize that restaurant-quality cooking equipment and supplies usually last longer than noncommercial cookware. So, included in this large—18,000 square feet—store are institutional-size spices (32 ounces of pure vanilla extract for $20.95); plastic and paper party supplies (fifty 9-inch plates for $8.49); and cooking "stuff" (10-quart aluminum Eagleware pot for $38.95). A Windy City family fixture since 1918. And one to warm the stove of any *Buying Retail Is Stupid!* cook's kitchen, with an extra-10%-discount coupon.

Northwestern Cutlery & Supply

810 W. Lake St.
Chicago, IL 60607
(312) 421-3662
Hours: Mon–Fri: 7–5; Sat: 7–4
AE, DISC, MC, V

West of the Loop is an odd mix of well-established businesses (many related to the food industry) and newly rehabbed loft condos and apartment rentals. Regardless of their residency, smart home chefs trek to Northwestern Cutlery, an old-line Chicago firm started in 1920. Here, good deals can be found on both professional and better-than-novice quality cookware and equipment, usually at a 25%–40% discount. A recent sale uncovered these bargains: two-piece Wusthof/Trident chef's cutlery set at $73.50; Le Creuset 5½-quart round French oven at $120 (was $200); and Henckel's four-piece steak-knife set from $110 (once about $192).

PICKARD FACTORY OUTLET

782 Covena Ave.
Antioch, IL 60002
(847) 395-3800
Hours: Mon–Sat: 8:30–4 (except holidays)
DISC, MC, V

Auctions sell some of Pickard's older patterns for good bucks. Settings have been purchased by residents of Washington D.C.'s White and Blair Houses, the U.S. Navy, and U.S. ambassadors around the world. Yet, no trip to our nation's capital is necessary, since Pickard is headquartered in Antioch, Illinois, and has an on-premises factory outlet, to boot. For 40%–50% off retail, minor flaws, undecorated pieces, and specialty seasonal items can be easily tolerated for the joy of owning Pickard. An example of the deals found on our visit: a 40-piece set of Washington china at $1,040 (retailing for $2,080).

ROMAN OUTLET STORE

2601 S. Lively Blvd.
Elk Grove Village, IL 60007
(847) 860-5657
Hours: Mon–Fri: 10–6; Sat: 10–4
AE, DISC, MC, V

Stuffed bunnies rub ears with Santa Clauses and wedding-cake ornaments. In Roman's 4,000-square-foot outlet, every day is literally a holiday. At the very front of the store are discontinued items; in the back (the warehouse) is irregular or imperfect merchandise. At least 50% off, so prices are nothing short of amazing: a porcelain bride-and-groom table decoration is $25 (retail at $210); and a plastic Kris Kringle, at $8 (was $38).

ROYAL INDUSTRIES
538 N. Milwaukee Ave.
Chicago, IL 60622
(312) 733-4920
Hours: Mon–Fri: 8–4
MC, V

A store with a split personality: sometimes, the name is Restaurant Supply House; at other moments, Royal Industries. What is not confusing, though, are the prices for the serious, bargain-minded home chef. Need a high chair for a guest's kid? It's sturdy and of commercial quality at $49.95 (compare to $89 retail). A major banquet for 40—and there's not enough glassware? Buy a 36-piece case of Libbey tumblers . . . and toast to the $54.05 price. Most everything that makes a kitchen work (except for extra help) is here, from bar stool seating and bone-porcelain dishes to KitchenAid attachments (great discounts) and heavy-duty aprons.

SAMPLES
1422 W. Webster Ave.
Chicago, IL 60614
(773) 244-6410
Hours: Mon–Sun: 10–6
MC, V

Just like the name says: the samples of Samples (really a factory outlet) include house- and giftwares from Copco, Le Creuset, Progressive, T-Fal, and so on, at prices 40%–60% lower than department and specialty stores. An oversized holiday cookie tin, found in the Container Store, costs $2.50, while big aluminum stockpots are generously priced at a smidge over $20.
Bridgman, MI—9709 Red Arrow Hwy. (at Lake St.), (616) 465-6559

1730 OUTLET COMPANY

1730 W. Wrightwood Ave.
Chicago, IL 60614
(773) 871-4331
Hours: Mon–Sat: 10–4
MC, V

Right around the corner from Stacy's Choice is the 1730 Outlet Company, its address-name a foil for TAG, or Trade Associate Group, a leading housewares importer/exporter. What's inside this cramped but well-merchandised space are wonderfully hued kitchen textiles, candles, lanterns, and other items of similar ilk, all of which are discounted, samples, and/or overstocks. Wooden bird barns that any feathered creature would be proud to call home are $8 (once $35); extra-padded potholders and mitts at $2 and $2.25 respectively (compare at $5 and $6); and slightly dinged seconds, iron prairie lanterns at $1.50 (were $20). Note: Crate & Barrel carries many TAG items in its retail stores.

DECORATOR ITEMS

BACK DOOR STORE (ENESCO)

2200 Busse Hwy.
Elk Grove Village, IL 60070
(847) 427-3660
Hours: Mon, Tues, Fri: 10–6; Wed & Thurs: 10–8; Sat: 9:30–5:30; Sun: 12–4
DISC, MC, V

All of the knickknacks, mementos, and just plain tchotchkes that parade across our mantels or beam through our china cabinets are what experts loosely term collectibles—and we as a nation spend five billion dollars on every year. Enesco, with national headquarters in Elk Grove Village, fuels our desire to amass and accumulate, with its imported lines of licensed figurines, giftware, clocks, and other, well, tchotchkes. Its highest renown emanates from Precious Moments, a line of wide-eyed porcelain cuties sculpted by artist Sam Butcher, caught in various activities and poses. With the opening of its one and only outlet in 1994, the Back Door Store (aka

Enesco) starts its discounts at 55%—with further reductions as necessary. What caught our eyes (and our hearts): minipandas at $2.99 (once $15); a $22.50 musical Coca-Cola vending machine (list is $50); and, of course, PM's "touch so many hearts" musical doll for $49.99 (retail $150). Memorabilia revisited.

GONE TO POT ★

1432 W. Irving Park Rd.
Chicago, IL 60613
(773) 472-2274
Hours: Mon–Fri: 12–6; Sat: 12–5
MC, V

It's part studio, part storefront: potter Marcy Glick more than makes do in a space that would cramp almost anyone else's style. On shelves, up the walls, and behind doors, dozens of artisan wares are displayed. And, if slightly distressed, they're tagged at least 50% lower than retail. One of the few seconds outlets for art ware in the entire country, Gone to Pot features pottery, glass, acrylic, metal, jewelry, and wood gifts, made by more than 80 practitioners across the country. Glick's own pastel ceramic pieces, for instance, are featured at some of the toniest boutiques and retailers in town. Two examples of savings: pearl-studded wood desk frames at $7 (originally $40); glazed ceramic working clocks at $20 (once $48). No tempest about teapots here. And great smiles about the additional 5% *Buying Retail Is Stupid!* coupon.

HAEGER POTTERIES FACTORY OUTLET

7 Maiden Lane
Dundee, IL 60118
(847) 426-3441
Hours: Mon, Thurs, Fri: 10–6; Sat & Sun: 11–5
DISC, MC, V

Few businesses remain as committed to independence—and to headquartering in the Chicago area—as Haegar Potteries, founded in 1871. The original owner helped rebuild the Windy City (via the Dundee Brickyard) after the Great Fire. Today, its outlet is situated right at the factory, on the Fox River, and offers Monday 30-minute tours as well as bargains on art pottery, silk foliage, and related decorative accessories. A few sample prices on Haeger's imperfects, one-of-a-kinds, and test pieces: ceramic table lamps at $55 (retail $110); $4.99 candlesticks; two-for-$8 cat or dog bowls. Many trek to Dundee for the company's annual June tent sale.

KOSMIC KANDLES ✪

2716 N. Elston Ave.
Chicago, IL 60647
(773) 252-6758
Hours: Mon–Fri: 10–6
AE, DISC, MC, V
◆ **Senior Discount:** 10% **Age:** 60+

Shades of the Grateful Dead, Haight-Ashbury, and the '60s Youth Revolution: scented 24-hour candles, factory seconds, and other illuminating home decor abound. Owner Mike Widmer offers pyramid-shaped candles with internal crystals for $5 or $8 each depending on size. Even greater discounts on larger purchases and/or with the 10% *Buying Retail Is Stupid!* coupon in hand.

LAST CALL

309 Old McHenry Rd.
Long Grove, IL 60089
(847) 821-8694
Hours: Mon–Sat: 9:30–5; Sun: 10–5:30
AE, DISC, MC, V

No, it's not the final season's sale of Neiman Marcus. Instead, owner Dave Mangel collects remnants, leftovers, and out-of-season gifts and holiday merchandise from his two Long Grove shops—Mangel's Gifts and Pine Cone Christmas Shop—and reduces original prices from 50% to 75%. It is truly finders keepers—and worth a trip every once in a while to discover, for instance, Christmas nutcrackers for $1.50 to $10 (once $6 to $40); brass trays at $11 (were $37.95); and $12 for one Bob Timberlake dinner plate. Celebrate the bargain season year-round.

NIEDERMAIER FACTORY OUTLET STORE

2828 N. Paulina Ave.
Chicago, IL 60657
(773) 528-1602
Hours: Wed–Fri: 10–5; Sat: 10–3
MC, V

There really is a Niedermaier, Virginia, and her name is Judy. Known by such well-heeled clients as Bloomingdale's, Saks Fifth Avenue, and Ralph Lauren Polo Stores, her display firm (primarily majoring in Christmas) also decorates the houses of Martha Stewart and Marissa Tomei with very tony, upscale, contemporary furniture. Within the factory outlet almost anything is possible—at 25%–50% off. Angel statues from $35 to $45; heart-shaped-back maple chairs at $225; a reproduction of a Greek tomb (in fiberglass) for $350.

NORCO ART PRODUCTS

670 W. Hubbard St.
Chicago, IL 60610
(312) 666-0019
Hours: Tues–Sat: 10–5:30
MC, V

So many customers bemoan the fact that craftsmanship, the practice of certain specialties, is dying out. Not so with Norco Art Products, since the Lucchesis have owned the cast-plaster business. Today, though, it's expanded beyond the Kewpie dolls carved for the now-demolished Riverview Park; merchandise includes some pretty fine-looking metal or wood chairs, tables, and other decorator accessories. Selections can be somewhat sparse, unless the Lucchesis are sprucing up for another sale; a bust of Beethoven or Shakespeare for $54.95; $98 for a Jason vase; a $219.95 upholstered wrought-iron side chair; a set of three tiered beechwood tables at $1,900.

ROYAL CRAFTS, INC.
437 Lively Blvd.
Elk Grove Village, IL 60007
(847) 640-8281
Hours: Mon–Fri: 8–4; Sat: 9–4; Sun: 10–3
MC, V

Gargoyles lurk. Religious statues sit serenely, awaiting purchase. Virtually every animal, vegetable, or mineral motif ever carved in plaster or stone has, at one time or another, appeared in this Elk Grove Village manufacturer's store. Beginning at a $12 price point and reflecting a 20%+ savings, more than 500 different styles could grace either a home's interior or exterior.

STACY'S CHOICE
2716 N. Paulina Ave.
Chicago, IL 60614
(773) 868-0123
Hours: Thurs & Fri: 10–5; Sat: 10–4:30; Sun: 12–4:30
DISC, MC, V
◆ **Senior Discount:** 10% **Age:** 60+

This address used to house the Silvestri Outlet, a manufacturer famed for its Christmas decorations. In spite of the name change, the merchandise is still of high quality—and much expanded. Find here anything for around the house, inside and outside: a faux silk bird of paradise at $2.57; aluminum chairs for $122 each; two-for-one taper candles; glorious Blenko glass vases for half of retail. At least 50% reductions on a literal potpourri of house "stuff." And . . . they've adopted our philosophy: a big sign by the cash register reads—"Friends don't let friends pay retail."

SASSAFRAS FACTORY OUTLET STORE
927 Lighthouse Pl.
Michigan City, IN 46380
(219) 872-4112
Hours: Mon–Sat: 9–8; Sun: 10–6
DISC, MC, V
◆ **Senior Discount:** 10% on Tues **Age:** 62+

To date, this Lighthouse Mall outlet of Sassafras is a solo one for the entire country. Which makes sense, since the parent company is headquartered in Chicago. Although the name gives few clues about its products, an in-store visit reminds shoppers of Crate & Barrel merchandise: brightly colored, well-designed imported/exported kitchen items, housewares, and miscellanea for the home. Most are marked down 20%, though a few out-of-season items are deeply discounted. Some recent savings: a package of educational foam blocks for toddlers at $19.95 (was $25); hand-painted dinnerware from $6.95 to $13.50; kids' bookends, $19.95 (once $27).

FURNITURE

Bedroom

AMERICAN MATTRESS
609 W. North Ave.
Chicago, IL 60610
(312) 587-7979
Hours: Mon–Fri: 10:30–8:30; Sat: 10–5; Sun: 11–5
DISC, MC, V
◆ **Senior Discount:** 10% **Age:** 65+

American Mattress, with its 30+ stores studding the Chicago area, is simply a different name for Serta, the one and only brand it carries. So, every mattress—from a foam futon to the top-of-the-line pillow-top Posturepedic—is discounted from 20% to 60%. Frequent specials and floor-model sales and closeouts ease wallet strain. Our North Avenue foray produced these prices: a complete futon (sans cover) for $649; a $349 metal-like headboard reduced to $299. Check the five clearance centers for best deals.

Over 30 locations; see the Yellow Pages

BED MART

Clybourn and Sheffield Aves.
Chicago, IL 60614
(312) 335-3336
Hours: Mon–Fri: 10:30–8:30; Sat: 10–6; Sun: 11–5
AE, DISC, MC, V
◆ **Senior Discount:** 10% **Age:** 65+

Comparison shopping for mattresses is a difficult task, simply because different national, regional, and local chains rename each model—although the Simmons, Sealy, Serta, et al. names remain the same. So, what's a smart shopper to do? Our advice: look for a straightforward, no-high-pressure salesperson to explain the differences—and test, test, test all of the beds. Check out delivery and disposal of unwanted mattresses. And finally, if you're buying bedding in quantity, why not ask for the best price? Bed Mart, we found, met all of the foregoing criteria—with 26 stores in greater Chicago, three of which are clearance centers—to check for best deals. Some sample ad prices: two-piece Beautyrest queen set at $399 and an ultra-premium luxury Simmons (queen size, again) for $659.

Call (800) KWIK BED for locations.
Clearance centers:
Chicago—5353 N. Broadway Ave., (773) 506-9696
Evergreen Park—2958 W. 95th St., (708) 636-8989
Hillside—4004 Roosevelt Rd., (708) 493-1928

THE BEDDING EXPERTS

1871 N. Clybourn Ave.
Chicago, IL 60614
(773) 528-9000
Hours: Mon, Tues, Thurs, Fri: 10:30–8:30; Wed: 11–8:30;
Sat: 10–5:30; Sun: 11–5
AE, BEDDING EXPERTS, DISC, MC, V

If there's one gripe common to consumers, no matter what location or age or household demographics, it is the inability of any retailer or repair person to indicate exact time of delivery/arrival—other than generic mornings or afternoons. Which is the one service that just might endear The Bedding Experts' merchandise to poten-

tial buyers: they promise delivery within 3-hour time slots. (No, we haven't tested them yet.) Mattresses are from the factories of Sealy and Stearns and Foster; frames, futons, and headboards are usually private label. Prices, from firm to luxury pillow-top, twin to king size, usually reflect a 50%+ savings over "retail"; continual weekly sales and 50+ Chicago-area locations could convince anyone to at least try out a Bedding Experts product.
Over 50 locations; call (888) EXPERTS

THE BEDPOST (HELLER BROTHERS BEDDING) ✪

2828 W. 48th Pl.
Chicago, IL 60632
(773) 376-9520
Hours: Mon–Fri: 8–3; Sat: 8–11:30
DISC, MC, V

The "bedst" deals from this private-label bedding manufacturer, claim the experts, are on odd sizes, custom orders, and cancellations. In practice, it's a great idea to hang around the Bedpost for top-quality mattresses at low-end prices. For instance, the Vertapedic Poly-Steel, Heller's top of the line, is a superfirm, quilted orthopedic construction. Also available: mattresses for cribs, institutional beds, futons. A sneak preview of mid-'97 prices: twin sets from $140 to $349; queen, $255 to $469; king, $299 to $595. And for those *Buying Retail Is Stupid!* readers who sleep better on a bargain, GM Randy Heller offers a free bed frame with every complete set purchased.

MATTRESS WORLD

3509 S. Halsted St.
Chicago, IL 60609
(773) 376-5396
Hours: Mon–Fri: 11–8; Sat: 11–5; Sun: 1–5
AE, MC, V

◆ **Senior Discount:** 15%–20% (depends on item) **Age:** 55+

What to say about naked mattresses? Mainly that, with the surfeit of national bedding dealers clamoring to make a sale, it's impossible not to buy at discount. (Unless, of course, you're not a devoted

reader of this book.) Ten-year-old Mattress World, with its 10 stores, specializes in Restonic, Sealy, and Spring Air. Typical of the prices offered: twin Restonic set (closeout) for $89; Sealy smooth-top twin bedding for $69; and top-of-the-line Sealy twin for $249. Always request free delivery, free setup, free removal of old bedding, and a free bed frame; it's part of the package.
10 locations, four in the Chicago area; see the Yellow Pages

Peppers Bedroom City Superstore Clearance Center

2755 W. Thomas
Melrose Park, IL 60160
(708) 343-3771
Hours: Mon–Fri: 10–5; Sat: 10–4
AE, MC, V

Peppers, with its advertising campaign, has by now become almost indelibly linked with water beds. But, step into its clearance center (not to mention the regular stores)—and discover conventional mattresses, futons, and air beds as well. At the Melrose Park outlet (home, it seems to us, of many other national "let's get rid of stuff" warehouses), we found good-quality bedroom furniture for decent prices—up to 50% reductions. Gathered together are overstocks, discontinueds, floor displays, and samples; futons start at $129 and bunk beds at $199.95. Other merchandise in cameo roles: dressers and chests, occasional tables, sheets and comforters.

Right-On-Futon ★

1184 N. Milwaukee Ave.
Chicago, IL 60622
(773) 235-2533
Hours: Mon–Sat: 11–7; Sun: 12–5
AE, DISC, MC, OPT, V

Though futons are the Japanese mattresses of choice, they still retain that hippie and '60s stigma and are often used as guest-room recliners or sleepers. President Mark Bello is out to change that image by educating customers about options, frames, mattress densities, and covers, while offering excellent prices. A comparison with other stores shows that most futons sell at similar tags (i.e., the manufacturer's price is almost always discounted). Yet, Right-On will tag 10% off the price of a cover with the purchase of a futon or frame, thanks to the *Buying Retail Is Stupid!* coupon.

SLEEP CENTERS WATERBEDS AND FUTONS TO GO ☆

137 North Ave.
Villa Park, IL 60181
(630) 279-3415
Hours: Mon, Tues, Thurs: 11–9; Fri: 11–3; Sat: 10–6; Sun: 12–5
AE, DISC, MC, V
◆ **Senior Discount:** 10% **Age:** 60+

Too much of any one thing today means it's time to sharpen pencils to figure out bargains. In this case, the savings are at Sleep Centers, which clears out overstocks of all types of beds, including futons and water beds, at some fairly decent prices. What we saw: an all-in-one water bed set with frame and headboard reduced by $250 (was $959.95); floor models of futons with frames from $149 to $399. And what you'll get: another 10% savings on any purchase with our *Buying Retail Is Stupid!* coupon.

UBIQUITOUS FUTON

1934 W. North Ave.
Chicago, IL 60622
No Telephone
Hours: Mon–Sat: 11–7:30; Sun: 12–6
AE, MC, V

Back to shades of the '50s: climb to the second floor of a Wicker Park storefront coffee bar—with no telephone—to find a collection of decently priced futons and bookcases. As well as two live-in felines, Oaxaca and Nickel, who belong to owner William Keller. Indeed, as the store name suggests, these futons are everywhere—and available at all prices, from $230 to $849 for full-size sleeping futons with frame, mattress, and cover. Cool containers for books, CDs, videos, and archaic record albums are all-wood and awesomely priced, from $20 for a CD rack to $179 for a 6-foot-high bookcase (and lifetime warranty). Dig it!

Home

AFFORDABLE PORTABLES

2608-10 N. Clark St.
Chicago, IL 60614
(773) 935-6160
Hours: Mon, Thurs: 10:30–8; Tues, Wed, Fri: 10:30–7;
Sat: 10:30–6; Sun: 12–5
DISC, MC, V

The Clark Street branch of this furniture-for-your-first-apartment store is literally piled to the rafters with take-with home furnishings. Remember the beanbag chair? It's here in multiple colors: $19.95 for small; $44 for large. Add a halogen lamp (starting at $39.95) and an unfinished-wood Mission-style frame and futon (beginning at $249.95) and, presto!, home number one is furnished. Well, sorta.

Arlington Heights—224 E. Golf Rd., (847) 718-1406,
Mon–Fri: 10:30–7; Sat: 10:30–6; Sun: 12–5
Evanston—924 W. Davis St., (847) 866-8124, Mon–Fri: 10:30–7;
Sat: 10:30–6; Sun: 12–5

THE BOMBAY COMPANY CLEARANCE CENTER

308 E. Rand Rd.
Arlington Heights, IL 60004
(847) 259-3583
Hours: Mon–Fri: 10–9; Sat: 10–6; Sun: 11–5
AE, MC, V

Four hundred Bombay Company stores coast to coast funnel their scratched and dented, bruised and discontinued, clearance and sample merchandise into one Arlington Heights store. So, find here 18th- and 19th-century-reproduction home furnishings—tables and chairs, prints, mirrors, lamps, and accessories—for 30%–70% off retail. Established in 1996, this outlet is already heavily trafficked, attractive because of its fairly frequent turnover of stock.

BUTCHER BLOCK FACTORY OUTLET SHOWROOM ✪
555 W. 16th St.
Chicago, IL 60616
(312) 666-9144
Hours: Mon–Fri: 8–4; Sat: 10–3
MC, V

A real butcher block, says Larry Grossman, is 100% wood; most butcher-block-style furnishings are made of laminated particleboard with a veneer of the real stuff. Which accounts for the higher prices seen in this factory showroom outlet, in existence for three decades. Maple, oak, and (sometimes) beechwood are the preferred materials; a 20% discount, the minimum savings. Here, a maple country worktable sells for $259 ($350 elsewhere); a round oak pedestal table, $579 ($725 retail). Certainly, don't table the extra 10% discount possible with the *Buying Retail Is Stupid!* coupon.

DESIGN WAREHOUSE
167 N. Racine Ave.
Chicago, IL 60607
(312) 773-5600
Hours: Wed–Fri: 9:30–6; Sat: 9:30–5; Sun: 11:30–5
MC, V
◆ **Senior Discount:** Depends on purchase **Age:** 60+

It's the southern brother of Chrome Yellow, that 25-year-old furniture-store fixture of Lincoln Avenue. And because of its location, buying clout, and Lincoln Park affiliation, Design Warehouse combines good style with good prices—at least 20% off. Shades-of-the-'50s vinyl stools, for instance, swivel at $79 each. Armoires at $395 and $595 beat others' tags, and couches at $895 price points (or thereabouts) make for comfy sittings, er, savings.

EUROPEAN FURNITURE WAREHOUSE

2145 W. Grand Ave.
Chicago, IL 60612
(312) 243-1955
Hours: Mon, Wed, Fri: 10–6; Tues, Thurs, Sat: 10–5; Sun: 12–5
DISC, MC, V

Housed in a former streetcar terminal, European Furniture Warehouse (or EFW for short) is truly a Merchandise Mart alternative—and consistently 20%–50% lower than decorator prices. In fact, it's expanded beyond the modern classics such as the Breuer black Barcelona chair to include an extensive Prairie collection, country-style furnishings, and a goodly selection of local artists' wares. Don't expect, however, two-digit prices; more typical is a sumptuous purple leather sofa for $2,024.25 (instead of its list $2,699) or funky black bungee chairs for $199.

FURNITURE CONNECTION

3128 N. Broadway
Chicago, IL 60657
(773) 281-7411
Hours: Mon–Fri: 10–8; Sat: 10–5; Sun: 11–5
AE, DISC, MC, OPT, V

Good prices on contemporary furniture is the sales pitch of Furniture Connection, along with a wide selection stuffed into 6,000 square feet on a second floor in New Town. Though not of Merchandise Mart quality, the bedding, wood, and upholstered furniture (along with lamps and a few other decorative accessories) are usually marked 25%–40% off. Englander bedding, for instance, ranges from a $254 twin to a $499 king luxury firm set (originally $738 to $3,398). And a light-cherry-finish rolling cocktail table appeals at $269.

Furniture Factory Outlet

2700 N. Elston Ave.
Chicago, IL 60647
(773) 276-3000
Hours: Mon–Fri: 10–7:30; Sat: 10–6; Sun: 12–5
DISC, MC, V

Up the stairs from Bill the Hatter is the Furniture Factory Outlet, a space so crammed with modern decorative options that it's difficult to find the exit. (Which might be a deliberate arrangement, after all.) Billing itself as a "purveyor of the upper part of lower-end furniture," this outlet shines with chrome, lacquer, glass, leather looks, and metallic highlights. A six-piece lacquer bedroom suite (an "as is" floor sample) goes for $1,200; sofa and love seat combinations start at $799; a contemporary floor lamp is priced $79. What you see here is definitely what you get.

Furniture Outlet

931 W. Irving Park Rd.
Itasca, IL 60143
(630) 875-6280
Hours: Mon–Fri: 10–9; Sat: 10–6; Sun: 11–6
DISC, MC, V

When your other half returns home absolutely raving about the prices and quality products at one store, it's a no-brainer: ya gotta go check it out. Sure enough, we found that the Furniture Outlet (the very unadvertised home for 11 stores' worth of Walter E. Smithe floor samples, discontinued items, and client returns) more than lives up to its billing. And if the quantities of America's best furniture names including Henredon, Lane, and Habersham Plantation don't floor you, the price tags will render you mute and dumbfounded (usually 40%–80% lower than retail). A few of the many tempting examples: pine-and-glass cupboard for $599.99 (once $1,770) and a red fabric-covered recliner at $499.99 (list was $1,486). Beats going to North Carolina anytime.

FURNITURE REP'S WAREHOUSE

700 E. Irving Park Rd.
Roselle, IL 60172
(630) 924-7632
Hours: Mon, Fri: 10–5:30; Tues–Thurs: 10–8; Sat: 10–4; Sun: 12–4
AE, DISC, MC, V

Why it's named the Furniture Rep's Warehouse is a mystery to us. As is the exact source of this store's merchandise. (We have a few ideas.) Major brands here are Kroehler, an old Chicago furniture manufacturer, and Stratolounger—as its name suggests, a recliner company. Other home decorating names occasionally join the 50%-discount lineup, such as Lexington (one of their "genteel" plantation chests was marked $1,170 from its original $2,145 tag). Some other savings: a three-piece dining room suite by Kroehler was marked at $1,065.

Five locations; see the Yellow Pages

GURNEE DISCOUNT FURNITURE

3535 W. Grand Ave. on Rte. 132
Gurnee, IL 60031
(847) 623-5060
Hours: Mon–Fri: 10–8; Sat: 10–6; Sun: 11–4
AE, DISC, MC, V

The "discount" in the store name is the tip-off: don't expect to find real wood furniture or major brand names here. Instead, Gurnee Discount offers some serviceable choices for turning empty boxes of rooms into a home of sorts, though the pieces probably won't last a lifetime. (Even most of its Magic Sleeps mattresses come with only a 5-year warranty.) If, indeed, the goal is disposable furniture, then the prices will definitely fit limited budgets: three-piece occasional table sets starting at $88; a $538 three-piece living room upholstered set (sofa, love seat, and chair); a six-drawer dresser at $89. Bargains daily—and inspect purchases carefully.

HARLEM FURNITURE SUPERSTORE AND CLEARANCE CENTER

North Ave. & Rte. 53
Northgate Shopping Center
Lombard, IL 60148
(630) 261-3900
Hours: Mon–Fri: 10–9; Sat: 10–6; Sun: 11–6
AE, DISC, HARLEM, MC, V

"As is" is the motto here at the only Harlem clearance center in the area (there are 10 retail stores). Therefore, caveat emptor—and inspect very carefully before you buy: there might be stains, dings, dents, and damage. On the other hand, it's hard to ignore some major furniture bargains: white curio cabinet for $99; honey-colored leather sofa at $799; bleached-wood china cabinet, $399. All sales are final!

HOME 1-2-3 ☆

222 W. Kinzie St.
Chicago, IL 60610
(312) 661-0124
Hours: Mon–Fri: 9:30–6; Sat: 11–6; Sun: 12–5
AE, DISC, MC, V

The word *discount* seems to be anathema to many retailers who prefer the term *off price*. But, in certain consumer products (such as bedding) it's also a truism that lower-than-list prices are SOP; that is, the never-ending "sale." Back of the Merchandise Mart, Home 1-2-3 always offers customers at least 30% off its home furnishings and decorative accessories—more during clearance, container, and alley sales. Owner Mark Rosenberg's stock is modern contemporary wood and all upholstered goods at excellent prices. On a recent visit we were taken with a Charles Rennie Mackintosh–like chair (sale price $59); a nifty metal-and-wood buffet credenza in the $600 range; and a blue and white squishy-soft sofa for $399. A designer look without the designer tags—but with an extra 10% off to bonafide *Buying Retail Is Stupid!* coupon carriers.

House of Teak Scandinavian ✪
830 North Blvd.
Oak Park, IL 60302
(708) 524-2300
Hours: Mon, Wed–Sat: 10–6; Sun: 12–5
AE, DISC, MC, V
◆ **Senior Discount:** 5% **Age:** 60+

The fine, elegant lines and glowing burnished woods of Scandinavian furniture do not necessarily come cheap. Still, they're less expensive at House of Teak's warehouse in Oak Park, where every day nets a great discovery. Sometimes, it's a one-of-a-kind piece, such as a rosewood wall unit for $2,100 (originally $5,000). During other expeditions, a well-known brand appearing in retail establishments will beg to be taken home, such as a honey-colored Natuzzi leather couch tagged at $1,499.95 (was $2,299.95). Twice-a-year clearance sales, when added to the 5%-discount coupon in *Buying Retail Is Stupid!*, help make any house a home.

Hufford Furniture ✪
310 W. Washington St.
Chicago, IL 60606
(312) 236-4191
Hours: Mon, Thurs: 8:30–7; Tues, Wed, Fri: 8:30–5:30;
Sat: 9:30–3:30
DISC, MC, V

One store, nearly 100 years in business, 30%–40% discounts, and a Loop location catering to the office lunchtime shopping crowd mean someone at Hufford Furniture is doing something right. And the reason for its success (aside from the lowered prices, of course) is the firm's emphasis on the customer . . . plus its considerable attention to cost efficiencies. Names include the furniture industry's finest, from American Drew and Baldwin Brass to Directional, Lexington, and Stiffel. A staff of 24 is ready, willing, and able to help with design questions and problems (free!)—and there's a flat $40 delivery charge no matter where the truck needs to go. We're already thinking about lining up for a little noon browsing—and taking advantage of the additional 10% discount offered to *Buying Retail Is Stupid!* readers.

MARJEN FURNITURE ★

8121 N. Milwaukee Ave.
Niles, IL 60714
(847) 966-1088
Hours: Mon–Fri: 10:30–8; Sat: 10–5; Sun: 11–5
DISC, MC, V

Family feud, part one: there is some sort of rift among three same-name Chicago-area stores, but no one's talking. The Niles and Libertyville versions of Marjen's stock almost every well-known brand, from American Drew and Berkline to Pulaski and Stanley, at a cool 40% savings (and occasionally more). Sealy bedding and upholstered and wood furniture crowd together on the floor without commissioned salespeople. And pocket another $20 when you spend $200 or more and use the *Buying Retail Is Stupid!* coupon.
Libertyville—526 N. Milwaukee Ave., (847) 549-7400

MARJEN OF CHICAGO ★

1536 W. Devon Ave.
Chicago, IL 60660
(773) 338-6636
Hours: Mon, Thurs: 10:30–8; Tues, Wed, Fri: 10:30–7; Sat: 10–6; Sun: 11–5
AE, DIN, DISC, MC, OPT, V
◆ **Senior Discount:** 10% **Age:** 55+

Family feud, part two: it is clear that Marjen of Chicago and Marjen Furniture in Niles and Libertyville once sold together. Today, though the merchandise is similar, the stores are completely autonomous, all featuring low-end furniture at major discounts (here, up to 70% off retail). This shop concentrates on mattresses and futons (though tables, chairs, and other furniture are also offered), delivered door to door on the purchase day. Owner Daniel Michell promises to beat any price at any store; all merchandise is brand new and under full warranty. What we saw: a four-piece black lacquer bedroom suite for $399; a two-chair Mission-style breakfast set for $149.95; and the "complete" living room—sofa, loveseat, and chair—for $399. Of definite note for *Buying Retail Is Stupid!* readers who are contemplating furnishing or redecorating: a $99 purchase comes with a free CD rack.

MARSHALL FIELD CLEARANCE CENTER
State St., 9th floor
Chicago, IL 60602
(312) 781-1000
Hours: Mon–Fri: 9:45–7; Sat: 9:45–6; Sun: 11–6
AE, DISC, MARSHALL FIELD'S, MC, V

Even locally famed interior designers have been spotted on the ninth floor of this Chicago retail institution. After all, where else could you find an exotic pale wood credenza (with a slight ding or two) from Baker for a mere $3,000? Lest some gasp at that audacious tag, there are other more reasonably priced furnishings to buy, at savings of 50%–70%, and sometimes more. Recognizable names, from Barcalounger and Bernhardt to Henredon and Simmons, are here in a variety of home forms: sofas, recliners, chairs, mattresses, tables, dining rooms, and the like. The best buys go fast; it pays to either make friends with a salesperson or visit regularly.

MONTALBANO MAJESTIC FURNITURE ✪
3000 St. Charles Rd.
Bellwood, IL 60104-1544
(708) 547-1010
Hours: Mon–Sat: 9–6; Sun: by appointment
DISC, MC, V

A name such as Montalbano Majestic simply rings with history: it's a family firm that opened its factory in 1929. The founder, at age 80-something, still continues to hand-carve elegant French and baroque furniture—and is probably the oldest active woodcarver in the United States. And a showroom offering old-world furnishings at a 30%–50% savings to customers from single parents to the consul general of Saudi Arabia. In addition to the remarkably ornate, 12-step-finish chairs and tables, sofas, and bedroom sets created in Bellwood, Montalbano now features other brands (e.g., Howard Miller clocks and curios, European imports), and its 20 craftspeople will reupholster, repair, restore, and refinish fine furniture. What does this elegance translate into? A gilded curio cabinet for $596 (once $1,296); a French grandfather clock at $896 (regularly $1,996); and a marble-top wood chest tagged $596 ($1,996 once). For *Buying Retail Is Stupid!* readers, the old-world (and new-world, too) furnishings will be reduced another 10%—and you'll be bombarded with gifts (buy a sofa, get a $300 oil painting; or purchase a bedroom set, and receive a $500 pair of lamps).

The Old Hacienda Furniture Store

4440B N. Elston Ave.
Chicago, IL 60641
(773) 777-7735
Hours: Mon–Sat: 10–6
AE, DISC, MC, V

Their ads say "wholesale." Though we wouldn't stretch the discounts of The Old Hacienda Furniture Store that far, still, prices are decent for handcrafted, primitive-rustic-style, all-pine furniture of the Southwest. A translation: don't expect the fine quality of, say, a Baker or Henredon. Doors do stick, and drawers may not fit exactly when pushed in and out. A glance at the furnishings showed these prices: carved bar stools at $52 each; small breakfront or china cabinet for $494; and a troika of tables, $247.

Plunkett's Warehouse

7224 N. Harlem Ave.
Niles, IL 60631
(773) 763-2300
Hours: Mon–Fri: 10–9; Sat: 11–5:30; Sun: 12–5
MC, Plunkett's, V

What happens to furniture showroom pieces when they outwear their welcome on the floor? At Plunkett's, all nine area stores funnel the display merchandise to Harlem and Touhy—at substantial savings. Most are simply being retired, not because they're shopworn, so the couches and chairs, living room, dining room, and bedroom suites, plus accessories, have usually been well cared for. Names such as Baker, Drexel Heritage, Henredon, and Lineage assemble in crowded minivignettes; discounts range from 30% to well over 50%. Our eyes lusted for a cheetah-covered wing chair ($699 from $1,080); a Drexel cane and wrought-iron chair ($249 from $809); and an unusual four-panel leather book screen ($839 from $1,245).

WICKES FURNITURE CLEARANCE & BUDGET CENTER ☆

167 Army Trail Rd.
Glendale Heights, IL 60139
(708) 529-7000
Hours: Mon–Fri: 10–8; Sat: 10–5; Sun: 12–5
AE, DISC, MC, V

Moderately priced furnishings have always been Wickes's forte. So, little changes at this Glendale Heights outlet but the tags, which are significantly lower here. Slight "bruises" notwithstanding, the sofas and tables and chests and rugs are usually 50% less than retail—and sometimes reduced even more. Walk atop a lush room-size area rug for $69.77 (once $299.97). Snooze peacefully on a white-lacquer contemporary six-piece bedroom suite at $899.77 (regularly $1,899.77); and lounge around on a four-piece beige leather sectional for $1,099.77 (a reduction of $1,700!). Stand behind us, please. (And start waiting for your gift with purchase—for *Buying Retail Is Stupid!* readers only.)

Resale

GABRIEL'S TRUMPET, INC. ☆

1163 E. Ogden Ave., #413
Naperville, IL 60563
(630) 420-2200
Hours: Mon–Wed, Sat: 10–5; Thurs & Fri: 10–8; Sun: 12–4
DISC, MC, V

Folks from as far away as Colonial Williamsburg drop by. And regular customers phone or visit from homes in Detroit, Iowa, and Minneapolis. In the few short years of its existence, Gabriel's Trumpet—owned by the Anderson family—has become the stomping ground for fans of fine consignment furniture. In fact, the store's seams are close to bursting; minivignetttes invite browsers to handle and touch. And prices, though definitely not in the inexpensive category, are much, much lower than the original retail. Well-manicured furnishings from Baker and Drexel to Lalique and Waterford simply cry to be carted home; most lean toward traditional styles, though country stuff does seep in. A December stroll-

through: Queen Anne mahogany highboy in impeccable condition for $2,750; 48 pieces of Royal Doulton's "Serebende" pattern for $950. And the extra-10%-discount *Buying Retail Is Stupid!* coupon could help make up your mind . . . quickly.
Wheaton—229 Rice Lake Sq., (630) 871-9500

HOUSE WALK FURNITURE ✪
1713 W. Golf Rd.
Mt. Prospect, IL 60056
(847) 640-0612
Hours: Mon–Thurs: 10–8; Fri & Sat: 10–6; Sun: 12–4
MC, V

Not only does Ronald Baker, president of House Walk Furniture, tag his gently used furniture at extremely low prices, he also schedules special sales where savings can be even sweeter. During our visit to the one and only location in Mount Prospect, we lounged in a regular-size love seat marked $120. Solid-wood end tables for propping up our tired shopping feet were listed at $35; dining room sets with four chairs, $225; a set with six chairs, $265. Some of the prices during House Walk's special sale last year: love seats for $60–$120; chairs and end tables, $16–$48; and dressers and chests, $70–$120 (regularly $175–$300). And we can easily envision a guest room full of House Walk items by wielding the 5% discount for *Buying Retail Is Stupid!* readers.

INTERIORS ON CONSIGNMENT ✪
2150 N. Clybourn Ave.
Chicago, IL 60614
(773) 868-0797
Hours: Tues–Sat: 10–6; Sun: 12–5
MC, V

"Pre-owned" is a description usually reserved for luxury cars, but it's certainly a great way to describe the mint-condition furnishings found at Interiors on Consignment, open since 1990. Store owners closely inspect all items prior to acceptance, so none of the wares show major damage. At one time or another, Gold Coast and Lincoln Park browsers can find the likes of Baker, Drexel, Henredon, even Roche Bobois, at 30%–50% savings. The best deals and highest-end housewares move quickly. Checking in frequently for the best selection is highly recommended. As is utilizing the 10% *Buying Retail Is Stupid!* coupon for extra savings.

Unfinished

NAKED FURNITURE ✪
5725 N. Broadway
Chicago, IL 60660
(773) 784-1616
Hours: Mon–Thurs: 10–8:30; Fri: 10–6; Sat: 10–5:30; Sun: 12–5
DISC, MC, V

A faux finisher's delight: real unadorned wood furniture with no particleboard in sight at reasonable prices—at least a 20% discount. All styles from contemporary and country to a streamlined traditional are represented; pine and oak predominate, as does the ubiquitous "hardwood." Opt for either do-it-yourself pieces or factory-finished (the latter at a higher price, of course). Regardless of the finish, complete your purchase by showing the additional-10%-discount coupon from *Buying Retail Is Stupid!*. (One note to avid couponers: though Naked Furniture is a national chain, only the store on North Broadway is offering the *Buying Retail Is Stupid!* discount.)

LAMPS & LIGHT FIXTURES

GRAHAM INDUSTRIES HOME FURNISHINGS ✪
300 E. Chestnut St.
Kankakee, IL 60901
(815) 932-0008
Hours: Mon–Thurs: 10–5; Fri: 10–6; Sat: 9–3
DISC, MC, V

OK, Kankakee is about an hour and a half (depending on your driving) south of the Loop. But in the midst of farm country, the all-in-one Big Lots combination discount–department–five-and-ten store, and some rather interesting antiques is lamp and shade manufacturer Graham Industries. VP Terry Graham says the lighting runs the full array of sizes (boudoir to floor) and styles (contemporary to country) for a very reasonable $10–$100. (Which represents a 20%–50% savings off retail.) Custom work's available too. And, before bemoaning the distance to Kankakee, remember that *Buying Retail Is Stupid!* readers will pocket even more savings, thanks to the extra-10%-discount coupon.

LAMP OUTLET ✪
3450 S. Racine Ave.
Chicago, IL 60609
(773) 650-7835
Hours: Fri: 11–6; Sat: 8–4
MC, V

No name-dropping allowed here, but it's probably enough to say that a major Chicago manufacturer of both lamps and occasional furniture (such as accent chairs) uses this store to unload its samples and overstocks. The result? At least 50% off retail for an assortment of pleated (and not) shades, ginger-jar lights, torchères, desk lamps, pickled-wood side chairs, and occasional tables in a variety of traditional and contemporary styles. And *Buying Retail Is Stupid!* readers will be able to light up their homes with another 10% discount.

LIT ART ✪
1201 W. Dundee Rd.
Wheeling, IL 60090
(847) 541-5310
Hours: Mon, Thurs: 10–8; Tues, Wed, Fri, Sat: 10–5
DISC, MC, V

It is a well-accepted fact within the home furnishings industry that MSRPS are never (well, rarely) adhered to. Still, Lit Art owner Glen Kaplan is extending *Buying Retail Is Stupid!* readers an offer few could refuse: namely, a 50%-off-list-price coupon discount. And when the brand names in the store include lighting and decorative accessories from such luminaries as George Kovacs, Frederick Raymond, and Stiffel, then we're permitted to say: "Such a deal!"

Linens

L&L Textile Co. ✪

351 W. Kinzie St.
Chicago, IL 60610
(312) 321-0034 or (800) 222-0266
Hours: Mon–Fri: 10–6; Sat & Sun: 9–5
AE, DISC, MC, OPT, V

It's in the basement. Stock is somewhat limited, and parking near the hip East Bank Club can be a nightmare. But L&L Textile Co. has endured such retail issues since 1981 . . . and so have its customers. Because price here is the object: towels, washcloths, potholders, and all kinds of domestics are truly offered with rock-bottom tags. Some examples: Jim Carrey leers on a velour beach towel version of *The Mask* for $8; dark solid-color cotton bib aprons hang for $3 each; and vinyl place mats—enough to tame any kid or pet spills—are tagged 95¢ apiece. And when the extra 5% *Buying Retail Is Stupid!* discount is applied, bargains certainly 'r' us.

Private Lives Bed and Bath Linens

56 E. Oak St.
Chicago, IL 60611
(312) 337-5474
Hours: Mon–Sat: 10–6; Sun: 12–5
AE, DISC, MC, V

What a difference a year makes! Local discount-domestics retailer Private Lives has consolidated multiple outlets into two stores and completely changed its wares into the ultra-upscale category (though still reduced by 20% and often more). Gone are the Ralph Laurens and Revsons; in their stead are expensive native and foreign names such as Designers Guild, Elve (part of Missoni), The Purists, and Schlossberg. Price discounts are color-coded, so sticker shock is gentle. One example: a multihued twin flat sheet from Tricia Guild is $38.99 (once $46). High quality extends to body-care lotions (from Nancy Koltes et al.) and boutique bathroom accessories.
Wilmette—1515 Sheridan Rd./Plaza del Lago, (847) 251-8236

TOWEL FACTORY OUTLET CENTER
7313 N. Harlem Ave.
Niles, IL 60714
(847) 647-7070
Hours: Mon–Fri: 9–6; Sat: 9–5; Sun: 11–5
DISC, MC, V

Downsizing happens to discount retailers, too. In the case of the Towel Factory Outlet Center, owned by Revere Mills, once there were five. Now only one—on busy Harlem Avenue in Niles—remains, with customers queuing up even at high noon. No wonder, because the prices are hard to match: a three-piece velourlike bath ensemble for $7.89; Ibena acrylic throws at about 12 bucks each; a $22.95 moire hamper. Decent towels and linens for utilitarian duties.

Jewelry

All that glitters is not necessarily gold—at discount. We've conducted an informal poll of antiques dealers, avid (and we mean fanatic) collectors, and well-known appraisers. All agree: you better either know your precious gems or be friendly with a jewelry retailer who will "work with you." Otherwise, some shop owners are likely to charge you retail. Including those at the famous "wholesale" buildings, like the Mallers edifice at 5 South Wabash.

Now, not all will gauge (or gouge) you by the size of your credit card case. But it pays in many ways to know who's who. Which is why we've circumvented many of the big, well-known advertisers and concentrated on those jewelers (as assessed by their peers) most likely to deal, whether in estate, new, or custom pieces.

Still, a little knowledge goes a long way. Though you may not want to spend the time and the trouble to be certified by the Gemological Institute of America (GIA), our panel of know-everythings contributed this advice:

- Feel the item's weight—and compare it with others. Platinum's the heaviest (and most expensive); gold next, depending on its karat weight. If it seems light, and the price seems somewhat out of line, listen to your instincts.

- Signed pieces do cost more. After all, a Cartier or Tiffany in hand is far preferable to (and infinitely more resellable than) a well-made no-name bracelet. There are, however, a ton of other hallmarks and artisans to be acquainted with, such as Black, Starr, Frost, Van Cleef, Oscar Heyman, and Hammerman Brothers.
- Chop the appraiser's estimate in more than half. An honest expert will figure replacement costs for your bauble—and quote you a retail price for insurance reasons. Which is generally twice the wholesale price. Those not as scrupulous may jack up the retail estimate even more, especially if they charge a percentage of the appraisal. The professionals' consensus: best seek out an appraiser who levies a flat rate.
- Style is not just a design "thing." Certain periods go in and out of favor (Georgian, for one), while others are always in demand, such as art deco. Ergo, the style of the jewelry may also dictate a premium price; an art nouveau plique-à-jour (enameled) dragonfly about 1 inch high, even unsigned, can command some pretty major bucks.

BENRUS WATCH AND JEWELRY FACTORY OUTLET

1550 W. Carroll Ave.
Chicago, IL 60607
(312) 243-3300
Hours: Mon–Fri: 8–4:30
AE, MC, V
◆ **Senior Discount:** 10% **Age:** 60+

Obviously, the most prominent brand of watches at this factory outlet is Benrus, all factory overruns. But, savings will also be found on names such as Seiko (chronograph from $450 to $399.99); Tag Heuer (compare $520 to $700 retail for a chronograph); and Movado (the Esperanza sells here for $797.99 versus $1,095 list price). Check the timepieces and jewelry carefully; there is, however, a 1-year warranty on all tickers.

BIJOUTERIE INTERNATIONAL ★

645 W. Grand Ave.
Chicago, IL 60610
(312) 733-5600
Hours: Mon–Fri: 10–6; Sat: 9–1
MC, V

There are discount retailers, and then there are shop owners who charge less than list price. We make the distinction because "service with a smile" belongs mainly in the second category. As do the folks at Bijouterie International, tucked away next to the Ohio Street entrance/exit for three of our major expressways. In a small space are packed literally thousands of pieces of costume jewelry—earrings, rings, bracelets, necklaces, belts—as well as sterling silver chains and beads from every part of the globe. The prices: '60s wood neon-hued dangly earrings for $7; $65 for a pair of well-constructed faux pearl and rhinestone drops; $3 for a real Limoges cameo or a Venetian Willifiore bead. And for *Buying Retail Is Stupid!* readers, an extra inducement: the coupon entitles you to 10% additional savings on any bead. The everyday discount: 50% off on all fashion jewelry.

CHICAGO DIAMOND CENTER

21 N. Wabash Ave., Booth 45
Chicago, IL 60602
(312) 609-0001
Hours: Mon–Wed, Fri: 10–5:30; Thurs: 10–6:30; Sat: 10–5
AE, DIN, DISC, MC, V

Six relatives behind one small jewelry counter? It's not that cramped at Chicago Diamond Center, since the family also owns a wholesale business down the street (in the Mallers Building). Which means that Tony, Phillip, Anna, Alex, Pete, and Willy don't fret about high overheads and large markups. Their merchandise also includes something old and something new; diamonds, of course, predominate along with some very well-priced estate pieces. One example: a white gold eternity band with six points of diamonds at about $500. As Pete Barshtak notes: "If we bought it cheap, we'll sell it cheap." A sister business to the Chicago Watch Center in the same mall.

CHICAGO WATCH BROKERS ☆

5 S. Wabash Ave., Suite 1207
Chicago, IL 60603
(312) 759-8777
Hours: Mon–Fri: 9:30–4:30
Cash, check

Considered the dealer of dealers, Jeff Cohen, owner of Chicago Watch Brokers, has some very discriminating customers. Such as Vanessa Williams, who, while in Chicago for the shoot of *Hoodlum*, sent one of her colleagues to Cohen in search of vintage silver cigarette cases. Cohen to the rescue as well with what he calls "gentlemen's accessories"—silver, gold, platinum, and gem-encrusted watches (Cartier, Piaget, Rolex, Tiffany), cufflinks, and occasional women's jewelry—and top-quality repair, too. Don't necessarily think "high prices"; Cohen's known to be fair and to want to "work with you." As evidenced by the extra 10% coupon for *Buying Retail Is Stupid!* readers.

GREAT LAKES JEWELRY

104 E. Oak St.
Chicago, IL 60611
(312) 266-2211
Hours: Mon–Sat: 10:30–5:30
AE, DISC, MC, OPT, V

An Oak Street basement stalwart since 1972, Great Lakes is the kind of jewelry store Cousin Bedell from Arkansas would adore. Or teens from Glenview. Prices, too, are irresistible on owner and manufacturer Nat Levy's modern sterling-silver beads, bangles, and baubles—50% off is the usual reduction. A few gold pieces are displayed; best gleamings, though, are on silver rings, bracelets, earrings, necklaces, cufflinks, money clips, perfume bottles, and letter openers.

LaRon Jewelers

5 S. Wabash Ave., Suite 806
Chicago, IL 60603
(312) 263-3898
Hours: Mon–Fri: 9–5; Sat: 10–1
MC, V

One glance at the Mallers Building's printed brochure, and you're hooked: everyone does custom jewelry design, it appears. Not so, says Larry Shtulman, owner of LaRon, since intricate handwork, from sculpting and wax carving to the actual setting of the gems and gold, is an art practiced by few. Creating animal figures, fashioning a personal cameo, or copying the engravings of a coin are all within his bailiwick; he learned the trade from his dad beginning at age 12. Trendy today, besides the one-of-a-kind pieces, are antique-looking bracelets, rings, and necklaces; platinum; and channel-set stones . . . all at reasonable prices (30%–50% lower than retail) here.

Lee-Kaye Jewelers

5 S. Wabash Ave., Suite 200
Chicago, IL 60603
(312) 236-9686
Hours: Mon–Fri: 9–5; Sat: 10–3
DISC, MC, V

Round diamonds, says Lee-Kaye owner Tony Liacone, are still the number-one shape for engagement rings, with marquise and princess styles the runners-up. Other than keeping their fingers on consumer trends (e.g., platinum is replacing gold as the precious metal of choice), the 50-year-old jeweler on the mezzanine of the Mallers Building thrives on word of mouth and recommendations. Custom, modern jewelry is its specialty; diamond, naturally, the top gem of choice—all at 30%–50% below retail prices.

MALNEKOFF & SON JEWELERS ✪

5 S. Wabash Ave., 12th Floor, Suite 1010
Chicago, IL 60603
(773) DIAMOND
Hours: Mon: 10–6:30; Tues–Fri: 10–6; Sat: 10–3
DISC, MC, V

Take time to talk with Peter Malnekoff . . . and you'll get an earful and eyeful of GIA education. Of the four Cs distinguishing a diamond (color, clarity, carat, and cut), far too little attention is paid to cut or shape, which can account for up to a 60% difference in price. He searches the world for the best in diamonds, offering customers from here to Hong Kong top-notch advice and 50%+ savings. A small portion of Malnekoff's showcases is devoted to antique jewelry; 90% is manufactured per customer request. His bangles, baubles, and beads gleam even brighter with the extra 10% discount to *Buying Retail Is Stupid!* readers.

MERRY RICHARDS JEWELERS

21 N. Wabash Ave., #22
Chicago, IL 60602
(312) 558-9188
Hours: Mon–Wed, Fri: 10–5:30; Thurs: 10–6:30; Sat: 10–5
AE, DISC, MC, V

Merry Cheng confesses: "My husband Richard was considered the black sheep. His mother is a doctor. His father is a lawyer. And Richard started as a salesman for fine jewelry." No road trips anymore, since this husband-and-wife team operates two stores, both extremely busy. What Merry Richards excels in is the ultramodern, supracontemporary jewelry, both custom and fashioned by world-known designers, sold at a good 30% discount. Of course, as with most of the Mallers and 21 North building occupants, diamonds are their best friends—which are sold here about 10%–15% lower than the Rapaport price (traditional cost guidelines for jewelers). Not necessarily low cost, but gems worth a longer look-see than a passing twinkle in your eye.
Oak Brook—1600 W. 16th St., (630) 990-1588

MONIQUE FINE JEWELRY, LTD.
5 S. Wabash Ave., Suite 807
Chicago, IL 60603
(312) 332-3762
Hours: Mon–Fri: 9–5; Sat: 9–3
AE, DISC, MC, V

A true sister act: Monique Zermatten and Rosalie Sciortino run Monique's Fine Jewelry as very experienced businesspeople, having owned and operated the now-defunct, then-posh Coiffeur de Paris on Rush Street. Their clientele are of the news-making variety as well as ordinary folks who stop by (via word of mouth) to secure a good price—usually 70% off department-store list. Custom design is one forte of these Casablanca-born siblings; diamonds, another. (Gold chains, they say, bring in no profit, since even street vendors can obtain very inexpensive gold ropes made in Italy.) We admired a 16-inch strand of dark gray pearls—the lighter, the less expensive, we were told—at an approximate cost of $4,000. Again, not inexpensive adornments, but good quality fairly priced.

P&J JEWELERS INC.
5 S. Wabash Ave., Suite 907
Chicago, IL 60603
(312) 236-1567
Hours: Mon–Fri: 9–6; Sat: 9–3
AE, DISC, MC, V
◆ **Senior Discount:** 10% **Age:** 65+

"Honesty" and "a good reputation," says P&J co-owner Jack Gamil, are the two most important qualities in a jeweler. (Or doctor, lawyer, accountant, we quickly add.) As one of the largest manufacturers in Chicago, with 45 craftspeople on staff, P&J works not only with individual customers but with large corporate accounts as well. Its biggest business is selling diamond engagement and wedding sets, with most of the gems imported from Israel. A bonus: about two to three tours weekly are booked to view P&J's "factory"; call ahead to inquire.

Swatch Outlet ☒

6170 W. Grand Ave.
Gurnee Mills Mall
Gurnee, IL 60031
(847) 855-8299
Hours: Mon–Sat: 10–9; Sun: 11–6
MC, V

The Swiss watch that revolutionized the industry with its quality and designer-trendy styling at a great price is now available at 30%–50% less than retail. In fact, says manager Spike Horton, his Gurnee Mills store is the "cheapest place in the universe to buy a Swatch." (There are four other outlets in the United States; this is the only store in the Midwest.) Same great merchandising and tickers at best prices; guard your newest purchase with this store's gift to *Buying Retail Is Stupid!* customers.

Worldwide Diamonds ☒

3703 W. Lake Ave.
Glenview, IL 60025
(847) 832-1000
Hours: By appointment only
AE, DISC, MC, OPT, V

Thanks to the World Wide Web, the fax, and the telephone, any jeweler in any city can buy diamonds from European and South African mining concerns and cutters. Which is why firms such as Worldwide Diamonds will cater to customer requests—and are open by appointment only. President Brian Harris runs a close-to-wholesale business, offering diamonds and diamond jewelry for about one-half of retail price. A sparkling purchase will net *Buying Retail Is Stupid!* reader customers an extra dividend: a free bottle of jewelry cleaner.

Medical & Optical Needs

DRUGSTORES & PHARMACIES

As is our wont, whenever we encountered a product whose bargain parameters flustered us, we consulted with the experts—colleagues and local advisers who know their way around the inside, say, of a jeweler's loupe.

Such is the case with drugstores and pharmacies. Doing the right kind of ℞ shopping is especially important if you consider that we as a nation spend more than 60 billion dollars each year on prescription drugs alone.

So, our guide to the world of meds and pills and ointments suggests the following money-saving strategies:

1. There are four "categories" of pharmacies, from least to most expensive. Top on the least-expensive list are the Wal-Marts, Targets, and Kmarts (Super Kmarts, too) of this country, all pricing drugs within pennies of each other. Next in line are two local-regional "value-priced" chains: Cub Foods and Omni (the latter is owned by Dominick's Finer Foods). Third: Dominick's, Osco, Walgreen. Fourth and most expensive: your independent, neighborhood, "Mr./Ms. knows your name and your family history" pharmacist.
2. However, many pharmacies, when asked, will match others' prices. So, Mr. Jones down the street may, indeed, be more than willing to give you the same or a similar price to keep your business. Just make sure you're comparing apples with apples—er, Valium with Valium. Ask these questions:
   - Is it the same number of pills, tablets, capsules, gel caps?
   - Is it the same potency as called for on the prescription?
   - Is it a comparison of brand name versus brand name, generic versus generic? (In other words, don't compare costs of brands with generics; almost always, the name you know is the name you'll pay more for.)
3. Not all generics are created equal. Though the ruler of the pharmaceutical world—the U.S. Food and Drug Administration

(FDA)—mandates that the generic drug must be equal in strength to the brand, sometimes there is a difference. And sometimes not. It depends, first and foremost, on the manufacturer of the no-name drug. And second, it depends on the excipients (the binders, fillers, preservatives, coloring, etc.) used; occasionally, those additives can alter the potency of the drug.

4. Whatever your decision, try to patronize the same pharmacy. It's never a good idea, warns our guide, to rush around from pharmacy to pharmacy, filling prescriptions at the cheapest stores. With your history of medications then scattered among many stores, it is difficult (if not impossible) for your pharmacist to advise you and/or your doctor if any of those pills might interact with other medication. Unless, of course, you freely and willingly volunteer your drug-taking history to *every* pharmacist.

   But that's a *real* pain. Instead, bite the bullet and keep your business at one pharmacy. That doesn't mean, however, that you *can't* comparison shop. After all, we must live up to our motto: "Buying retail is stupid!"

Health Foods & Nutritional Supplements

Blue Sky Market ✪

39 Huntington Lane
Wheeling, IL 60090
(847) 541-8118
Hours: Mon–Fri: 9–8; Sat: 9–7; Sun: 9–5
DISC, MC, V
◆ **Senior Discount:** 10% **Age:** 65+

The newfound cachet of alternative medicine means herbs and vitamins are flying off the shelves. In an age also dominated by superstores and category killers, Blue Sky Market stands out as one of the few independent and extremely knowledgeable retailers of most things natural. Either John or owner Janet Angel (a doctor of nutrition) can help you compare brands and choose supplements from well-known manufacturers such as Carlson, Nature's Plus, and TwinLab—and save at least 20%. Pocket an extra 10% savings on supplements when you present the *Buying Retail Is Stupid!* coupon.

BROADWAY VITAMINS ★

3321 N. Broadway
Chicago, IL 60657
(773) 404-9000
Hours: Mon–Fri: 11–7; Sat: 10–6; Sun: 12–5
AE, DISC, MC, OPT, V

The aging of the baby boomers could be a veritable gold mine for feel-good products and retailers; vitamins and health foods could potentially profit from this lucrative market. Most natural herb and vitamin products are not discounted more than 20%, so Broadway Vitamins and its two Chicago siblings, by offering 15% off, are neck and neck with their competitors. Find here well-known brands such as Champion Nutrition, Nature's Way, Schiff, Source Naturals, and TwinLab. Bonus one: a licensed, certified nutritionist is ready, willing, and eager to answer questions. Bonus two: a $3-off *Buying Retail Is Stupid!* coupon on a $15+ purchase.

Chicago—True Nature Foods, 6034 N. Broadway, (773) 465-6400, Mon–Sat: 10–7; Sun: 12–5

Chicago—Morse Avenue Natural Foods, 1527 W. Morse Ave., (773) 743-7190, Mon–Sat: 10–7; Sun: 12–5

CORNER HEALTH FOODS ★

502 N. Seymour
Mundelein, IL 60060
(847) 566-4888
Hours: Mon, Tues, Fri: 9–7; Wed: 9–6; Thurs, Sat: 9–5
DISC, MC, V

◆ **Senior Discount:** 10% on supplements **Age:** 62+

One of the primary reasons consumers tend to favor one store over another is the quality of information delivered with a smile. And when the store discounts 15%–30% regularly, so much the better. Corner Health owner Anne Johnson prides herself in offering shoppers updated health data via books, computers, and employees; her products, too, represent some of the best vitamin and nutritional supplement names—Carlson, Country Life, Nature's Way, NOW, and Solgar (just to mention a few). Ask for a supplement discount card for additional savings. Plus, utilize the 10% *Buying Retail Is Stupid!* coupon.

The Fruitful Yield
5005 W. Oakton St.
Skokie, IL 60077
(847) 679-8882
Hours: Mon: 10–7; Tues, Fri: 10–6; Thurs: 10–8; Sat: 10–5
DISC, MC, V

Juniper berries will help clear the air of germs. Caffeine, according to research, can increase PMS symptoms. And bilberry preparations, used by World War II British pilots, have been shown to improve eyesight. One of the better health food/vitamin stores (along with, in our estimation, Blue Sky, Corner Health, Sherwyn's) in our area to offer up-to-date information is the eight-store Fruitful Yield chain. Because, in addition to how-to-use data and advice, the Yield folks provide good savings on a variety of vitamins, herbs, and natural foodstuffs. One recent weekly special featured Hain peanut oil for $4.59 (once $6.95); Schiff's single-day at $13.49 (60 tabs were $17.99); $7.99 for 100 Siberian ginseng (list $10.80). And, at the Skokie store, ask for Alan; tell him we sent you.
Eight stores; call (800) 469-5552 for locations

Sherwyn's Health Food Shop ✪
645 W. Diversey Pkwy.
Chicago, IL 60614
(773) 477-1934
Hours: Mon–Fri: 9–8; Sat: 9–7; Sun: 11–7
DISC, MC, V

Stop by anytime, day or night, and you'll find Sherwyn's teeming with an amazing melting pot of customers. Opened in 1973, this one-of-a-kind store, located on busy Diversey Parkway, carries every natural food, cosmetic, supplement, and herb known to man (and woman). Typical discounts run from 10% to 50% on such recognizable brands as TwinLab, Country Life, Solaray, Hain, Kiss My Face, and the like. Consult with Sherwyn's resident nutrition expert, Dr. Bill, a retired biochemist. And don't forget the $2 off coupon in the back of *Buying Retail Is Stupid!*.

Vitamin House, Inc. ☒
7036 W. Higgins Rd.
Chicago, IL 60656
(773) 631-1720
Hours: Mon, Wed–Fri: 9–5; Tues: 9–4; Sat: 9–2
MC, V

Close to O'Hare, this unassuming storefront houses one of the largest and oldest private-label manufacturers of glandulars, minerals, and vitamins sold under the name of Brothers Pharmaceuticals. These products are an obvious path to saving 20%–50%. One example: 100 capsules of natural vitamin E (400 I.U.) goes for $5.95; 250 for $14.20. An additional mental boost might be the 20% extra savings offered to *Buying Retail Is Stupid!* readers.

Optical Services

Sun King Optical ☒
826 W. Armitage Ave.
Chicago, IL 60614
(773) 975-7867
Hours: Mon–Thurs: 11–7; Fri: 11–6; Sat: 10–6; Sun: 12–5
AE, MC, OPT, V

Shades of spring and summer: Sun King Optical will protect anyone's eyes from hot rays with a top-quality, brand-name selection of sunglasses at 20%–50% lower than retail. Trendy shoppers can find Ray Ban's round metal glasses for $99 (instead of $166) or Vuarnet's cool-cat wraps for the same price (once $139). Other designers represented: Armani, Calvin Klein, Revo, among others. And cool down further with Sun King's $10- and $20-off offers to *Buying Retail Is Stupid!* readers (see coupon for details).
Chicago—44 E. Chicago Ave., (312) 649-9110
Evanston—522 W. Dempster Ave., (847) 864-5200

Music, Movies & Live Entertainment

Unlike Manhattan (the city, not the movie from director Woody Allen), Chicago does discount even its first-run movies . . . if you can make the first weekend show or the last Monday-through-Friday reel starting before, normally, 5:00 P.M. Prices are usually a tad more than half price (as of summer 1997, about $5). Still, once you munch a bunch and sip a little, that flick will set one person back about a ten-spot, much more than a Blockbuster night.

Are there less expensive alternatives? You bet . . . if you don't need to be a Siskel and Ebert clone who *must* review first-run films the minute they open. In fact, in 1978, Willis Johnson, new owner and president of Tivoli Enterprises, began a second-run movie kingdom by accident—when his acquisition of the Downers Grove Tivoli theater almost went belly-up. He then introduced the idea of bargain flicks to the western suburbs—and 29 second-run screens (out of a total 69 in 17 movie houses) and 19 years later, cheap movies are among his biggest moneymakers.

Here, then, is the list of movie theaters showing second-run films (usually right before they're released onto video) at prices *Buying Retail Is Stupid!* readers will applaud—usually at or below the magic $4 mark. (Do check ticket prices in advance; with the cost of moviegoing now hovering dangerously close to 10 bucks for one shot in New York City, who knows when our prices will increase?)

- Barrington—Catlow, 116 W. Main St., (847) 381-0777
- Carpentersville—Cinema 12, Meadowdale Center, (847) 428-6131
- Chicago—Chestnut Station, Clark & Chestnut Sts., (312) 337-7301
- Chicago—Davis, 4614 N. Lincoln Ave., (773) 784-0893
- Chicago—Harlem Corners, (708) 598-5559
- Chicago—Logan, Milwaukee and Kedzie Aves., (773) 252-0627
- Chicago—Portage, 4050 N. Milwaukee Ave., (773) 202-8000
- Chicago—Village, Clark St. and North Ave., (312) 642-2403
- Chicago—Village North, 6746 N. Sheridan Rd., (773) 764-9100

- Des Plaines—1476 Miner St., Des Plaines, (847) 298-6715
- Downers Grove—Tivoli, 5021 Highland Ave., (630) 968-0219
- Downers Grove—Tivoli South, 2119 63rd St., (630) 968-0219
- Elgin—Casino, 250 S. Grove, (847) 608-9401
- Elk Grove—Elk Grove, Biesterfield and Arlington Heights Rds., (847) 228-6707
- Elmhurst—York, 150 N. York Rd., (630) 834-0675
- Fox Lake—Fox Lake, 115 Lakeland Plaza, (847) 973-2800
- Glen Ellyn—Glen, 540 Crescent Ave., (630) 469-0780
- Hanover Park—Tradewinds, Barrington and Irving Park Rds., (630) 289-6707
- Highland Park—Highland Park, 445 Central, (847) 432-3300
- Hoffman Estates—Barrington Square, 2330 W. Higgins Rd., (847) 843-7606
- Libertyville—Liberty 1&2, 708 N. Milwaukee Ave., (847) 362-3011
- Lombard—Northgate Theaters, I-355 and North Ave., (847) 627-1010
- Morton Grove—Morton Grove, 7300 W. Dempster St., (847) 967-6010
- Mundelein—Mundelein Cinema, 155 N. Seymour, (847) 566-2490
- Naperville—Ogden, 1227 E. Ogden Ave., (630) 357-5050
- Park Ridge—Pickwick, 5-17 S. Prospect, (847) 518-3333
- Skokie—Skokie Theater, 7924 N. Lincoln Ave., (847) 673-4214
- Vernon Hills—Show Place 8, Milwaukee Ave., (847) 247-8958
- Wheaton—Wheaton, 123 N. Hale St., (847) 668-1680

Live Entertainment

Grant Park Music Festival

235 S. Columbus Dr.
Chicago, IL 60603
(312) 742-4763
Hours: Hours for performances vary
AE, MC, V

That Chicago has become second to none in terms of cultural affairs is due, in large part, to the emphasis of top city officials on things musical, theatrical, and otherwise entertaining. Hence the Grant Park District Music Festival, a Chicago Park District institution since 1935—and, according to its sponsors, the nation's only remaining free, municipally funded, classical music festival. Pomp and circumstance aside, for at least a few of the 10 weeks, we diligently trot down to the bus, picnics in hand, to eat and listen to such luminaries as Herb Alpert, Ian Anderson, Jethro Tull, baritone Dimitri Hvorostovsky, and other known and soon-to-be-famous talents. And if you truly feel like contributing (or avoiding the inevitable grass stains on your clothing), check out the membership pass—$40 for one person means a for-sure seat near the Petrillo Bandshell, plus other discounts.

HOT TIX

108 N. State St.
Chicago, IL 60602
(312) 977-1755
Hours: Mon–Sat: 10–6; Sun: 12–5; hours vary at other locations
AE, MC, V

Supported by Chicago-area theaters, Hot Tix offers seats to shows and performances at discount rates. (Similar deals are available in Manhattan and other big U.S. cities.) When picked up in person, at any of the five Hot Tix locations, your tickets are half price! (Tickets are never sold over the phone, nor can they be forwarded by mail.) With shows such as *All the Rage*, *Defending the Cave Man*, the Joffrey Ballet of Chicago, *Merrily We Roll Along*, *Sheer Madness*, and *Sunset Boulevard* appearing in the summer months of '97, it's hard not to sing along. Four Tower Records stores (two in Chicago, one each in Bloomingdale and Schaumburg) also support the half-price theater arts. Since hours, credit cards, locations, and ticket prices vary, call the State Street Hot Tix box office for more information.
Chicago—Michigan and Chicago Aves. at the historic Water Tower
Evanston—1616 Sherman Ave. (City Parking garage)

Ravinia Festival

Lake Cook and Green Bay Rds.
Highland Park, IL 60635
(847) 266-5100
Hours: Box office: Mon–Fri: 10–6; Sun: 1–6; hours for performances vary
AE, DISC, MC, V

With a different concert every day from June 1 until September 1, Ravinia has our vote as one of the area's best summer activities. Situated in a northern suburb a hop, skip, and a jump from the train, the acreage of Ravinia alone is enticing—especially since cheap seats (and the best, in our opinion) are on the grass. Yes, it's the summer home of the CSO (Chicago Symphony Orchestra, to you). But there's also music for everyone: classical, jazz, country, contemporary, and even appearances by such acts as Peter, Paul & Mary and the Temptations. Pavilion seats run from $15 to $40; and lawn seats $8 to $10, depending on the concert. On average, though, inside tickets run about $30. For complete concert information and a brochure of upcoming performers, call (847) 266-5100.

Second City

1616 N. Wells St.
Chicago, IL 60614
(312) 337-3992
Hours: Mon–Sat: 10:30–10:30
AE, DISC, MC, V

Here's one piece of theatrical history we proudly claim: improvisation started here. And no one does it better than Second City. (OK, OK, we're biased.) Then again, think of the names associated with this Wells Street landmark: Mike Nichols and Elaine May, Jim and John Belushi, George Wendt, and other comedic and acting and directing legends. And almost every weeknight at 10:30 (Saturdays and Sundays, too) after the scheduled revue, the Second City troupe does free improvs—sometimes based on audience suggestions, sometimes on their own whims and whimsies. To our mind, this is the truest, purest form of the art . . . and the hardest, since it relies on sheer wit and physical presence. Drop in—it's easy to get hooked.

THEATRE ON THE LAKE
Lake Shore Dr. at Fullerton Ave.
Chicago, IL 60614
(773) 742-7994
Hours: Box office: Tues–Sat: 1–6; hours for performances vary
AE, DISC, MC, V

Right on the magnificent Drive, with breezes blowing through the stage, is the Theater on the Lake—open from June to August. The cast is as close to professional as community actors can be—plus the directors and top pros are all paid by the Park District. In the last year or so, the stage has been populated by local theater companies—or plays borrowed from them. Best yet, any seat in the house costs $9—or $60 for a season's subscription (nine plays). What starred in summer '97? *It's Your Fault* from Second Songs of the Spanish Civil War; *Golden Boy* from Steppenwolf.

MUSIC & MOVIES

DR. WAX
2523 N. Clark St.
Chicago, IL 60657
(773) 549-3377
Hours: Mon–Sat: 11–9; Sun: 11–6
DISC, MC, V

How many used music stores constitute too many? Obviously, Dr. Wax, with its four locations, suffers no lack of customers for its well-priced, already-heard LPs, CDs, and cassettes . . . and some new "vinyls" too. There's certainly gold in recycling music for both retailer and customer. Used CDs (the majority of the stock) range from $2.99 to $9.99, while new records play at a considerable discount: $4.99 to $13.99.

Chicago—1203 N. State St., (312) 255-0123
Chicago—5210 S. Harper Ave., (773) 493-8696
Evanston—1615 Sherman, (847) 475-8848

DOG EAR MUSIC & MOVIES
117 W. Rockland Rd.
Libertyville, IL 60048
(847) 362-5666
Hours: Mon–Thurs: 10–9; Fri & Sat: 10–10; Sun: 11–9
AE, DISC, MC, V

"If you insist upon buying cassettes at places like Musicland and Record Town, then you don't understand discounts and bargains." That's the philosophy of Dog Ear, specializing in both used and new audios and videos in different formats. Expect a 30% savings on new CDs, while used will run from $1.99 to $8.99. Previously heard cassettes, too, are reduced to $2.99 to $7.99. Weekday movie rentals cost $2.50 each, jumping to $3 on Friday, Saturday, and Sunday.

JAZZ RECORD MART ★
444 N. Wabash Ave.
Chicago, IL 60611
(800) 684-3480
Hours: Mon–Sat: 10–8; Sun: 12–5
AE, DISC, MC, V

It swings here—not only with the sounds of music, but also with occasional late nights, free films, and lots of hip folks. One of the best places for all things jazz and blues too, especially "cut-outs" or those items no longer being manufactured. A few examples of the buys: Sarah Vaughan's *Crazy and Mixed Up* imported CD at $9.99 (once $16.99); and a Modern Jazz *The Last Concert* two-CD set now priced at $12.99 (normally $27.99). Also uncovered are soon-to-be antique LPs, 78s, and 45s; a mail-order catalog and a Web site complete their top-notch customer service. Add to your hip-ness by flashing your 10% *Buying Retail Is Stupid!* coupon.

MUSIC RECYCLERY ✪

4104 N. Harlem Ave.
Norridge, IL 60634
(708) 583-0903
Hours: Mon–Sat: 10–9; Sun: 11–6
MC, V
◆ **Senior Discount:** 10% **Age:** 65+

In the spirit of being environmentally considerate is the five-store Music Recyclery, housed in major Chicagoland shopping malls. Having started the business in 1993, entrepreneurial owner Paul Frischer not only will sell, but also is eager to buy any and all music-related items—yes, even pre-owned Walkmans, video games, and stereo equipment. From country to reggae, blues to soul, the Recyclery's music will sing out in record, CD, cassette, laser disc, and 45 formats for 40%–80% off retail. And in keeping with the '90s, the chain promotes a Web site catalog that changes every day. What won't change is the 20% additional discount offered to *Buying Retail Is Stupid!* readers.

Gurnee—6170 W. Grand Ave., #681, (847) 855-7844
Mt. Prospect—999 Elmhurst Rd., (847) 670-0903
Rolling Meadows—1400 E. Golf Rd., (847) 228-9399
West Dundee—1072 Spring Hill Mall, (847) 836-1162

2ND HAND TUNES

2604 N. Clark St.
Chicago, IL 60614
(312) 929-6325
Hours: Mon–Sat: 11–8; Sun: 12–7
DISC, MC, V

Two of the eight 2nd Hand Tunes specialize in vinyl. Period. Two others feature only CDs or cassettes. But the growth of this chain (and others like it) is a testimonial to the strength of the recycling movement—and to the eternal appeal of all kinds of music. Some of the better prices on pre-listened-to notes are here: used CDs and vinyls, from 99¢ to $10; cassettes, 49¢ to five bucks; and eight-tracks about the same.

Eight locations; see the Yellow Pages

VIDEO BEAT
2616 N. Clark St.
Chicago, IL 60614
(773) 871-6667
Hours: Mon–Sat: 11–8:30; Sun: 12–8
AE, DISC, MC, V

First the used record stores debuted. Then, those dealing in previously owned audiocassettes, followed by outlets specializing in CDs. Now comes Video Beat, truly a retailer for the MTV generation, with its gently watched music videos (along, of course, with all the new and used forms of recordings). Lee and Steve and Greg offer a new buying niche for the dedicated music lover, with used videos averaging from $1 to $20; vinyls, $2.50 to $7; cassettes, $3 to $4.50; CDs, $2 to $7.50. Supply-and-demand economics, of course, determine exact prices.

Musical Instruments

So, little Jane or John falls in love with a piano or saxophone or guitar. And you, as a devoted parent or relative, decide to indulge the child. Stop . . . and check with our musician-counselor, who has identified six key elements of purchasing.

1. Follow the title of this book—religiously.

   After all, buying retail *is* stupid; never, ever pay list price (or retail) for any musical instrument—from an 85-key-er to guitar or drum or saxophone, among others.

   There is one exception: handmade or custom-designed instruments. That includes violins, violas, cellos, bassoons, or harps—any instrument that is not mass-produced on assembly lines. So, all of this advice pertains only to non-handcrafted instruments.
2. Remember the magic number of 30%. It's the standard discount on musical instruments—even pianos and organs.
3. Become a sales hound.

   Some *Buying Retail Is Stupid!* stores hold annual or biannual sales and discount instruments 50% or more. Guitar Center is one example. Other retailers limit their sales to invitation-only events, which means finding out how to get on the mailing list. See The Music Gallery.

4. Practice, practice, practice price knowledge.

   Compare prices at three different stores. And make sure it's an exact match—for example, the cost of a Gibson Les Paul custom model guitar against the cost of a Gibson Les Paul custom model guitar, not against the price of a standard or studio or deluxe model. Or consider drum sets: some dealers might confuse consumers by adding or subtracting cymbals, bass drum pedals, or a drummer's throne of varying brands. In guitars, the substitute could be an amplifier of not-as-good quality.
5. If the discount is only 30%, ask for 42%–47%.
6. Confirm *everything*.

   There's certainly no harm in simply shopping around. But, if you don't plan to buy right away, get price quotes in writing, including exact brand, model, color, accessories, freebies, and so on. And while we're discussing our favorite subject—freebies—here are the gratuities to ask for when buying a piano or an organ: a seat and free tunings *every* year (usually, three for the first 12 months and then one to two annually). If that request hits the proverbial brick wall, then negotiate, at the very least, for free delivery and setup.

MUSIC STORES

FATBOYS MUSICAL OUTLET ✪

9010 N. Milwaukee Ave.
Niles, IL 60714
(847) 297-2350
Hours: Mon–Fri: 12–9; Sat: 10–6; Sun: 12–4:30
AE, MC, V

Musical instruments at prices almost guaranteed to make a band member's fingers itch are the stock in trade at this oddly named store. Names such as Washburn (guitars), Trace Elliot (amps), and Tama (drums) dominate; service is professional—and friendly; and discounts are decent (20%–50% off retail). Watch for the occasional back-to-school, Christmas, and blowout sales for higher price reductions. Or prepare to conduct your own orchestra by using the 10%-extra *Buying Retail Is Stupid!* coupon.

FLATS & SHARPS
6749 N. Sheridan Rd.
Chicago, IL 60626
(773) 465-5233
Hours: Mon, Wed–Fri: 11–6; Tues: 11–8; Sat: 11–5
AE, DISC, MC, V
◆ **Senior Discount:** Depends on item **Age:** 62+

Though the hours are clearly listed, better call first: creative types—musicians, artists, writers, and so on—sometimes don't adhere to schedules. Nonetheless, it could be worth a visit to pluck the strings of a mandolin or sitar at Flats & Sharps, with its rather iconoclastic selection of used and new instruments. Close to the Rogers Park campus of Loyola University, the store keeps its audience and their limited budgets in mind. Guitars, for instance, start at $148, many accompanied by a free carrying case; amps, at $104.99 and up, discounts averaging about 30%. Available too are accessories, repairs, and lessons for the budding James Taylor of the family.

THE MUSIC GALLERY ★
2558 Green Bay Rd.
Highland Park, IL 60035
(847) 432-6350
Hours: Mon–Fri: 12–8; Sat: 10–5
AE, DISC, MC, V

Understand the association of refretting, level, and crowns with guitars? Then, the 20-something-year-old music gallery, filled with acoustic and electric guitars from production pieces to one-of-a-kind, will most definitely pluck your heartstrings. Next to names such as Fender, Gibson, and Yamaha are also amplifiers and drum sets; two rooms filled with instruments invite musicians to take a test drive. Service doesn't end with the sale; the Gallery offers multitrack and sound-system rentals as well as the expertise of two guitar technicians, who, together, have worked on more than 15,000 instruments. Our best bet (other than redeeming the 20% *Buying Retail Is Stupid!* coupon)? Make sure you're on the list for the invitation-only July sale . . . and get in line early.

Musician's Network

5505 N. Clark St.
Chicago, IL 60640
(773) 728-2929
Hours: Mon–Fri: 11–7:30; Sat: 10:30–6; Sun: 12–5
AE, DISC, MC, V

In the spirit of "some buys are more equal than others" is the Musician's Network, a North Side store of used/refurbished and new musical instruments. We suspect that the Network's price determination depends heavily on the price paid. Antiques dealers perpetually explain to customers that two identical pieces may not be priced identically because they were purchased at different times, at different price tags. Whatever the case, we rummaged through the stock and found good names, decent prices. Examples from the Network's wares: $600 for a used Ensonia keyboard; a Peavey electric guitar for $379; and drumsticks at $2.95 a pair. The store's good turnover at the lower end ensures "new" merchandise presented at every new visit.

Pianos & Keyboards

Conn Music Center

1492 Townline Rd.
Mundelein, IL 60060
(847) 949-0977
Hours: Mon, Thurs: 10–8; Tues, Wed, Fri: 10–6; Sat: 10–5
DISC, MC, V
◆ **Senior Discount:** 5% **Age:** 60+

One almost "for-sure" investment, according to Tim Case of Conn Music Center: pianos, since they've been increasing 15%–18% in value each and every year. His recommendation? Young Chang, the only vertical console piano still manufactured with hardwoods.

Nonetheless, those 85 keys don't come cheap, even with discounts; a new grand sells here for $9,503 (listed at $11,879) and an ebony console for $3,451 (was $4,314). Other brands also get play: Technics and Kurzwell digitals as well as Howard Miller clocks. Do ask for the lowest price . . . and about all warranties.

FIELD'S PIANO SUPER WAREHOUSE ★

3143 W. 95th St.
Evergreen Park, IL 60805
(708) 424-4845
Hours: Mon, Thurs: 9–8; Tues, Wed, Fri, Sat: 9–4:30; Sun: 12–4 and anytime by appointment
AE, DIN, DISC, MC, OPT, V
◆ **Senior Discount:** 10% **Age:** 55+

From Bechstein to Yamaha, both old and new pianos, digital keyboards, and organs find a home in Field's Piano Super Warehouse. Though the sales hype can be thick and staccato, typical savings are around 48%, which, when you're considering a purchase the size of a Bosendorfer grand, could be substantial. Besides, this all-in-the-family store (now operated by the third generation) will service its own musical wares too. Plunk the Field's keys even more sonorously with the $300-minimum-purchase *Buying Retail Is Stupid!* coupon. This entitles a buyer to free delivery and four free lessons!

KURT SAPHIR PIANOS

310-322 W. Chicago Ave.
Chicago, IL 60610
(312) 440-1164
Hours: Mon–Sat: 10–5:30
MC, V

News is when a family-owned business passes the five-decade mark. It's true history if a firm succeeds through a century . . . or more. Actually, Kurt Saphir Pianos started making music in Vienna; wars and other atrocities forced emigration to Chicago. All to our good fortune, since the sixth generation of Saphirs continues to ply its skills on both new and rebuilt pianos of some renown, from the elegant Bosendorfer grand to the utilitarian Charles Walter console.

The average savings is about 30%–40%; free are benches and local delivery within range of its three stores. An instant orchestra in 85 keys.

Barrington—117 E. Northwest Hwy., (847) 381-3050

Wilmette—123 Green Bay Rd., (847) 256-5225

Pickle Piano Company ✪

104 W. Lake St.

Bloomingdale, IL 60108

(630) 894-2992

Hours: Mon–Fri: 11–8; Sat & Sun: 11–4

AE, DISC, MC, V

A name such as Pickle is difficult to forget. Owner Matt Bechteler rebuilds, restores, and repairs (and then sells) some of the finest pianos and organs extant. In fact, the names sound like European composers: Bechstein, Hoffman, Niemeyer, Petrov, Weinbach, all at 25% savings. New instruments, too, including electronic versions, are available at a discount. (Alert to avid key-ticklers: set your metronomes for the additional *Buying Retail Is Stupid!* savings—25% on new, 10% on used ebonies and ivories.)

Repairs

Admiral Music Co.

5951 N. Clark St.

Chicago, IL 60660

(773) 271-4400

Hours: Mon, Thurs: 9–9; Tues, Wed, Fri, Sat: 9–5; Sun: 11–4

AE, DISC, MC, V

The waiting list is 27 months long—to restore private customers' pianos. Which makes sense, given the incredible handwork necessary for reconditioning and Admiral's 48-year reputation. Every piano name appears in silent concert here at one time or another; what we coveted was a 1926 Baldwin ebony lacquer full grand . . . at $12,900 (new, Admiral manager Dick Femke said, would cost $21,900). Don't despair, however; there is truly a piano for every household: spinets begin at $1,200; consoles, $1,500; and grands at $5,500. Music to our ears.

Office & Business Needs

NEW & USED PRODUCTS

AMERICAN OFFICE FURNITURE

805 N. Milwaukee Ave.
Chicago, IL 60622
(800) 300-6779
Hours: Mon–Fri: 9–5:30; Sat: 10–3
AE, MC, V

On February 15, 1936, "Machine Gun" Jack McGurn, one-time leader of Capone's gang, was fatally shot at a Milwaukee Avenue bowling alley, now the site of American Office Furniture. Obviously, this stigma hasn't affected the owners, since small business folks, home workers, and corporate types regularly buy office furniture here at a 50%–70% discount. New Hon metal files are usually 50% discounted (e.g., a four-drawer runs $109, compared to $225). Merchandise Mart samples, appearing after the huge NEOCON trade show in June, sell quickly at 60%–70% off retail—with absolutely no signs of a forced-shotgun marriage.

DIRECT OFFICE FURNITURE WAREHOUSE

5041 N. Western Ave.
Chicago, IL 60625
(773) 271-3000
Hours: Mon–Sat: 9:30–6
AE, DISC, MC, V

Many Chicago-based authors call this store a godsend, with its sometimes jungle-resembling mixture of old and new desks, file cabinets, chairs, credenzas, and office furnishings. Here is home for some of the best prices on Hon file cabinets, ready-to-assemble workstations (e.g., Sauder and O'Sullivan), and comfy, ergonomic chairs from the likes of Herman Miller and Steelcase. Even upscale, slightly used reception and conference furnishings land in one or both locations, including a sale-priced $12,000 all-in-one matched cherry-and-mahogany wood office system. Merchandise turns quickly; watch for ads heralding a 10% extra discount on used items.
Chicago—7232 N. Western Ave., (773) 465-3300

GENERAL OFFICE FURNITURE

529 N. Milwaukee Ave.
Chicago, IL 60622
(312) 421-4265
Hours: Mon–Fri: 8:30–5
MC, V

Hats off to a businessman who's been around for 44 years—and continues to manage his store almost daily. Owner Don Hoffberg, promoting via modest classified ads, identified the home-office boom way before corporate downsizing was included in Webster's lexicon. New or used, whether the intent is to buy, sell, or rent/lease, General Office is as competitive as the next—with the pre-owned stuff, obviously so, trading hands for mere pennies ($75 and up for used desks; $20+ for used chairs). Our look at the nouvelle home goods: a Global ergonomic exec's chair for $390 (regularly $578) and a three-piece blond maple desk set for $2,700 (was $4,500). So, expect up to 50% reductions on the new.

GENTLY USED OFFICE FURNITURE ✪

1300 W. North Ave.
Chicago, IL 60622
(773) 736-6200
Hours: Mon–Fri: 10–6; Sat: 10–4
AE, DISC, MC, OPT, V

Sometimes, in excellent weather, chairs will sit invitingly, right on North Avenue, between Home Depot and the Kennedy expressway, waiting for the first taker. At other times, the headquarters of "GUOF," as it's known, is filled with both new and used office furniture at major discounts: 50%–70% off new, and even greater reductions on pre-owned stuff. Hunting reveals brands such as Alina, Herman Miller, Steelcase, et al. Overstock, truckload, and coupon sales throughout the year net the best savings along with a judicious application of the extra-10% *Buying Retail Is Stupid!* coupon.

RSI/OFFICE FURNITURE OUTLET
1060 E. Ogden Ave.
Naperville, IL 60563
(630) 778-7900 or (888) 2-GET-RSI
Hours: Mon–Fri: 9–6; Sat: 10–3
DISC, MC, V

More than ever before, home workers in both suburbs and city have quite a few outlets from which to choose for new and used office furniture. The four-store RSI chain, in fact, offers a new twist on options available: using a 10-step process, they remanufacture previously owned furniture and panel systems and sell or rent pieces at a fraction of the original cost. New, used, or remanufactured, 40 furniture brands are represented—on display or through RSI's catalog. Sample values: four-drawer Global file cabinet, $171 ($285 retail); 8-foot racetrack conference table, $503 (was $839); high-back Global leather tilt-and-swivel chair, $372 (was $620).
Aurora—2115 E. New York St., (630) 978-0500
Chicago—570 W. Jackson Blvd., (312) 669-9600
Palatine—546 E. Northwest Hwy., (847) 358-7100

Paper & Party Goods

CARD AND PARTY WAREHOUSE ★
4126 W. Belmont
Chicago, IL 60641
(773) 736-4400
Hours: Mon, Wed–Fri: 9–9; Tues: 9–8; Sat: 9–6; Sun: 9–5
DISC, MC, V

Think elephant and donkey: five locations of the Windy City's largest party and balloon supplier serve a variety of individual and institutional customers with 50% off on favors, costumes and accessories, and custom invitations. No party is too big to outfit; buyers include nightclubs and restaurants, plus affairs in connection with the Democratic and Republican National Conventions. Plastered all over their stores are wares from American Greetings, Disney, Hallmark, and Warner; savings reflect some mighty good deals: blown-up bunch of birthday helium balloons for $19.95 and Halloween costumes priced as low as $9.96. Hosts with the most will also remember the 5% extra *Buying Retail Is Stupid!* discount on selected purchases over $20 when planning parties (the savings increase with amount of purchase).

Chicago—1265 N. Milwaukee Ave., (773) 232-7900
Chicago—1880 W. Fullerton Ave., (773) 342-1500
Chicago—6254 N. McCormick Ave., (773) 478-6200
Mundelein—405 W. Townline Rd., (847) 566-1111

Card Carousel ★

3336 Ridge Rd.
Lansing, IL 60438
(708) 474-0696
Hours: Mon–Thurs: 9:30–5:30; Fri: 9:30–8; Sat: 9:30–5
AE, DISC, MC, V

The number of occasions requiring at least one greeting card (if not a gift) has risen exponentially. It makes sense, then, to stock up on those sentimental mailers, especially if the price is right. At the two south Chicagoland stores owned by Jack Wilson—Card Carousel and The Villager—it's virtually impossible to say no to half-price cards (some are only 39¢) as well as to the well-discounted party goods, invitations, and bridal accessories. (Plus, we know no better way to say "thank you" than with the 15% *Buying Retail Is Stupid!* coupon.)

Lansing—The Villager Discount, 3322 Ridge Rd., (708) 474-4949

PDT Printing ★

3532 W. 63rd St.
Chicago, IL 60629
(773) 776-7774
Hours: Mon–Fri: 1–10; Sat: 1–5
DISC, MC, V

We voted this—unanimously—the most unusual store-with-great-prices in *Buying Retail Is Stupid!* Its nickname alone ("The Cop Shop") might give you a clue. Once you're inside, owner Patrick Gutkoeska's off-the-wall merchandise is bound to give you a terminal case of the giggles . . . and an insatiable desire to buy a lot of stuff. Such as the $14 nightshirts, "Feel Safe; Sleep with a Cop." Or the $10 for-women-only T-shirt saying, "I've got a badge, a gun, and PMS. Any questions?" More serious items—a $7.50 pepper spray, search gloves, even $24.25 handcuffs (a Mother's Day bestseller)—also relate to the men and women in blue. Though Gutkoeska does daylight as a printer, we strongly suspect that The Cop Shop part of the store will prevail. Especially when *Buying Retail Is Stupid!* readers cash in on the extra 10% discount offered on any merchandise. In professional lingo: "19 Paul says it all." (In consumer language: "This is a nuisance call no one wants to handle.")

Pets & Animal Supplies

PET FOOD OUTLET

1476 Townline Rd.
Mundelein, IL 60060
(847) 566-3321
Hours: Mon–Fri: 10–8; Sat: 10–5; Sun: 11–4
DISC, MC, V

Three felines—Gibson, Mia, and Vincent—rule the store roost here, with occasional visible signs of their mischievousness. But, who could blame them, with all the less-than-retail (about 10% off) toys and num-nums? Almost any companion-animal owner will discover something to buy, from national brands such as Iams and Science Diet to local and natural manufacturers (Solid Gold Herbal, Fromm Family Excel) as well as books, bones, chew toys, leashes, shampoos, and other pet-phernalia.

Photography

We've heard horror tales about wedding and special-occasion photographers that would simply curl the edges of any good glossy. What do consumers do, we wondered, who don't know professionals—or who buy based on price alone? So, we turned for advice to one of our business buddies, Lee Balgemann, who spent umpteen years learning the trade at Associated Press and now has his own flourishing photo studio. (We nicknamed this the Top Five List for Photo-Finish Pix.)

1. Word of mouth is best.

   But, don't just gather one or two names. Call the ASMP (American Society of Media Photographers), the APA (Advertising Photographers of America), and/or the PPA (Professional Photographers of America). Tell them what you want—and your budget.
2. Make thorough checks into references—and portfolios.

   Anyone who can't give you two or three names of satisfied clients should be avoided. Definitely give all references a call, with specific questions uppermost in your mind: Did she or he listen to you and supply what you wanted? Was he or she prompt for all meetings? Were you comfortable with him or her? And so forth. And look through the photographer's portfolio—as well as through pix owned by clients (if at all possible).
3. Price should not be your only determinant.

   In fact, if cost matters a lot, we strongly suggest you supply the most talented member of your family with an idiot-proof point-and-shoot camera. Because good photography is *never* cheap. Our best advice: shop quality—*and* price.
4. Deals are not always what they seem.

   Sometimes, photographers have been known to charge less money for the actual shoot—hoping they'll make it up on the quantity reprints or enlargements. Don't let them. See what professional labs such as Gamma here charge for color, slides, processing—and compare fees. Examine all parts of a package, especially its inclusions and exclusions. Then you're better prepared to counter-offer or negotiate.
5. Professionals are known by the company they keep—and by their behavior.

   "Be prepared" is a motto with wider applications than the Boy Scouts. Remember Tom and Marge's wedding when the lights and flashes didn't work? Or when little cousin Mickey somehow got hold of a camera . . . and dropped it? Always, always, *always* make sure your photographer carries more than one camera and lens and flash, and so on, along with tons of film. And once the happy event is finished, and you have the proofs in your hands, ask if you now have all the shots taken or whether any have been left out.

"Life-milestone" pictures are truly worth many words—and every penny.

A Camera Store

634 S. Wabash, 2nd floor
Chicago, IL 60605
(312) 431-0050
Hours: Mon–Fri: 9:30–6; Sat: 9–5
DISC, MC, V

Wouldn't you guess that a jack-of-all-trades photographer (Mark Orenstein, by name) had to open Chicago's only all-used camera store? Right around the corner from Columbia College, and a huff and a puff up a rather steep flight of stairs is a surprisingly orderly and well-kept shop with everything photographic at your fingertips. In the back is a wide assortment of darkroom stuff—lights ($375 for a Bowen's 15000 mono) and developing equipment. In the front, a visual artist's dream, from point-and-shoot for novices to a Minolta 300SI ($249) for pros. Even better than the standard discount (typically 50%) is the care and feeding of customers; Mark and his staff work with everyone very patiently, answering all manner of questions.

Calumet Photographic

520 W. Erie
Chicago, IL 60610
(312) 440-4920
Hours: Mon–Fri: 8–6
AE, DISC, MC, V

The hours alone at Calumet's Chicago store indicate its primary audience: the 8–6, Monday through Friday are geared to practitioners and near-serious amateurs. In fact, the River West outlet is split in half: one for the equipment, the other for sundries. And though prices on their new and used merchandise reflect competitive dis-

counts (at least a 25% savings), other Calumet programs promise even greater reductions. Especially their Calumet preferred customers club. For $15 each year, members enjoy exclusive one-day sales, free admission to monthly seminars, and bonus dollars, among other perks. And, of course, the brands carried are of the highest caliber: a Minolta autometer for $328.95; a Nikon body with a 105 mm lens for $199; and a well-loved Woodfield 4 × 5 for $899.
Bensenville—890 Supreme Dr., (630) 860-7447

CENTRAL CAMERA COMPANY

230 S. Wabash Ave.
Chicago, IL 60604-2396
(312) 427-5580
Hours: Mon–Fri: 8:30–5:30; Sat: 8:30–5
AE, DISC, MC, V

Semiprofessional photographer friends swear by Central as one of the three camera stores for best deals. (The other two? Helix and Calumet.) What is critical to remember, they say, is that bargains will be found in purchases over $500, where the retailer has some "wiggle room." Any items priced lower than that magic number will be the same at any store, local or national. A strictly Chicago business since 1899, Central offers discounts on both new and used equipment—lenses of all shapes and sizes, tripods, and camera bodies, as well as film and other photographic needs.

HELIX CAMERA & AUDIO

310 S. Racine Ave.
Chicago, IL 60607
(312) 421-6000
Hours: Hours vary
DISC, MC, V

"Popcorn stuff," laughed one salesperson when we asked about the competition. Helix has become a home of sorts for serious amateur and pay-for-hire photographers, with its occasional seminars and workshops by outside experts on matters of visual import, such as wedding-picture tips and digital imaging. Too, it boasts probably the best variety and prices on underwater equipment, should that be your metier. At all of its nine stores, not only are discounts gener-

ous (30% and more) on brand-name new and used cameras, lenses, lighting, and the like, but their service is very personal also . . . and geared to long-term relationships. (We overheard one conversation: the customer loudly thanked the clerk for his efficiency in saving him money on processing.)
Nine stores; call (800) 621-6471 for locations

Plants, Lawn & Garden

RENTOKIL OUTLET STORE
855 E. Aptakisic Rd.
Buffalo Grove, IL 60089
(847) 634-4108
Hours: Tues–Sat: 9–5
DISC, MC, V

We agree: it's an extremely odd name for a business renting tropical plants to offices. On the other hand, prices are so terrific on Rentokil's "used" green leafy (and flowering) things that we won't comment further. (Plus, our "black thumb" is well known to local greenhouses.) Our stroll in their outlet yielded these oxygen producers: $3.99 for a 4.5-inch kalanchoe; a $12.75 tag on a foot-high jasmine; a small Rieger begonia for $3.99; and 4-inch geraniums at half a buck each. Ask about their trees and containers.

SMITH & HAWKEN OUTLET
1780 N. Marcey St.
Chicago, IL 60614
(312) 266-1988
Hours: Fri: 10–7; Sat: 10–6; Sun: 1–5
AE, MC, V

The catalog name that literally smells garden-fresh now has established one of its two outlets in Chicago (number two is in Mill Valley, California). Open Friday through Sunday, next to its retail neighbor, Smith & Hawken's outlet features random selections from its catalog pages. Christmas wreaths, men's and women's casual clothing, kids' toys, and body lotions were all sighted on one recent visit—for at least 50% off. Specials such as $58 wool floral scarves for $19 will please hearty shoppers. Even better discounts are found by rummaging through two wire bins (try $5 for a black corduroy skirt, originally $78).

Special Sales

That Chicago has now become the home for many small manufacturers is due to the efforts of Mayor Richard Daley. But, more than a nod of the head must also be given to Dorothy Fuller, fashion maven extraordinaire of the Apparel Center, and to the considerable time she's spent luring prospective Seventh Avenue-type businesses to our town. Consequently, the good news for our *Buying Retail Is Stupid!* readers: manufacturers' sales on discontinueds, overstocks, overruns, and past-season merchandise do occur with relative frequency—at least once a week. Many of the larger firms' sales are listed here.

There is another way to find out best deals on fashion "leftovers": check (believe it or not) the bulletin boards in the Apparel Center's lower-level restrooms. There, showrooms with merchandise to sell post notices about dates and times.

Don't, however, even think of wandering the corridors of the Center, sniffing out sample sales. The area is pretty security conscious; we even got stopped (with a press badge, no less!) to ask about our destination.

A Month of Sundays

363 W. Erie St.
Chicago, IL 60610
(312) 642-5700
Hours: Once a year
Cash, check

For years, Chicago's Apparel Center has spearheaded a concerted effort to keep apparel manufacturers or lure them to our city. That ploy is obviously working, witnessed by A Month of Sundays, headquartered in River North. And once a year, usually the first Saturday in December, there's a warehouse sale on men's and women's soft-as-silk casual cotton knits—jackets, sweaters, dresses, tops, sweats, shorts, skirts from extra small to extra large. Past-season and sample merchandise sells here for more than 50% off retail: men's polos for $25–$35 (originally $78–$85); dresses at $20–$35 (retail $64–$88). Get on the mailing list for official notification.

Amy Rigg Clothing Co.

1807 W. Sunnyside Ave., G3
Chicago, IL 60640
(773) 271-3112
Hours: Two or more times a year
Cash, check

Hoosier schoolteacher-turned-clothing-designer Amy Rigg does the slightly funky, specialized women's boutique kind of look: unusual fabrics in muted colors cut slightly full for tops, coats, pants, skirts, and dresses. About two or three times a year, announced by postcards and direct mail, she opens her workroom/showroom to sell overruns and "as-is" wearables at 25%–40% (and sometimes more) less than retail. A fuzzy-wuzzy warm black chenille knee-length coat was $425 (compare at $525); a gray-and-red chenille striped dress, $140 ($185 retail).

Annual Mammoth Music and Record Mart

Golf and Skokie Rds.
Skokie, IL 60202
(847) 674-MART
Hours: Once a year; hours vary
DISC, MC, V

In the mid-1970s, Les Turner—then afflicted with amyotrophic lateral sclerosis (ALS), Lou Gehrig's disease—developed the idea of having a sale for used music after he had thrown away some old LPs and saw kids scavenging for them. Now held yearly, for 10 days in late September/early October, this sale, known as the Mammoth Music and Record Mart, directs almost all proceeds to ALS research ($8 million has already been raised). Expect up to 75% savings—and to be a sport; it all goes to a good cause. More info? Call for times and dates for the upcoming Mart.

BRANDEIS UNIVERSITY'S BOOK SALE
Old Orchard Center
Skokie, IL 60077
(847) 604-1919
Hours: Once a year; hours vary
Cash

For about 10 days in June, a sprawling yellow-and-white-striped tent decorates part of the parking lot at Old Orchard Center in Skokie. As do hundreds of area book addicts, haunting the bins of Brandeis University's annual book sale. Close to half a million used books are priced for immediate sale—and the last 2 days of this Brandeis-sponsored fest become a reader's delight, when all remaining items are half a buck or less.

THE DESIGN ALLIANCE
c/o Peg Walt of Walt Dyas
Sycamore, IL 60178
(815) 895-4078
Hours: Once a year; hours vary
Payment varies by designer

At least once a year, maybe twice, the Design Alliance, a network of 22 Chicago-area fashion and furnishings designers, brings together overruns, samples, and discontinued merchandise to sell to the public. Members are headquartered from as far north as Milwaukee to the western reaches of Sycamore. The group's special sale features whimsically painted animal clocks, jewelry, softly dyed pillows and scarves, other home decorator accessories, and a wealth of women's apparel from business conservative to downright funky in all types of textiles and sizes. Prices hover dangerously close to wholesale; the samples sale is usually followed by a fabrics and notions closeout. (P.S. They're always looking for a nonprofit sponsor; in the last few sales, the Bottomless Closet and the House of the Good Shepherd benefited.) Look for ads and publicity announcing future sales.

ELLIE BEGONIA
1539 Old Deerfield Rd.
Highland Park , IL 60035
(847) 831-0900
Hours: Once a year; hours vary
Cash

As of our last visit, Ellie Giller, owner of Ellie Begonia, hadn't figured out where to relocate her design studio. (The building on Old Deerfield Road had just been sold.) But rest assured, anywhere Ellie goes, we'll faithfully follow for her yearly sale—with some of the most imaginative kids' apparel extant. Selling to the classy department stores and boutiques across the country, she manufactures on the South Side—our gain, since overruns and overstocks are nearby. A sampling of the close-to-wholesale sample items, fitting baby to size 14: daisy-yellow patent girl's jumper with black and white flowers; Polartec top/sweats with sun and moon appliqués and complementary buttons; and decorated teeny "owie" blankies for tots who need to hang on to a material object. And adults, take heart: other fringed and appliquéd, design-worthy Polartec throws are especially for grown-ups.

EUROPEAN IMPORTS LTD.
2475 N. Elston Ave.
Chicago, IL 60647
(773) 227-0600
Hours: Thurs–Sat: 9–3:30—occasional weekends per year
Cash, check

Faithful customers of this producer/packager of gourmet foods and goodies have patronized European Imports' sales through three owners and two moves—and always line up before 9:00 A.M. of the first sale day. Depending on the season (and the leftovers), the wares (and prices) vary. Out-of-code 1-pound hunks of Swiss cheese go for $3; overstocks of spices, soups, and seasonings are a minimum of 25% off; even deluxe holiday food baskets, cookies, and crackers are in the affordable range. Open at least three Thursday-to-Saturday weekends a year; best get on the mailing list for advance notification.

GRASS ORCHIDS

2141 N. Southport Ave.
Chicago, IL 60614
(773) 342-8055
Hours: Once a year; hours vary
Cash, check

The kind of delicate, arty, ultrafeminine gowns that might have been favored by Laura Winfield in Tennessee Williams's *The Glass Menagerie* are Grass Orchids's stock in trade. Owner-designer Shirley Shoup regularly sells her mother-of-the-bride and evening dresses and hand-painted leathers, silks, and crepes to very high-end retailers. About two or three times a year, overstock, samples, and occasional returns are offered in Shoup's work space/showroom for dramatically low prices: elegant silk palazzo pants for $100, one-of-a-kind painted leather belts for $65, lace-encrusted outfits for $300–$500 (retail is usually in the four-figure range). Getting on the mailing list is the surest way to be notified of upcoming sales.

HART SCHAFFNER & MARX

101 N. Wacker Dr.
Chicago, IL 60606
(312) 372-6300
Hours: Once a year; hours vary
MC, V

Once or twice a year, around the lunch hour, streams of immaculately dressed executive men and women of all sizes and all ages file into 101 North Wacker. Upon their ascending to the designated floor and handing over the appropriate pass, the organized melee begins: the Hart Schaffner & Marx "employee" sale. People working in the building and Barrie Pace catalog subscribers/purchasers are issued passes, which also admit friends and family. And yes, for those shoppers preferring conservative and well-constructed business apparel, savings are spectacular: $35 for skirts; $75+ for men's slacks (depending on label); $150 for men's suits (again, priced according to label); $85 for women's overcoats. Selection and sizes vary; names include Austin Reed, Krizia (men), and Maggy London, among others.

The Learning Tree Parent & Teacher Store
4419 N. Ravenswood Ave.
Chicago, IL 60640
(773) 769-3737
Hours: Dates and hours vary
AE, DISC, MC, V

The results are in: the family that reads together does better in school . . . and in life. With that in mind, we strongly recommend a foray to the yearly sale of The Learning Tree Parent & Teacher Store. After all, educational goods are not only teacher necessities, but parental requirements too. During their annual warehouse sale, items are reduced to 20%–60% off their regular retail value. Some of the goods spotted at last year's sale include: helper workbooks, $1.50 (were $2.99); sticker packages (once $1.25–$1.50) discounted to 65¢–90¢; and assorted notepads, $1.50 (were $2.95). Call regarding dates . . . or watch the newspapers.

Maria V. Pinto Designs, Inc.
1006 S. Michigan Ave., 4th floor
Chicago, IL 60605
(312) 360-1330
Hours: Two times a year; hours vary
MC, V

From Chicago to New York and back: Art Institute grad Maria V. Pinto sharpened her considerable design skills under the tutelage of Geoffrey Beene, then returned home to ply feminine wares coveted by many of the tip-top tony retailers (no names here). Twice a year, she opens her studio-cum-workshop to sell samples to women very appreciative of European fabrics and classic lines; four-ply satinlike charmeuse tank tops pair with mixing or matching jackets, skirts, pants, and et ceteras in textiles such as tissue-thin silks, papery linens, metal tulles, and Venise laces. Prices are tantamount to a clearance, from $10 to $250, well below suggested retail. Call to join the mailing list.

THE SHELL GAME

1444 Old Skokie Rd.
Highland Park, IL 60035
(847) 831-4480
Hours: Twice a year; hours vary
Cash

Twice a year, in June and December, The Shell Game opens its doors to a ready, eager, and willing public. Why? One trek to the Highland Park suburb will disclose the reason for the queues: belts, hats, gloves, and scarves found in specialty stores across the country are now marked at wholesale prices. Examples from a recent winter sale: gloves from $4 to $8 (were $16 to $20); leather belts at $5 to $10 (once $20 to $50). A mailing-list postcard notifies prospective shoppers.

SMART CREATIONS INC. ★

3354 Commercial Ave.
Northbrook, IL 60062
(847) 272-3451
Hours: Twice a year; hours vary
MC, V

Even though this almost 40-year-old manufacturer of costume jewelry isn't open year-round, special shopping days do arise for the buying public—two each year, to be exact. Sales occur conveniently close to some special gift-buying occasions, such as Mother's Day and the Thanksgiving/Christmas season. Manufacturers' samples and overruns on necklaces, earrings, pins, bracelets, even women's belts can adorn you and your loved ones for mere bucks (say, three or five of 'em) instead of the retail price of $6 to $40. Plus, with the purchase of $15 or more, *Buying Retail Is Stupid!* readers are gifted with a pair of earrings. Call to ask about future sale dates and times.

WEBER-STEPHENS

200 E. Davis St.
Palatine, IL 60067
(847) 934-5700
Hours: Once a year; dates and hours vary
AE, MC, V

Tales grow tall when you ask about the origins of the patented round Weber kettle. Some say George Stephens, owner of this multimillion-dollar barbecue manufacturer, grabbed the round lid of a garbage can to slow down the coal fires. Others claim he sold it out of the back of a station wagon. Regardless, we're fortunate enough to be the headquarters for this innovator-producer. Once a year, during the best of summer, people from all over Illinois travel to stake out quality outdoor barbecue products at quality reductions. Hundreds of Weber grills are reduced from 40%–60% for the public during this gigantic tent sale. Hours and times of sale vary—call Weber-Stephens to determine schedules of future sales.

WILTON INDUSTRIES, INC.

2240 W. 75th St.
Woodridge, IL 60517
(630) 963-7100
Hours: Nine-day sales twice a year; hours vary
DISC, MC, V

The tents are visible from several blocks away, as are the lines of cars to be parked and hordes of people checking in and out. The occasion? A kitchen-boggling assortment (at equally mind-boggling prices) of bakeware, cake decorating equipment, photo frames, kitchen tools, and teakettles from Copco, Rowoco, and Western Gallery, all brands operating under the Wilton banner. Held twice a year (May and October) on the grounds, er, parking lot of corporate headquarters, this 9-day sale attracts literally hundreds to pore through 2,000 different products. Some of the real deals (they do change daily): $10 for a cow teakettle; $2.60 for a high-tech kitchen zester; $15 for a wooden bread box—usually all up to a 75% savings. Cooking up a storm.

ZSCH STUDIO
1807 W. Sunnyside Ave.
Chicago, IL 60640
(773) 878-0208
Hours: Twice a year; hours vary
Cash, check

Often in concert with Amy Rigg, sometimes solo, Lisa Zschunke of Zsch sells her hat, scarf, and jacket samples. The lines are simple; materials are elegant—such as an unusually patterned piqué, a sturdy polished cotton, or a tissue-thin linen. Since she's started to experiment with pants and skirts, an occasional item or two is for sale as well. Find, for instance, a hip-long black burlap jacket for $70 and a linen-rayon shirt for $40, well under wholesale.

Sports & Recreation

EXERCISE EQUIPMENT

FITNESS FACTORY OUTLET ✪
2875 S. 25th Ave.
Broadview, IL 60153
(800) 383-9300
Hours: Mon–Fri: 11–7; Sat & Sun: 11–5
AE, DISC, MC, V
◆ **Senior Discount:** 15% **Age:** 60+

That treadmill gathering dust in your closet could be joined (or replaced) by other exercise equipment . . . at much-reduced prices, thanks to the Fitness Factory Outlet. Only a few years old, this discounter actually started life as a mail-order catalog, then expanded to one retail store (with more to come). Plus, its more-than-80,000 square feet allow even nonexercisers to begin a wish list; factory-direct means a top-quality recumbent bike is $999 and home gyms start at $299. All equipment (including free weights, treadmills, and steppers, too) is tagged at up to 70% off. And *Buying Retail Is Stupid!* readers can work out another 10% discount by using the coupon in the back of the book.

GOLF

A GOLF OUTLET INC.

334 Georgetown Sq.
Wood Dale, IL 60191
(630) 227-0700
Hours: Tues–Fri: 10–6:30; Sat: 10–5
AE, DIN, DISC, MC, OPT, V

Tee up for one or for a foursome: golf, obviously, is the only sports specialty at A Golf Outlet. Owner Susan Raines, who calls her shop the bargain basement for serious amateur and pro golfers, acquires most of her first-quality wares from country-club golf shop liquidations. Apparel to wear on the links is usually 40%–75% off retail, boasting brands such as Fila, Izod, Polo, and Tommy Hilfiger. And equipment (including books and videos) starts at a 30% discount from such manufacturers as Ping, Taylor Made, Titleist, and Slazenger. Watch for her mega-blowouts during the first week of December and the third week of March; expanded hours during the season.

GOLF CLUBS FOR LESS ☆

650 E. Roosevelt Rd., Unit 111
Glen Ellyn, IL 60137
(630) 790-1201
Hours: Tues–Fri: 12–8; Sat: 10–5; Sun: 12–4
DISC, MC, V
◆ **Senior Discount:** 5% **Age:** 62+

Although Golf Clubs for Less specializes in "off brands" instead of pro-line golf clubs, deals are still there for the knowing—and the knowledgeable. Here, the latest technology is marked at huge savings. During our visit, we swung around the following: a set of irons for the low price of $179; graphites for only $280; and a set of three woods or graphites, $175 to $600. (Figure a normal discount of 40%–65% below retail.) Regardless of whether you live for the weekend links, any duffer will appreciate the extra $25 savings on any set of woods . . . available to *Buying Retail Is Stupid!* readers.

PRO SHOP WORLD OF GOLF

8130 N. Lincoln Ave.
Skokie, IL 60077
(847) 675-5286
Hours: Mon–Thurs: 10–8; Fri & Sat: 10–6; Sun: 11–5
AE, DISC, MC, V

Few nongolfers realize the importance of ranges to test equipment, let alone the distinction between men's and ladies', right- and left-hand clubs. (We pleaded total ignorance until a friend-player enlightened us.) The Pro Shop, established in 1953, caters to both novice and near-professional with services above and beyond low, low prices. Such as special manufacturers' days, featuring gifts with purchase, factory representatives, and raffles; willingness to take trade-ins; and the four test ranges. Some names and prices we witnessed: $9.99 for a dozen Wilson golf balls (originally $36); an extra 20% off all putters; $299.99 for a set of Spalding midsize irons.

SPORTING GOODS

CHICAGO SPORTS EXCHANGE ☆

4159 N. Western Ave.
Chicago, IL 60640
(773) 583-7283
Hours: Tues–Fri: 9–7; Sat: 9–3
DISC, MC, V

Where else but in this Land of Lincoln could you find a store specializing in new and used sports equipment—and live bait?! (No, we didn't sample the latter.) A precursor to Play It Again Sports by some 9 years, the Chicago Sports Exchange's rule of thumb: 50% less than retail on all previously owned stuff. Not only are team game accessories available, but the CSE guys also sell equipment for biking, camping, fishing, and skating (in addition to the "we got tired of" NordicTrack-ing and rowing machines). All products are reconditioned and raring to go; we snuck glances at $20+ adult Rollerblades in-line skates and a $40 Master Step. Flex your muscles, ladies and gents. And it gets even better with the 10% *Buying Retail Is Stupid!* coupon in hand, good on a $100 minimum purchase.

Sportmart Clearance Center

1800 N. Harlem Ave.
North Riverside, IL 60546
(708) 366-2439
Hours: Mon–Sat: 10–7; Sun: 10–6
DISC, MC, V

It's a day-to-day event at the Sportmart Clearance Center, since great prices on both apparel and equipment are quickly snatched up by eager buyers. Whether past-season or not, most of the merchandise is reduced by at least 50%, a boon to parents of rapidly growing kids. (As well as to adults adopting a new sport, changing sizes, or simply searching for deals on sports stuff.) What we saw on the floor: New Balance running shoes at $19.96 (were $39.96); $29.98 Astroblade in-line skates (retail is $59.96); and bunches of good-quality T-shirts starting at $5.

Winter & Water Sports

Pool-A-Rama Warehouse Outlet

3535 W. Ridge Rd.
Gary, IN 46408
(219) 980-0101
Hours: Mon–Fri: 10–8; Sat: 10–6; Sun: 11–5
AE, DISC, MC, V
◆ **Senior Discount:** 10% **Age:** 60+

The Midwest's outdoor summer swimming season is, unfortunately, way too short for many of the aquatically inclined. But the two warehouse outlets of Pool-A-Rama balance products for hot weather with other seasonal and year-round merchandise: spas, pool tables, artificial Christmas trees, foosball, and the like. The bonus, of course, is discounted wares, sometimes up to 50% off retail. A few samples: an 18-foot Trevi pool for $999 (elsewhere $1,250); a $1,399.99 solid oak, slate-topped Hercules pool table (retail $1,699.99); brand-name spas from $2,000 (three seats) to $4,200 (seven seats). Installation of pools is, of course, an additional charge.

South Holland, IL—Universal Pool City, 2 W. 166th St., (708) 339-6060

Surplus

AMAZING SAVINGS WAREHOUSE OUTLET

6141 N. Lincoln Ave.
Chicago, IL 60659
(773) 539-4000
Hours: Mon–Sat: 9–9; Sun: 10–7
MC, V

Closeout items at prices well below suggested wholesale price (SWAP) are the major draw at the four Chicagoland locations of this regional chain. Selection varies with every visit, and brand names dominate: Lego 266-piece building set for $9.99; Jockey sports bras for $2.99 and $3.99; Foster Grant and other name-brand specs for $2.49. Fragrances, cosmetics, housewares, and toys are just a few of the one thousand offerings.

Broadview—17th and Cermak Rd., (708) 343-8080
Morton Grove—7204 Dempster St., (847) 965-2929
Wheeling—889 W. Dundee Rd., (847) 537-1000

CREATIVE REUSE WAREHOUSE

721 W. O'Brien St.
Chicago, IL 60607
(312) 421-3640
Hours: Tues, Thurs, Sat: 9–5; Sun: 12–4
Cash, check

An environmentally friendly gold mine for kids, students, teachers, and anyone with a creative bent (though in a less-than-desirable urban location). Creative Reuse, "where discards become discoveries," offers excess or surplus corporate "stuff" at literally pennies. With a few exceptions, shopping bags can be loaded with everything officelike—paper, clips, tweezers, binders, and lots of et ceteras—for about $3. Other examples: 25¢ legal pads, $5 rubber stoppers, 50¢ hospital food trays, $3 used bowling shoes. A new kind of archeological dig.

THE OUTLET STORE ★

5402 N. Elston Ave.
Chicago, IL 60630
(773) 685-5770
Hours: Mon–Fri: 9–5; Sat: 10–5
DISC, MC, V

Leftovers, in this case, make for great "cents": "If you find it cheaper elsewhere, it's yours free," insists Ben Kiernan, owner of this Outlet outlet. What's here? A ton of stuff, mainly overstocks from top-notch companies, direct merchants, bankruptcies, auctions. Family clothing and shoes; household and garden materials; and bedding and electronics. Prices generally represent at least a 60% discount, and sometimes more. Items, because of the excellent savings, do turn over rapidly. Available the day we stopped in: a Panasonic wet/dry shaver (regularly $219.95) for $59.95; $9.75 kids' Keds in your basic white ribbed oxford (were $24.95); and must-have doggie bomber jackets at $4.99 (list is $24.99). To ensure that all experience the thrill of the hunt, The Outlet Store is offering *Buying Retail Is Stupid!* readers an additional 10% discount.

Z WALLIS/ARMY/NAVY SURPLUS DEPOT

4647 N. Broadway
Chicago, IL 60640
(773) 275-1386
Hours: Mon–Thurs, Sat: 9–5:45; Fri: 9–6:45; Sun: 10–4
AE, DISC, MC, V

Although the grunge look has passed into the annals of classic fashion mistakes, it is still possible to emulate the "not much money" look for, yes, not much money. Best places to find those kinds of duds, dudes? Army-Navy Surplus stores. And, for our dollars, some of the better bargains are found at Z Wallis in the Uptown neighborhood. Even those weighing in against U.S. military bureaucracy won't have much to complain about here: patchwork-leather fanny packs at $2.99; camouflaged H_2O bottles at $1.49; paratrooper jackets starting at $15. Being patriotic pays.

Toys, Dolls & Games

CHILDREN'S GIFT OUTLET ★

289 Northfield Rd.
Northfield, IL 60093
(847) 441-5975
Hours: Mon–Sat: 9–5; Sun: 12–5
MC, V

McDonald's, move over: those hot and trendy Beanie Babies coveted by the younger set are plentiful here at last report, as are a host of other toys, games, books, party favors, and accessories. Markie Carlson, president of this national wholesale distributor, buys primarily with the ages of birth to 9 or 10 years in mind, but a few adult items (suede bridge cloths, scissor chatelaines) slip in too, with discounts ranging from 20% to 50%. Add to these savings some unusual services: gift wrapping, hand-painted personalization, monogramming, and a birthday club. And mark your road maps for a Northfield trip with the grandkids—especially with another 10% savings from *Buying Retail Is Stupid!*.

CUT-RATE TOYS

5409 W. Devon Ave.
Chicago, IL 60646
(773) 763-5740
Hours: Mon–Sat: 9–5:30; Sun: 11–3
DISC, MC, V

To quote one of our most highly esteemed bargain hunters: "If Cut-Rate has what you're looking for, there's a good chance they'll have the lowest price anywhere." Believe it: owner-operator and chief dolly-discounter Marvin Hecht's been in business since 1953—and his toy prices are among the best. His selections span the globe; both imports and exports get the reduced-price treatment. A few April '97 examples: $16.99 Russian Barbie; Crayola tabletop easel at $11.99; Little Tikes farm for $19.99; a wondrous Playmobil dollhouse at $149.99. And look on the dollar table for rock-bottom bargains.

DEVON TOYS

2424 W. Devon Ave.
Chicago, IL 60659
(773) 973-0194
Hours: Mon–Sat: 9–8; Sun: 10–6
Cash, check

Their full-page advertising is unmistakable. As are their prices: a Pioneer Shopkeeper Barbie for $14.99 ($29.99 regularly); Beanie Babies for $3.99 (we didn't find any of the "most wanted"); and salon hairbrushes for 99¢ (instead of $5). Though best known for its toys, this "heart of Devon discount" store also features gifts, party goods, greeting cards, and miscellanea at prices up to 75% less than retail. Or, if a particular doll or plaything is destined to be on a favorite niece, nephew, or grandchild's list, Devon Toys has a prepay, preorder policy to ship the latest Barbie or toy craze when available.

Travel

LUGGAGE & TRAVEL ACCESSORIES

IRV'S LUGGAGE WAREHOUSE

3139 Dundee Rd.
Northbrook, IL 60068
(847) 205-5585
Hours: Mon–Wed, Fri: 9–6; Thurs: 9–8; Sat: 10–5; Sun: 10–4
AE, DISC, MC, V
◆ **Senior Discount:** 10% **Age:** 60+

The folks at Irv's make absolutely no bones about their discount status—from 20% to 70% off retail every day, 7 days a week, 12 months a year. Plus, they carefully point to differences among luggage sets, explain irregulars (no guarantees), and ferret out bargains that *best* match your needs. All the big bag names are present: Hartmann, Andiamo, Briggs & Riley, Delsey, Tumi, Dakota (a Tumi cousin), Samsonite, et al. Get ready to pack your bags!

Chicago—820 W. North Ave., (312) 787-4787
Elk Grove Village—2408 E. Oakton St., (847) 437-4787

Kaehler Luggage Outlet

176 S. Waukegan Rd.
Deerfield, IL 60015
(847) 498-1888
Hours: Mon–Fri: 10–9; Sat: 10–5:30; Sun: 12–5
AE, MC

Buying discount luggage can sometimes be dicey. Is it irregular, discontinued, or just leftover stock? Part of the appeal of the Kaehler outlet is that the firm has been in business since 1920; obviously, then, they stand behind the merchandise. Find here traveling bags for 20%–50% (sometimes more) off retail. An irregular tweed Hartmann garment bag was priced at $359.50 (once $535). And check the tag on an Atlantic floral suitcase, reduced from $140 to $49. Briefcases, leather goods, and a few handbags are also discounted.
Elm Grove, WI—13315 Watertown Plank Rd., (414) 784-3315, Mon–Fri: 9:30–5:30; Sat & Sun: 9:30–5

Travel Services

Condominium Holidays

11470 Sparrow Dr.
Woodstock, IL 60098
(815) 334-8333
Hours: Mon–Fri: 9–5; Sat: 10–5
MC, V

Want to visit your children who've just moved but refuse to stay at their house? How about a romantic getaway to some far-off island? However attractive the location, the site becomes even more alluring with the vision of savings dancing in our heads. (All the more bucks to squander on native souvenirs.) The answer? Condominium Holidays. By specializing in rental of condos, cottages, and sometimes houses, this travel service company takes away the pain of booking an overpriced hotel from Hawaii to Australia. For instance, a Maui studio condo, on the beach with a kitchenette and a pullout bed, $89 a day. (PS: This is the lowest, rock-bottom deal available.) Or the land of Disney in Orlando starts at $49, extending into the hundreds, depending on your wallet.

Hot Rooms
1 E. Erie St., Suite 225
Chicago, IL 60611
(773) 468-7666
Hours: 24-hour hot line
AE, DISC, MC, V

Finding a decent hotel room at a decent price in our fair town can sometimes produce more stress than it's worth—especially during prime convention times. Hot Rooms, on the other hand, does everything possible to provide a quality night's sleep for a quality price. They work with Chicago hoteliers and a few here and there around O'Hare. Prices depend on dates and availability; both single rooms and doubles are offered. Some of the better prices worth noting: a single at the Best Western for $75, a double for $85; and at the Executive Plaza, singles and doubles with a river view at $94 per night. The highest price? The Renaissance Hotel in Leo Burnett's headquarters for $195 per night.

Variety & Thrift Stores

By now, the average astute, inquisitive, and perspicacious *Buying Retail Is Stupid!* reader has discovered that certain areas in Chicago are simply loaded with bargain stores.

That reader is right. Roosevelt Road is one obvious destination; Devon Avenue, another. But there are other strips and streets that might yield savings we overlooked. Two that come to mind: up and down the extremely long stretch of Harlem Avenue, south to north. And Milwaukee Avenue, starting at 1200, to 3000 north (though there may be a few worthy *Buying Retail Is Stupid!* outlets on the southern end of this street). And don't forget Belmont Avenue, from about 1800 west to the Kennedy Expressway—teeming with merchandise of the antiques and collectibles variety.

Since everything in the land of discount can change in a heartbeat (we just noted, for instance, the opening of a Church's Shoe Outlet on State Street downtown), let us know if you've discovered any new, slash-to-the-bones, below-wholesale outlet or area flea market we haven't included.

AMERICAN SCIENCE & SURPLUS

Milwaukee at Foster and Central
Gladstone Corners Shopping Center
Chicago, IL 60646
(773) 763-0313
Hours: Mon–Fri: 10–6; Thurs: 10–9; Sat: 9–5; Sun: 11–5
DISC, MC, V

A bold warning should appear on the American Science & Surplus door: "Enter with curious kids at your own risk." With a store slogan such as "Incredible stuff, incredible prices," parents' wallets will rapidly be depleted. A recent trip (with two kids in tow) netted slimy-brain-look-alike key chains, music box innards, yellow and black plastic crime scene tape, and fish scale bracelets, each well under $10. Since 1937, a day's delight for children and adults.

Geneva—33 W. 361, (630) 232-2882
Milwaukee, WI—6901 W. Oklahoma, (414) 541-7777
Orland Park—15142 LaGrange Rd., (708) 873-9270

CHICAGO AVENUE DISCOUNT

1637 W. Chicago Ave.
Chicago, IL 60622
(312) 226-0004
Hours: Mon–Fri: 9:30–7; Sat: 9:30–6; Sun: 10–6
AE, DISC, MC, V

Regimented clothing for work has, for the most part, been banished from the corporate scene (except, of course, for certain industries). Yet, at times uniforms are still needed for the younger set—boys and girls attending parochial or private schools, as one example. One place to shop? Chicago Avenue Discount, which offers much more than the standard pants, shirts, jumpers, and skirts (from $5.94 to $19.93 each piece). Other family members will be outfitted here too: infant necessities (e.g., $29.93 Graco walker); male and female steel-toed work shoes ($8.93 to $16.93); bed linens (a king sheet set for $22.93); even a $13.79 old-time breeze box if summer air-conditioning goes on the fritz. An inexpensive, any-season, stock-up-on-basics store.

DAVECO DOLLARS AND CENTS ☆
2454 W. Devon Ave.
Chicago, IL 60659
(773) 743-1058
Hours: Mon, Thurs: 10–8; Tues, Wed, Fri: 10–6; Sat: 9:30–6; Sun: 11–5; Holidays: 11–5
MC, V

A name such as Daveco Dollars and Cents, plus its two locations on nearly wholesale Devon Avenue, virtually assures consumers of some good deals on household and health and beauty aids closeouts. Among the February sales: 2.5 ounces of Norell cologne for $19.99 (once $44); a 6.4-ounce tube of Crest toothpaste for $2; an urban-life wire-and-wheeled shopping cart at $21.99. Or how about 200 square feet of slightly damaged (the box, that is) Glad Wrap for $2? Make sure you carry enough of the green stuff, since they prefer no credit cards. *Buying Retail Is Stupid!* readers with a $10+ purchase (and the Daveco lucky-dollar coupon) will get a buck back at the cash register.

Dollars & Sense, Chicago—2455 W. Devon Ave., (773) 743-2708

GREAT DOLLAR VALUE ☆
4200 W. Belmont Ave.
Chicago, IL 60641
(773) 286-5203
Hours: Mon–Fri: 10–9; Sat: 9–7; Sun: 10–6
AE, DIN, DISC, MC, V

In 1986 it began life as Sportique. Today it's known as Great Dollar Value, reflecting this store's expansion into housewares and giftwares. Among the brands found at Stuart Timoner's shop are The Limited and Rubbermaid, wares that realize savings from 30% to 50%. (And *Buying Retail Is Stupid!* readers will pocket another 10% with the coupon if their purchase is $25 or more.)

JP Electronics of Illinois

2425 W. Devon Ave.
Chicago, IL 60659
(773) 761-4422
Hours: Mon–Sun: 10:30–7:30
MC, V
◆ **Senior Discount:** 5% **Age:** 62+

Another Chicago shopping stop on the way to Europe and points east: down the street from International Video is a similarly stuffed store, JP Electronics (was JP's Super Store), featuring primarily electronics to be shipped overseas (220 volts). In fact, except for a larger quantity of bigger-screen TVs, the merchandise is virtually identical to that of its competitor—audio and video equipment, appliances, some luggage, and the famous bric-a-brac, potpourri, or whaddayacallit. Watch for unpriced items; it might be best to check costs elsewhere first. One of the tags we did see indicated a good deal: 13-quart DuPont Silverstone heavy-gauge stockpot at $39.

Star Distributors

3500 N. Milwaukee Ave.
Chicago, IL 60641
(773) 725-7770
Hours: Mon–Sat: 9–6; Sun: 10–5
AE, DISC, MC, V

Star distributes a veritable panoply of the items that, at least once in a while, every household needs. Things such as irons, luggage, extension cords, kitchen miscellanea, and other small appliances (some wired for the USA, others for overseas). And everything's priced to sell in the old-fashioned variety-store kind of format. Diligent (and patient) shoppers can find an eight-language translator for $29.90; 26-inch canvas pullman luggage at $13.50; a large duffel bag for $9.50; and a small Gold Star microwave (with turntable) at $99.90. In the heart of yet another Windy City discount district.

SUBURBAN NEWS

3300 W. Devon Ave.
Lincolnwood, IL 60659
(847) 679-5577
Hours: Mon–Sat: 8–9; Sun: 9–6
MC, V

How many convenience stores can also truthfully claim to be discounters? Suburban News certainly can. Close to Chicago and south Evanston, this nondescript store specializes in selected grocery items, health and beauty aids, and cigarettes—all at good prices. Recent weekly specials: a four-pack of Cottonelle bathroom tissue at 89¢; three 32-ounce spritz bottles of Fantastik for $5; and eight 20-ounce bottles of Coke for $2.99. Stock varies; expect at least a 20% savings.

Elmwood Park—Discount People, 2900 N. Harlem Ave., (708) 453-2433
Niles—Goldfinger, 7227 N. Harlem Ave., (847) 647-7460

WORLD DISTRIBUTORS

3420 N. Milwaukee Ave.
Chicago, IL 60641
(773) 777-2345
Hours: Mon–Sat: 9–6; Sun: 11–5
DISC, MC, V
◆ **Senior Discount:** Depends on item **Age:** 60+

Forget buying electronics here. (Besides, ABT and the megastores give the best deals.) Instead, focus on World for the stuff that makes a house a home, for the wares and toys and equipment that can transform an any-age human into a kid again. (We, at least, had a great deal of fun meandering around different aisles and saying to each other: "What about?" or "Whaddaya think?") Brand names nestle next to knockoffs; the products—toys, housewares, fragrances, equipment—are as varied as the store's shoppers. We giggled at $2.50 for a 3.3-ounce Claudio eau de toilette (a sure substitute for Giorgio), and stocked up on individual pieces of silverware for 33¢ and a host of kitchen gadgets (from 99¢ to $1.19). Also on our "maybe buy" list: a 30-piece highway car set for $8.99; a life-size doll for $9.50. We are the World!

B

Local Stores of Regional and/or National Discounters

Many of our top personal choices for shopping are national or regional chains and are difficult to categorize. Here's one example: should Marshall's be included in clothing & accessories, food & beverages, or home furnishings? Obviously, there are many chain discounters with a variety of merchandise.

We tackled our problem by the strategy "divide and conquer." Just as Section A is strictly local stores, Section B represents Chicagoland discounters with a tie to regional or national store chains. Use both sections when you're truly hunting for that one-of-a-kind item. Or consult the Index or Contents if you're puzzled.

Appliances

Sears Retail Outlet Store

2065 N. George
Melrose Park, IL 60160
(708) 216-2870
Hours: Mon–Sat: 9–5:30; Sun: 12–5
AE, DISC, MC, Sears, V

The harder side of Sears is well represented in this giant retailer's four outlet stores in the suburbs of Chicago. Appliances or furniture

with slight dings, dents, or scratches find a new home (and new prices) in the 40,000-square-foot Melrose Park or the 28,000-square-foot Carol Stream warehouse or in Matteson. Showcased along with the Kenmore name are other top brands such as Amana, GE, and Zenith. A sample of the discounts: a 27-cubic-foot Amana refrigerator at $899 (was $1,599) and a Kenmore electronic washing machine at $399.98 (was $909.99). According to our sources, Sears has outlets in many areas of the country; check with a local Sears.
Carol Stream—455 S. Schmale Rd., (630) 690-0380
Crestwood—155th St. and Cicero Ave., (708) 429-6738
Matteson—600 Lincoln Mall, (708) 283-4000

Art

THE GREAT FRAME UP
280 Hawthorn Corners
Vernon Hills, IL 60061
(847) 680-1880
Hours: Mon–Fri: 10–9; Sat: 10–6; Sun: 12–5
AE, DISC, MC, V

It sure doesn't look like a 25-year-old franchise. But Franklin Park–headquartered The Great Frame Up, now with stores in 30 states (and 26 in our area), claims a quarter century of expertise in helping folks mat and frame posters and artwork themselves. Beginning at about $3 a foot, you can indeed mount a picture yourself (they cut the materials to spec). Or if nothing aesthetic suits your fancy, all stores have their own selections of discounted, ready-to-hang wall art. There's the Chicago skyline ($89.95); a Michael Jordan slam-dunking ($29.95); and a Michael–Scottie Pippen–Dennis Rodman photo pose for $80.95 (was $110). And yes, other graphics besides Bulls team members are available as well.
26 locations in Chicagoland; see the Yellow Pages

Arts, Crafts & Hobbies

Art Supplies

Pearl

225 W. Chicago Ave.
Chicago, IL 60610
(312) 915-0200
Hours: Mon–Sat: 9–7; Sun: 12–5
AE, DISC, MC, V

Henri Matisse would be thrilled: just picture a portable, totable wood French Julian easel at $169.95, instead of the $500 list price. Similar deals on other arts and crafts supplies are what make Pearl one of the fastest-growing discount art supermarkets. Now with 19 independent stores in 11 states (this is the only Heartland outlet), Pearl started as a New York house paint supplier in the '50s. The rest, as they say, is history: at least a 20% discount on all books and supplies, an inventory including virtually all known arts and crafts manufacturers (imagine a dozen different lines of oils alone), artist salespeople, and weekend demos.

Craft & Floral Supplies

Michael's

7225 W. Dempster St.
Niles, IL 60714
(800) MICHAELS
Hours: Mon–Sat: 9–9; Sun: 10–6
AE, DISC, MC, V

Almost anything that makes a house a home can be bought at Michael's—at a good price. Even "regular" prices here sometimes beat the "low, low costs" other discounters advertise. Knitting yarn, for instance, usually sells at $1.39 for 4 ounces; a host of wicker accents, from a magazine rack to a vanity with mirror, is tagged at $12.99 each piece. With 21 Chicagoland stores, this national Texas-based chain stocks both seasonal holiday (Easter, Christmas) and evergreen items ready to make or accessorize with.
20 stores in Chicagoland; call (800) MICHAELS for locations

FABRICS & NOTIONS

CALICO CORNERS
1525 N. Wells
Chicago, IL 60610
(312) 280-9707
Hours: Mon–Thurs: 10–7; Fri & Sat: 10–6; Sun: 12–5
DISC, MC, V

There are two major differences between Calico Corners and its nearest competitor (other than slightly higher prices at Calico): one, all fabrics are clearly tagged either first quality or quality seconds. And two, they reveal actual mill names (e.g., Cyrus Clark, P. Kaufmann, and Ralph Lauren). Here, one of the famed Mr. Polo textiles (a Kensington tartan) is marked $31.99, while almost imperceptible seconds of a major mill are priced $8.99 per yard (instead of the regular $24). Fabrications and custom furniture, called "Brandywine," along with the trims and accessories of home furnishings, are also available.

Barrington—400 W. Northwest Hwy., (847) 304-0080
Deerfield—495 Lake Cook Rd., (847) 480-1900
Hinsdale—777 N. York Rd., (630) 920-1955
Wilmette—105 S. Green Bay Rd., (847) 256-1500

LOOMCRAFT
640 N. LaSalle St.
Chicago, IL 60610
(312) 587-0055
Hours: Mon–Thurs: 10–8; Fri & Sat: 10–6; Sun: 11–5

On our initial foray into Loomcraft, we couldn't help but notice a "hold" sign on a bolt of fabric marked for Gordon's restaurant. The secret of Loomcraft, then, is out: incredible savings (from 30% to 70% off) on no-name, high-end fabrics where in-stock merchandise is usually not priced more than $29.99 a yard. Here and there a few mills print their names: Anju, Portfolio, P. Kaufmann. But, with the goal of saving major bucks and knowing that your fabric of choice is a (pick one) Colefax & Fowler, Schumacher, Waverly, or other status textiles, it's worth buying anonymously—and bragging later.

16 stores in Chicagoland; call (800) LOOMCRAFT for locations

Minnesota Fabrics
3326 W. Belmont Ave.
Chicago, IL 60618
(773) 463-0180
Hours: Mon–Fri: 9:30–9; Sat: 9:30–6; Sun: 11–5
DISC, MC, V
◆ **Senior Discount:** 10% first Wed of each month **Age:** 55+

Business and national magazines report that the sewing revolution has returned, perhaps a nod to the cocooning movement. No matter the reason, Minnesota Fabrics stores always seem to be busy—with continual sales on their already discounted merchandise. In fact, the name of this national chain is somewhat of a misnomer, since wares also include drapery fixtures, yarns, crafts, seasonal decorations, and notions. Bargain bins add even further luster to sewers' savings.

26 locations in Chicagoland; see the Yellow Pages

Automobile Needs

Because we pride ourselves on being gear-phobes (i.e., knowing zip about the interior workings of a car), the numbers in the advertisements for national tire discount chains didn't faze us in the least.

That is, until car-racing aficionados (and friends) explained that we really, truly ought to understand the system of numerals and letters. So, we pass that knowledge along to you, dear *Buying Retail Is Stupid!* readers, for edification, information, and success in winning the game of Trivial Pursuit.

Here's the sequence, to take an example:

97S P225/70R15 M/S

- **97S:** This initial section is called the "service description"; 97 is the tire's load index, showing the maximum weight a tire can carry at its speed rating or S. 97S means the tire could carry 1,609 pounds at its certified top speed of 112 mph.
- **P225:** The following letter—in this case, P—indicates the kind of vehicle the tire fits; P is for passenger. There are at least two other

designations: LT means light truck, and T means Temporary Spare. 225 is the tire's width in millimeters.

- **70:** This two-digit number is called the "aspect ratio," or the tire's sidewall height as a percentage of its width. A low ratio means a shorter sidewall, which can improve steering response.
- **R15:** This letter-number set stands for tire construction and rim diameter. First, the R stands for radial, which comprises close to 100% of the passenger tire market. Second, 15 is the tire's rim diameter in inches, which could range from 12 to 20.
- **M/S:** Last, but definitely not least in the Midwest, is mud and snow certification, signaling improved starting, stopping, and driving performance in foul weather.

Parts & Accessories

Forest City Auto Parts

4952 S. Cicero Ave.
Chicago, IL 60632
(773) 284-8787
Hours: Mon–Fri: 8–10; Sat: 8–9; Sun: 9–6
DISC, MC, V

Among the big three—Murray's, Pep Boys, and the 67 stores of Forest City—are literally pennies of differentiation. What one may sell for $3.79 is priced $3.84 by another. And so on. What you will find at Forest City are continual sales, tons of brand-name choices, and generally helpful advice. (Unless, of course, you really can't tell batteries from belts . . . and then we strongly suggest a course in Car 101.) Rebates, either mail-in or instant, are abundant; prices, from combo wrench sets to enamel paint, highly competitive. A June sampling: 84¢ for STP oil treatment; $2.29 for your choice of liquid or paste Turtle Wax; and Zymol car polish for $13.99.
66 locations in Chicagoland; see the Yellow Pages

J.C. WHITNEY CO.

2319 S. Throop St.
Chicago, IL 60608
(312) 431-6000
Hours: Mon, Thurs: 9–7; Tues, Wed, Fri, Sat: 9–6; Sun: 9–4:30
AE, DISC, MC, V

You could choose to walk in and be mesmerized by the 55,000 auto parts and accessories offered by J.C. Whitney (formerly known as Warshawsky . . . and idolized by mechanics and collectors). Or select, instead, a specific item from one of their many thick catalogs and let your fingers (and credit cards) do the shopping. Known since 1915 for providing hard-to-find older-car thingamabobs, Whitney offers an incredible assortment of choices—at better prices (from 10% to 40% discount) than the standard car dealer. A $2.98 VX-6 battery additive (regularly $3.98) fights the dead-battery syndrome. And a 30-piece screwdriver bit set for $8.99 (rather than $11.99) guarantees that do-it-yourselfers will have versatile tools in one convenient place.

MURRAY'S DISCOUNT AUTO STORES

2120 S. Oak Park Ave.
Berwyn, IL 60402
(708) 484-4220
Hours: Mon–Fri: 8–9; Sat: 8–7; Sun: 9–5
AE, DISC, MC, V
◆ **Senior Discount:** Depends on item **Age:** 65+

A car boy's delight: headquartered in Bellville, Michigan, and operating in five major markets with 64+ stores, Murray's offers both basic and the more sophisticated parts for deliberate auto know-nothings as well as amateur mechanics. Forget buying car essentials at gas stations; we found necessities such as wiper blades, motor oil, filters, spark plugs, and windshield washer fluid at excellent prices here. (And though we know that Murray's tags on products such as long block engines and disc brake pads are decent, experts have advised that remanufactured and reconditioned parts are probably less expensive.) A recent auto stop at one of our 12

Murray's reveals: window washer solvent for 79¢ a gallon; Valvoline motor oil at 66¢ a quart (after rebate).
12 locations in Chicagoland; see the Yellow Pages

PARTS USA AUTO WAREHOUSE

2255 W. Touhy Ave.
Chicago, IL 60645
(773) 743-9474
Hours: Mon–Fri: 7–9; Sat: 7–8; Sun: 9–6
AE, DIN, DISC, MC, V

Once upon a time, and not so long ago either, rebates and coupons were unofficially declared dead. But, they live on at the auto parts discounters, who'll fight for every consumer penny and haggle best prices from every manufacturer. Good news for us *Buying Retail Is Stupid!* readers looking to find accessories at decent savings whether we shop at Pep Boys or Parts USA. This national chain, with five stores here, offers pretty much the same mix of gearhead merchandise—from oils and waxes and lubricants to heavy metal stuff such as headlights and radiators and engines. More than 1,700 parts, branded and not, as well as repair manuals (Chilton and Haynes diagnostics): zoom in on AC Delco oil filters starting at $2.99 or LeBra front headlights/bumper protection from $49.99 up.
Six locations in Chicagoland; see the White Pages

PEP BOYS

2604 N. Elston Ave.
Chicago, IL 60647
(773) 395-4444 or (800) PEP-BOYS
Hours: Mon–Fri: 7–9; Sat: 7–8; Sun: 9–6
AE, DISC, MC, V

No, it's not a new kind of cheerleading team. Pep Boys, an East Coast stalwart (aka at one time Manny, Moe & Jack), has invaded the Midwest to threaten both discount auto parts warehouses and installation specialists. Because, with a smile, a set of certified technicians will cheerfully give you estimates on labor, such as tune-ups ($44.99 and up), an AC quick check ($19.99), and brake service

beginning at $79.99. They also sell the stuff that makes our cars purr, hum, and run, from Castrol gear oil ($3.39) to AC spark plugs ($1.14) and sets of tires.
15 stores in Chicagoland; call (800) PEP-BOYS for locations

TRAK AUTO, SUPER TRAK, SUPER TRAK WAREHOUSE

5415 N. Broadway
Chicago, IL 60640
(773) 728-0505
Hours: Hours vary; check with individual stores
DISC, MC, V

There's Trak Auto, Super Trak, and Super Trak Warehouse. And, if you're anything like the average car owner, you'll head for the latter two—with greater selections. Almost any product that makes automobiles go faster, smoother, without noises or bumps in the day or night is here at a discount, which will make under-the-hooders' work much easier. Like Wal-Marts, these stores stand by their everyday low prices: "We will meet any competitor's price—advertised or not, on identical items." And we especially like their offer of free "loaner tools," available at Super Trak and its warehouse (though, quite frankly, we'd never borrow them being un-handy by nature). Well-respected names and private labels populate their floors: Bosch wiper blades from $5.59 to $11.99 (20% savings); your choice of Trak brake fluid, engine degreaser, or oil treatment for 88¢; Heet antifreeze at two for 98¢.
35 Trak Auto, 36 Super Trak, 9 Super Trak Warehouse stores in Chicagoland; see the Yellow Pages

RENTALS

ENTERPRISE RENT-A-CAR

6200 Touhy Ave.
Niles, IL 60174
(847) 647-9695
Hours: Mon–Fri: 7:30–6; Sat: 9–12
AE, DISC, MC, V

Wheels are rented for simple reasons: an unfortunate car crash, a complete auto reengineering, or cousin Bob decided to hog your vehicle for the weekend. Whatever, we vote for Enterprise. First, we love to be picked up and dropped off at our high-rise home (sorta like having your own chauffeur). Second, the prices won't dent our checkbook; there's at least a 10% savings off regular car rental rates—and even more, if someone else is footing the tab (such as your insurance company). And third, weekend rates are usually the best in the area. Start your weekend anytime on Friday and end it by 10:00 A.M. Monday for savings like: A Ford Escort with 500 free miles for $59.97; a Pontiac Grand Am or Chevy Corsica for $74.97; and an Altima for the low rate of $89.97. Weekly rates vary. Anyway, smooth savings help pave the way for a smooth ride.

16+ locations in Chicagoland; see the Yellow Pages, or call (800) RENT-A-CAR for locations

Rent-a-Wreck
3519 N. Lincoln Ave.
Chicago, IL 60635
(773) 281-1111 or (800) 616-6886
Hours: Hours vary
All major credit cards

Got a dead battery but need to be somewhere at noon—and our beloved CTA/Metra public transportation is out of the question? Well, apply to Rent-a-Wreck to abolish car worries. And no, don't let the name scare you—the autos supplied are simply slightly dinged or dented or scratched, not totaled, usually with a high five-digit odometer—lots of miles. (Should you rent a wreck for more than a day or two, our advice: ask for the best car and rate available.) Weekly rates include: a Chevy Cavalier for $24.95 a day (this averages out to $140 a week) plus 100 miles free per day and 20¢ a mile thereafter. A Ford Escort for a weekend jaunt will run $69.95 with 300 miles free (20¢ for each mile after 300). Pickup for weekend rates begins at your convenience on Friday, and the car must be returned Monday by noon.

9+ locations in Chicagoland; see the White Pages, or call (800) 616-6886 for locations

Repairs

All Tune and Lube

900 N. Lake St.
Mundelein, IL 60060
(847) 566-6100
Hours: Mon–Fri: 8–6; Sat: 8–4
DISC, MC, V

Sometimes franchisees act independently of their parent company . . . and charge very different prices from colleagues, even those in neighboring suburbs. Which is one reason why recommending auto service technicians in any metropolitan area can be so precarious. (Another reason is that service of any kind, because of its dependence on the individual technician and individual customer, is extremely quirky. One car owner could have a great tune-up; a second, a completely horrific experience.) On our own, we favor the Mundelein branch of All Tune and Lube, a national franchise chain based in Metairie, Louisiana (with 19 stations in our area). With a direct-mail coupon, their oil change and lube runs about $12.90 (it's $20 at our dealership). And their technical services range from free brake inspections to 30/60/90 factory-scheduled maintenance. Check each store for policies, hours, and prices.

18 stores in Chicagoland; call (800) 935-8863 for locations

Tires

Discount Tire Co., Inc.

18W520 Roosevelt Rd.
Lombard, IL 60148
(630) 953-9091
Hours: Mon–Fri: 8:30–6; Sat: 8:30–5
AE, DISC, MC, V

Consider your driving habits before purchasing tires, advise our car experts. It may be, for instance, that all four tires don't need to be replaced if you have front-wheel drive. Or that high-performance tires aren't really necessary if the auto is driven only on weekends or

does only a 10-mile daily round-trip to work. Armed with that information, get in the groove with one of the three national tire discount retailers—this time, Discount Tires Co. with 300+ stores nationally and four in our area. Though they do promote brands such as BF Goodrich, Michelin, and Pirelli, much of their advertising centers on no-name tires with low prices (four steel radials for $60, indeed). Make sure you ask about extras such as state environmental or disposal fees, aligning, and balancing.
Bloomingdale—86 Stratford Dr., (630) 529-2003
Countryside—5505 S. LaGrange Rd., (708) 579-9438
Joliet—2845 Plainfield Rd., (815) 436-0906

JUST TIRES
3400 N. Lincoln Ave.
Chicago, IL 60657
(773) 348-5433
Hours: Mon–Fri: 7–8; Sat: 7–6; Sun: 9–5
AE, MC, V

The only way, we've found, to truly compare prices is to clip ads and travel from store to store, looking at similar products and listening to the "what we offer" spiel. Unlike most of its competitors, Just Tires lives up to its billing: no brakes or discs, struts or shocks sold—simply deals on wheels. Many of the familiar brand names are stocked, with the emphasis on Goodyear and private labels; plus they feature a 125% price guarantee as well as certified technicians and mechanics. Fifteen Chicagoland locations for this 65-store national chain mean that their offer of "low prices . . . fast service" is probably justified.
14 stores in Chicagoland; call (800) TIRES-FAST for locations

Tire America
6520 W. Fullerton Ave.
Chicago, IL 60635
(773) 622-2212
Hours: Mon–Fri: 7:30–8; Sat: 7:30–5; Sun: 10–4
AE, DISC, MC, Sears, Tire America, V
◆ **Senior Discount:** 5% **Age:** 65+

The worst place to buy tires, according to our racing car expert, is at any car dealer's shop, since all equipment must be marked up a certain percentage to ensure profits. On the other hand, some of the better deals for tires fitting non-motorsport cars will be found at one of three national discounters. In the process of a name change to NTB National Tire & Battery, Tire America, owned by Sears and headquartered in Chicago, has all the major brands at a 30% savings. Certified mechanics mount, balance, and align. New services—brake discs and drums, shocks and struts—are continually being offered (and couponed). And chances are, one of the 18+ Chicagoland locations is nearby.

18+ locations in Chicagoland; see the Yellow Pages

Beauty Supplies

The Cosmetic Center
2817 N. Broadway
Chicago, IL 60657
(773) 935-2600
Hours: Mon–Fri: 10–9; Sat: 10–7; Sun: 11–6
DISC, MC, V

An alert to the Makeup Brigade: the hunt for cosmetics and fragrance savings on national brands such as Estee Lauder, Lancôme, and Revlon has ended. Because the regional (in Maryland, New Jersey, North Carolina, Pennsylvania, and Virginia, in addition to Illinois) Cosmetic Center chain, although it doesn't exactly slash prices, does cut a modest 15%–20% off retail tags. Discounts are higher during special sales (such as Mother's Day) and in couponed news-

paper supplements; frequent free or low-cost premium-with-purchase deals also lift our countenances. Our primping for prices revealed: 1.75-ounce Lancôme night skin treatment for $39.99 (regularly $54); Red cologne for $34.99 (retail $55); and a $3.99 Maybelline's Great Lip (was $6.50).
20+ locations in Chicagoland; see the White Pages

SALLY BEAUTY SUPPLY

1300 N. Ashland Ave.
Chicago, IL 60622
(773) 276-4580
Hours: Hours vary
AE, MC, V
◆ **Senior Discount:** Depends on item **Age:** 65+

If you want to set up a beauty salon in the confines of your own home, then check with Sally for professional-quality equipment such as electric nail tools, trolleys, and shampoo bowls. In addition, its dozens of retail outlets in Chicagoland are truly best bets for discounted manicure, hair, and skin care products—amazing not only for prices, but also for an incredible selection. Pick, for example, from 20+ shades of brown in Aurelle, Bigen, Clairol Complements, Fanci-Full, Wella, and others from $3.49 to $4.29 each. And 100 oversized cotton puffs at 89¢ beats even national drugstore prices.
36 locations, 9 in Chicagoland; see the Yellow Pages

ULTA3 COSMETICS & SALON

North and Sheffield Aves.
Chicago, IL 60622
(312) 664-0732
Hours: Mon–Fri: 10–9; Sat: 10–7; Sun: 11–6
AE, DISC, MC, V

The beauty biz is notorious for sinking its money into advertising and packaging . . . with the conclusion by many that deep discounts are rare. Ulta3 Cosmetics effectively ducks that issue by encouraging consumers to sign up for "the Ultimate Beauty Club" and by regularly offering special GWPS —gifts-with-purchase—to those in the know. A recent visit yielded about a 20% savings: Paul Mitchell hair

care three-pack at $15.99 (once $18.40); a free Nailtiques conditioner with purchase; Cover Girl makeup at $3.99 (was $6.50).
17 locations in Chicagoland; see the Yellow Pages

Books

BARGAIN BOOKS INC.

49 E. Chicago Ave.
Chicago, IL 60611
(312) 642-6416
Hours: Mon–Fri: 9–8; Sat: 9–7; Sun: 12–5
MC, V

What happens to unsold books? (No, they don't go to publishing heaven.) Instead, many are purchased by outfits such as Bargain Books, which then resell these "remainders," as they're called by the trade, to consumers. Very, very few of these tomes, now at 50%–90% off retail, are current bestsellers. Many bookstore chains, like Crown, feature a few tables of remainders, but Bargain Books is the first outlet we've seen to sell 100% remainders (with a few extraneous items, such as posters and calendars, thrown into the mix). An example or two: James Michener's *Centennial* in hardcover for $8 (priced at $40); a recent Weight Watchers' cookbook, $8.99 (was $23).
6 stores in Chicago, Montana, Missouri, Indiana, Wyoming; most locations found in the Yellow Pages

CROWN BOOKS AND SUPER CROWN

26 N. Wabash Ave.
Chicago, IL 60602
(312) 357-1150
Hours: Mon–Fri: 9–7; Sat: 10–6; Sun: 12–5
AE, DISC, MC, V

More than 30 Chicago-area locations of Crown offer discounted books—but no cappuccino or biscotti. With stores generally smaller than rivals Borders and Barnes & Noble, Crown eschews coffee

shops and CDs to concentrate on lower prices. Recent *New York Times* bestsellers, for example, are 40% off. Though Crown doesn't stock as many titles as the competition (85,000 versus 150,000), they'll special order—and still give you a bigger discount than the other two. Plus, we understand that the smaller, 6,000- to 10,000-square-foot outlets will eventually be replaced by Super Crowns—obviously, the bigger, better, bolder version at 15,000 square feet each. Given that the $12 billion industry is forecast to grow 4.5% annually, we predict that more Super Crown customers will say: "One book, straight up, lowest prices, please."
30+ locations in Chicagoland; see the Yellow Pages

Building & Remodeling

CERAMIC & STONE TILE

COLOR TILE & CARPET

2917 N. Ashland Ave.
Chicago, IL 60657
(773) 929-4943
Hours: Hours vary; check with individual stores
AE, DISC, MC, V
◆ **Senior Discount:** Depends on item **Age:** 60+

Used to be, Color Tile had no "& Carpet" after its name. We suspect that increased competition among floor covering retailers promoted the additional moniker. Prices are about equal to others, whether locally owned or part of a national chain; what is unusual is the inclusion of installation fees for wood and laminate floors. (Watch for the exact wording on installation, however: Does the work include removal of the old flooring? Is padding preferred, even required, for wood or laminate? And is it part of the package?) All the usual brands, from Armstrong to Pergo and DuPont Stainmaster, are here; samples of summer savings: $639 for 40 square yards of berber carpeting (was $1,479); Pergo laminate at $6.99 per square foot installed.
18 locations in Chicagoland; see the Yellow Pages

THE TILE SHOP

980 W. Algonquin Rd.
Arlington Heights, IL 60005
(847) 342-9500
Hours: Mon–Fri: 7–9; Sat: 9–5:30; Sun: 11–5
AE, DISC, MC, V

On Manhattan trips, we constantly fall in love with the artisan tiles at Country Floors—but not with the prices. Now the Windy City's found a way to offer top-notch home ceramics—or porcelain, marble, granite, slate, or limestone—at less than retail prices, usually from 10% to 30% discount: The Tile Shop in Arlington Heights, part of a national chain. It's definitely not a do-it-yourself store, though there are how-to-install seminars on Saturday mornings. Vignettes suggest a wide possibility of applications; products are all top of the line from 30 to 50 different manufacturers, many European.

National; 10 locations throughout the United States, only 1 in Chicagoland; see the Yellow Pages

FLOOR COVERINGS

CARPETLAND USA

6900 W. North Ave.
Chicago, IL 60635
(773) 745-3500
Hours: Mon–Fri: 10–8; Sat: 10–6; Sun: 11–5
Carpetland, MC, V
◆ **Senior Discount:** 10% **Age:** 60+

We'll be the first to admit: it is very difficult to judge the sales prices touted by floor covering stores. The only rule of thumb? Let your fingers be your guide in touch tests, and make sure the brands you're deciding on are comparable. Given that caveat, Carpetland USA, with about 16 stores in our area, promotes some of the lowest prices we've seen: Pergo laminate starting at $2.99 a square foot; private-label wear-dated carpet at $779 for 40 square yards; remnants

beginning at $39 to $99. Of special note: an extended installation guarantee; service free for the life of the carpet.
16 locations in Chicagoland; see the Yellow Pages

ONE-STOP SUPPLIERS

BUILDERS SQUARE

2400 Main St.
Evanston, IL 60202
(847) 869-0303
Hours: Hours vary
AE, DISC, MC, V
◆ **Senior Discount:** 10% on Tues **Age:** 55+

It's a one-stop, service-oriented home-improvement and home-decor specialty store, akin to the late and lamented Handy Andy and its archrival Home Depot. And, with 174 stores in 21 states (including more than a dozen here), Builders Square is fiercely, aggressively competitive: 109,000+ square feet of electrical, plumbing, lumber, painting, hardware, and decorative merchandise; 30,000 to 40,000 square feet of gardening and building materials. Check the Idea Center sporting full-scale kitchens, bathrooms, and family entertainment rooms—literally, design ideas for every room in the house (and trained "consultants" to help figure out plots and plans). Other services we're impressed with: "barrier-free" products for people with disabilities; gift registry ("But, honey, I wanted a Makita power saw!"); free delivery; try-before-purchase tool center; learning center; free lumber and glass cutting (up to five cuts). Phew! Think we'll go nap before tackling the next DIY project.
14+ stores in Chicagoland; see the Yellow Pages, or call (800) 634-5940 for locations

CRAFTY BEAVER HOME CENTERS

1522 W. Lawrence Ave.
Chicago, IL 60640
(773) 271-2288
Hours: Hours vary
AE, DISC, MC, V
◆ **Senior Discount:** 10% **Age:** 62+

The emphasis here, as the name suggests, is on lumber—stacks and stacks of it. But, judging the store as a home center, we've found that the Crafty Beaver's staff is usually much more knowledgeable than much of the competition—which helps when you're all thumbs. All of the gidgets and gadgets displayed in the average hardware store are here, along with seasonal items such as lawn equipment and gardening materials. Prices are competitive, and, when coupons appear in newspaper supplements, discounts are positively, well, handy. Some examples: $5 daily carpet cleaner rental (originally $19.99); three single-cut keys for a buck.

Chicago—3850 W. Montrose Ave., (773) 478-5510
Chicago—4306 N. Central Ave., (773) 625-4432
Skokie—4810 W. Oakton Ave., (847) 673-3000

THE HOME DEPOT

2201 Oakton St.
Evanston, IL 60202
(800) 553-3199
Hours: Mon–Thurs, Sat: 6:30–10; Fri: 6:30–11; Sun: 8:30–7
AE, DISC, MC, V

Whether you are a do-it-yourselfer or a construction/building maintenance professional, Home Depot caters to you. Based in Atlanta, with 15+ stores in our area, Home Depot is North America's largest home-center retailer; it operates 411 warehouse-style home centers in 32 states. Each store stocks approximately 40,000 to 50,000 different kinds of building materials, home-improvement supplies, and lawn and garden products at prices substantially below retail. Brand names include Kohler, Delta, Disston, Skil, Stanley, Ortho, Owens, Corning, PPG, and more. All stores have knowledgeable sales associates as well as professional designers offering

free in-store consultations for home-improvement projects, from lighting to computer-assisted designs for kitchens and bathrooms. Most Home Depot stores have a 20,000- to 28,000-square-foot garden center and offer installation services. Services can range from single-item installations, such as ceiling fans or carpeting, to more expensive projects—such as installation of kitchen cabinets.
15+ locations in Chicagoland; see the Yellow Pages

MENARDS
2601 N. Clybourn Ave.
Chicago, IL 60614
(773) 880-5954
Hours: Mon–Fri: 7–10; Sat: 7–8; Sun: 8–6
DISC, Menards, MC, V

So-called category killers such as Home Depot are hard to beat, but a few hardware chains such as the 130-store Menards do promote their savings in semiweekly circulars and sales. (Of course, best deals anywhere go to professional remodelers and contractors.) Even if you're all thumbs and simply prefer to buy, not do it yourself, typical discounts are at least 20% on tools, building materials, lawn and garden supplies, and even ready-to-construct homes (a three-bedroom, 2½ bather was recently advertised at $34,368). Their advertising spokesperson, 70-year-old Ray Szmanda of Antigo, Wisconsin, has become a cult figure of sorts—and clearly states (believe it or not) that he's not a do-it-yourselfer. Good quality, not high-end brands.
28 locations in Chicagoland; see the Yellow Pages

WALL & WINDOW TREATMENTS

EDDIE Z'S EXPRESS BLINDS

818 W. North Ave.
Chicago, IL 60622
(312) 951-0400 or (800) 57EDDIE
Hours: Mon, Thurs: 10–8; Tues, Wed, Fri: 10–6; Sat: 10–5; Sun: 12–5
AE, MC, V
◆ **Senior Discount:** 5% **Age:** 63+

Deciding to buy window coverings can be a "blind" purchase, especially considering that most brand names, such as Hunter Douglas and Levolor, among others, are usually heavily discounted. Nonetheless, Eddie Z's, a regional string of window wear retailers, will provide good prices on shutters, shades, blinds, and drapery. Best bets for savings are the nonbranded, private-label coverings. It's also a smart move to pay a bit extra to have their installers measure.
15 stores in Chicagoland, plus Wisconsin and Indiana; call (800) 57EDDIE for locations

Clothing & Accessories

BRIDAL & FORMAL

DAVID'S BRIDAL

4512 N. Harlem Ave.
Norridge, IL 60656
(708) 583-1740
Hours: Mon–Fri: 11–9; Sat: 10–6; Sun: 12–5
AE, DISC, MC, V

Being a bride is fun—for exactly one day. The preparations before the Big Event, though, can be fraught with problems, hassles, and downright mayhem. In at least one department, though, a fairly new national chain is solving wedding issues: the 50-store (and growing) David's Bridal, with four locations here. From size 4 to 26, gowns in the hundreds are ready to buy—as are all the accoutrements, such as shoes, handbags, garters, cake servers, headpieces, and bridesmaid dresses. Discounts range from 20% to 50% off on gowns at $199 to $1,000; alterations are extra. There's a limited selection of "David's Express" bridesmaid dresses; three styles in any size in 3 weeks. One recent happily-ever-after story: a 20-something woman walked in on Monday, selected a size 16, and was married in that gown on Friday in Las Vegas.

Burbank—7706 S. Cicero Ave., (708) 636-6100
Lombard—421 E. Roosevelt Ave., (630) 932-7333
Schaumburg—500 E. Golf Rd., (847) 884-8990
Call (800) 399-BRIDE for other locations

FAMILY APPAREL

BURLINGTON COAT FACTORY

7340 W. Foster Ave.
Chicago, IL 60656
(773) 763-6006
Hours: Mon–Sat: 10–9; Sun: 11–6
AE, DISC, MC, V

With a name like "Coat Factory," it stands to reason that outerwear is one of Burlington's best buys. And it's a fact: they offer 10 to 15 times more coats, coats, coats than the Mr. and Mrs. Joe Average department stores, from as many as 300 manufacturers. Shoppers at Burlington can expect to save up to 60% on more than 1,000 design and name-brand fashions for the whole family. All locations feature an impressive selection of the latest first-quality ladies' designer dresses, suits, sportswear, and accessories; top-name men's suits and sportswear; famous-label clothes for children of all ages; and, of course, coats—10,000 to 20,000 outer garments in each and every location all-year-round. Look also at their extensive selection of infant and toddler apparel, furniture, and accessories in Baby Depot. A P.S.: We've heard from very good sources that special orders of the "coat" kind are welcome . . . and discounted at least 25%.

Burbank—8320 S. Cicero Ave., (708) 636-8300
Chicago—4520 S. Damen Ave., (773) 254-0054
Call (800) 444-COATS for other locations

GAP OUTLET

2778 N. Milwaukee Ave.
Chicago, IL 60647
(773) 252-0594
Hours: Mon–Sat: 10–8; Sun: 11–6
AE, DISC, MC, V

One of the first stand-alone Gap outlets, this store, occupying the corner of Milwaukee, Kimball, and Diversey, has been joined by 30 others nationwide, with more to come. Definitely a discounter's delight at 30% less than retail, the Gap Outlet features not only its own label for the entire family, but also selections from Old Navy Clothing Company and Banana Republic. Frequent visits do pay; a recent stop revealed two-for-one infant "onesies" at $6.99, slightly irregular women's overalls for $34.99, and men's all-cotton tees for under $10.

Gurnee—6170 W. Grand Ave., (847) 855-9311
Huntley—Huntley Factory Shops, (847) 669-9100
Michigan City, IN—Lighthouse Place Outlet Center, 601 Wabash, (800) 866-5900

LORD & TAYLOR CLEARANCE CENTER

445 E. Palatine Rd.
Arlington Heights, IL 60004
(847) 259-4211
Hours: Mon–Fri: 10–9; Sat: 10–8; Sun: 11–6
AE, DISC, MC, V

Rising young women executives in major Chicagoland corporations swear by it. This Lord & Taylor center, filled with clothing for men, women, and children, resembles a barn with racks more than a real store. Digging through the disorganized jumble, however, nets real dividends: Andrea Jovine, Adrienne Vittadini, Liz Claiborne, and DKNY, among others, for about 25% off the original suggested retail price (and usually more). Men's and kids' wearables boast similar savings, though instantly recognizable brand names are scarcer. Most apparel is at least one, usually two seasons old. One of 10 nationally, though the only L&T in our neck of the woods.

Nine locations throughout the United States

MARSHALLS, INC.

1834 W. Fullerton Ave.
Chicago, IL 60614
(773) 296-4494
Hours: Mon–Sat: 9:30–9:30; Sun: 12–6
AE, DISC, MC, V

If you're tired of the big price tags that go along with designer clothes, then Marshalls is the place for you. With over 490 stores nationwide and 13 just in our area, Marshalls is probably now the largest off-price retailer in the country (with the recent TJ Maxx merger) and offers a savings of 20%–60% off top-of-the-line men's, women's, and children's clothing. And those who haunt these superstores will agree that certain locations are more equal than others—that is, better deals and bigger labels just happen to crop up in specific stores in different neighborhoods. (Hey, a girl's gotta have some secrets!) Marshalls also has a menswear department with fantastic savings on suits, sportscoats, ties, and dress shirts, as well as an expansive shoe department.

13 locations in Chicagoland; see the Yellow Pages

SYMS

9840 N. Milwaukee Ave.
Niles, IL 60714
(847) 699-8484
Hours: Mon–Fri: 10–9; Sat: 10–6:30; Sun: 12–5:30
AE, DISC, MC, Syms, V

Perhaps the major reason Sy Syms and his daughter promote so heavily their trademarked slogan—"An educated consumer is our best customer"—is that some of their discounts are better than others. And knowing the actual, not the suggested, retail prices helps to calculate the savings—usually 10%–30%, and occasionally more. Syms is truly a national discount apparel store, with merchandise for the family from underwear to topcoats. Best buys are unadvertised sale items (e.g., all raincoats another $10 off), end-of-season bargains, and high-end designer wares that might have escaped general notice.

Addison—280 W. North Ave., (708) 620-6445
Gurnee—6170 W. Grand Ave., (847) 855-0600

TJ Maxx

1 N. State St.
Chicago, IL 60602
(312) 553-0515
Hours: Mon–Sat: 9:30–9:30; Sun: 10–6
AE, DISC, MC, V

With more than 580 stores across the country, TJ Maxx lives up to its non-minimalistic ad slogan: "The Maxx for the minimum." Hailed as our largest off-price retailer (10 are in our own backyard), Maxx, with its purchase of Marshalls, makes for some powerhouse buying to and savings too. All stores offer brand-name family apparel, domestics, giftware, accessories, shoes, and jewelry at prices from 10% to 60% below list. We regularly browse and do TJM runs for great buys on Ralph Lauren sheets, Donna Karan lingerie (used as sportswear), and perfumes and other scents-ible products. The Loop store, especially, attracts both intriguing shoppers and interesting products.
10+ locations in Chicagoland; see the Yellow or White Pages

Infants' & Children's Apparel

Babies "R" Us

16 E. Golf Rd.
Schaumburg, IL 60193
(847) 781-8889
Hours: Mon–Sat: 9:30–9:30
AE, DISC, MC, V

Having recently been swallowed by Toys "R" Us, the once and former Baby Superstore has just been christened (what else?) Babies "R" Us. No matter, because the discounts are still alluring, netting customers from 10% to 25% off suggested retail prices. All four Chicagoland stores, like their parent, offer aisles of merchandise in every category, usually a dozen models of playpens, for instance, instead of just two or three. Everything is here for the newborn, infant, and toddler; you'll find diapers and formula in addition to toys and clothing.

Burbank—7750 S. Cicero Ave., (708) 424-8755
Lansing—17675 S. Torrence Ave., (708) 474-3222
Naperville—1955 Glacier Park Ave., (630) 416-2225

CHOCOLATE SOUP

602 Green Bay Rd.
Winnetka, IL 60093
(847) 446-8951
Hours: Mon–Wed, Fri, Sat: 10–5:30; Thurs: 10–8; Sun: 12–5
MC, V

The name alone is enough to entice doting grandparents, aunts, uncles, and other relatives to stop by. Once in, you're mesmerized by the crowded racks and racks of great-looking kids' wearables—many made in Missouri under the Chocolate Soup label (and carrying a 40% discount). Other labels, such as French Toast and OshKosh, appear—with slightly smaller reductions. But, what truly sells are the eponymous clothes, such as a spaceship-appliquéd-and-printed toddler's summer jumpsuit on major sale for $12.

13 stores throughout the United States; next closest is located in Indianapolis

THE EXCLUSIVE OILILY STORE

123 Lighthouse Place
Michigan City, IN 46360
219/872-3577
Hours: Mon–Sat: 9–8; Sun: 10–6
AE, DISC, MC, V

The only Oilily outlet in the United States is right in Chicago's backyard. Though fanciers of the colorful Netherlands apparel for kids and women are not widespread, we predict that, once exposed, few will be able to resist the trademark pattern-on-pattern, mix-and-match clothing. True, this Lighthouse store features 12-month-old merchandise, but the 50%+ savings and the evergreen styling will delight bargain shoppers anywhere. A playful toddler's sundress sells for $47 (once $96), while an all-weather boy's coat of many colors is tagged at about $90 (previously $175).

HANNA ANDERSSON

215 Lighthouse Place
Michigan City, IN 46360
(219) 872-3183
Hours: Mon–Sat: 9–8; Sun: 10–6
AE, DIN, DISC, MC, OPT, V
◆ **Senior Discount:** 10%, some restrictions **Age:** 55+

Portland, Oregon–based cataloger Hanna Andersson quickly rose to fame through the "Hannadowns" program—returning your outgrown Hanna kids' clothes for a 20% credit toward new purchases. Now there's a second way to save on these wonderfully colored, Swedish-inspired cotton clothes for babes, kids, moms, and dads: expect at least a 25% discount (usually more) at the line's Midwest outlet. Sizes are based on height; merchandise normally lags one season behind, but designs are classic and made to last.

Two outside of Chicago: one in New Hampshire, the other in Oregon

KIDS "R" US

10 S. State St.
Chicago, IL 60603
(312) 857-0727
Hours: Mon–Fri: 9:30–7; Sat & Sun: 9:30–6
AE, DISC, MC, OPT, Toy's card, V

State Street, that Great Street, has now become the avenue of discounters, boasting not only TJ Maxx and Filene's Basement, but also Toys "R" Us and its sibling. Close to two dozen "Kids" are strategically placed in Chicago and suburban neighborhoods; national brands, frequent sales promotions, and low prices do draw crowds. Of special note are licensed merchandise (the 101 Dalmations apparel, a big fave, was reduced 25% right before Thanksgiving 1996) and classically appealing labels such as Carter, Levi's, Nike, and OshKosh.

18+ stores in Chicagoland; call (800) KIDS R US for locations

LARGER SIZES FOR WOMEN

THE ANSWER

180 N. Wabash Ave.
Chicago, IL 60601
(312) 419-1801
Hours: Mon, Thurs: 10–7; Tues, Wed, Fri: 10–6; Sat: 10–5
AE, DISC, MC, V

In the old days (before the Revolution of the Female Variety), the polite term was "Rubenesque." Today, it's been deep-sixed in favor of the politically correct BBW (Big Beautiful Woman) and the fuller-sized figure. No longer forgotten is this group wearing 14–26 sizes; even top retailers are scurrying to incorporate high-end large-size salons and styles in their stores. But, what's the average Extra-Misses to do? We found The Answer, a nearly 100-store national chain (owned by Catharine's Corporation) catering to BBWS exclusively—with prices about 20% lower than retail. In fact, their selection, which also features hosiery and costume jewelry, now includes petites as well. A few examples: a John Meyer dressy pink suit with beads for $219 (regularly $249) and a once-reduced Rena Rowan jacket for $99.99 (originally $162).

Six others in Chicagoland strip malls; see the Yellow Pages

LEATHER GARMENTS & FURS

ANDREW MARC COMPANY STORE

11211 120th Ave.
Lakeside Marketplace
Kenosha, WI 53142
(414) 857-4655
Hours: Mon–Sat: 10–9; Sun: 11–6
AE, MC, V
◆ **Senior Discount:** 15% **Age:** 55+

The oh-so-chic nylon outer garments popularized by Italy's Prada are oh-so-quietly emulated in the designer styling of Andrew Marc garments for both men and women. Available now in colors other than black, the outerwear showcased by this company outlet store—one of only four in the United States—usually is short, and accom-

panied by leather, fur, or furlike fabrics, at 20%+ savings. Accessories such as wallets, purses, and belts from other manufacturers echo similar discounts. (An oversized nylon tote, once $150, was marked $100 in a special sale.)
Four locations in the United States

LEATHERMODE ☆

6170 W. Grand Ave., Suite 563
Gurnee, IL 60031
(847) 855-8775
Hours: Mon–Sat: 10–9; Sun: 11–6
AE, DIN, DISC, MC, V

Almost anything cloaked in leather—jackets, accessories, luggage—is featured at Leathermode, usually for a 30%–60% savings from retail prices. Moderately priced goods from the likes of Kenneth Cole, Guess?, and Jones New York sell well here; two of the national chain's 22 outlets are located in Chicago suburbs. And a bonus: a purchase of $150+ (accompanied by our coupon, naturally) entitles *Buying Retail Is Stupid!* readers to a gift.
Huntley—11800 Factory Shops Blvd.
22 stores in the United States; call (800) 600-4555 for locations

MATERNITY CLOTHES

DAN HOWARD'S MATERNITY FACTORY OUTLET

4245 N. Knox Ave.
Chicago, IL 60641
(800) 9-MONTHS
Hours: Hours vary
AE, MC, V

An empire grows in Chicago: 30+ years ago, Dan Howard started as one store for expectant mothers' clothing. Today, over 320 stores (125 are outlets) do business in the United States and Canada under both the parent and Mothertime names. Pregnant as well as nursing moms will find prices hard to resist (wearables are usually of 100% cotton); nursing tops at $18; pajamas from $18 to $44; shirts for $38.
Nine in Chicagoland; call (800) 9-MONTHS for locations

MEN'S APPAREL & ACCESSORIES

THE MEN'S WEARHOUSE

2070 N. Clybourn Ave.
Chicago, IL 60614
(773) 525-5942
Hours: Mon–Sat: 10–9; Sun: 12–6
DISC, MC, V

The Men's Wearhouse offers a full selection of designer, well-known brand-name, and private-label menswear and accessories: suits, sports coats, slacks, shirts, shoes, ties, belts, socks, formal wear, and outerwear. Prices typically reflect 20%–30% savings from tags at department and specialty stores. Expect a high level of customer service and quick turnaround on alterations (each location has its own tailor). And just imagine: there's free pressing for the life of your Wearhouse suit.

Chicago—38 E. Walton St., (312) 482-9303
Chicago—25 E. Washington St., (312) 263-2306

TOMMY HILFIGER

Lighthouse Place
Michigan City, IN 46360
(219) 878-9888
Hours: Mon–Sat: 9–8; Sun: 10–6
AE, DISC, MC, V

At retail, the Tommy Hilfiger label has infiltrated the domain of women's wear and home bedding. But the label's outlets (43 coast to coast, at last count) still carry men's merchandise only. This particular heartland outlet, the sole representative within our shopping area, features its famed classic shirts, slacks, sweaters, and sportswear at a 20% reduction—less of a reduction, quite frankly, than some of the superstore discounters. Then, again, sales are another matter: at least twice a year, at season's end (usually February and July), visit for substantial savings.

MEN'S & WOMEN'S APPAREL

BURBERRY FACTORY OUTLET

805 Lighthouse Place
Michigan City, IN 46360
(219) 874-7777
Hours: Mon–Sat: 9–8; Sun: 10–6
AE, DISC, MC, V

That famous English plaid popularized in raincoat linings and umbrellas is now on sale—almost permanently—in seven U.S. outlet stores, only one of which is located in America's Midwest. Fine fabrics, attention to the minutest of details, and classic styles make any Burberry purchase a long-lasting investment. Though still not an inexpensive buy, their wares, when discounted, do considerably less damage to the credit card and wallet—definitely a 25% minimum reduction and often much more. Like their brolly for $29 (was $55), a range of men's sports shirts for $39–$49 on second sale (were $75 to $95), and end-of-season ladies' clearance at $79–$499 (originally $195–$1,650).

Seven locations throughout the United States

FILENE'S BASEMENT

One North State St.
Chicago, IL 60602
(312) 553-1061
Hours: Mon–Fri: 9–7; Sat: 9–6; Sun: 11–5
AE, DISC, MC, V

A downtown Boston fixture for decades, Filene's Basement has now moved west to conquer even more male and female shoppers' hearts. Four Chicago locations—most in affluent or near-affluent zip codes—carry similar discounted brand-name merchandise from retailers and manufacturers (e.g., Calvin Klein, Chetta B., Jones New York, Liz Claiborne, Dockers) with some differences. Michigan Avenue tends to feature more of the higher-end wares, such as Desmo leather handbags for 60%–75% off and phenomenal prices on leftovers from exclusive boutiques such as Barneys, Henri Bendel, and Holt Renfrew. Preadvertised sales such as $250+ designer

bridal gowns witness early-morning queues and TV crews. Rumor has it the Loop store is expanding, adding a children's department and a larger housewares/domestics section.
Chicago—830 N. Michigan Ave., (312) 482-8918
Oak Brook—2155 W. 22nd St., (630) 954-1388
Skokie—4831 Golf Rd., (847) 674-0069

OFF FIFTH—SAKS FIFTH AVENUE OUTLET

6170 W. Grand Ave.
Gurnee, IL 60031
(847) 662-0988
Hours: Mon–Sat: 10–9; Sun: 11–6
AE, DIN, DISC, MC, Saks, V

This discount subsidiary of the famous New York City landmark has truly gone global, with over 200 stores and still counting. Sure, this clearinghouse is the dumping grounds for its retail parent, but who cares? The deals are great, ranging from 40% to 70% markdowns on mainly high-end apparel for men and women. What we saw: $239.90–$349.90 for Ferragamo handbags (retail $400–$600); $59.90 sleeveless linen Harvé Bernard dresses ($109.90); $79.90 Ungaro Studio slacks (once $135); Kieselstein-Cord ties for $29.90 (were $125). Both petite and Salon Z sizes are well represented. Note: Watch for red stars indicating further reductions (usually substantial). And of the two Chicagoland stores, Schaumburg resembles more of a department store in its display; Gurnee, closer to a bargain basement.
Schaumburg—1430 E. Golf Rd., (847) 413-8803
Call (800) 221-8340 for other locations

SHOES

Family

DSW SHOE WAREHOUSE

3131 N. Clark St.
Chicago, IL 60657
(773) 975-7182
Hours: Mon–Fri: 11–9; Sat: 11–8; Sun: 12–6
AE, DISC, MC, V

This ever-expanding regional chain (25+ stores, with three—and soon four—representatives in our area) claims it's a "better way to buy better shoes." Well, maybe, but there's a lot of competition. About 20%–50% is the markdown range for such popular and well-known footwear as Bandolino, Bruno Magli, Doc Martens, Cole-Haan, and Johnston & Murphy, all displayed atop stacks of shoe boxes for self-service convenience. Accessories such as socks and handbags, too, are featured, but in much more limited quantities and selections. Membership in the DSW Club saves you even more.
Oakbrook—2155 W. 22nd St., (630) 571-9313
Skokie—Skokie Fashion Square, 9454 Skokie Blvd., (847) 674-2772

FAMOUS FOOTWEAR

7173 Central Ave.
Skokie, IL 60077
(800) 40-FAMOUS
Hours: Mon–Fri: 10–9; Sat: 10–8; Sun: 11–6
DISC, MC, V

It started nearby, in Madison, Wisconsin, over 35 years ago, bearing the banner of Neil's Factory Outlet Shoe Store. Now Famous Footwear is among our largest chains of shoe stores selling brand-name footwear for the entire family, with 785 retail stores in 44 states (60+ in our Midwest locale). Famous Footwear owes its success to the concept it introduced in 1961: brand-name shoes for the entire family . . . for less. (Our story: a great pair of black-and-white Reebok high-tops for $30, far less than even the wholesale price.) Get 10%–50% off on brands such as Nike, Reebok, Dexter, Nunn

Bush, Rockport, Westies, Timberland, Naturalizer, Buster Brown, and Bass.
60+ stores in Chicagoland; call (800) 40-FAMOUS for locations

FOOTLOCKER OUTLET
216B Ridge Rd.
Griffith, IN 46319
(219) 838-2071
Hours: Mon–Fri: 10–8; Sat: 10–5:30; Sun: 11–5
AE, DISC, MC, V

Just do it (which is our philosophy of discount deals . . . with due apologies to Nike)! And two south Chicagoland outlets of the national Footlocker chain will permit each and every one of us to save quite nicely, thank you, on name-brand bargains on athletic wares for the entire family. Expect a 10%–50% reduction on all clothing, shoes, and caps. For instance, NBA/NFL (etc.) team down jackets sell here for $39.90; sweatshirts, $19.90; men's Reebok high-step cross trainers, $29.90 (were $59). An upfront bargain table showcases even sportier discounts (e.g., shoes at $19.90). Michael Jordan would be proud.
Palos Heights—12801 S. Harlem Ave., (708) 361-3040

FOOTQUARTERS
1506 Golf Rd.
Schaumburg, IL 60173
(847) 413-1526
Hours: Mon–Fri: 10–9; Sat: 10–8; Sun: 10–6
AE, DISC, MC, V

It is a sad and not-so-savvy shopper who can't find a good buy on shoes, we contend. (Yes, even if your foot's a quadruple-E in width and a 16 in size. Because someone, somewhere can fit you at a discount.) Here's yet another example of a national chain opening in a strip mall near you: Footquarters, with seven (and maybe more to come) stores in greater Chicago. Casual and sports shoes are the ticket here, with well-known men's and women's sneaks and sandals and mocs and the like priced about 40% below retail. Samples of savings: $89 for a pair of men's Rockport mocs (list is $130)

and $49 for women's Nike Air Gridstar (regularly $75). If the shoe fits, buy it!
Check Yellow Pages for locations

Payless Shoe Source
16 N. State St.
Chicago, IL 60602
(312) 201-1344
Hours: Mon–Fri: 8–8; Sat: 9–8; Sun: 9–6
AE, DISC, MC, V

Remember Fayva, Thom McAn, and Shoetown? You can bet that national chain Payless won't go the way of these retail dinosaurs. Payless specializes in producing dirt-cheap knockoffs of best-selling styles such as clogs (here, $9.99), ballet flats ($9.99), and work boots ($40). Once owned by the May Department Stores Company and headquartered in Topeka, Kansas, this shoe-it-yourself discounter has 4,300 outlets nationally (and 100+ in greater Chicago) and is responsible for selling one out of every five pairs of shoes in the United States.
Call (800) 444-SHOE for locations
Corporate HQ: (913) 233-5171

Women's

Nine West Outlet
2739 N. Clark St.
Chicago, IL 60614
(773) 281-9132
Hours: Mon–Fri: 9–9; Sat: 9–7; Sun: 11–6; hours vary at other locations
AE, DISC, MC, V

It's difficult to tell anymore the true "manufacturer's suggested retail price," since a number of discounters have been rumored to mark up, then down. Nonetheless, national companies such as Nine West, with their own outlet chains, do post regular prices. This stand-alone Lincoln Park store, with others located in Chicagoland shopping malls, offers 30%+ discounts not only on its flagship

brand, but also on siblings Callico, Nine & Co., and Enzo Angiolini. Samples of first-quality savings: spring sandals at $39 (were $59); women's dress pumps at $44.97 (once $64).
Gurnee—6170 W. Grand Ave., (847) 855-1313
Huntley—Factory Store 1800, (847) 669-8572
Call (800) 260-2227 for other locations

PARADE OF SHOES

105 W. Adams St.
Chicago, IL 60647
(800) 4-PARADE
Hours: Hours vary
AE, DISC, MC, V

Francesco Bardini. Courtney Taylor. Planet. Sounds like some of the higher-priced spreads in women's shoes, but at the national Parade of Shoes outlets, with nine representatives in greater Chicago, we've never yet had to spend more than two Andrew Jacksons (or 40 bucks) on one pair of shoes. Fashion forward is the appeal here; find knockoffs of the latest footwear—say, wedgies, clogs, and comfort walkers—for prices ranging from mid-teens to about $29.98. The usual accompaniments appear, too, such as stockings, socks, handbags, belts, and hosiery.
Nine stores in Chicagoland; call (800) 4-PARADE for locations

WOMEN'S APPAREL

CLOTHESTIME

614 W. Diversey Ave.
Chicago, IL 60657
(773) 327-6655
Hours: Mon–Fri: 10–9; Sat: 10–8; Sun: 11–6
AE, DISC, MC, V

Ready for funk and flash and the latest hip and trendy stuff? Since 1974, Clothestime stores have specialized in first-quality, brand-name women's clothing at prices from 10% to 50% less than department and specialty stores. Clothestime caters to young, fashion-conscious juniors in the 18–34 age bracket and offers private

dressing rooms, attentive sales staff, layaway plans, and a 30-day money-back guarantee with a customer receipt.
12 locations in Chicagoland; see the Yellow Pages

DOTS

6560 W. Fullerton Ave.
Chicago, IL 60635
(773) 889-8600
Hours: Mon–Sat: 10–9; Sun: 12–5
DISC, MC, V

If a major portion of your paycheck goes on your back, then stop . . . by DOTS. (We're lucky to have 10 in Chicagoland.) There, first-quality, name-brand fashions including Limited, Express, Cherry Stix, Jordache, Mickey Mouse, Currants, and No Excuses sell for about 10 bucks each. All sizes proliferate; some outlets carry girls' sizes—in sportswear, career, separates, and accessories. Unsure about a fit? Just ask. Store associates are trained in service, service, and more service; DOTS' unconditional return policy is a no-risk. Inventory is continually changing; twice a week, shipments arrive.
10+ locations in Chicagoland; see the Yellow Pages

ELLEN TRACY

Lighthouse Place, #803
Michigan City, IN 46360
(219) 879-6452
Hours: Mon–Sat: 9–8; Sun: 10–6
AE, MC, V

Though this high-end women's clothing manufacturer boasts at least 15 other discount outlets throughout the United States, Ellen Tracy at Lighthouse Place is the only one in the tristate area. Typically, the bright-colored and subdued corporate mix-and-match suits, dresses, blouses, skirts, and pants—as well as the sportier and lower-end Company line—are displayed 13 weeks behind regular retail store availability . . . and about 30% lower in price. Bigger savings occur when merchandise has been in-store for a while; best prices are during semiannual clearances (notification by postcard). A newer feature, when available: a goodly selection of women's sizes for elegant business dressing.

FITIGUES

1535 N. Dayton St.
Chicago, IL 60622
(312) 255-8866
Hours: Mon–Sat: 10–6; Sun: 12–5
AE, MC, V

Fitigues concept of waffle-wear/thermal-wear cotton casual clothing actually started as a brainstorm of Chicago couple Andrea and Steven Rosenstein. And true to the founders' roots, the line's first outlet stores are also located here. Expect anywhere from 30% to 50% off, with weekly specials discounted further: a women's striped pullover sells for $63.99 (regularly $128); infant "onesies" for $27.99 ($56); and distressed leather bomber jackets for women and men at $259 (once $529).

Buffalo Grove—398 W. Half Day Rd., (847) 634-3020

Fox's

2336 N. Clark St.
Chicago, IL 60614
(773) 281-0700
Hours: Mon–Fri: 11–8; Sat: 10–6; Sun: 12–5
MC, V

Headquartered in Florida with two stores now in Chicagoland, Fox's has adopted the policy pioneered by Loehmann's: cut out the clothing labels to offer shoppers even deeper discounts. Though the quantity of women's wear by no means equals that of its competitor, Fox's offers high, high-fashion suits, pants, coats, dresses, and casual clothing at suitable savings. Chenille sweaters in the dead of winter were priced at $29, while cashmere pullovers sported tags of $38.

Skokie—9432 Skokie Blvd., (847) 673-8516

GROUP USA

14 N. Wabash Ave.
Chicago, IL 60602
(312) 857-1808
Hours: Mon–Fri: 10–7; Sat: 10–6; Sun: 11–5
AE, DISC, MC, V

Call it one-stop shopping for women's wear, if you will. (Though we find it interesting that the downtown Group USA is cheek to cheek with Filene's Basement and, to a lesser extent, with TJ Maxx.) Based in Secaucus, New Jersey, this eight-state, 10-year-old chain promotes au courant fashions at an average 30% discount. Unfamiliar names from Europe (Rina Rossi, Taiga) join Annie Alexander, Gloria Vanderbilt, and Kenar; shoes are sized European style (e.g., footwear fits in the 40-something ranges). Handbags, costume jewelry, belts, coats, and evening wear complete the merchandise mix. A *Buying Retail Is Stupid!* sneak peek: a Cotton Framework hot-coral zippered jacket for $49.99 (regularly $78); slide-into-summer canvas shoes at $32.99 (retail $44).

Gurnee—6170 W. Grand Ave., (847) 855-1660
Call (800) 624-6246 for other locations

HIT OR MISS

1830 W. Fullerton Ave.
Chicago, IL 60657
(773) 404-5255
Hours: Hours vary
AE, DIN, DISC, MC, V

One of the original off-price stores (before "discount" was incorporated permanently into America's vocabulary), Hit or Miss has become a stalwart for great deals on hosiery and casual wear. Once upon a time, when it first started in the 1970s, this national chain featured high-end labels. Today, the wares are distinctly mid-scale, such as Gloria Vanderbilt and knockoffs of more expensive fashions (e.g., Synari instead of Tahari, we assume). Prices still remain faithful to the original off-price concept: Reed Hunter cotton polos for $19.99 (retail $28); two-for-$12 Ellen Ashly tights; and Alias cotton T-dresses at $19.99 (compare at $39).

15 locations in Chicagoland; see the Yellow Pages

LOEHMANN'S
7234 Dempster St.
Morton Grove, IL 60053
(847) 966-1350
Hours: Mon–Sat: 10–9; Sun: 11–6
AE, DISC, MC, V

They pioneered group dressing rooms—and, probably, launched the entire concept of labels (discretely removed, in some cases) for less. With two outlets in Chicagoland, Loehmann's is the one discounter where women can always find consistently well-made career, casual, and dressy clothes to wear. The Back Room, usually distinguished by signage and a physical separation (a wall, room, etc.), is the holding arena for both European and American designers, with prices slashed a good 35% and more.
Downers Grove—1524 Butterfield Rd., (630) 495-4333

TALBOT'S OUTLET
670 N. Northwest Hwy.
Park Ridge, IL 60068
(847) 823-7700
Hours: Mon–Fri: 10–9; Sat: 10–6; Sun: 12–5
AE, MC, V

It's hard to know where to look first in this one of 10 Talbot's outlets nationwide. Does baby need a gaily printed cotton corduroy "onesie" for $12 (was $30)? Or Mom, a pair of Italian suede heels for $39 (originally $88)? How about a linen short-sleeved dress for Sis at $49 (compare at $148)? Savings at this no-frills outlet always seem to be at least 50%, though a few boys' items, clearance racks, and special sales reflect even lower prices.

Computers

Would you buy a used computer at a flea market?

Don't scoff. Increasingly, for small businesses and solo home workers, the answer is yes—because they simply don't need megamegabytes of power or extremely sophisticated machines upgraded to the nth degree. Then, they turn to a broker or refurbisher; the latter is a firm that handles nearly new computers, recertifies them, and sells them with the original manufacturer warranties. Often, the refurbished equipment was returned to dealers in the first 30 to 90 days for either repair or exchange (coming with an out-of-the-box failure rate at less than 3%). And the savings—depending on make, model, and year—can be substantial: a laptop originally listed at $2,300 sells for $1,250 refurbished and $1,050 used.

What else to know or ask?

- Determine your most important software programs and most critical functions, such as access to the Internet.
- Make sure there's enough disc space and memory—a minimum 810 megabyte disc and 16 mb of RAM.
- How about manuals . . . and service? Post-purchase, individuals might need to pore through printed instructions or talk with technicians about a problem.
- Finally, what's the warranty? On used, it runs from 2 to 90 days. Refurbished equipment can be 1 year or more, same as new.

Look at Boston Computer Exchange ([800] 262-6399), Computer Renaissance (a national chain listed in the Yellow Pages), or Atlanta Computer Exchange for all the used cyber-stuff. For refurbished machines? Contact Dell Factory Outlet ([800] 336-2891) and Rumerson Technologies, among others. And surf the Web for specific addresses and contact information for these refurbished and used computer companies.

CompUSA

7011 N. Central Ave.
Skokie, IL 60076
(847) 677-3644
Hours: Mon–Sat: 9–9; Sun: 11–6
AE, CompUSA, DIN, DISC, MC, V

There's a high-tech war in progress. And it's already elicited some casualties here: Best Buy has almost completely dissociated itself from selling computer products. And Elek-Tek, a Chicago institution for many years, is fighting off a possible Chapter 11 bankruptcy. It is, thus, the clout of national giants that drives down prices; CompUSA is one. With 123+ stores in the USA and 4 in our immediate

area, this chain offers the works: software, hardware, and accessories. Instant rebates and special sales help reduce costs, as does their promise to beat other retail prices. What we liked at a recent promotion: 16 mb of PC memory for $69.99; VirusScan for $40; and all floor models of office furniture (lamps, too) at 50% off.
Downers Grove—3000 Finley Rd., (630) 241-1144
Naperville—324 Rte. 59, (630) 548-0300
Schaumburg—1057 E. Golf Rd., (847) 619-1221

Computer City

352 W. Grand Ave.
Chicago, IL 60610
(312) 840-5900
Hours: Mon–Sat: 10–9; Sun: 11–6
Computer City, DISC, MC, V

These days, the margins on personal computers and accessories are pretty slim, so all the national chains are slugging it out in price wars. Fort Worth, Texas-headquartered Computer City is no exception. Brands featured at 20% (and more) savings include Apple, Compaq, Hewlett-Packard, Packard Bell, Sony, and the like; further discounts are possible through manufacturer rebates, charge card specials, their 110% price guarantees, and returned in-the-box unused merchandise. (We bought a full-page swivel monitor for $750, a 25% savings.)
Deerfield—99 S. Waukegan Rd., (847) 509-4400
Naperville—193 Glacier Park Ave., (630) 548-8000
Schaumburg—950 E. Golf Rd., (847) 310-5800
Call (800) THE-CITY for other locations

Computer Discount Warehouse

315 W. Grand Ave.
Chicago, IL 60610
(312) 527-2700
Hours: Mon–Fri: 8–7; Sat: 10–5
AE, DISC, MC, V

The brainchild of Chicago native Michael Krasny (a former used car salesman), Computer Discount Warehouse—CDW for short—now commands a great deal of respect from consumers and indus-

try alike for its aggressive growth and rock-bottom prices. The firm started in 1984 as a mail-order catalog for small businesses and today operates two Chicago-area showrooms. They'll match any PC or Mac hardware, software, or peripheral prices, including such brand names as IBM, Motorola, NEC, and U.S. Robotics. Plus, telephone support is for a lifetime; customers' questions are answered by certified, trained technicians and engineers. Geek-dom pays off.
Buffalo Grove—1020 E. Lake Cook Rd., (847) 419-6100,
Mon–Fri: 8-8; Sat: 9–5

MEI/Micro Center
2645 N. Elston Ave.
Chicago, IL 60647
(773) 292-1700
Hours: Mon–Sat: 10–9; Sun: 12–5
AE, DISC, MC, Micro Center, V

Does Chicago really need another discount computer retailer? The answer's moot, since MEI/Micro Center of Columbus, Ohio, just moved into the Elston neighborhood. Its claim to fame? Walk in or dial up your order (there's a catalog); choose from 34,000+ products with names you know and trust (including MEI-labeled accessories and refurbished Sony monitors). What is truly new and different is breadth of product line and emphasis on educating the customer; there's a separate classroom at 200 West Adams in the Loop. And lower prices certainly aid Micro's appeal: find the "Dummies" series of books for close to half price; a 15-pack of diskettes for 99¢; and a U.S. Robotics modem for $105.40.

Department & Warehouse Stores

JCPENNEY OUTLET STORE
250 W. North Ave.
North Park Mall
Villa Park, IL 60181
(630) 279-1700
Hours: Mon–Sat: 9–9; Sun: 10–6
AE, DISC, JCPenney, MC, V

We're fortunate, indeed: 2 of the 17+ national outlets for JCPenney catalog "stuff" are located in our backyard—specifically, in Gurnee Mills and Villa Park. Overstock and discontinueds for the family and the house galore turn over rather regularly in these two stores, spurred on by specials and promotions slashing prices even further than the 20%–60% initial discounts. Though prices certainly weren't confusing, we found ourselves stumped by the initials LTP—which stand for Less Than Perfect—on certain tags. Still, the merchandise's serviceable, wearable, and of good quality. Mickey Mouse was on sale when we visited ($6.99 to $9.99 for the Disney rodent's appearance on tops and shorts). As were an LTP king-size comforter ($19.99); bridesmaid dresses starting at $49.99; and the unbeatable Bulls jerseys at $7.99.
Gurnee—6170 W. Grand Ave., (847) 855-0470

NORDSTROM RACK
Woodfield Village Green Center
Schaumburg, IL 60173
(847) 413-2121
Hours: Mon–Sat: 10–9; Sun: 11–6
AE, MC, Nordstrom, V

The Midwest invasion of Seattle-based Nordstrom would not be complete without the opening of its outlet, Nordstrom Rack. In fact, the Northbrook cousin of the Schaumburg store has proven to be so popular that lines of North Shore shoppers wait patiently for new merchandise to be unloaded. So, the pickings are from the leftovers of the mother stores and include men's, women's, kids', plus sizes,

some decorative accessories, and, of course, the famed selection of shoes. Wearables from Isaac Mizrahi, Donna Karan, Hickey Freeman, Sonia Rykiel, et al. show up from time to time, as do Nordstrom's private label, London Fog, and other brand names. Expect at least 30%–40% savings, with more at end-of-season clearance time.
Northbrook—1999 Skokie Blvd., (847) 205-0890

SAM'S CLUB

2450 N. Main St.
Evanston, IL 60202
(847) 491-9000
Hours: Mon–Fri: 10–9; Sat: 9:30–8:30; Sun: 10–6
DISC

A brother of Wal-Mart, Sam's Club is the nation's leading members-only warehouse club, with 435 locations in 48 states. In each, you'll find tremendous savings on business and office supplies, televisions, VCRS and camcorders, large and small appliances, home furnishings, clothing, watches, jewelry, sheets, towels, and more. Sam's Club depends on high-volume sales compensating for very narrow profit margins, resulting in prices substantially below retail. All items are first quality and include the best brand names. There are two types of membership offered. Business members pay $25 annually—and six additional cardholders at $10 each are permitted. Individuals pay $25 annually and can add one card for $10. Call the store nearest you for membership qualifications.
10+ stores in Chicagoland; (800) 925-6278 for locations

SERVICE MERCHANDISE

3240 N. Ashland Ave.
Chicago, IL 60657
(773) 472-3940
Hours: Mon–Sat: 9–9
AE, DISC, MC, Service Merchandise, V

More than 26 Service Merchandise stores in Chicagoland (and representatives in 37 states) equal savings on a variety of household and personal items. Best known for its wide (and inexpensive) array of gold and gem-set jewelry, this national discount chain offers both brand and no-name merchandise at distinct savings—though it is

often difficult to figure out the exact percentage of reduction, since many products are priced similarly by its competitors. Some samples: a Mr. Coffee espresso maker for $34.99; O'Sullivan ready-to-assemble work center at $69.99; and halogen torchères for $12.99 each.
26 stores in Chicagoland; call (800) 251-1212 for locations

SPIEGEL OUTLET STORE

6170 W. Grand Ave.
Gurnee, IL 60031
(847) 855-1787
Hours: Mon–Sat: 10–9; Sun: 11–6
MC, V
◆ **Senior Discount:** 15% on Wed **Age:** 60+

Manhattan's Seventh Avenue is hundreds of miles away (800, to be more precise). Yet, the number of fashion and consumer products manufactured in and around our fair city never fails to amaze. Headquartered in Downers Grove, a western suburb, Spiegel, a mail-order merchandiser, sends its overstocks, discontinueds, past seasons, et al. to various locations, two in Chicagoland, to be exact. So, this mini-department store has now become the happy hunting grounds for all kinds of body and home furnishings, at a good savings. Here, we let our eyes do the walking: 200-thread-count Dan River queen sheet set at $39.99; $5.99 polyester/cotton dress shirts; 50% reduction on selected women's wearables from the catalog.
Naperville—2781 Aurora Ave., (630) 961-4980
Call (800) 645-7467 for other locations

SUPER KMART

600 Meacham Rd.
Elk Grove, IL 60007
(847) 584-3600
Hours: Open 7 days a week, 24 hours
AE, DISC, MC, V

The parent company has, for years, been the butt of many jokes. All will agree, however, that Kmart offers terrific prices on everyday household items. Enter (quietly) Super Kmart, a 24-hour grocery in Chicago's suburbs (and, of course, throughout the country) with

deals that are hard to beat. Here's just a sampling from main aisles in one week, most valid only with a $20 purchase: $3.97 for a 24-pack of Coca-Cola; 47¢ per can of Star-Kist chunk light tuna; 99¢ per pound for ground turkey; two Colombo light yogurts for 88¢; and 68¢ for a pint of fresh strawberries. A double-your-money-back product/meat/deli guarantee makes shopping at this superstore difficult to resist.
Broadview—800 Broadview Village Sq., (708) 344-0101
Homewood—17550 S. Halsted St., (708) 922-1500
Vernon Hills—413 N. Milwaukee Ave., (847) 816-8600

TUESDAY MORNING
1880 W. Fullerton Ave.
Chicago, IL 60614
(773) 384-2559
Hours: Mon–Sat: 10–6; Thurs: 10–8; Sun: 12–6
DISC, MC, V

The exact reason for the moniker of this national closeout chain remains somewhat obscure—except that stores are shuttered four times a year for restocking. When they open for 6 to 10 weeks at a stretch, it's anyone's guess as to what merchandise will appear—from $7.99 art sets to $59.99 21-inch wheeled luggage, all from famous makers. Markdowns range from 50% to 80% (sometimes more toward the end of a selling season). It's best to get there during the opening week, since pickings can be slim and scattered afterward.
13 locations in Chicagoland; see the Yellow Pages

WAL-MART STORES, INC.
1300 S. Des Plaines
Forest Park, IL 60130
(800) 925-6278
Hours: Hours vary
AE, DISC, MC, V

The late Sam Walton has forever left his imprint on American retailing: friendly people greeters, top-notch customer service, and low, low prices. Each Wal-Mart has more than 36 departments,

including family apparel, health and beauty products, housewares, and toys, at below-retail prices. And because Wal-Mart carefully controls expenses to maintain its low price structures, sales need never occur. More than 2,200 stores populate America's suburbs, exurbs, and farm country, rather than city streets. Plus, the corporation's regional distribution centers permit personalization of the merchandise mix; locally made products are frequently (and proudly) displayed in-store. And 240 Wal-Mart Supercenters feature full-service groceries as well as the usual "stuff."
17+ stores in Chicagoland; call (800) 925-6278 for locations

Electronics

Best Buy
1000 W. North Ave., west of Sheffield
Chicago, IL 60622
(312) 988-4067
Hours: Mon–Sat: 10–9; Sun: 11–6
AE, Best Buy, DISC, MC, OPT, V

The aptly named Minnesota-based Best Buy originally specialized in electronics—and then gradually added accompanying products, such as recorded music, computer hardware and software, and office equipment (though they've distanced themselves from most cyber-merchandise). Its 26+ stores in the Chicago area promote different discounts almost every week—and 365 days a year, they'll beat any competitor's price (and refund another 10%). Store clerks are helpful but not necessarily product specialists. A few holiday examples of brand-name bargains: \$8.99 movie videos; 900 MHz Panasonic cordless telephone for \$149.99; 19-inch remote Magnavox TV at \$179.99.
26+ locations in Chicagoland; see the Yellow Pages

CIRCUIT CITY
2500 N. Elston Ave.
Chicago, IL 60647
(773) 772-0037
Hours: Mon–Sat: 10–9; Sun: 11–6
AE, DISC, MC, V

Take advantage, whenever offered, of the birthday and anniversary celebration specials from national discounters. Many of the deals may indeed be loss leaders, but if the product's a household necessity, we say "buy." Such is the case with Circuit City, which honored its 48th year in business in 1997—and usually has an anniversary sale each year. Price and selection, certainly, are its strong points, but for knowledgeable, informed sales staff, Circuit City's hit-or-miss. Brand names, warranties, and rebates all apply, as does its 110% low price guarantee. Sample deals at the 28 stores here: a GE Potscrubber for $299.99; $89.99 for a Hoover upright; a 21.6-cubic-foot Whirlpool fridge at $899.99.

28 stores in Chicagoland; call Elston Ave. store for other locations

Flowers

SILKCORP FACTORY STORES
1439 W. Webster Ave.
Chicago, IL 60614
(773) 529-0912
Hours: Mon–Fri: 10–8; Sat: 10–6; Sun: 11–5
AE, MC, V

A scents-ible promise: this is one florist whose fragrances and blooms won't overwhelm consumers when they first walk in. Most fake flowers have absolutely no connection to reality; it's clear that the owner is either allergic or has a black thumb. The 10-store regional Silkcorp Factory, though, produces blooms and trees and arrangements that even interior designers buy. Their tulips-sans-smell, when artfully displayed in a vase, are difficult to distinguish from the real thing. With silks from China and a factory/headquar-

ters in Chicago's backyard (Broadview), the prices, although a bit high, represent savings: a basket of blushingly pink peonies for $107.70 (retail $249.99) and a 6-foot-high ficus tree at $117.70 (once $259.99). Opening specials and seasonal discounts will make Silkcorp's ever-fresh look even more fragrant.
Nine stores in Chicagoland; call (800) THE SILK for locations

Home Furnishings

China, Cookware, Crystal, & Silver

Dansk

Lighthouse Place, #105
Michigan City, IN 46360
(219) 879-8300 or (800) 624-5678
Hours: Mon–Sat: 9–8; Sun: 10–6
AE, DISC, MC, V
◆ **Senior Discount:** 10% on Tues **Age:** 62+

Occasionally grouped with Gorham and Lenox China and Tabletop in other outlet malls, Dansk stands alone in Lighthouse Place—and within the geographic boundaries covered by *Buying Retail Is Stupid!*. All the streamlined Scandinavian modern wood, stoneware, flatware, china, glassware, and linens are now at least 30% off; seasonal items (holiday mugs, for instance), slightly damaged goods, and nonselling wares are reduced even further. Since a number of Dansk patterns remain constant, nearly- and newlyweds, as well as folks adding to their collections, are known to haunt this store.

Lechter's Housewares

23 E. Madison St.
Chicago, IL 60602
(312) 629-2611
Hours: Mon–Fri: 8–7; Sat: 10–6
AE, DISC, MC, V

Housewares is one of those catchall words that seem to defy exclusions. Or, as one not-to-be-identified industry sales rep said, it

includes "everything but the kitchen sink . . . and sometimes that too." That is, indeed, Lechter's specialty, from salt and pepper shakers to wood picture frames. Depending on the brand name (and the buyer's clout), discounts run from 25% to 77%, and occasionally more. Recent price samples: a 12-cup Krups coffeemaker for $29.99; all Rubbermaid at 25% off; and $69.99 for a 102-piece flatware set from Farberware.
25+ stores in Chicagoland; call (800) 60-KITCHEN for locations

MIKASA
161 Skokie Valley Rd.
Highland Park, IL 60035
(847) 831-8820 or (800) 489-2200
Hours: Hours vary
AE, DISC, MC, V

Mikasa has always been cited for its quality china, silver, and kitchenware. And its national factory outlets, both freestanding and located in malls, usually offer different wares from those found at full price in department and specialty stores. Regardless of the specific inventory, all are still marked "Mikasa" . . . and the quality remains. We won't dish about the prices: five-piece stainless place-setting for $22.99 (regularly $50); a $17.99 Wild Lily Flower vase (was $35); and a 20-piece set at $29.99 closeout (reduced from $250). Five locations in Chicagoland ensure that no one will ever miss a Mikasa deal.
Huntley—11800 Factory Shops Blvd., (847) 669-0077
Kenosha, WI—Lakeside Marketplace, (414) 857-2003
Oak Brook—2155 W. 22nd St., (630) 572-6578
Wheaton—131 Towne Sq., (630) 752-0970

Waccamaw

Skokie Village Crossing Center, Touhy and Central Aves.
Skokie, IL 60077
(847) 675-3595
Hours: Mon–Fri: 10–9; Sat: 10–7; Sun: 11–6
AE, DISC, MC, NOV, V
◆ **Senior Discount:** 10% on Wed **Age:** 55+

One of our shopper-friends regularly patronizes Waccamaw to purchase her annual supply of plain, microwave-friendly plates, or to pick up a hostess gift or two. This regional chain, though, does stock more than porcelain and dishes; its all-home-furnishings merchandise is priced well for budget-conscious and first-apartment consumers. Such as its eight-piece "bed in a bag" for $70 (instead of $150). Or a six-pack of institutional white bath towels for $19.99. Mid-price points reign; well-known manufacturers from Cuisinart and Pfaltzgraff to Krups and Wamsutta sell their lower-end wares here.

Gurnee—6170 Grand Ave., (847) 855-0480
Naperville—856 S. Rte. 59, (630) 778-7718
Rolling Meadows—1400 E. Golf Rd., (847) 806-6105

Decorator Items

Crate & Barrel Outlet Store

800 W. North Ave.
Chicago, IL 60614
(312) 787-4775
Hours: Mon–Fri: 10–7; Sat: 10–6; Sun: 11–5
AE, DISC, MC, V

Most shoppers will recognize the clean lines, good quality, and trendy colors in Gordon Segal's acclaimed home-design store. All welcome its discount buys. In the same merchandise environment as its full-price siblings, each outlet offers a range of cost reductions: 20%–35% off classic jelly-jar and crystal glasses, dinnerware, canvas bags, and pots and pans—with further discounts on seasonal items (Christmas ornaments, patio furniture) and "shtickle," damaged or one-of-a-kind wares. Post-holiday sales, well-advertised, herald more dramatic discounts. When Crate & Barrel began to offer furniture in select stores, it was only a matter of time until rejects, returns, and slightly damaged sofas, tables, chairs, and so forth showed up in the outlets. To date, the Buffalo Grove outlet specializes in furnished goods; discounts are not that hefty (20% to 30%); the colors, occasionally odd; and the "as is" tags need to be inspected carefully.

Buffalo Grove—225 McHenry Rd., (847) 541-7700
Michigan City, IN—Lighthouse Place, Store 117, (219) 878-0200

Furniture

Leather Center

233 W. Huron St.
Chicago, IL 60610
(312) 943-9415
Hours: Mon–Thurs: 10–8; Fri & Sat: 10–6; Sun: 12–6
AE, DISC, MC, OPT, V

Mmm, the suppleness of leather. That feeling has seduced both the home furnishings industry and the consumer, broadening a selection once confined to Granddad's wing chair. Today, colors and grades of seating leather rival any fashion house—and prices are fiercely competitive. National factory outlet Leather Center offers fair prices for good-quality merchandise (a traditional-style five-cushion couch sells for about $1,500 plus tax) . . . and better, a lifetime warranty and 2-week delivery. Different provisions throughout the year, and sample sales will net eagle-eyed buyers even greater discounts.

Deerfield—495 Lake Cook Rd., (847) 564-0503
Lombard—2968 Finley Rd., (630) 916-9165
Schaumburg—168 E. Golf Rd., (847) 884-0900

LINENS

BED BATH & BEYOND

1800 N. Clybourn Ave.
Chicago, IL 60614
(312) 642-6596
Hours: Mon–Sat: 9:30–9; Sun: 10–6
AE, DISC, MC, V

Started in 1971 by New Yorkers Leonard Feinstein and Warren Eisenberg as Bed 'n' Bath, today's monster housewares, kitchen, and so forth discount retailer Bed Bath & Beyond, now with seven representatives in the Chicago area (and probably more to come), is designed to amaze, astound, and otherwise dazzle shoppers into buying. The enormous assortment guarantees that prices will be lower than retail (about 20%–40% reduced), and in-store and seasonal specials promise further savings. Some examples: Fieldcrest/Adrienne Vittadini king sheets for $39.99; J.A. Henckels seven-piece knife block set for $59.99; Dirt Devil hand vac at $39.99. Every name you know and trust for less—with 109+ stores in 25 states.

Seven stores in Chicagoland; see the Yellow Pages

LINENS 'N THINGS

600 N. Michigan Ave.
Chicago, IL 60611
(312) 787-0462 or (800) LNT-8765
Hours: Mon–Fri: 10–8; Sat: 9–7; Sun: 10–6
AE, DISC, MC, V

Having recovered from the initial foray of Filene's Basement, august Michigan Avenue has become fair game for all kinds of national discounters. One of the latest to join the fray is Linens 'N Things, sandwiched between a Marshalls and a movie complex. It is a curious mix of Bed Bath and Lechter's merchandise; domestics, for instance, features mid-scale wares (Wamsutta, Royal Velvet, et al.) at competitive prices: boldly colored full-size sheet sets for $59.99; Martex towels (the first set for $30.97; the second, 50% off). Yet, in the cooking and housewares departments the products definitely lean toward the higher end: Calphalon (seven pieces for $239.99); Cuisinart ($49.99 for a blender); tilt-top bed tray for $9.99. Compare and contrast, smart shoppers say.

150+ stores throughout the United States, 12+ in Chicagoland; call (800) LNT-8765 for locations

Jewelry

Jewelry Exchange

1313 N. York Rd.
Elmhurst, IL 60126
(630) 530-9490
Hours: Mon, Thurs: 10–8; Tues, Wed, Sat: 10–5:30; Sun: 11:30–5
AE, DISC, MC, V

A four-store firm that stretches from L.A. to New York (and stops here in suburban Elmhurst), the Jewelry Exchange not only guarantees its merchandise, but also manufactures pieces right at its facility-factory. Diamonds, especially, can be difficult to buy, because quality is, quite frankly, in the eyes of the knowledgeable beholder. Some of the wares displayed during our look-see: a 14K-gold heart pendant with 1 carat total weight (TW) of diamonds was tagged $199. And 1-carat TW diamond stud earrings, again set in 14K gold, were priced $399.

Medical & Optical Needs

AMERICA'S BEST
520 N. Michigan Ave.
Chicago, IL 60611
(312) 329-9750 or (800) TWO-PAIR
Hours: Mon–Fri: 9–7; Sat: 9–5
MC, V
◆ **Senior Discount:** 10% **Age:** 65+

The eyes have it: price wars for the consumer dollar have extended to optical exams and supplies, with the growth of chains such as Lenscrafters and Pearle Vision. And America's Best does its darnedest to compete, including a vow to offer "guaranteed lowest prices." A sample of current prices: two pairs of bifocals for $59.99 and disposable contacts for $49.99 (limited to new patients and to two six-packs).

Downers Grove—2934 Finley Rd., Main St. Sq., (630) 916-4770
Mundelein—Rte. 60, east of Rte. 45 by Menards, 62 Oak Creek Plaza, (847) 949-1212
Oak Lawn—Green Oaks Shopping Center, (708) 423-2020
Schaumburg—520 E. Golf Rd., (847) 781-1022

FOR EYES OPTICAL
635 Chicago Ave.
Evanston, IL 60202
(847) 864-8176 or (800) FOR-EYES
Hours: Mon–Thurs: 9–8; Fri–Sat: 9–6; Sun: 11–5
DISC, MC, V
◆ **Senior Discount:** 10% **Age:** 60+

There is something to be said for the old-fashioned optician who painstakingly measures, grinds, and fits the near- and farsighted. Yet, baby boomers, close to bifocal age, will also appreciate the 20%+ savings offered by larger chains such as For Eyes Optical. One week it's a storewide sale at 25%–50% off; another, the ad reads $69—one pair. Consistently good service, too, though not promised in 60 minutes.

Eight stores in Chicagoland; call (800) FOR-EYES for locations

Musical Instruments

Guitar Center
2375 S. Arlington Heights Rd.
Arlington Heights, IL 60005
(847) 439-4600
Hours: Mon–Fri: 10–9; Sat: 10–6; Sun: 12–6
AE, DISC, MC, V

It is devoted to guitars—but not to the exclusion of other musical instruments. In this 28-store national chain (outlets are located in California, Florida, Massachusetts, Michigan, Texas, and Wisconsin . . . and, of course, our grand state), anything even vaguely sound-related is featured, including books on artists and styles (peruse the RockWalk 10th-anniversary book at $49.95 for photographic peeks at some of the greats, such as Jimi Hendrix, Led Zeppelin, among others). Most musical brands are represented, and, though discounts vary, special and occasional catalog sales promise even greater bargains . . . such as a Zildjian stick bag for $9.99 (was $19.95).

Burbank—8250 S. Cicero Ave., (708) 422-1400
Chicago—3225 N. Clark St., (773) 327-5687
Villa Park—298 W. Roosevelt Rd., (630) 832-2800

Music Go Round
862 W. Main St.
West Dundee, IL 60118
(847) 426-1223
Hours: Mon–Fri: 10:30–8; Sat: 10–5; Sun: 12–4
AE, DIN, DISC, MC, V

Watch this space: Music Go Round, a franchise business owned by the parent of Computer Renaissance, Disc Go Round, Once Upon a Child, and Play It Again Sports, now has only two outlets in the Chicago area—Aurora and West Dundee, to be specific. But, just like its siblings, it'll grow; right now, there are 30 Music Go Round stores coast to coast. The idea: to buy, sell, and trade in new or used musical instruments, all in very good or mint condition. Though prices

can lean toward the high side, there are some decent bargains to be had: $175 Conn trombone with case; $379.99 Takamine acoustic guitar ($729 new); new five-piece Yamaha drum set at $699.99 (list is a grand). We especially appreciate the family-plan discount: after you buy a band instrument for one kid, the rest of your children get an extra 10% discount. Music to the wallet.
Aurora—4436 E. New York St., (630) 585-1066
30 locations throughout the United States

Office & Business Needs

ONE-STOP SUPPLIERS

ARVEY'S OFFICE SUPPLY

661 N. LaSalle St.
Chicago, IL 60610
(312) 951-5051
Hours: Suburban stores—Mon–Fri: 7:30–9; Sat: 9–5; Sun: 11–5
Hours: Downtown stores—Mon–Fri: 7–7; Sat: 9–5; Sun: 12–5
AE, DISC, MC, V

The players in the seemingly lucrative home-office market seem to either multiply—or merge. So, it's hard to tell who's the best for what product, when, and where. Regardless, Arvey's will remain the best lower-than-retail source for colored paper and envelopes as well as a wide selection of laser stationery. Of course, all the usual merchandise appears at good prices: computers, furniture, mailing and packaging materials, and a potpourri of supplies.
Arlington Heights—900 W. Algonquin Rd., (847) 870-0075
Chicago—3555 N. Kimball Ave., (312) 463-0822
Downers Grove—1306 Butterfield Rd., (630) 953-2727
Niles—8526 Golf Rd., (847) 956-4701

Office Depot

2928 N. Ashland Ave.
Chicago, IL 60657
(800) 557-3376
Hours: Mon–Fri: 7–9; Sat: 9–9; Sun: 10–6
AE, DISC, MC, Office Depot, V

What did home workers and small businesses do before the advent of the office superstore? No longer set to be the biggest (since the Federal Trade Commission disallowed its merger with East Coast Staples), Office Depot generally matches the below-retail prices offered not only by direct competitors such as Arvey's and Office Max, but also by computer discounters. Top brand names are discounted only 10%–20%. And certain omissions (there are few if any Apple products) are rather conspicuous. On the other hand, this national chain backs its prices with a 155% guarantee.

20+ stores in Chicagoland; see the Yellow Pages, or call (800) 557-3376 for locations

Office Max

2255 Howard St.
Evanston, IL 60202
(847) 492-0662
Hours: Mon–Fri: 7–9; Sat: 9–9; Sun: 10–6
AE, DISC, MC, V

As office superstores go, each has its own array of best products to buy. And national Office Max, with its 30+ Chicago-area stores, specializes in paper stuff, a rather decent array of ready-to-assemble office furniture from major manufacturers (Bush and O'Sullivan), and AT&T products. Its computer lines are roughly comparable to Office Depot's in terms of variety, brand names, and price. As are other business supplies. Check out these samples: 25 Pendaflex colored hanging file folders for $9.99 (once $17.95); $129.99 AT&T cordless phone; and a surprisingly good-looking cherry-laminate office suite to assemble at $399.99.

30 stores in Chicagoland; call (800) 788-8080 for locations

New & Used Products

Cort Furniture Rental Clearance Center

955 E. Algonquin Rd.
Arlington Heights, IL 60005
(847) 981-1450 or (800) 589-2678
Hours: Mon, Thurs: 9–7; Tues, Wed, Fri: 9–6; Sat: 10–5
AE, DISC, MC, V

Office furniture at a discount is readily available—and even cheaper when it's been used. National chain Cort specializes in the rentals of desks and chairs, so when customers return, trade in, or retire the goods, deals can reflect rock-bottom prices. And corporate-type residential furniture is also ready to buy—especially if you don't mind mixing and matching dining room chairs. Our tip: check carefully for dings, dents, scratches, and nonworking parts; if something's slightly out of kilter (and you either don't care or can fix it), negotiate, negotiate, negotiate! Some advertised specials: desks from $199 and $229; chairs starting at $99 and $129.

Chicago—22 W. Ontario St., (312) 266-8719
Naperville—25W221 Ogden Ave., (630) 355-4664

Paper & Party Goods

Paper Supplies

Lewis Paper Place

705 S. Jefferson St.
Chicago, IL 60607
(312) 922-2000
Hours: Mon–Fri: 7–5
MC, V

Here's our submission for the Guinness Book of World Records: the only drive-through discount retailer of quality papers for printing (because there's absolutely zip parking on Jefferson Street). Headquartered in Lisle, with four other stores in Chicago as well as in South Bend, Kalamazoo, and Denver/Fort Collins, Lewis Paper

Place specializes in "forest products" for graphic designers and printers—names such as Wausau, Howard Linen, Starwhite Vicksburg, and others. How could anyone resist the colorful appeals of lively ivory, moonstone blue, rocket red, or star sapphire grey? Seriously, though reams intended for photocopying use are also stocked here (and at prices competitive with the office superstores), the best deals are on top-notch papers: Astrobright 60# text in letter size at $10.99 (for one K's worth) and 80# Howard Linen cover at $31.49. Save bucks; print with a friend.

Six locations in Chicagoland; some in the Yellow Pages

Party Goods

Factory Card Outlet

2585 N. Elston Ave.
Chicago, IL 60614
(773) 486-0948
Hours: Mon–Sat: 9–9; Sun: 10–6
DISC, MC, V
◆ **Senior Discount:** 10% on Wed **Age:** 55+

Based in Bensenville, Illinois, Factory Card Outlet boasts more than 125 stores, with more to be launched soon. The eight or so locations in and around Chicago offer the now-famous 39¢ greeting cards, along with party supplies, gift wraps, and special-occasion items at excellent savings. A few examples: $3.88 for a 100-count pack of plastic cutlery; Easter tissue paper at $1.49 (was $1.99); and 10-oz. Valentine mugs for 99¢ each. Quite a change from its 1980s beginnings as a greeting-card showroom.

Eight locations in Chicagoland; see the Yellow Pages

Party City
3417 N. Western Ave.
Chicago, IL 60618
(773) 871-3500
Hours: Mon–Fri: 9–9; Sat: 9:30–8; Sun: 10–5
AE, DISC, MC, V

Does the ever-increasing number of party-ware discounters indicate that Americans are entertaining more? Probably not. But, with over 175 stores nationally, New Jersey–based Party City lays claim to being one of the oldest superchains that supply plastics and paper, streamers, and decorations for any and all occasions. Prices are consistently 30%–50% below retail; at Halloween, for instance, kids can choose to ape Wolfman or emulate Spiderella for a mere $19.99. Corporate headquarters: Rockway, NJ, (201) 983-0888; see the Yellow Pages

Pets & Animal Supplies

Pet Care
143 Skokie Valley Rd.
Highland Park, IL 60085
(800) 394-4PET
Hours: Mon–Sat: 9–9; Sun: 10–6
DISC, MC, V

Any store that allows your pet to accompany you shopping is, well, the cat's meow. And on special occasions, national discounter Pet Care will even sell some of the smaller beasts, such as fancy hamsters ($3.99) and guinea pigs ($16.99), even baby iguanas and ferrets. All the grocery store and premium pet foods are available at about a 20%–30% savings; brand-name accessories, grooming tools, and treats are also found on the shelves at similar savings. Weekly sales advertised in newspaper circulars stretch dollars further, as does their promise: "low price guaranteed; we'll match any competitor's advertised price."

Pet Supplies/Plus

5435 N. Harlem Ave.
Chicago, IL 60634
(773) 594-1717
Hours: Mon–Sat: 9–9; Sun: 10–6
MC, V

Any household claiming more than one pet deserves a major discount by our humane standards—whether it be on food or litter or treats. And not only does national chain Pet Supplies/Plus reduce the prices on supplies for our companion animals with a smile, but it also doubles manufacturers' coupons (up to $1) on its storehouse of more than 10,000 items. Besides, the prices are seductive: four cans of 9 Lives cat food for $1; two 25-pound bags of Cats' Pride litter for $5; a 37.5-pound bag of Purina dog chow at $12.88. (Pet Supplies/Plus delivers all your pets' needs right to your door for a charge of about $15. Prices may exceed this amount depending on your purchase.)

13 locations in the Chicago area; see the Yellow Pages

PetSmart

291 Skokie Blvd.
Northbrook, IL 60062
(800) 785-0557
Hours: Mon–Fri: 9–9; Sat: 10–9; Sun: 11–7
DISC, MC, V

With 30 locations in Chicago, PetSmart superstores offer a "double-the-difference" price guarantee on over 12,000 pet-related items, including pet foods and treats: Science Diet, Iams, Authority, Ralston Purina, Friskies, and Alpo. Or make sure your companion animal is collared and leashed; shampooed; cologned; protected from fleas and ticks; and supplied with vast quantities of playthings. There are also over 500 varieties of tropical fish. Pets are more than encouraged to visit to sample new foods and treats, learn obedience, be groomed, or get vaccinated (the doctor's always in, since PetSmart leases space to independently owned and operated veterinary clinics). Since 1987, PetSmart has donated over $2.5 million to local and national animal charities, such as the American Humane

Association. Plus, no puppy or kitty mills here; each store features a "Luv a Pet" adoption center—operated by local animal shelters and rescue groups. Woof!
30 stores in Chicagoland; call (800) 785-0557 for locations

Plants, Lawn & Garden

Frank's Nursery & Crafts
1920 W. Dempster St.
Evanston, IL 60201
(847) 866-6988
Hours: Mon–Sat: 9–9; Sun: 9–6
AE, MC, V
◆ **Senior Discount:** 10% **Age:** 65+

Nursery is the name at Frank's; the rest seems somewhat incidental (such as its crafts and decorations). But this national chain offers hard-to-find garden fungicides and herbicides, manufactured by Greenview et al., which are reasonably priced with formulas equal or superior to the national brands. Too, check the tags on fledgling trees and shrubs against local greenhouse prices; Frank's will exchange or refund if its tree won't grow in Brooklyn—er, Berwyn.
Deerfield—497 Lake Cook Rd., (847) 498-0146
Morton Grove—6715 W. Dempster St., (847) 966-2611

Special Sales

J. Tiras Handbags
6101 Royalton, Suite 106
Houston, TX 77081
(800) 460-1999
AE, MC, V

Once a year, Texan Jerome Tiras comes to town—two days in Chicago, two in a northern suburb—to tout his handbag impostors, all at substantially lower prices. Look-alikes cost from 50% to 80%+ off the prices of the original designs; for example, a Judith Lieber minaudière or evening purse copycat is $425 (compared to $1,000). Other imitated designers include Bottega Veneta, Finesse, and Salvatore Ferragamo.

Kids Catalog

Locations vary
(800) 826-0619
Hours: Hours vary
AE, DISC, MC, V

It's a traveling road show: overstocks, nonsellers, and past-season merchandise from four mainly kids' clothing catalogs—After the Stork, Little Feet, Playclothes, and Sun Skins—are collected, then sold at up to 70% reductions at various locations around the country. In May 1997, baby through teen wares starred for one weekend in Westmont—one of our western suburbs—at the Inland Meeting & Expo Center (strollers were also welcome). Fall 1997 appearances were expected in Baltimore; Boxborough, Massachusetts; Edison, New Jersey; and Minneapolis. Call (800) 826-0619 to request a free copy of their sales-alert newsletter.

Sports & Recreation

Exercise Equipment

Play It Again Sports

2101 W. Irving Park Rd.
Chicago, IL 60618
(773) 463-9900
Hours: Hours vary; check with individual stores
AE, DISC, MC, V

What's the best-selling equipment at Play It Again Sports? Ironically enough, exercise equipment (at least at this Irving Park outlet), since barbells and rowing/biking/treadmill machines are also the first to be sold. Started in the late 1980s in Minnesota, this national

franchise is now the largest retailer of new and used sports equipment, numbering nearly 700 stores, with 12 to 15 representatives here (all individually owned and operated). Recycled products usually sell for about 50% of retail; new items reflect a smaller discount. A sampling of summer 1997 sports fan choices: $14.99 for a pair of used in-line skates; about eight bucks for an 8-pound vinyl weight; well-loved baseball catcher knee pads for $5.99. Other services: skate sharpening ($3); lessons of all kinds; and a golf driving range at $3 a bucket. Services, prices, and hours vary from store to store.
12–15 locations in Chicagoland; see the Yellow Pages

GOLF

LAS VEGAS DISCOUNT GOLF & TENNIS

687 E. Golf Rd.
Schaumburg, IL 60173
(847) 781-0737
Hours: Mon–Fri: 10–7; Sat: 10–6; Sun: 11–5
AE, DISC, MC, V

Whether the score's 40–love or a handicap under 5, those needing a racket or club—for sports reasons only!—best check Las Vegas Discount Golf & Tennis. With more than 21 years of experience, and 65 locations in 20 states (though only 1 site in the Chicago area), it has weathered both drought and flood of demand to outfit amateur Jack Nicklauses and Steffi Grafs. Find here not only retail golf and tennis equipment, but also apparel and other related merchandise from manufacturers such as Cole, Taylor Made, Cobra, Ping, Wilson, Hogan, Foot-Joy, and more. Sales mean even greater savings, such as a free three-pack of Penn balls with every tennis racket purchase or a gratis Cutter & Polo shirt with any Alien Wedge buy. All merchandise is clearly displayed and identified to enable a rapid transition to the links and the clay (or grass) courts.

NEVADA BOB'S DISCOUNT GOLF AND TENNIS

60 E. Lake St.
Chicago, IL 60601
(312) 726-4653
Hours: Hours vary; check with individual stores
AE, DISC, MC, V

One man, Tiger Woods, has done more for the sport of golf than any other individual to date. So, expect the 25 million Americans now enjoying tees for four to double, maybe even triple, in the next decade. Then, yes, worldwide discounters such as Nevada Bob's (300 stores) will literally rake in the greens. With 11 locations in our neighborhood, Nevada Bob's usually proffers a range of equipment and apparel ready for beginning and prime-time players at a 40% discount. Some of the values we spied: $9.99 for closeout Spalding golf shoes; 15 Pinnacle Gold golf balls for $13.99; two all-cotton Equus men's shirts for $29.99 (usually $24.99 each).
11 locations in Chicagoland; see the Yellow Pages

WINTER & WATER SPORTS

BOAT-U.S. MARINE CENTERS

567 E. Roosevelt Rd.
Lombard, IL 60148
(630) 792-1550
Hours: Mon–Thurs, Sat: 9–8; Fri: 9–9; Sun: 9–5
AE, DISC, MC, V

Lake Michigan, say confirmed sailors, is one of the trickiest waters to navigate—due to mercurial weather that can storm or shine at a moment's notice. That watery challenge has inspired boaters here; there's always a years-long waiting list for slips in Chicago proper. Not surprising, marine stores are popping up in and around our fair city. Enter, then, two outlets of BOAT-U.S. Marine Centers, the retail division of the 510,000-member BOAT-U.S., the nation's largest organization of recreational boaters. Here, 8,000 items of sailing stuff—equipment, electronics, accessories, even clothing—are sold at 50% off retail. Membership does have its rewards, such as boat loans and charter bargains. If you find a lower price—anywhere—

they'll match it on the spot! Annual dues are $17; call (800) 395-2628 for more information.
Arlington Heights—63 W. Rand Rd., (847) 398-0606

BOATER'S WORLD (CHICAGO YACHTING & NAVIGATION)
1661 N. Elston Ave.
Chicago, IL 60621
(773) 227-7900
Hours: Mon–Sat: 9–8; Sun: 10–5
AE, DISC, MC, V

Ahoy, confirmed landlubbers: here is the one place not to shop if you're water-phobic, you hate boats, or you're simply immune to the pleasures of sailing. On the other hand, we can't think of many stores we'd rather poke around in. Boater's World—the old Chicago Yachting & Navigation on Elston—soon will have two representatives in our area, bringing to 81 the number of stores nationwide. Owned by Ritz Cameras, this discount marine center carries wares from anchors to trailers, interesting stuff such as premium golden teak oil, white polo rags, and lulu teasers (we kid you not; they're fishing lures). Better yet, all hands are experienced and will help you decide best brands or put together a halyard. They regularly offer about a 10%–15% discount, and more with special sales, coupons, and an annual Captain's Club membership.

WEST MARINE
627 W. North Ave.
Chicago, IL 60614
(312) 654-1818
Hours: Mon–Sat: 9–9; Sun: 9–5
AE, DISC, MC, V

Rich Steams of Doyle Sail on spinnaker trim and handling . . . Wednesday-evening fleet nights with discounts to all attending. It's clear from a glance at the events board, the depth of merchandise, and the knowledgeable staff (everyone either sails or, in Chicago vernacular, "stinkpots") that West Mariners know their stuff. Based in California with 162 stores nationally in strategic waterfront areas, West Marine has four in our area, each stocking over 32,000 items.

Discounts vary (but they will meet/beat others' prices): Bose environmental speakers for $239 (list $279); mooring whips for a 17-footer at $219 (retail $309); $59.95 for a stainless-steel destroyed wheel ($100 regularly). It's worth buying the catalog for five bucks; hints and tips from the West Advisor (e.g., about fuel filters and anchor windlasses) provide invaluable information.
Fox Lake—2 W. Grand Ave., (847) 973-2221
Michigan City, IN—3221 Franklin St., (219) 874-9722
Racine, WI—427 S. Main St., (414) 637-3500

Surplus

Dollar Bills

3339 W. Belmont Ave.
Chicago, IL 60618
(312) 588-3386
Hours: Mon–Sat: 9–9; Sun: 11–6
Cash, check

Remember when Mom and Dad reminisced about the good ole days . . . and the good ole prices, like 5¢ for a loaf of bread? Since today's dollar is probably close to yesterday's nickel, national franchise Dollar Bills promotes the buying power of a buck . . . and amazes even the most jaded of us with its offerings. Every store of the 20+ in Chicagoland features some items over the magic dollar line—a pounder-plus jar of Prego spaghetti sauce for $1.50, Quaker Life cereal for $2.50—but most merchandise falls within the 1-buck-or-less guidelines. A sampling of the generic and branded savings, all for 100 pennies each: 3.7-ounce Crest toothpaste, two Jell-O packets, two Campbell's tomato soups, paper and cleaning products, gift wrap, even tool sets.
20+ locations in Chicagoland; see the Yellow Pages

Everything's $1.00
4125 Harlem Ave.
Norridge, IL 60634
(708) 457-8300
Hours: Mon–Sat: 10–9; Sun: 10–6
Cash, check

Everything's $1.00 provides value to customers by offering quality closeout merchandise for just $1. For a mere 100 pennies, find books, food and snacks, gifts, health and beauty aids, stationery . . . all at 20%–50% below retail. Why so low a price tag? Because of manufacturers' overruns, changes in packaging, inaccurate market forecasts, or financial distress (read: Chapter 11 bankruptcies and the like). Plus, there are no defectives, seconds, or impaired merchandise.
13 locations in Chicagoland; see the Yellow Pages

MacFrugal's Bargains Close-Outs
785 W. Golf Rd.
Des Plaines, IL 60016
(847) 228-1254
Hours: Mon–Sat: 9–9; Sun: 11–8
DISC, MC, V

What a manufacturer might lose is our gain at MacFrugal's, with five locations in our area. Here are the sources of the Mac's largesse: packaging changes, overruns, customs appropriations, factory downtimes, warehouse relocations, canceled orders, discontinueds, buybacks, and media brokers (among others). But, quite frankly, our concentration is on the 30,000+ different items . . . and the 70% savings. On the day we visited, we grabbed the following: a 40-quart Sterilite wastebasket at $3.99; $1.59 for 36 sheets of Bounce; $7.99 for Farberware nonstick fry pans; and Anchor-Hocking food storage systems starting at 99¢.
Glendale Heights—203 E. Army Trail Rd., (847) 539-0914
Lombard—441 E. Roosevelt Rd., (708) 953-9420
Niles—7215 W. Dempster St., (847) 966-2709
Woodridge—7340 Woodward Ave., (630) 852-6639

Toys, Dolls & Games

TOYS "R" US

State and Madison Sts.
Chicago, IL 60608
(773) 247-4411
Hours: Hours vary
AE, DISC, MC, NOV, V

It is as difficult to compete with a mega retailer the size and stature of Paramus, New Jersey–based Toys "R" Us as it is to refuse kids who beg for one more Barbie accessory or the newest game. (We know from personal experience.) There's also no denying that this superstore, with more than 26 individual representatives (and a downtown State Street branch) established here, offers some of the best prices and broadest variety of merchandise around. Every brand name is well ensconced in at least one of its aisles: find Fisher-Price, Huffy, Nintendo, Sega, and dozens of others. Plus its "low price guaranteed" assures customers that Toys "R" Us will match any advertised price (with a few restrictions, of course). Some springtime savings: a Sony analog joystick for $69.99; swing sets from $99.99; and in-line skates from $19.99.

27+ locations in Chicagoland; see the Yellow Pages

U.S. TOY CO./CONSTRUCTIVE PLAYTHINGS ✪

5314 W. Lincoln Ave.
Skokie, IL 60077
(847) 675-5900
Hours: Mon–Wed, Fri: 8:30–6; Thurs: 8:30–9; Sat: 8:30–5; Sun: 12–5
Institutional accounts, MC, V

Another name for kid heaven: the only Chicagoland outlet of U.S. Toy Co. (aka Constructive Playthings), though five others exist in Colorado, Florida, Kansas, Pennsylvania, and Texas. So, better make sure you explore sans the young set; discounts from 5% to 20% on lines from Brio and Crayola to Milton Bradley and Ravensburgers are common. Better yet are the wholesale tags on carnival prizes and supplies and the spring/fall and sidewalk sales. Teachers' alert: this catalog outlet also offers crafts, goody-bag ideas, day-care/preschool furniture, resources, and other helpful merchandise. Another 10% goes to eager parent-readers of *Buying Retail Is Stupid!* with coupon.

C

Factory Mall Outlets

The impetus for constructing an outlet mall in a town, at least here in Chicago, is not necessarily to bolster consumer spending. Rather, the additional revenues projected to tumble in are eyed hungrily by town officials—and, of course, the developers.

Such may be the case with Monee, situated between Park Forest to the north and Peotone to the south (and thus within *Buying Retail Is Stupid!—Chicago*'s shopping grounds). In December 1996, this town of 1,800 citizens announced plans for a new $200 million mega-mall—200 stores and restaurants, 20 movie screens, and parking for 10,000 vehicles, not to mention an anticipated $4.5 million in yearly sales taxes.

Is there a real need for a seventh outlet mall? Yes, say retail experts, since the six million consumers within a 40-mile radius are not saturated with *this* particular type of shopping format. In fact, Off Fifth—Saks Fifth Avenue Outlet was the first to sign on with Monee—even though they have two other stores in Illinois (Schaumburg and Gurnee). Expect Monee Mills to open in 1999.

And with number seven solidly on the drawing boards, are numbers eight and nine far behind? Kankakee and Morris, Illinois, have both announced mega-mall plans, too.

Gurnee Mills

6170 W. Grand Ave.
Gurnee, IL 60031
(847) 263-7500
Hours: Mon–Sat: 10–9; Sun: 11–6
AE, DISC, MC, V

Gurnee Mills features 229 outlet stores, including: Totes Factory Store, Baby Guess?/Guess? Kids Factory Store, Levi's Outlet, Carter's Childrenswear, Bugle Boy Factory Store, Corning/Revere Factory Store, ACA Joe, Casual Male Big and Tall Outlet, L'eggs/Hanes/Bali/Playtex, Etienne Aigner, Athletes Foot Outlet, Champs Outlet, Ann Taylor Factory Store, Bass Apparel, London Fog Factory Store, Mondi, PS Plus Sizes, Tahari Outlet, Bentley's Luggage Outlet, Lands' End Outlet, Barbizon Lingerie Co., Van Heusen, Westport Woman/Westport Ltd., and more!

This nonsmoking indoor mall provides wheelchairs, strollers, and Smartcart rentals at no charge. Only minutes away from Six Flags Great America Theme Park.

See also Bed Bath & Beyond, Burlington Coat Factory, Gap Outlet, JCPenney Outlet Store, Kids' Express, Leathermode, Music Recyclery, Nine West Outlet, Off Fifth—Saks Fifth Avenue Outlet, The Sharper Image, Spiegel Outlet Store, Swatch Outlet, Syms, and TJ Maxx

Huntley Factory Shops

11800 Factory Shops Blvd.
Huntley, IL 60142
(847) 669-9100
Hours: Mon–Sat: 10–9; Sun: 11–6
Credit cards accepted depend on store

More than 60 stores, including: Bose Factory Store, Petite Sophisticates, Geoffrey Beene, Casual Corner Woman, Westport Woman, Cape Isle Knitter, Royal Doulton Outlet, Baldwin Brass Home Accents, American Eagle Outlet, Toy Liquidators, Britches Great Outdoor Outlet, American Tourister Factory Outlet, Big Dog Sportswear, Carter's Childrenswear, Aileen Bass Company, Levi's Outlet, Bugle Boy Factory Store, Corning/Revere Factory Store, County Seat Outlet, Jones New York Factory Finale, Champion Hanes, S&K

Menswear, Fila, Van Heusen, Famous Brands Housewares Outlet, Reebok, Rockport, The Paper Factory, and more.

See also Gap Outlet, Leathermode, Mikasa, and Nine West Outlet

KENOSHA FACTORY OUTLET

7700 120th Ave.
Kenosha, WI 53142
(414) 857-7961
Hours: Mon–Sat: 10–9; Sun: 10–6
Credit cards accepted depend on store

This site features 105 outlet stores, including: Bugle Boy, Champion Hanes, The Company Store, Eddie Bauer Outlet, The Jockey Store, Van Heusen, Baby Express, Toy Liquidators, Golden Books Factory Store, Buxton, The Paper Factory, Totes and Sunglass World, Welcome Home, Shoes to Boot, Sony Factory Outlet Center, Fieldcrest Cannon, Rue 21, C.S.O., and much more.

See also Famous Footwear, Hit or Miss, and Kids' Express

LAKESIDE MARKETPLACE OUTLET CENTER

11211 120th Ave., Suite 19A
Kenosha, WI 53142
(414) 857-2101
Hours: Mon–Sat: 10–9; Sun: 11–6
AE, DISC, MC, V (also depends on store)

Here you'll find 76 outlet stores, including: Donna Karan Company Store, Black & Decker, NordicTrack, Fila, Van Heusen, Anne Klein Factory Store, Izod/Gant, Avia, J H Collectibles, Liz Claiborne Outlet Store, American Tourister Factory Outlet, Maidenform, Carole Little, Timberland Factory Outlet, Enzo Angiolini, Bass Company, Dansk Factory Outlet, Benetton, Brooks Brothers Factory Store, Joan & David, Cambridge Dry Goods Company, Polo Ralph Lauren Factory Store, J. Crew Factory Store, B.U.M. Equipment, Big Dog Sportswear, OshKosh B'Gosh Factory Store, Genuine Kids, Boot Factory, Leslie Fay, Nike Factory Store, and more.

See also Andrew Marc Company Store, and Chicago Cutlery, Etc., Mikasa

LIGHTHOUSE PLACE OUTLET CENTER

601 Wabash
Michigan City, IN 46360
(219) 879-6506 or (800) 866-5900
Hours: Mon–Sat: 9–8; Sun: 10–6 (Jan. 1 through Feb. 29: Mon–Sat: 9–6; Sun: 10–6)
AE, DISC, MC, V

Lighthouse Place offers 110 outlet stores, including: Ann Taylor, American Eagle Outlet, Van Heusen, Toy Liquidators, Timberland Factory Outlet, Anne Klein Factory Store, Bass Company, Benetton, Stone Mountain Handbags, Boston Traders, Jones New York, Pfaltzgraff Factory Store, Oneida Factory Store, Bugle Boy Factory Store, Brooks Brothers Factory Store, Carole Little, Maidenform, Carter's Childrenswear, London Fog Factory Store, J H Collectibles, J. Crew Factory Store, Izod/Gant, Guess? Factory Store, Eddie Bauer Outlet Store, Donna Karan Company Store, Corning/Revere Factory Store, and much more.

See also Crate & Barrel Outlet Store, Ellen Tracy, The Exclusive Oilily Store, Gap Outlet, Hanna Andersson, Maternity Works, Mikasa, Nine West Outlet, Sara Lee Outlet Store, Sassafras Factory Outlet Store, Spiegel Outlet Store, and Tommy Hilfiger

THE PIANO FACTORY OUTLET MALL

410 S. First St.
St. Charles, IL 60174
(630) 584-2099
Hours: Mon–Fri: 10–9; Sat: 10–6; Sun: 11–5
Credit cards accepted depend on store

More than 20 special shops averaging 20%–70% off retail including: American Tourister, Banister/Easy Spirit Outlet, Izod, Corning/Revere Factory Store, The Housewares Outlet Store, The Leather Manor, Temptations Jewelry, Kitchen Collection, and more.

See also Misty Harbor

D

Antiques and Collectibles

Every little town (and big city, too) now boasts at least one antique mall filled to the ceiling with tchotchkes. For *Buying Retail Is Stupid!—Chicago*, we focused primarily on Chicago co-ops with a lot of sellers—obviously, to offer smart shoppers a lot of choices.

There are, however, many, many more to shop, too numerous for inclusion here. The best guide, in our opinion, to the who, what, where, and when of antiques and collectibles malls in the tristate area is *AntiqueWeek's Central Antique Shop Guide*. Issued yearly by *AntiqueWeek*, it's a mere $3.50 postpaid. (There's an Eastern edition, too.) Call (800) 876-5133 for ordering information, or write the editorial folks at P.O. Box 90, Knightstown, IN 46148.

Antique Stores & Malls

Armitage Antique Gallery
1529 W. Armitage Ave.
Chicago, IL 60622
(773) 227-7727
Hours: Mon–Sun: 11–6
MC, V

Dealers come and dealers go in this very citified mall of 10 different antiques and collectibles proprietors. But, the merchandise is always varied enough to poke, peek, and prod to uncover something worth purchasing. At last visit, costume jewelry was much on display, along with 1940s furnishings, textiles, and accessories such as hammered aluminum, Czech pottery, and assorted potpourri. Occasionally, fine jewelry sneaks in (former Guv Big Jim Thompson showed a few antique watches). And a real find, despite interior designers who haunt this place, appears at times, such as the incomplete green-and-white set of Clarice Cliff dinnerware for $750 (one piece alone can sell for that much).

Belmont Antique Mall

2041 W. Belmont Ave.
Chicago, IL 60618
(773) 549-9270
Hours: Mon–Sun: 11–6
AE, DISC, MC, V

We absolutely adore this mall owner's attitude: make an offer on any item tagged at $100 (or more) . . . and we'll communicate it to the dealer. Open in two locations, the Belmont Antique Mall boasts 40 dealers, some fairly heavy customer traffic, and a mixed bag of bargains, from vintage clothes in good repair to Victorian-era furniture. The nooks and crannies will intrigue the hardiest of treasure hunters. We got excited about a set of Blue Ridge pottery (signed by Paul McCobb, a highly collectible 1940s–1950s designer) for $150, while we were puzzled by a $460 tag on a walnut dresser. Then again, the motto of an antiquer always prevails: buy low, sell high.
Chicago—2229 W. Belmont Ave., (773) 871-3915

Chicago Antique Centre, Ltd. ★

3045 N. Lincoln Ave.
Chicago, IL 60657
(773) 929-0200
Hours: Mon–Sun: 11–6
AE, DISC, MC, V

The nooks and crannies of an urban antiques mall are definitely worth a second, even third, look, since stock (and dealers) can turn over at a rapid rate. Not as heavily trafficked as Wrigleyville malls and featuring lower prices is the 35-dealer Chicago Antique Centre. On a recent visit, hidden among the hordes of crystal beads and sturdy oak and pine furniture were a few Italian glass vases, reasonably priced. Other categories found: pottery, costume jewelry, textiles, African artifacts, collectibles (i.e., anything mass-produced and less than 100 years old), pictures, silver, china, vintage apparel. And parking behind the building makes a visit (or two or three) very accessible—and appealing. Adding to that accessibility is the mall's 10%-additional-discount coupon just for *Buying Retail Is Stupid!—Chicago* readers.

INTERNATIONAL ANTIQUES ✪

2300 W. Diversey Ave.
Chicago, IL 60647
(773) 227-2400
Hours: Mon–Sun: 11–6
AE, MC, V

In a surprisingly commodious space, 20-something antiques dealers trade their wares, ranging from country pine to 1940s and 1950s signed furniture. The accent here is on the "bigs" rather than the "smalls" (i.e., items easily carried in hand or knapsack), so enterprising shoppers will find roomfuls of furniture in a few vignettes and displays. "Let's make a deal" is the name of the game here, with *Buying Retail Is Stupid!—Chicago* readers profiting from an extra 10% discount.

KOHLER'S TRADING POST

638 E. St. Charles Rd.
Lombard, IL 60148
(630) 620-1220
Hours: Tues–Sat: 10–5
MC, V

Filmmakers instinctively gravitate to the barns and yards of Kohler's—like the set designers for *Dennis the Menace* and *Baby's Day Out.* In fact, it's not that unusual to find an English telephone booth ($3,100) or a pair of cannons waiting for an enterprising (and brave) buyer. More than 65 years of collecting, through three generations, have spurred Kohler's growth—and simply, an incredible potpourri of stuff: a mélange of porcelain sinks and toilets, *National Geographics*, old 78 RPM records, furniture, and et ceteras.

LINCOLN ANTIQUE MALL ★

3141 N. Lincoln Ave.
Chicago, IL 60657
(773) 244-1440
Hours: Mon–Sun: 11–7
AE, DIN, DISC, MC, OPT, V

An array of 60 dealers and ever-changing antique and collectible merchandise almost guarantee that sharp-eyed bargain hunters sometimes find a great deal. Or, at least, a fair one. Unfortunately, with the proliferation of price books on various antique categories, even old buttons and cigarette cases, finding a Picasso in the trash is a rare, winning-the-lottery type of experience. But, here in the Lincoln Antique Mall are good buys on furniture and accessories as well as the "smalls"—lunch boxes, quilts, costume jewelry, '50s and '60s paraphernalia. And a true lust to uncover the next copy of the Declaration of Independence can be sated, in part, by the use of the additional-10%-off *Buying Retail Is Stupid!—Chicago* coupon.

LOOK WHAT I FOUND ★

2907 N. Broadway
Chicago, IL 60657
(773) 472-7202
Hours: Mon–Fri: 12–7; Sat & Sun: 10–7
MC, V

The name's a clear giveaway: once a kid's exuberant chant, "Look What I Found" in the heart of New Town is now a retail mix of vintage, resale, and antique home and body furnishings. Dresses and suits, inner wear and outerwear from the fine salons of Marshall Field's and Saks Fifth are usually priced at a 40% discount (though manager Diane Skolnique indicates a willingness to negotiate). Costume jewelry fans will gladly paw through the stash of pins and earrings, even complete parures hallmarked Coro, Eisenberg, Hobe, Hattie Carnegie, Vendome, and Weiss (among others). An even better incentive for *Buying Retail Is Stupid!—Chicago* readers: a $20 minimum purchase qualifies for a free pair of artisan-made earrings.

Phil's Factory Antique Mall
2040 W. Belmont Ave.
Chicago, IL 60618
(773) 528-8549
Hours: Mon–Sun: 11–6
MC, V

"Phil" is Phyllis, in reality, and she manages a barn of a 14-dealer antiques mall right in the heart of "Collectibles Central." Best known for furniture, the mall posts reasonable prices: $225 for a good condition '50s kitchen dinette set; an unusually ornate hand-carved wood chair at $500; and a wood chest of unspecified origin for $150. Tucked in one conspicuous corner is a paper goods dealer, trading in soon-to-be-extinct commodities such as old sheet music and Superman comics.

Wrigleyville Antique Mall ✪
3336 N. Clark St.
Chicago, IL 60657
(773) 868-0285
Hours: Mon–Sat: 11–6:30; Sun: 12–6
AE, DISC, MC, V

More than 50 dealers on two levels with all types of merchandise, great and small, are found in this spacious antiques and collectibles mall. Coproprietor Danny Alias has attracted some of the best and brightest antiques traders in town with pre–baby boomer items: chrome Chase accessories, Czech pottery, '50s dining sets, even art deco furniture. Prices are fair, and if you have a resale tax number, even fairer. And the fairest of them all is the 10% extra *Buying Retail Is Stupid!—Chicago* savings on any $10 minimum purchase.

Flea Markets & Antique Shows

Shopping flea markets is a very serious business here in the Midwest. Devotees of this pastime have been known to drive two and a half hours beginning at 3:00 A.M. to trek through oozing mud and large-enough-to-drown-a-rottweiler rain puddles to find a treasure.

Why? Maybe because our official "hunting" season is so short—from April through October. Or maybe it's because collectors from the East and the West (not to mention from overseas) have converged on the heartland, discovering that our prices and merchandise are reasonable and unusual, respectively. Or maybe because we're just a little bit more fanatic about the antiquing process.

Whatever. There are a ton of unwritten rules and regulations surrounding negotiations, timing, prices, and the exact nature of the collectible.

To acquire that kind of knowledge, we suggest subscribing to one of the weeklies or monthlies covering the business. (*AntiqueWeek* is our current favorite; see page 302 for ordering information.) Look for, in particular, Harry Rinker's column; he's a sort of Jimmy Breslin equivalent in antiques and collectibles. We find his humor refreshing amidst those who take themselves (and their collections) way too seriously.

There is one flea market topic, however, that begs to be covered. That is, what to take along and wear. Here, then, is our own personal list-to-end-all-other-lists:

1. Layered clothing.

   One minute hot. Next minute, not. The vagaries of weather here are impossible to predict (one reason why our local TV networks run through so many meteorologists). Seriously, be prepared to add or subtract apparel as need be.
2. Comfortable walking shoes.

   Need we say more?
3. A poncho with hood.

   The lightweight kind that fits in a purse or pocket is best.
4. A sun/rain hat.

   Don't underestimate the powerful protection a well-brimmed hat provides. And if you can't find a topper that double-functions, then go with the headgear that shields from Uncle Sun.
5. Cash—and lots of it.

   Hey, you *can* leave home without them—American Express, MasterCard, Visa, and the like. Because the minute you mention credit or plastic, the price increases. And cards are harder to haggle and negotiate. Traveler's checks are OK in some markets, not in others.

6. A magnifying glass and a jeweler's loupe.

   Let's face it: tired baby-boomer eyes are afflicted with presbyopia (read: we need bifocals). So, any aid to vision deserves to be included—especially if you're searching for hallmarks, logos, brands, or signatures.

7. Tape measure(s).

   One is usually not enough. (Ours are either permanently misplaced or twisted beyond repair.) It's important to verify that the armoire for the guest bedroom will not only suit the decor, but also accommodate the room's (and the door opening) dimensions.

8. A pocketknife.

   We're definitely pacifists—and proponents of nonviolence. Still, a mini-knife helps with the hunt . . . to scrape off flakes of paint . . . to pry open unwilling drawers . . . to cut off a reluctant tag.

9. Notebook and pen.

   Documenting prices and purchases and great and lousy dealer names, addresses, and phone numbers helps make us all better antiquers.

10. A magnet.

    Only schlep this if you're testing for brass (it clings) and copper and other base metals (it doesn't).

11. An instant camera.

    Spy a piece that you just aren't ready to buy yet? Searching for inspiration on redecorating? Need to record an event for posterity? Then, by all means, take along an instant camera—but it should be extremely lightweight.

12. Diapers.

    You read it right: softer-than-soft cloth diapers, if the collectible is at all fragile. Dealers may or may not have bubble plastic or newspapers to wrap around your new possessions. Ergo, BYOD.

13. Walkie-talkies.

    Traveling in pairs to a flea market can be hazardous to your friendship. Especially if you're both seeking the same merchandise. On the other hand, in vast fields and with large numbers of dealers, two is definitely not a crowd. Split up to cover more of the market . . . with walkie-talkies in hand.

14. Food (we couldn't end on the number 13).

    It is our uniform rule not to eat anything sold at flea markets. (There are a few exceptions, but only a few.) Instead, we lug plenty of yuppie water and diet sodas (it can be a dehydrating experience), plus some fruit. But, if your taste buds tingle at the very mention of overpriced elephant ears, funnel cakes, sweet rolls, major fried chicken, and the like, be our guest.

In the end, though, the idea of shopping flea markets and antique shows should be considered an adventure, an experience to be enjoyed, and a great way to learn about the art of buying and bargaining and deal making.

THE BUYER'S FLEA MARKET

4545 W. Division St.
Chicago, IL 60651
(773) 227-1889
Hours: Sat & Sun: 8–5
50¢ adults; 25¢ seniors; kids under 6 free

Most weekly flea markets in the Midwest—as opposed to monthly gatherings of antiques and collectibles dealers—comprise folks peddling inexpensive new merchandise; sometimes groceries as well. In essence, the 17+-year-old Buyer's Flea Market represents lower-end, one-stop shopping for the entire family (limited foodstuffs are offered). With space for 500 dealers, both inside and out, this Division Street market includes all the stuff—shoes, clothes, bedding, perfumes, vitamins, and even occasional furniture (such as dinettes, lamps, and end tables of the modern variety). Weekend entertainment, from face painting to clowns, helps draw a steady crowd from A.M. to P.M. Unfortunately, it's not as handicapped-accessible as other markets.

Double Outdoor Flea Market

2800 W. Columbus Ave.
Chicago, IL 60652
(773) 925-9602
Hours: Sat & Sun: 5:30–3
No charge on Sat; Sun: 75¢ adults

Located near Marquette Park on Chicago's Southwest Side, this large outdoor market attracts Windy City denizens from every conceivable neighborhood. (As well it should, given the array of merchandise displayed every week.) Half old and half new, items range from shoes to electronics. Some of the buys worth mentioning: an unopened 42-inch ceiling fan, $15; shoes for the entire family (though mainly children), $5; and removable car radios, $13. "Handicapped accessible" is not a phrase well known by this group of vendors. Food stands and outdoor johns are easy to find, though parking is a different story. A word to the wise . . . arrive as early as possible to save walking time for the market itself.

DuPage Antique Flea Market

2015 Manchester Rd.
Wheaton, IL 60143
(630) 455-6090
Hours: Third Sunday of each month: 7–4
$3 adults; kids 11 and under free

A smallish show (under 100 dealers in winter) that's not frequented as much as Kane or Sandwich, DuPage nonetheless does attract its share of regular buyers the third Sunday of every month. Indoors is room for about 75 dealers, including some of our favorite jewelry sellers, a Russian poster booth, and great old toys. (Of course, dealers do come and go; we make no promises about exact booths.) In the summer, their great out-of-doors is heavily trafficked, especially with an all-night Saturday extravaganza in August. Admission's a cool three bucks—and if you can pass for 11 and under, it's free. Forget the food. Disabled people will find this an easy-to-negotiate market.

Heart of the Park Antique Show/Sale

State Fair Park
Milwaukee, WI 63280
(414) 968-2995
Hours: Sat: 9–5; Sun: 10–5 (held about every other month)
$3.50 adults; $3 seniors; kids 12 and under free

Though Milwaukee is oh-so-slightly out of the range of the Chicago version of *Buying Retail Is Stupid!—Chicago* (it's a good 2-hour drive from the Loop), this five-times-a-year show is too good to omit. A little over 100 dealers consistently display their wares; though country furniture and glassware predominate, we've uncovered a few finds here. Such as an old sterling-silver watch fob in the $50–$75 range (New York dealers usually charge at least double that price). And occasional folk items—tramp-art frames, painted-wood primitive statues—that are becoming more and more difficult to locate, let alone buy. Parking is not pretty; unless you arrive in the early hours, be prepared to walk and walk and walk from satellite lots. Or get a parking ticket. And one of our friends' parents, who uses a wheelchair, declares that this is one of the most disabled-friendly shows around.

Kane County Flea Market

Kane County Fairgrounds, between Rtes. 64 and 38
St. Charles, IL 60174
(630) 377-2252
Hours: Sat: 1–5; Sun: 7–4 (first Sunday and preceding Saturday of each month)
$4 adults; kids under 12 free

Now celebrating its 30th birthday, the Kane County Flea Market is primarily an inside flea market with about 1,000 dealers in the best of months; there are outside booths during the summer only (weather permitting). Antiques and collectibles reign, making this an ideal place for any dealer or interior decorator or simply a crazed collector of "stuff." We've found that booths featuring knockoffs and imitations of, say, Gucci handbags and Polo T-shirts are a bit too prevalent at times, but occasional bargains more than make up for the lapse. There is a $4 admission charge for the public, and food, parking, and restrooms are available. (Handicapped spaces are available as well.)

RACINE ANTIQUES FAIR

County Fairgrounds–Rtes. 45 and 11
Union Grove, WI 53182
(847) 540-7750
Hours: Every Sunday from June to September: 8–4
$3 admission

The all-too-short season that defines a typical Chicago summer also witnesses an overly heavy schedule of flea markets and antique shows, both regular and seasonal. So, the choice of which to attend always depends on a coin toss—and the health of our feet. The few times we've attended the monthly Sunday-only Racine Antiques Fair, running from June to September, we've noted that the 65 dealers seem to concentrate on country and folk merchandise, with fair prices. (An unusually elongated small tramp-art frame was ours for $100.) Wander in and out of bucolic barns for a $3 admission . . . and bring your own food.

SANDWICH ANTIQUES MARKET

Fairgrounds, Rte. 34 west of town
Sandwich, IL 60548
(773) 227-4464
Hours: One Sunday each month from May through October: 8–4
$4 admission

No, it's not a piece of meat between two hunks of bread. Rather, it's one of our favorite seasonal (May through October) monthly antique haunts, even though it means rising at 3:00 A.M. to travel two hours west. Bob Lawler, manager of this and the Caravan market in Michigan (among others), has gathered a juried group of 500+ dealers inside barns and on the grass. Prices do not reflect great bargains, but here and there reasonable deals pop up: a black-and-white African quilt for $300; a mission-style umbrella stand priced under $200; decent signed costume jewelry at less than $100 each item. Food tends toward the greasy and caloric (ham, eggs, sausage for breakfast; elephant ears as snacks)—and tramping through the extensive grounds can be wearing.

SWAPORAMA
4600 W. Lake St.
Melrose Park, IL 60160
(708) 344-7300
Hours: Sat & Sun: 7–4; plus one weekday, which differs among locations
50¢ adults; kids under 12 free

What could be better than an indoor-and-outdoor flea market? With about 70 booths (including those in the great out-of-doors), this market deals mainly in clothes and accessories—from hairpieces to hairspray. Some of the savings we gathered: a cordless Panasonic phone for $75; leather belts for $4 or two for $7; unopened packages of glam girl Barbies for $6.99; sunglasses, $2–$6; a glass end table for $187; luggage of all sizes from $5 to $20; sports jerseys priced at $40; and leather handbags beginning at $7. Plus produce: one pound of jalapeño peppers, one pineapple, and/or one pound of tomatoes . . . only a buck! Other conveniences: tons of free parking and indoor restrooms. A tiny food court at the back awaits appetites, offering every kind of food imaginable (pizza, stuffed peppers, hot dogs, hamburgers, even burritos). People with disabilities may have some trouble with the narrow aisles inside, though the paved ground makes traveling easy.

Alsip—4350 W. 129th St., (708) 344-7300
Chicago—4100 S. Ashland Ave., (708) 344-7300

TWIN FLEA MARKET
Between Dundee and Willow on Hintz Rd.
Wheeling, IL 60090
(847) 229-0909
Hours: Sat & Sun: 7–4
75¢ adults; 50¢ seniors and kids under 12

Once a week, we guarantee you, expect all male members of the family—especially handy individuals—to quietly vanish in the

A.M. . . . only to reappear later with say, a 13-piece power bit set for $12.50 and a 22-piece screwdriver set for only $11.50. While visiting, we spotted substantial savings on 70% used and 30% new merchandise. Some deals: Fila, Nike, and Calvin Klein T-shirts, $2; a large piece of luggage, $15 (once $95); T-shirts with sports logos, four for $10; and a brand-new Hoover Dirt Devil for only $60—with a 1-year warranty! Produce, too: 12 limes, or 3 pounds of tomatoes or bananas (take your pick) for only a buck! Parking is very limited, so start shopping early. On the other hand, portable toilets and food stands are conveniently located, though not as handicapped-accessible as some—the gravel-strewn roads promote a bumpy ride.

WOLFF'S FLEA MARKET

6920 N. Mannheim Rd./Rosemont Horizon
Rosemont, IL 60018
(847) 524-9590
Hours: Every Sunday from April to October: 7–3
$1 adults; 50¢ senior citizens and kids under 12

In 1991, David Wolff set up shop and has managed to create one of the largest outdoor flea markets here. This outdoor "rummage-'o-rama," held every Sunday beginning in April to the end of October, is home for 300 booths full of merchandise—ranging from toys for tots to antiques for collectors. There is a true mix of goods available—60% of the items are new; 40% used. Snack bars, indoor restrooms, handicap accessibility, and free parking are just a few of the bonuses to this find. Best call ahead, though—the market is closed during special events at the Rosemont Horizon.

WORLD'S LARGEST GARAGE SALE

1616 Sherman
Evanston, IL 60202
(847) 328-1500
Hours: Last weekend of July
$1 admission

Downtown Evanston is blocked for, quite literally, miles as residents and folks from surrounding communities as well as the city shop the one-weekend-only "World's Largest" garage sale. Held the last full weekend in July, this 180+-booth sale probably doesn't live up to its adjectives—but it's sure fun browsing for the small admission charge of 1 dollar. It's a curious mix of real dealers and home owners, selling merchandise from slightly used and dinged pots and pans to a sprinkle of antiques and collectibles. (We discovered a well-carved black Bakelite bracelet for under $50.) All floors of the garage at Church and Davis are covered with tables; parking nearby is impossible (though public transportation is next door). And a very slow elevator awaits people with disabilities.

4

Directory of Consumer Resources

Bargain Hunter's Reference Library

About Consumer Resources

Becoming a "smart shopper" involves rational (rather than emotional) decision making. Whether you're purchasing a product or seeking services, there are a number of questions to be asked: How do I get the best value for my money? What do I need to know to make an informed decision? What pitfalls do I need to avoid? What recourse do I have when I am dissatisfied?

Fortunately, an increasing number of excellent publications are available to assist you in answering these questions. The smart shopper will create a home consumer library of pertinent books, periodicals, catalogs, pamphlets, and articles. Offered at a nominal cost (in many cases free), these publications can help you become a knowledgeable shopper, one who is more likely to make sound decisions, avoid mistakes, and save thousands of dollars.

This Directory of Consumer Resources contains brief descriptions of more than 35 such publications, including *Consumer Reports*, a monthly magazine reporting results of comparative field tests of a wide variety of products; the Better Business Bureau's *A to Z Buying Guide*, and *The Frugal Shopper* by Ralph Nader and Wesley J. Smith (both provide consumers with essential information to make sound, economical purchasing decisions on hundreds of products and services); U.S. Government catalogs containing hundreds of printed materials to assist with living more wisely, effectively, economically, and healthily (most of these are free or inexpensive); *Consumer Action*, a guide that details resources available for dissatisfied consumers; *The AAA Auto/Graph Book*, containing information about getting the most for your money when buying a new or used car.

Of special interest in this chapter are several books that tell you how to obtain a wide variety of goods and services free. You may want to start your home reference library by writing for both free publications and those available at minimal cost (usually government publications), as well as those that discuss ways of acquiring things free.

Upon obtaining any of the materials described in this chapter, become familiar with them by glancing through the table of contents and skimming the texts. You are certain to find some interesting and intriguing information. Even this casual reading will make you a more knowledgeable consumer and enable you to know where to look for more specific information before buying. Over the course of a year, you will probably refer to these resources often and find them invaluable.

Books with older publication dates are listed because the material has remained pertinent. Some may be out of print and no longer available in bookstores; however, your local library may have them. The library may be your source of first choice anyway—the price is right—and you may gradually acquire publications for home use to which you would expect to refer more frequently.

Consumer Resource References

A to Z Buying Guide
Publisher: Council of Better Business Bureaus
4200 Wilson Blvd., Arlington, VA 22203
Latest Edition: 1991 ($9.95)

This guide's 300 pages provide essential information for making sound, economical purchasing decisions on hundreds of products and services. It can be obtained at Better Business Bureaus and bookstores, or by writing directly to the Council. Also includes information about Better Business Bureau's consumer education books, pamphlets, and other publications and services designed to help you make informed buying decisions.

The AAA 1996 Auto/Graph Book
Publisher: American Automobile Association
1000 AAA Dr., Heathrow, FL 32746
Call your local AAA office
Latest Edition: 1996 ($12.95)

The AAA Auto/Graph Book provides you with the facts you need to walk into a dealer's showroom with the confidence of a wise and prudent shopper. It will help you make the right decision with less confusion and more peace of mind. You will be privy to the test results of 112 of the most popular foreign and domestic car models. Each vehicle's performance, comfort, convenience, workmanship, and value are reported. Lists of each vehicle's best and worst features are provided along with pictures of each car's exterior, interior, dashboard, and cargo area. Price lists are also included. Introductory chapters deal with analyzing your needs, test driving, understanding your warranty, negotiating, maintaining your vehicle, and resolving disputes. You can obtain the book at any local AAA office. It's well worth the investment.

Absolutely Free!
Publisher: Prima Publishing
P.O. Box 1260BK, Rocklin, CA 95677
(916) 632-4400
Latest Edition: 1995 ($9.95)

This book gives inside information on a wealth of free products and services in the areas of crafts, clothes and jewelry, food, beauty and health, toys and games, and much more. *Absolutely Free!* tells you where to find nearly 300 top-quality products that you and your entire family will want. As a bonus, most of the products and resource guides promote the kind of safe, natural lifestyle that enhances your family's well-being and our environment. The value of the free products you will receive far outweighs the cost of the book!

Baby Bargains
Publisher: Windsor Peak Press
1223 Peakview Circle, Suite 7000, Boulder, CO 80302
(800) 888-0385
Latest Edition: 1996 ($11.95)

A big question about having a baby is how to afford it. The average cost of caring for a baby has been estimated at $5,000 for the first year. Economy-minded parents or parents-to-be will be interested in the many ways to save money described in *Baby Bargains.* Denise and Alan Field, authors of the popular *Bridal Bargains*, provide information on how and where to save 20%–50% on baby furniture, equipment, clothes, toys, maternity wear, and much more. A no-questions-asked, money-back guarantee is offered to anyone who doesn't save at least $250 on baby expenses by using this book.

The Best Bargain Family Vacations in the U.S.A.
Publisher: St. Martin's Press
175 5th Ave., New York, NY 10010
(800) 288-2131, (212) 674-5151
Latest Edition: 1993 ($13.95)

Time to load the kids in the Winnebago and head for some fun in the sun? Imagine going face-to-face with the mild-mannered manatee in Florida's Homosassa Springs State Wildlife Park. Or maybe your family would like to help professional archaeologists uncover a prehistoric pueblo in Arizona's White Mountain Archaeological Center. *The Best Bargain Family Vacations in the U.S.A.* offers over 250 affordable, kid-friendly, nationwide vacation spots, with accommodation prices ranging from around $6 to $75 a night. Everything from resorts to dude ranches to family camps is covered in the book, which provides vacation-spot descriptions and cost and accommodation information. A two-part appendix offers information on budget hotels and U.S. tourist offices.

Bridal Bargains
Publisher: Windsor Peak Press
1223 Peakview Circle, Suite 7000, Boulder, CO 80302
(800) 888-0385
Latest Edition: 1996 ($11.95)

According to *Bridal Bargains*, the average U.S. wedding costs over $19,000. In this book, Denise and Alan Fields describe creative and innovative solutions for planning a wedding on a realistic budget. They tell you how to save 20%–50% off brand-new, nationally advertised bridal gowns. In addition, information and strategies are provided that can save you hundreds of dollars on wedding pictures, catering, flowers, invitations, rings, entertainment, the wedding site, and more. The authors offer the following money-back guarantee: "If *Bridal Bargains* doesn't save you at least $500 on your wedding, we will give you a complete refund on the cost of this book! No questions asked!"

Consumer Action Guide
Publisher: Consumer Action
116 New Montgomery St., San Francisco, CA 94105
(415) 777-9635 (Complaint Hot Line)
Latest Edition: 1993 ($3)

The *Consumer Action Guide* is a useful reference when you run into legal problems. It includes the addresses and telephone numbers of regulatory and law enforcement government agencies, business-sponsored complaint-resolution offices, nonprofit information and referral organizations, and agencies that offer free or low-cost legal assistance.

The Consumer Bible
Publisher: Workman Publishing Company, Inc.
708 Broadway, New York, NY 10003
(212) 254-5900
Latest Edition: 1995 ($14.95)

This book supplies consumers with the knowledge they need to shop smart—from how to get the edge on buying essential goods and services, to avoiding scams and schemes. Used for every purchase, *The Consumer Bible* is like giving yourself and your family a 20% pay raise—effective immediately. It includes everything you need to know to get the best value on food, health care, home, clothing, repairs, legal advice, phones, vacations, banks, pets, and more. The author, Mark Green, served as the highly effective consumer affairs commissioner of New York City (1990–1993), and became the city's first public advocate. This comprehensive book will save you both time and money daily.

Consumer Information Catalog
Publisher: Consumer Information Center
P.O. Box 100-6A, Pueblo, CO 81002
(719) 948-4000
Latest Edition: 1996 (Free)

This 13-page catalog lists free and low-cost publications of consumer interest. Topics include car care, children and parenting, employment, federal program benefits, food and nutrition, medicine and health, money and finance, small business, travel, hobbies, and much more. The publications described in this U.S. government catalog are packed with valuable information and can improve anyone's personal or business lifestyle.

Consumer Reports ***1998 Buying Guide***
Publisher: Consumers Union
P.O. Box 51166, Boulder, CO 80321
(800) 500-9760
Latest Edition: 1998 ($8.99)

Providing up-to-date buying advice and evaluations on hundreds of brand-name products, this yearly guide gives the consumer ready access to information on topics such as automobiles, audio and video gear, home workplace equipment, and yard and garden machines. Featuring a "better to worse" rating system, frequency-of-repair charts, and additional information on product recalls and reliability, the *1998 Buying Guide* also includes a one-year index to *Consumer Reports* magazine at the back of the book, following the guide index. A new edition is published yearly.

Consumer Resource Handbook
Publisher: Consumer Information Center
Pueblo, CO 81009
(719) 948-4000
Latest Edition: 1996 (Free)

This is a U.S. government publication of nearly 100 pages listing many consumer affairs contact names; also lists addresses and phone numbers of hundreds of manufacturers, and county, state, and federal agencies handling a wide variety of consumer problems. A worthwhile addition to your consumer information library.

A Consumer's Guide to Renting a Car
Publisher: Alamo Rent-A-Car, Public Affairs Department
McCool Communications, P.O. Box 13005, Atlanta, GA 30324
(404) 768-4161
Latest Edition: 1995 (Free)

This 24-page guide provides information that will help you rent a car less expensively and more conveniently. It will facilitate your asking the right questions and making the correct decisions about reserving your vehicle, club discounts, fuel policies, mileage charges, special equipment, one-way rentals, potential surcharges, additional charges, responsibility for rental vehicles, car rental protection options, loss of use, liability insurance, where to pick up your car, returning your car, mechanical problems, accidents, and travel safety. Enclose a self-addressed, stamped (55¢ postage) business-size envelope when requesting this free publication.

Cut Your Bills in Half
Publisher: Smithmark Publishers Inc.
16 E. 32nd St., New York, NY 10016
(212) 532-6600
Latest Edition: 1994 ($8)

The editors of *Cut Your Bills in Half* offer many cash-saving tips, including "First Aid for Gardening Tools" and "Avoiding Flashy Accessories." This guide covers a wide range of topics: travel bargains, affordable furniture, and lower insurance rates, to name only a few. Did you know that your car will last longer if you don't follow your owner's manual timetable for an oil change, or that your canvas shoes will last a lot longer with a spray of silicone?

Don Wright's Guide to Free Campgrounds
Publisher: Cottage Publications
420 S. 4th St., Elkhart, IN 46516
(800) 303-7833, (219) 293-7553
Latest Edition: 1994 ($16.95)

Before you pack the family station wagon and roll off for the Rockies, or plan that yearly excursion to Yellowstone, you'll definitely want to look at *Don Wright's Guide to Free Campgrounds.* Written for experienced campers and rookies alike, the guide lists thousands of campgrounds across the United States where you can stay absolutely free, or almost free. National forests, county and state parks, and long-term visitor areas are just some of the vacation sites providing that perfect, fun, and economical getaway.

Don't Go to the Cosmetics Counter Without Me
Publisher: Beginning Press
4065 Hollis St., Emeryville, CA 94608
(415) 658-3453
Latest Edition: 1996 ($16.95)

Designed to prove that the female consumer doesn't have to spend a fortune on skin care and makeup, *Don't Go to the Cosmetics Counter Without Me* sets out to demystify the inflated claims and price tags on the 300 cosmetic lines available in the United States and Canada. In addition to taking aim at such brand names as

Revlon and Cover Girl, the book covers everything from shopping techniques and overviews of ingredients, to sifting through celebrity model double-talk. The book differentiates between companies and manufacturers that use animal testing and those that don't.

Fit Pregnancy Buyer's Guide
Publisher: Shape/Weider Publications
21100 Erwin St., Woodland Hills, CA 91367
(818) 884-6800
Latest Edition: 1997 ($3.95)

This 120-page guide is a must-have directory to nearly 400 products of interest to expecting and brand-new parents. Color-coded sections cover fashions, underwear, shoes, beauty products, and books for the pregnant woman; and, for new parents, strollers, car seats, cameras, backpacks, play yards, activity centers, baby furniture, toys, books, and videos. You can also use it as a gift-buying guide for friends and family. Written by experts as well as parents who have been there, each section is illustrated with colorful photos and an easy-to-use box of "Tips Before You Buy." Published annually; available on newsstands.

Free Food . . . & More
Publisher: Probus Publishing Co.
1925 N. Clybourn Ave., Chicago, IL 60614
(800) PROBUS-1 (776-2871)
Latest Edition: 1992 ($9.95)

Did you know that every year the American family throws away almost $2,000 worth of cash refunds and rebates for products they use every day? An ideal guide for bargain hunters and coupon clippers alike, *Free Food . . . & More* alerts you to discounts and freebies on food and entertainment, as well as health and household goods. From slashing the monthly energy bill to video rental savings, this book teaches you how to turn daily budget-busting headaches into major savings.

The Frugal Shopper
Publisher: Center for Study of Responsive Law
P.O. Box 19367, Washington, DC 20036
Latest Edition: 1992 ($10)

Coauthored by consumer advocate Ralph Nader, *The Frugal Shopper* helps you win the consumer game. It enables you to make smart decisions on major expenses, professional services, utilities, credit, and marketplace negotiations. You'll learn to discern between credit cards and "credit checks," or how the "fair plan" can help you overcome the restrictions that insurance companies place on "hazardous areas." In coping with difficult times, *The Frugal Shopper* is a valuable consumer companion.

Goodridge's Guide to Flea Markets
Publisher: Adams Media Corporation
Jim Goodridge, P.O. Box 510085, St. Louis, MO 63129
(314) 296-0990
Latest Edition: 1995 ($9.95 each)

What do a deserted airplane hangar, a parking lot at a major university, and the world-famous Rose Bowl stadium have in common? All are sites of one of America's favorite venues—the flea market. In his four-book series, author Jim Goodridge presents a comprehensive directory of flea markets. Each edition is packed with all the "need-to-know" information, including size of markets, directions, average daily attendance, types of merchandise, hours of operation, booth rates, and advice on how to get the best bargains. Four regional editions are available covering the Southeast, Northeast/Mid-Atlantic, West/Southwest, and Midwest.

Guide to Free Tax Services—Publication #910
Publisher: Internal Revenue Service
Department of the Treasury, Washington DC 20224
(800) 829-1040
Latest Edition: 1994 (Free)

This guide describes numerous IRS tax services, publications, tax tips, and information about many IRS programs. Materials and information programs are free and most are available year-round.

Additionally, *Guide to Free Tax Services* lists toll-free IRS telephone numbers and IRS mailing addresses.

How to Clean Practically Anything
Publisher: Consumers Union
101 Truman Ave., Yonkers, NY 10703
Latest Edition: 1993 ($11.95)

How to Clean Practically Anything tells you how to remove more than 54 common stains, and get the best value from hundreds of cleaning products and appliances. Rating products on a "better" or "worse" scale, the pocket-sized guide provides the consumer with money-saving and safety tips on every imaginable cleaning agent.

How to Keep Your Car Looking Young
Publisher: Car Care Council
One Grand Lake Dr., Port Clinton, OH 43452
(419) 734-5343
Latest Edition: 1995 (Free)

Many of us spend as much time in our cars as we do in our living rooms. Keeping your car looking young improves driving pleasure and safety and increases the value of your vehicle. This eight-page pamphlet has numerous valuable tips for getting the job done.

How to Protect Yourself Against Ripoffs
Publisher: Retirement Living Publishing Co., Inc.
28 W. 23rd St., New York, NY 10010
(212) 366-8850
Latest Edition: 1991 ($4)

This 27-page booklet discusses many of the most common rip-offs and provides information on how to protect yourself against them. Topics include Real Estate Fraud, Free Vacation Offers, Insurance Come-Ons, Health Quacks, Door-to-Door Con Artists, Car Repair Rip-offs, Check Tampering, Cash Register Cheats, Telemarketing Frauds, Credit Cons, Mortgage Scalpers, and the Newest Scams.

Motorist's Tire Care and Safety Guide
Publisher: Tire Industry Safety Council
P.O. Box 3147, Medina, OH 44258
Latest Edition: 1995 (Free)

This 17-page pamphlet provides information you need to know about auto and light truck tire care and safety. Included are sections on inflation pressure, tire inspection, good driving habits, vehicle conditions affecting tires, the sidewall story, replacement tire selection, cold-weather driving, service assistance, and storage tips.

1996 AT&T Toll-Free National 800 Directory
(Consumer Edition)
Publisher: AT&T
Five Century Dr., Parsippany, NJ 07054
(800) 562-2255
Latest Edition: 1996 ($14.99)

Reach out and save some money! A comprehensive phone guide to consumer savings, the *AT&T Toll-Free National 800 Directory* includes a Consumer White Pages section containing alphabetical listings by name of businesses, organizations, and government agencies that provide toll-free 800 numbers to the public; it also includes section numbers that indicate under what product or service heading a listing may be found in the Consumer Yellow Pages. A new edition is published yearly.

The Official Freebies for Families
Publisher: Lowell House Juvenile
2029 Century Park E., Suite 3290, Dept. VH,
Los Angeles, CA 90067
(310) 552-7555
Latest Edition: 1995 ($4.95)

The Official Freebies for Families lists more than 250 "freebie" mail offers, ranging from carryalls for the kids to tips on horseshoes rules. Filled with concise, readable catalog descriptions, the handbook can easily slide into your glove compartment or knapsack. Costs and company addresses are listed at the bottom of each entry.

The Official Freebies for Kids
Publisher: Lowell House Juvenile
2029 Century Park E., Suite 3290, Dept. VH,
Los Angeles, CA 90067
(310) 552-7555
Latest Edition: 1996 ($5.95)

Keeping the kids busy and happy doesn't have to be a costly Nintendo nightmare. In *The Official Freebies for Kids* you can choose from more than 130 freebie mail offers designed for your children. Crafts, games, toys, and magazines are just some of the items to be found in this slim, handy book. Treat your kids to "Dinosaur Fourus wooden craft plans" or "Spifey Spider and Belfry Bat pins." Entertaining your children needn't be a burden to the budget.

The Official Freebies for Teachers
Publisher: Lowell House Juvenile
2029 Century Park E., Suite 3290, Dept. VH,
Los Angeles, CA 90067
(310) 552-7555
Latest Edition: 1996 ($4.95)

The latest edition of *The Official Freebies for Teachers* describes clever classroom crafts, activities, games, and educational items available to teachers, including more than 100 freebies that cost nothing or next to nothing. Most of the selections are fun items to share with students. Some of the freebies are ideas for science fair projects, rubber stamps, maps, challenging puzzles, stickers, and personalized award certificates.

The Official Guide to Buying, Connecting, and Using Consumer Electronics Products
Publisher: Electronics Industries Association, Consumer Electronics Group/CE Book
2500 Wilson Blvd., Arlington, VA 22201
Latest Edition: 1995 ($9 + $6.95 shipping & handling)

This 172-page book covers every aspect of consumer electronics products—from pre- to postpurchase. It answers questions such as:

What do I look for when purchasing a personal computer? How do I hook up my VCR to watch one TV program and record another while connected to cable? Are large and small speakers really the same? What type of alarm system should I buy for my car? Product categories covered are computers, audio, video, home theater, auto sound, mobile electronics, telecommunications, home office, and home control.

The Official Guide to Government Auctions
Publisher: Crown Publishers
210 E. 50th St., New York, NY 10022
Latest Edition: 1992 ($25)

This 494-page book tells you everything you've ever wanted to know, or might want to know, about auctions. In great detail, it explains where and how to find out about auctions and how to participate effectively in them. It illustrates the possibilities of finding great deals (up to 80% off) on cars, office equipment, televisions, and almost every type of merchandise imaginable. It also describes pitfalls to avoid. It is a basic reference for anyone who is interested in auctions—both beginners and seasoned auction goers.

1,001 Free Goodies & Cheapies
Publisher: Information USA, Inc.
P.O. Box E, Kensington, MD 20895
(301) 924-0556
Latest Edition: 1994 ($19.95)

Who doesn't love a freebie? This book contains all the neat stuff you can get your hands on and put to use for gifts, self-help, teaching aids, toys, investment decisions, and more. The offers are either free or priced less than $10. Take note, though: these freebies are not really free—you already paid for them with your tax dollars. Just another reason for you to take full advantage of the opportunities described in this book.

1001 Ways to Cut Your Expenses
Publisher: Bantam Doubleday Dell
2451 S. Wolf Rd., Des Plaines, IL 60018
(800) 323-9872
Latest Edition: 1992 ($9.95)

There's no doubt these days that saving money across-the-board is a high priority on everyone's agenda, and financial planning guru Jonathan D. Pond has written the sort of dollar-slashing guide that most shoppers want to use. Filled with savvy step-by-step tips on saving on everything from utilities to courtships, the book includes self-tests, case studies, and budget tables that will help you cut expenses on every front. Did you know that you might be able to get a college degree under your employer's tuition program, or that you can save by taking your own bags to the grocery store? Some of the subchapters have a commonsense ring to them ("Don't Lend Money to a Thief," "Buy Artificial Plants Instead of Live Ones").

Phil Lempert's Supermarket Shopping and Value Guide
Publisher: NTC/Contemporary Publishing Group
4255 W. Touhy Ave., Lincolnwood (Chicago), IL 60646-1975
(800) 323-4900
Latest Edition: 1996 ($9.95)

Phil Lempert, nationally known as the "Supermarket Guru," has created this unique handbook to help shoppers make their way through the maze of modern supermarkets while getting the absolute best deals on each and every item. Readers will learn thousands of invaluable insider tips and helpful hints, including how to tell if a product is really on sale, what to do to get in and out of a store fast, how to get freebies from stores and manufacturers, how to decipher food labels, which products a shopper should never buy, and many more. Each chapter contains a concise top-10 list of values as well as the answers to the most commonly asked consumer questions. Also featured are hints from supermarket managers and an appendix of food information. No cost-conscious consumer can afford to do without this book.

The Practical Guide to Practically Everything
Publisher: Random House, Inc.
New York, NY 10022
(800) 733-3000
Latest Edition: 1998 ($13.95)

This is an expert, no-nonsense guide to the most important developments in everything from health and nutrition to money management, education, career planning, travel, entertainment, and consumer technology. Expert Picks, Tips, Lists, Q & As, and Sources will help to clear the fog and give you the truth about what you, the consumer, need to know.

The Safe Shopper's Bible
Publisher: Macmillan/Simon & Schuster
1633 Broadway, New York, NY 10019
(800) 223-2348
Latest Edition: 1995 ($14.95)

Can coloring your hair cause cancer? Which apple juice is safest for your baby? Is furniture polish making your asthma worse? Where can you find meat without hormones and additives? Here at last is a comprehensive guide to answer all your questions about thousands of brand-name household products, personal-care products, foods, and beverages. Because many items you buy every day contain ingredients that can cause allergic reactions, breathing difficulties, dizziness, cancer, birth defects, and other problems, *The Safe Shopper's Bible* is a must for those who care about their health.

Shopping for a Better World
Publisher: Ballantine Books
201 E. 50th St., New York, NY 10022
(800) 733-3000, (212) 751-2600
Latest Edition: 1994 ($14)

A shop-smart text with a social conscience, *Shopping for a Better World* rates companies on their performances on such vital issues as animal testing and the environment, to name only two. A bracing clarion call for the consumer activist, this pocket-sized paperback grades each company's social awareness and responsibility with a demanding, issue-conscious, 12-column checklist. In keeping with this spirit, the volume also lists the addresses, phone numbers, and names of chief company executives, encouraging consumers to exercise their duty to defend our "endangered ecosystem" by writing to the companies directly.

Shopping for a Safer Car
Publisher: Insurance Institute for Highway Safety
Publications Box 1420, Arlington, VA 22210
(703) 247-1500
Latest Edition: 1995 (Free)

Safety should rank high on the list of considerations when you're purchasing a car. In simple, jargon-free language, this 14-page booklet answers questions regarding what to look for in safety features. Anyone interested in safety will find useful information here. Include a self-addressed, stamped business-size envelope.

The Super Coupon Shopping System
Publisher: Hyperion
114 5th Ave., New York, NY 10011
Latest Edition: 1994 ($5.95)

Shop smart by turning coupon clipping into bonafide cash clout! *The Super Coupon Shopping System* shows you how to cut your supermarket bills by up to 80% by earning hundreds, even thousands, of dollars annually using manufacturers' refunds. A valuable guide to such shopper-friendly information as coupon organization, shoppers' trading networks, and the retail structure, this book provides easy, step-by-step methods to reducing your cost on product prices.

Trash or Treasure
Publisher: Treasure Hunt Publications
P.O. Box 3028, Pismo Beach, CA 93448
(800) 549-7500
Latest Edition: 1995 ($29.95)

You can make major bucks from unwanted items gathering dust in your basement, garage, or attic. Subtitled "How to Find the Best

Buyers of Antiques, Collectibles and other Undiscovered Treasures," *Trash or Treasure* is to selling what *Buying Retail Is Stupid!* is to buying. The nation's oldest and most reliable guide to locating honest and knowledgeable buyers of everything from stuffed aardvarks to zeppelin parts worth $1,500, lace worth $50 an inch, or Hot Wheels you can sell for $1,000. Includes names, addresses, and phone numbers of top expert buyers in 3,500 categories of antiques and collectibles, plus a simple four-step process for getting fair prices for anything you own.

Unbelievably Good Deals & Great Adventures That You Absolutely Can't Get Unless You're Over 50
Publisher: NTC/Contemporary Publishing Group
4255 W. Touhy Ave., Lincolnwood (Chicago), IL 60646-1975
(800) 323-4900
Latest Edition: 1998 ($9.95)

If you are over 50, you qualify for hundreds of money-saving offers from vacation adventures to everyday benefits. Now in its 10th edition, this bestselling guide has been revised, expanded, and packed with up-to-date information about trips, clubs, programs, and special deals. The latter includes travel adventures; price breaks on airfares; up to 50% off at hotels, motels, and restaurants; exclusive tours; big discounts on trains, buses, and car rentals; tax and insurance breaks; and much more. A new, updated edition is published every year.

Smart Shopper's Quiz

Find Out How Smart You Are, or Could Be, at "Buying More for Less"

Part I

How to Shop

Mark each statement below by checking either the *Yes* or *No* column. If your behavior "more often than not" (or often enough in your view) agrees with the statement, check *Yes*. Otherwise, check *No*.

	YES	NO
1. Before buying a high-priced product, I check the ratings of several models in a magazine such as *Consumer Reports*.	☐	☐
2. Before buying a high-priced product, I avoid pitfalls by checking books such as the Better Business Bureau's *A to Z Buying Guide*.	☐	☐
3. I comparison shop by calling retail stores for prices and checking newspaper ads.	☐	☐
4. I check on a store's return policy before buying.	☐	☐
5. I buy items I don't need because they're a bargain.	☐	☐
6. I buy items after holidays for next year's holidays to take advantage of sizable discounts.	☐	☐

	YES	NO
7. I spend too much time shopping for low-priced items.	☐	☐
8. I take enough time when shopping for high-priced items.	☐	☐
9. I do major grocery shopping once a week to save time and energy.	☐	☐
10. I use a pocket calculator when grocery shopping to determine which size of product is the best buy.	☐	☐
11. I check the grocery store receipt to make sure the scanned prices agree with the shelf prices.	☐	☐
12. When buying small appliances, I test them before leaving the store to make sure they work.	☐	☐
13. I grocery shop from a list to cut down on impulse buying.	☐	☐
14. I use discount coupons to save money.	☐	☐
15. I buy generic or store brands for some products.	☐	☐
16. When buying clothes I plan a basic wardrobe to ensure that I have a minimum of all essentials.	☐	☐
17. When buying clothes, to ensure they are well made, I check seams, zippers, stitching, buttons, jacket lapels, and the comfort of skirts or pants when sitting and walking.	☐	☐
18. When I buy shoes, they must fit in the store. (I don't buy tight shoes expecting them to stretch later.)	☐	☐
19. Before buying a high-priced item, I do some research on it.	☐	☐
20. If I need clothing for a special event—to be worn only once or twice—I consider renting instead of buying.	☐	☐
21. I generally inform myself of return policies of businesses from which I buy.	☐	☐
22. I keep receipts to make returning purchases easier.	☐	☐
23. I complete and return warranty cards promptly and file them for easy access.	☐	☐

	YES	NO
24. When going on a big shopping trip, I make a list and a budget to avoid impulse buying.	☐	☐
25. I frequently have my spouse or a friend accompany me when shopping for high-priced products.	☐	☐
26. As a woman, when shopping for clothing, I wear a leotard and tights to save the time and trouble of changing clothes frequently.	☐	☐

PART II

WHAT I KNOW ABOUT DISCOUNT SHOPPING

Mark each statement below by checking either *True* or *False*. If you believe the statement is for the most part true, check *True*; otherwise, check *False*.

	TRUE	FALSE
27. Manufacturer outlet malls have many name-brand stores offering goods at discounts from approximately 10% to 80%.	☐	☐
28. Only a few states have manufacturer outlet centers.	☐	☐
29. It may not pay to visit a manufacturer outlet mall to make only one purchase.	☐	☐
30. It's wise to visit garage sales early in the day.	☐	☐
31. You can negotiate price with the seller at a garage sale.	☐	☐
32. Near the end of a garage sale, prices will be reduced greatly.	☐	☐
33. You can sometimes get a great buy at a garage sale.	☐	☐
34. You can find out where and when garage sales will take place by consulting newspaper classified sections.	☐	☐

	TRUE	FALSE
35. Some flea markets offer a tremendous variety of merchandise.	☐	☐
36. You should not assume that everything for sale at a garage sale or flea market is a bargain.	☐	☐
37. Most resale stores take clothing from individuals on consignment and keep a percentage of the sale price for themselves.	☐	☐
38. At resale stores you sometimes can buy high-end clothes—worn once or not at all—at bargain basement prices.	☐	☐
39. Shopping resale stores for children's clothes is an excellent way to save money.	☐	☐
40. Clothes for sale at resale stores have almost always been laundered or dry cleaned.	☐	☐
41. Only business owners may participate in government auctions.	☐	☐
42. Government auctions offer only military equipment for sale.	☐	☐
43. Pre-auction inspection is an important means of not overpaying for an item.	☐	☐
44. Police auctions of unclaimed stolen goods are available in many cities.	☐	☐
45. The '90s sometimes have been called the "decade of discount shopping."	☐	☐

SMART SHOPPER'S QUIZ SCORING

INSTRUCTIONS

The following are the correct answers for each item in the quiz. Circle each item you answered correctly. You get one point for each correct answer. Add them up and record your total score of correct answers. Then read the interpretation of your score below.

Correct answers:

1. Y	2. Y	3. Y	4. Y	5. N	6. Y
7. N	8. Y	9. Y	10. Y	11. Y	12. Y
13. Y	14. Y	15. Y	16. Y	17. Y	18. Y
19. Y	20. Y	21. Y	22. Y	23. Y	24. Y
25. Y	26. Y	27. T	28. F	29. T	30. T
31. T	32. T	33. T	34. T	35. T	36. T
37. T	38. T	39. T	40. T	41. F	42. F
43. T	44. T	45. T			

Total correct answers: ________

INTERPRETATION OF SCORES

Total score:

41–45 You could write your own book, but don't compete with us.

31–40 You could probably be a shopping consultant. Think about it.

24–30 Always review the "Smart Shopping" section of this book before shopping.

11–23 Never shop alone.

1–10 We hope you have more money than you know what to do with. Have someone else in your family do the shopping. If you don't change your shopping habits, you may eventually have to consider declaring bankruptcy.

Indexes

Discount Stores and Outlets

Companies Offering Discount Coupons

Consumer Resources by Publication Title

Buying Retail Is Stupid! Discount Coupons

Take the coupon, book, or page (photocopy not accepted) along to any of the stores listed here for your discount. The store will initial the coupon and return the page or book to you.

Discount may not be valid on certain items or with any other offers. Valid for one purchase per store. Expires 12/31/99.

BUYING RETAIL IS STUPID!—CHICAGO
ABC Auto Parts & Sales, Inc.
10% Off Purchase (Used Auto Parts Only)
Redeemed:

BUYING RETAIL IS STUPID!—CHICAGO
Abt Electronics & Appliances
5% Off Purchase
Redeemed:

BUYING RETAIL IS STUPID!—CHICAGO
Adams Shoe Factory Outlet
10% Off Purchase
Redeemed:

BUYING RETAIL IS STUPID!—CHICAGO
Alamo Shoes
10% Off Purchase
Redeemed:

BUYING RETAIL IS STUPID!—CHICAGO
American Kitchen and Bath Outlet
10% Off Purchase
Redeemed:

BUYING RETAIL IS STUPID!—CHICAGO
The Bedpost (Heller Brother Bedding)
Free Bed Frame with Every Complete Bed Purchased
Redeemed:

Obtain your discount by redeeming this ***Buying Retail Is Stupid!—Chicago*** coupon at the store listed on opposite side. Discount may not be valid on certain items or with any other offers. Valid for one purchase per store.
Expires 12/31/99.

Obtain your discount by redeeming this ***Buying Retail Is Stupid!—Chicago*** coupon at the store listed on opposite side. Discount may not be valid on certain items or with any other offers. Valid for one purchase per store.
Expires 12/31/99.

Obtain your discount by redeeming this ***Buying Retail Is Stupid!—Chicago*** coupon at the store listed on opposite side. Discount may not be valid on certain items or with any other offers. Valid for one purchase per store.
Expires 12/31/99.

Obtain your discount by redeeming this ***Buying Retail Is Stupid!—Chicago*** coupon at the store listed on opposite side. Discount may not be valid on certain items or with any other offers. Valid for one purchase per store.
Expires 12/31/99.

Obtain your discount by redeeming this ***Buying Retail Is Stupid!—Chicago*** coupon at the store listed on opposite side. Discount may not be valid on certain items or with any other offers. Valid for one purchase per store.
Expires 12/31/99.

Obtain your discount by redeeming this ***Buying Retail Is Stupid!—Chicago*** coupon at the store listed on opposite side. Discount may not be valid on certain items or with any other offers. Valid for one purchase per store.
Expires 12/31/99.

BUYING RETAIL IS STUPID!—CHICAGO
Berry-Cutler Hosiery
10% Off Purchase
Redeemed:

BUYING RETAIL IS STUPID!—CHICAGO
Bijouterie International
10% Off on Beads; 50% Off on Fashion Jewelry
Redeemed:

BUYING RETAIL IS STUPID!—CHICAGO
Blue Sky Market
10% Off on Supplements Only
Redeemed:

BUYING RETAIL IS STUPID!—CHICAGO
Broadway Vitamins
$3 Off on Purchase of $15 or More
Redeemed:

BUYING RETAIL IS STUPID!—CHICAGO
Burnham Glove
10% Off Purchase
Redeemed:

BUYING RETAIL IS STUPID!—CHICAGO
Butcher Block Factory Outlet Showroom
10% Off Purchase
Redeemed:

Obtain your discount by redeeming this ***Buying Retail Is Stupid!—Chicago*** coupon at the store listed on opposite side. Discount may not be valid on certain items or with any other offers. Valid for one purchase per store.

Expires 12/31/99.

Obtain your discount by redeeming this ***Buying Retail Is Stupid!—Chicago*** coupon at the store listed on opposite side. Discount may not be valid on certain items or with any other offers. Valid for one purchase per store.

Expires 12/31/99.

Obtain your discount by redeeming this ***Buying Retail Is Stupid!—Chicago*** coupon at the store listed on opposite side. Discount may not be valid on certain items or with any other offers. Valid for one purchase per store.

Expires 12/31/99.

Obtain your discount by redeeming this ***Buying Retail Is Stupid!—Chicago*** coupon at the store listed on opposite side. Discount may not be valid on certain items or with any other offers. Valid for one purchase per store.

Expires 12/31/99.

Obtain your discount by redeeming this ***Buying Retail Is Stupid!—Chicago*** coupon at the store listed on opposite side. Discount may not be valid on certain items or with any other offers. Valid for one purchase per store.

Expires 12/31/99.

Obtain your discount by redeeming this ***Buying Retail Is Stupid!—Chicago*** coupon at the store listed on opposite side. Discount may not be valid on certain items or with any other offers. Valid for one purchase per store.

Expires 12/31/99.

BUYING RETAIL IS STUPID!—CHICAGO
Buy Popular Demand
15% Off Purchase (on Full-Price Items Only)
Redeemed:

BUYING RETAIL IS STUPID!—CHICAGO
Buy-A-Tux Superstore
10% Discount
Redeemed:

BUYING RETAIL IS STUPID!—CHICAGO
Card and Party Warehouse
5% Off on Purchase over $20; 10% Off on Purchase over $100; 15% Off on Purchase over $200 (Helium Balloons and Sales Items Excluded)
Redeemed:

BUYING RETAIL IS STUPID!—CHICAGO
Card Carousel
15% Off Purchase
Redeemed:

BUYING RETAIL IS STUPID!—CHICAGO
Carpet Styles Co.
$3 Off per Square Yard
(Excluding Specialty Items, Closeouts, and Already Discounted Items)
Redeemed:

BUYING RETAIL IS STUPID!—CHICAGO
Casey's Liquors
5% Off Purchase
Redeemed:

Obtain your discount by redeeming this ***Buying Retail Is Stupid!—Chicago*** coupon at the store listed on opposite side. Discount may not be valid on certain items or with any other offers. Valid for one purchase per store.
Expires 12/31/99.

Obtain your discount by redeeming this ***Buying Retail Is Stupid!—Chicago*** coupon at the store listed on opposite side. Discount may not be valid on certain items or with any other offers. Valid for one purchase per store.
Expires 12/31/99.

Obtain your discount by redeeming this ***Buying Retail Is Stupid!—Chicago*** coupon at the store listed on opposite side. Discount may not be valid on certain items or with any other offers. Valid for one purchase per store.
Expires 12/31/99.

Obtain your discount by redeeming this ***Buying Retail Is Stupid!—Chicago*** coupon at the store listed on opposite side. Discount may not be valid on certain items or with any other offers. Valid for one purchase per store.
Expires 12/31/99.

Obtain your discount by redeeming this ***Buying Retail Is Stupid!—Chicago*** coupon at the store listed on opposite side. Discount may not be valid on certain items or with any other offers. Valid for one purchase per store.
Expires 12/31/99.

Obtain your discount by redeeming this ***Buying Retail Is Stupid!—Chicago*** coupon at the store listed on opposite side. Discount may not be valid on certain items or with any other offers. Valid for one purchase per store.
Expires 12/31/99.

Buying Retail Is Stupid!—Chicago
Chernin's Shoes, Inc.
10% Off Regular Price in Full-Line Stores; 10% Off Current Price in Outlets
Redeemed:

Buying Retail Is Stupid!—Chicago
Chicago Antique Centre, Ltd.
10% Off on Purchase of $25 or More
Redeemed:

Buying Retail Is Stupid!—Chicago
Chicago Fur Outlet
5% Off on Purchase of $500 or More
Redeemed:

Buying Retail Is Stupid!—Chicago
Chicago Shoe Market Shoe Bazaar
10% Off Purchase (Shorts and Socks Excluded)
Redeemed:

Buying Retail Is Stupid!—Chicago
Chicago Sports Exchange
10% Off on Minimum Purchase of $100
Redeemed:

Buying Retail Is Stupid!—Chicago
Chicago Watch Brokers
10% Off Purchase
Redeemed:

Obtain your discount by redeeming this ***Buying Retail Is Stupid!—Chicago*** coupon at the store listed on opposite side. Discount may not be valid on certain items or with any other offers. Valid for one purchase per store.

Expires 12/31/99.

Obtain your discount by redeeming this ***Buying Retail Is Stupid!—Chicago*** coupon at the store listed on opposite side. Discount may not be valid on certain items or with any other offers. Valid for one purchase per store.

Expires 12/31/99.

Obtain your discount by redeeming this ***Buying Retail Is Stupid!—Chicago*** coupon at the store listed on opposite side. Discount may not be valid on certain items or with any other offers. Valid for one purchase per store.

Expires 12/31/99.

Obtain your discount by redeeming this ***Buying Retail Is Stupid!—Chicago*** coupon at the store listed on opposite side. Discount may not be valid on certain items or with any other offers. Valid for one purchase per store.

Expires 12/31/99.

Obtain your discount by redeeming this ***Buying Retail Is Stupid!—Chicago*** coupon at the store listed on opposite side. Discount may not be valid on certain items or with any other offers. Valid for one purchase per store.

Expires 12/31/99.

Obtain your discount by redeeming this ***Buying Retail Is Stupid!—Chicago*** coupon at the store listed on opposite side. Discount may not be valid on certain items or with any other offers. Valid for one purchase per store.

Expires 12/31/99.

BUYING RETAIL IS STUPID!—CHICAGO
Chicago's Discount Cleaner
30% Off Regular Price on Four or More Dry-Cleaned Garments
Redeemed:

BUYING RETAIL IS STUPID!—CHICAGO
Children's Gift Outlet
10% Off Purchase
Redeemed:

BUYING RETAIL IS STUPID!—CHICAGO
Corner Health Foods
10% Off Purchase
Redeemed:

BUYING RETAIL IS STUPID!—CHICAGO
Cyber Exchange Computer Centers
Free Software; No Minimum Purchase
Redeemed:

BUYING RETAIL IS STUPID!—CHICAGO
Daveco Dollars and Cents
$1 Off on Purchase of $10 or More
Redeemed:

BUYING RETAIL IS STUPID!—CHICAGO
Designer Resale of Chicago, Inc.
10% Off Purchase
Redeemed:

Obtain your discount by redeeming this ***Buying Retail Is Stupid!—Chicago*** coupon at the store listed on opposite side. Discount may not be valid on certain items or with any other offers. Valid for one purchase per store.

Expires 12/31/99.

Obtain your discount by redeeming this ***Buying Retail Is Stupid!—Chicago*** coupon at the store listed on opposite side. Discount may not be valid on certain items or with any other offers. Valid for one purchase per store.

Expires 12/31/99.

Obtain your discount by redeeming this ***Buying Retail Is Stupid!—Chicago*** coupon at the store listed on opposite side. Discount may not be valid on certain items or with any other offers. Valid for one purchase per store.

Expires 12/31/99.

Obtain your discount by redeeming this ***Buying Retail Is Stupid!—Chicago*** coupon at the store listed on opposite side. Discount may not be valid on certain items or with any other offers. Valid for one purchase per store.

Expires 12/31/99.

Obtain your discount by redeeming this ***Buying Retail Is Stupid!—Chicago*** coupon at the store listed on opposite side. Discount may not be valid on certain items or with any other offers. Valid for one purchase per store.

Expires 12/31/99.

Obtain your discount by redeeming this ***Buying Retail Is Stupid!—Chicago*** coupon at the store listed on opposite side. Discount may not be valid on certain items or with any other offers. Valid for one purchase per store.

Expires 12/31/99.

BUYING RETAIL IS STUPID!—CHICAGO
Disgraceland
10% Off on Purchase of $25 or More (Not Valid on Sale Items)
Redeemed:

BUYING RETAIL IS STUPID!—CHICAGO
Edward Don Outlet Store
20% Off Purchase Plus Gift
($5 Minimum Purchase; One Gift per Customer)
Redeemed:

BUYING RETAIL IS STUPID!—CHICAGO
Eileen Fisher Outlet
10% Off Purchase
Redeemed:

BUYING RETAIL IS STUPID!—CHICAGO
Eli's Cheesecake World
10% Off Purchase ($10 Minimum Purchase)
Redeemed:

BUYING RETAIL IS STUPID!—CHICAGO
Elite Audio
10% Off on Minimum Purchase of $100
Redeemed:

BUYING RETAIL IS STUPID!—CHICAGO
Entre Nous
5% Off Purchase
Redeemed:

Obtain your discount by redeeming this ***Buying Retail Is Stupid!—Chicago*** coupon at the store listed on opposite side. Discount may not be valid on certain items or with any other offers. Valid for one purchase per store.

Expires 12/31/99.

Obtain your discount by redeeming this ***Buying Retail Is Stupid!—Chicago*** coupon at the store listed on opposite side. Discount may not be valid on certain items or with any other offers. Valid for one purchase per store.

Expires 12/31/99.

Obtain your discount by redeeming this ***Buying Retail Is Stupid!—Chicago*** coupon at the store listed on opposite side. Discount may not be valid on certain items or with any other offers. Valid for one purchase per store.

Expires 12/31/99.

Obtain your discount by redeeming this ***Buying Retail Is Stupid!—Chicago*** coupon at the store listed on opposite side. Discount may not be valid on certain items or with any other offers. Valid for one purchase per store.

Expires 12/31/99.

Obtain your discount by redeeming this ***Buying Retail Is Stupid!—Chicago*** coupon at the store listed on opposite side. Discount may not be valid on certain items or with any other offers. Valid for one purchase per store.

Expires 12/31/99.

Obtain your discount by redeeming this ***Buying Retail Is Stupid!—Chicago*** coupon at the store listed on opposite side. Discount may not be valid on certain items or with any other offers. Valid for one purchase per store.

Expires 12/31/99.

BUYING RETAIL IS STUPID!—CHICAGO
Eurodirect International
Free Tie with Purchase of Suit, Sports Coat, Leather, or Pants
Redeemed:

BUYING RETAIL IS STUPID!—CHICAGO
Expectations Outlet
10% Off on $50 Minimum Purchase
Redeemed:

BUYING RETAIL IS STUPID!—CHICAGO
Exposition Carpet Co., Inc.
10% Off Purchase
Redeemed:

BUYING RETAIL IS STUPID!—CHICAGO
Fatboys Musical Outlet
10% Off Purchase (Not Valid on Orange-Tagged or Half-Off Items)
Redeemed:

BUYING RETAIL IS STUPID!—CHICAGO
Field's Piano Super Warehouse
Free Delivery, Four Free Lessons with $300 Minimum Purchase
Redeemed:

BUYING RETAIL IS STUPID!—CHICAGO
Fitness Factory Outlet
10% Off on $100 Minimum Purchase of Regularly Priced Merchandise
(Floor Models Not Eligible for Coupon Discount)
Redeemed:

Obtain your discount by redeeming this ***Buying Retail Is Stupid!—Chicago*** coupon at the store listed on opposite side. Discount may not be valid on certain items or with any other offers. Valid for one purchase per store.

Expires 12/31/99.

Obtain your discount by redeeming this ***Buying Retail Is Stupid!—Chicago*** coupon at the store listed on opposite side. Discount may not be valid on certain items or with any other offers. Valid for one purchase per store.

Expires 12/31/99.

Obtain your discount by redeeming this ***Buying Retail Is Stupid!—Chicago*** coupon at the store listed on opposite side. Discount may not be valid on certain items or with any other offers. Valid for one purchase per store.

Expires 12/31/99.

Obtain your discount by redeeming this ***Buying Retail Is Stupid!—Chicago*** coupon at the store listed on opposite side. Discount may not be valid on certain items or with any other offers. Valid for one purchase per store.

Expires 12/31/99.

Obtain your discount by redeeming this ***Buying Retail Is Stupid!—Chicago*** coupon at the store listed on opposite side. Discount may not be valid on certain items or with any other offers. Valid for one purchase per store.

Expires 12/31/99.

Obtain your discount by redeeming this ***Buying Retail Is Stupid!—Chicago*** coupon at the store listed on opposite side. Discount may not be valid on certain items or with any other offers. Valid for one purchase per store.

Expires 12/31/99.

Buying Retail Is Stupid!—Chicago
Flower Bucket, Inc.
Six Free Carnations with $10 Minimum Purchase
Redeemed:

Buying Retail Is Stupid!—Chicago
Frame Factory
10% Off Purchase (Not Valid with Other Coupons)
Redeemed:

Buying Retail Is Stupid!—Chicago
Gabriel's Trumpet, Inc.
10% Off Purchase (Sale Items Excluded)
Redeemed:

Buying Retail Is Stupid!—Chicago
Gently Used Office Furniture
10% Off Purchase; No Minimum
Redeemed:

Buying Retail Is Stupid!—Chicago
Golf Clubs for Less
$25 Off on Any Set of Woods
Redeemed:

Buying Retail Is Stupid!—Chicago
Gone to Pot
5% Off Purchase
Redeemed:

Obtain your discount by redeeming this ***Buying Retail Is Stupid!—Chicago*** coupon at the store listed on opposite side. Discount may not be valid on certain items or with any other offers. Valid for one purchase per store.

Expires 12/31/99.

Obtain your discount by redeeming this ***Buying Retail Is Stupid!—Chicago*** coupon at the store listed on opposite side. Discount may not be valid on certain items or with any other offers. Valid for one purchase per store.

Expires 12/31/99.

Obtain your discount by redeeming this ***Buying Retail Is Stupid!—Chicago*** coupon at the store listed on opposite side. Discount may not be valid on certain items or with any other offers. Valid for one purchase per store.

Expires 12/31/99.

Obtain your discount by redeeming this ***Buying Retail Is Stupid!—Chicago*** coupon at the store listed on opposite side. Discount may not be valid on certain items or with any other offers. Valid for one purchase per store.

Expires 12/31/99.

Obtain your discount by redeeming this ***Buying Retail Is Stupid!—Chicago*** coupon at the store listed on opposite side. Discount may not be valid on certain items or with any other offers. Valid for one purchase per store.

Expires 12/31/99.

Obtain your discount by redeeming this ***Buying Retail Is Stupid!—Chicago*** coupon at the store listed on opposite side. Discount may not be valid on certain items or with any other offers. Valid for one purchase per store.

Expires 12/31/99.

Buying Retail Is Stupid!—Chicago
Graham Industries Home Furnishings
10% Off Purchase; No Minimum
Redeemed:

Buying Retail Is Stupid!—Chicago
Grand Appliance
$20 Off on Purchase of $350 or More
Redeemed:

Buying Retail Is Stupid!—Chicago
Great Dollar Value
10% Off on $25 Minimum Purchase
Redeemed:

Buying Retail Is Stupid!—Chicago
Home 1-2-3
10% Off Purchase (Excluding Sale Items)
Redeemed:

Buying Retail Is Stupid!—Chicago
House of Teak Scandinavian
5% Off Purchase
Redeemed:

Buying Retail Is Stupid!—Chicago
House Walk Furniture
5% Off Purchase
Redeemed:

Obtain your discount by redeeming this ***Buying Retail Is Stupid!—Chicago*** coupon at the store listed on opposite side. Discount may not be valid on certain items or with any other offers. Valid for one purchase per store.

Expires 12/31/99.

Obtain your discount by redeeming this ***Buying Retail Is Stupid!—Chicago*** coupon at the store listed on opposite side. Discount may not be valid on certain items or with any other offers. Valid for one purchase per store.

Expires 12/31/99.

Obtain your discount by redeeming this ***Buying Retail Is Stupid!—Chicago*** coupon at the store listed on opposite side. Discount may not be valid on certain items or with any other offers. Valid for one purchase per store.

Expires 12/31/99.

Obtain your discount by redeeming this ***Buying Retail Is Stupid!—Chicago*** coupon at the store listed on opposite side. Discount may not be valid on certain items or with any other offers. Valid for one purchase per store.

Expires 12/31/99.

Obtain your discount by redeeming this ***Buying Retail Is Stupid!—Chicago*** coupon at the store listed on opposite side. Discount may not be valid on certain items or with any other offers. Valid for one purchase per store.

Expires 12/31/99.

Obtain your discount by redeeming this ***Buying Retail Is Stupid!—Chicago*** coupon at the store listed on opposite side. Discount may not be valid on certain items or with any other offers. Valid for one purchase per store.

Expires 12/31/99.

Buying Retail Is Stupid!—Chicago
Hufford Furniture
10% Off Purchase (Excluding Clearance Merchandise)
Redeemed:

Buying Retail Is Stupid!—Chicago
I. B. Diffision: The Warehouse
10% Off Purchase
Redeemed:

Buying Retail Is Stupid!—Chicago
I Do, Inc.
$25 Off Veil with Gown Purchase;
Does Not Apply with Other Discount Incentives
Redeemed:

Buying Retail Is Stupid!—Chicago
Imperial Clothiers
5% Off Purchase of $100 or More
Redeemed:

Buying Retail Is Stupid!—Chicago
Interiors on Consignment
10% Off on First Purchase Only
Redeemed:

Buying Retail Is Stupid!—Chicago
International Antiques
10% Off Purchase
Redeemed:

Obtain your discount by redeeming this ***Buying Retail Is Stupid!—Chicago*** coupon at the store listed on opposite side. Discount may not be valid on certain items or with any other offers. Valid for one purchase per store.

Expires 12/31/99.

Obtain your discount by redeeming this ***Buying Retail Is Stupid!—Chicago*** coupon at the store listed on opposite side. Discount may not be valid on certain items or with any other offers. Valid for one purchase per store.

Expires 12/31/99.

Obtain your discount by redeeming this ***Buying Retail Is Stupid!—Chicago*** coupon at the store listed on opposite side. Discount may not be valid on certain items or with any other offers. Valid for one purchase per store.

Expires 12/31/99.

Obtain your discount by redeeming this ***Buying Retail Is Stupid!—Chicago*** coupon at the store listed on opposite side. Discount may not be valid on certain items or with any other offers. Valid for one purchase per store.

Expires 12/31/99.

Obtain your discount by redeeming this ***Buying Retail Is Stupid!—Chicago*** coupon at the store listed on opposite side. Discount may not be valid on certain items or with any other offers. Valid for one purchase per store.

Expires 12/31/99.

Obtain your discount by redeeming this ***Buying Retail Is Stupid!—Chicago*** coupon at the store listed on opposite side. Discount may not be valid on certain items or with any other offers. Valid for one purchase per store.

Expires 12/31/99.

BUYING RETAIL IS STUPID!—CHICAGO
IRCO Art Products Co., Ltd.
10% Discount; No Minimum Purchase
Redeemed:

BUYING RETAIL IS STUPID!—CHICAGO
Irv's Clothing
10% Off Purchase
Redeemed:

BUYING RETAIL IS STUPID!—CHICAGO
Jazz Record Mart
10% Off Purchase
Redeemed:

BUYING RETAIL IS STUPID!—CHICAGO
King of Tile, Inc.
10% Off Purchase
Redeemed:

BUYING RETAIL IS STUPID!—CHICAGO
Kosmic Kandles
10% Off on Purchase of $10 or More
Redeemed:

BUYING RETAIL IS STUPID!—CHICAGO
Krasny & Company
10% Off Purchase
Redeemed:

Obtain your discount by redeeming this ***Buying Retail Is Stupid!—Chicago*** coupon at the store listed on opposite side. Discount may not be valid on certain items or with any other offers. Valid for one purchase per store.

Expires 12/31/99.

Obtain your discount by redeeming this ***Buying Retail Is Stupid!—Chicago*** coupon at the store listed on opposite side. Discount may not be valid on certain items or with any other offers. Valid for one purchase per store.

Expires 12/31/99.

Obtain your discount by redeeming this ***Buying Retail Is Stupid!—Chicago*** coupon at the store listed on opposite side. Discount may not be valid on certain items or with any other offers. Valid for one purchase per store.

Expires 12/31/99.

Obtain your discount by redeeming this ***Buying Retail Is Stupid!—Chicago*** coupon at the store listed on opposite side. Discount may not be valid on certain items or with any other offers. Valid for one purchase per store.

Expires 12/31/99.

Obtain your discount by redeeming this ***Buying Retail Is Stupid!—Chicago*** coupon at the store listed on opposite side. Discount may not be valid on certain items or with any other offers. Valid for one purchase per store.

Expires 12/31/99.

Obtain your discount by redeeming this ***Buying Retail Is Stupid!—Chicago*** coupon at the store listed on opposite side. Discount may not be valid on certain items or with any other offers. Valid for one purchase per store.

Expires 12/31/99.

Buying Retail Is Stupid!—Chicago
L&L Textile Co.
5% Off Purchase; No Minimum
Redeemed:

Buying Retail Is Stupid!—Chicago
Lady Joyce Co.
10% Off Purchase
Redeemed:

Buying Retail Is Stupid!—Chicago
Lamp Outlet
10% Off Purchase
Redeemed:

Buying Retail Is Stupid!—Chicago
Leather Outlet
10% Off Purchase; No Minimum
Redeemed:

Buying Retail Is Stupid!—Chicago
Leathermode
Gift with Purchase of $150 or More
(Not Valid on Layaways, Gift Certificates, Previously Purchased Merchandise, or with Any Other Offer)
Redeemed:

Buying Retail Is Stupid!—Chicago
Lincoln Antique Mall
10% Off on Items Priced at $20 or More
Redeemed:

Obtain your discount by redeeming this ***Buying Retail Is Stupid!—Chicago*** coupon at the store listed on opposite side. Discount may not be valid on certain items or with any other offers. Valid for one purchase per store.
Expires 12/31/99.

Obtain your discount by redeeming this ***Buying Retail Is Stupid!—Chicago*** coupon at the store listed on opposite side. Discount may not be valid on certain items or with any other offers. Valid for one purchase per store.
Expires 12/31/99.

Obtain your discount by redeeming this ***Buying Retail Is Stupid!—Chicago*** coupon at the store listed on opposite side. Discount may not be valid on certain items or with any other offers. Valid for one purchase per store.
Expires 12/31/99.

Obtain your discount by redeeming this ***Buying Retail Is Stupid!—Chicago*** coupon at the store listed on opposite side. Discount may not be valid on certain items or with any other offers. Valid for one purchase per store.
Expires 12/31/99.

Obtain your discount by redeeming this ***Buying Retail Is Stupid!—Chicago*** coupon at the store listed on opposite side. Discount may not be valid on certain items or with any other offers. Valid for one purchase per store.
Expires 12/31/99.

Obtain your discount by redeeming this ***Buying Retail Is Stupid!—Chicago*** coupon at the store listed on opposite side. Discount may not be valid on certain items or with any other offers. Valid for one purchase per store.
Expires 12/31/99.

BUYING RETAIL IS STUPID!—CHICAGO
Lit Art
50% Off Purchase
Redeemed:

BUYING RETAIL IS STUPID!—CHICAGO
Long Grove Confectionary Co. Outlet
10% Off Purchase
Redeemed:

BUYING RETAIL IS STUPID!—CHICAGO
Look What I Found
Free Artisan-Made Earrings with Purchase of $20 or More
Redeemed:

BUYING RETAIL IS STUPID!—CHICAGO
Malnekoff & Son Jewelers
10% Off; No Minimum Purchase
Redeemed:

BUYING RETAIL IS STUPID!—CHICAGO
Marjen Furniture
$20 Off on Any Purchase of $200 or More
Redeemed:

BUYING RETAIL IS STUPID!—CHICAGO
Marjen of Chicago
Free CD Rack with Purchase of $99 or More
Redeemed:

Obtain your discount by redeeming this ***Buying Retail Is Stupid!—Chicago*** coupon at the store listed on opposite side. Discount may not be valid on certain items or with any other offers. Valid for one purchase per store.

Expires 12/31/99.

Obtain your discount by redeeming this ***Buying Retail Is Stupid!—Chicago*** coupon at the store listed on opposite side. Discount may not be valid on certain items or with any other offers. Valid for one purchase per store.

Expires 12/31/99.

Obtain your discount by redeeming this ***Buying Retail Is Stupid!—Chicago*** coupon at the store listed on opposite side. Discount may not be valid on certain items or with any other offers. Valid for one purchase per store.

Expires 12/31/99.

Obtain your discount by redeeming this ***Buying Retail Is Stupid!—Chicago*** coupon at the store listed on opposite side. Discount may not be valid on certain items or with any other offers. Valid for one purchase per store.

Expires 12/31/99.

Obtain your discount by redeeming this ***Buying Retail Is Stupid!—Chicago*** coupon at the store listed on opposite side. Discount may not be valid on certain items or with any other offers. Valid for one purchase per store.

Expires 12/31/99.

Obtain your discount by redeeming this ***Buying Retail Is Stupid!—Chicago*** coupon at the store listed on opposite side. Discount may not be valid on certain items or with any other offers. Valid for one purchase per store.

Expires 12/31/99.

BUYING RETAIL IS STUPID!—CHICAGO
Marlo Warehouse Outlet
$5 Off on Purchase of $25 or More
Redeemed:

BUYING RETAIL IS STUPID!—CHICAGO
Max Gerber
10% Off Purchase
Redeemed:

BUYING RETAIL IS STUPID!—CHICAGO
Midwest Discount Yarns
10% Off Purchase
Redeemed:

BUYING RETAIL IS STUPID!—CHICAGO
Montalbano Majestic Furniture
10% Off; or $300 Oil Painting with Any Sofa Set; or $500 Pair of Lamps with Any Bedroom Set (Not Valid on Sale Prices or with Other Coupons)
Redeemed:

BUYING RETAIL IS STUPID!—CHICAGO
Moo & Oink
5% Off on Purchase of $10 or More
Redeemed:

BUYING RETAIL IS STUPID!—CHICAGO
Mort Cooper Ltd.
Free Silk Tie ($40 Value) **with Purchase of Suit**
Redeemed:

Obtain your discount by redeeming this ***Buying Retail Is Stupid!—Chicago*** coupon at the store listed on opposite side. Discount may not be valid on certain items or with any other offers. Valid for one purchase per store.

Expires 12/31/99.

Obtain your discount by redeeming this ***Buying Retail Is Stupid!—Chicago*** coupon at the store listed on opposite side. Discount may not be valid on certain items or with any other offers. Valid for one purchase per store.

Expires 12/31/99.

Obtain your discount by redeeming this ***Buying Retail Is Stupid!—Chicago*** coupon at the store listed on opposite side. Discount may not be valid on certain items or with any other offers. Valid for one purchase per store.

Expires 12/31/99.

Obtain your discount by redeeming this ***Buying Retail Is Stupid!—Chicago*** coupon at the store listed on opposite side. Discount may not be valid on certain items or with any other offers. Valid for one purchase per store.

Expires 12/31/99.

Obtain your discount by redeeming this ***Buying Retail Is Stupid!—Chicago*** coupon at the store listed on opposite side. Discount may not be valid on certain items or with any other offers. Valid for one purchase per store.

Expires 12/31/99.

Obtain your discount by redeeming this ***Buying Retail Is Stupid!—Chicago*** coupon at the store listed on opposite side. Discount may not be valid on certain items or with any other offers. Valid for one purchase per store.

Expires 12/31/99.

BUYING RETAIL IS STUPID!—CHICAGO
The Music Gallery
20% Off Purchase
Redeemed:

BUYING RETAIL IS STUPID!—CHICAGO
Music Recyclery
20% Off Purchase
Redeemed:

BUYING RETAIL IS STUPID!—CHICAGO
My Mother's Closet
10% Off Purchase
Redeemed:

BUYING RETAIL IS STUPID!—CHICAGO
My Sister's Closet
10% Off Purchase (Not Valid During Storewide Sale)
Redeemed:

BUYING RETAIL IS STUPID!—CHICAGO
Naked Furniture
10% Off on Regularly Priced Items; Labor Excluded
Redeemed:

BUYING RETAIL IS STUPID!—CHICAGO
Nine Months New
15% Off on Any One Item, Excluding Children's Furniture and Breast Pumps
Redeemed:

Obtain your discount by redeeming this ***Buying Retail Is Stupid!—Chicago*** coupon at the store listed on opposite side. Discount may not be valid on certain items or with any other offers. Valid for one purchase per store.
Expires 12/31/99.

Obtain your discount by redeeming this ***Buying Retail Is Stupid!—Chicago*** coupon at the store listed on opposite side. Discount may not be valid on certain items or with any other offers. Valid for one purchase per store.
Expires 12/31/99.

Obtain your discount by redeeming this ***Buying Retail Is Stupid!—Chicago*** coupon at the store listed on opposite side. Discount may not be valid on certain items or with any other offers. Valid for one purchase per store.
Expires 12/31/99.

Obtain your discount by redeeming this ***Buying Retail Is Stupid!—Chicago*** coupon at the store listed on opposite side. Discount may not be valid on certain items or with any other offers. Valid for one purchase per store.
Expires 12/31/99.

Obtain your discount by redeeming this ***Buying Retail Is Stupid!—Chicago*** coupon at the store listed on opposite side. Discount may not be valid on certain items or with any other offers. Valid for one purchase per store.
Expires 12/31/99.

Obtain your discount by redeeming this ***Buying Retail Is Stupid!—Chicago*** coupon at the store listed on opposite side. Discount may not be valid on certain items or with any other offers. Valid for one purchase per store.
Expires 12/31/99.

BUYING RETAIL IS STUPID!—CHICAGO
The Outlet Store
10% Off Purchase
Redeemed:

BUYING RETAIL IS STUPID!—CHICAGO
Payless Appliance Warehouse, Inc.
10% Off on Any Purchase of $275 or More
Redeemed:

BUYING RETAIL IS STUPID!—CHICAGO
PDT Printing
10% Off; No Minimum Purchase
Redeemed:

BUYING RETAIL IS STUPID!—CHICAGO
Pickle Piano Company
25% Off on New Items; 10% Off on Used Items
Redeemed:

BUYING RETAIL IS STUPID!—CHICAGO
Plass Appliance Outlet Store
Normal Delivery and Installation Free with Purchase; Excludes Built-In Appliance Installation
Redeemed:

BUYING RETAIL IS STUPID!—CHICAGO
Right-On-Futon
10% Off Any Futon Cover with Purchase of Any Futon or Frame
(Not Valid with Other Discounts or on Sale Items)
Redeemed:

Obtain your discount by redeeming this ***Buying Retail Is Stupid!—Chicago*** coupon at the store listed on opposite side. Discount may not be valid on certain items or with any other offers. Valid for one purchase per store.

Expires 12/31/99.

Obtain your discount by redeeming this ***Buying Retail Is Stupid!—Chicago*** coupon at the store listed on opposite side. Discount may not be valid on certain items or with any other offers. Valid for one purchase per store.

Expires 12/31/99.

Obtain your discount by redeeming this ***Buying Retail Is Stupid!—Chicago*** coupon at the store listed on opposite side. Discount may not be valid on certain items or with any other offers. Valid for one purchase per store.

Expires 12/31/99.

Obtain your discount by redeeming this ***Buying Retail Is Stupid!—Chicago*** coupon at the store listed on opposite side. Discount may not be valid on certain items or with any other offers. Valid for one purchase per store.

Expires 12/31/99.

Obtain your discount by redeeming this ***Buying Retail Is Stupid!—Chicago*** coupon at the store listed on opposite side. Discount may not be valid on certain items or with any other offers. Valid for one purchase per store.

Expires 12/31/99.

Obtain your discount by redeeming this ***Buying Retail Is Stupid!—Chicago*** coupon at the store listed on opposite side. Discount may not be valid on certain items or with any other offers. Valid for one purchase per store.

Expires 12/31/99.

BUYING RETAIL IS STUPID!—CHICAGO
Sagrani Clothiers
10% Off Purchase
Redeemed:

BUYING RETAIL IS STUPID!—CHICAGO
Saturday Audio Exchange
Free Headphones with Purchase of Stereo System
Redeemed:

BUYING RETAIL IS STUPID!—CHICAGO
Second Vogue
10% Off Purchase
Redeemed:

BUYING RETAIL IS STUPID!—CHICAGO
Sherwyn's Health Food Shop
$2 Off Purchase
Redeemed:

BUYING RETAIL IS STUPID!—CHICAGO
Singer Factory Distributor
Carrying Case Free with New-Machine Purchase
Redeemed:

BUYING RETAIL IS STUPID!—CHICAGO
Sleep Centers Waterbeds and Futons to Go
10% Off Purchase
Redeemed:

Obtain your discount by redeeming this ***Buying Retail Is Stupid!—Chicago*** coupon at the store listed on opposite side. Discount may not be valid on certain items or with any other offers. Valid for one purchase per store.

Expires 12/31/99.

Obtain your discount by redeeming this ***Buying Retail Is Stupid!—Chicago*** coupon at the store listed on opposite side. Discount may not be valid on certain items or with any other offers. Valid for one purchase per store.

Expires 12/31/99.

Obtain your discount by redeeming this ***Buying Retail Is Stupid!—Chicago*** coupon at the store listed on opposite side. Discount may not be valid on certain items or with any other offers. Valid for one purchase per store.

Expires 12/31/99.

Obtain your discount by redeeming this ***Buying Retail Is Stupid!—Chicago*** coupon at the store listed on opposite side. Discount may not be valid on certain items or with any other offers. Valid for one purchase per store.

Expires 12/31/99.

Obtain your discount by redeeming this ***Buying Retail Is Stupid!—Chicago*** coupon at the store listed on opposite side. Discount may not be valid on certain items or with any other offers. Valid for one purchase per store.

Expires 12/31/99.

Obtain your discount by redeeming this ***Buying Retail Is Stupid!—Chicago*** coupon at the store listed on opposite side. Discount may not be valid on certain items or with any other offers. Valid for one purchase per store.

Expires 12/31/99.

Buying Retail Is Stupid!—Chicago
Smart Creations Inc.
Free Pair of Earrings with Purchase of $15 or More; One Free Pair per Customer
Redeemed:

Buying Retail Is Stupid!—Chicago
Steve Austin
15% Off Plus Free Necktie with Suit Purchase
Redeemed:

Buying Retail Is Stupid!—Chicago
Style & Substance
10% Off Purchase
Redeemed:

Buying Retail Is Stupid!—Chicago
Suitsmart
10% Off Purchase (No Discount on Alterations)
Redeemed:

Buying Retail Is Stupid!—Chicago
Sun Harvest Market
10% Off on Purchase of $25 or More
Redeemed:

Buying Retail Is Stupid!—Chicago
Sun King Optical
$10 Off on Purchase over $50; $20 Off on Purchase over $150
(Certain Restrictions Apply)
Redeemed:

Obtain your discount by redeeming this ***Buying Retail Is Stupid!—Chicago*** coupon at the store listed on opposite side. Discount may not be valid on certain items or with any other offers. Valid for one purchase per store.

Expires 12/31/99.

Obtain your discount by redeeming this ***Buying Retail Is Stupid!—Chicago*** coupon at the store listed on opposite side. Discount may not be valid on certain items or with any other offers. Valid for one purchase per store.

Expires 12/31/99.

Obtain your discount by redeeming this ***Buying Retail Is Stupid!—Chicago*** coupon at the store listed on opposite side. Discount may not be valid on certain items or with any other offers. Valid for one purchase per store.

Expires 12/31/99.

Obtain your discount by redeeming this ***Buying Retail Is Stupid!—Chicago*** coupon at the store listed on opposite side. Discount may not be valid on certain items or with any other offers. Valid for one purchase per store.

Expires 12/31/99.

Obtain your discount by redeeming this ***Buying Retail Is Stupid!—Chicago*** coupon at the store listed on opposite side. Discount may not be valid on certain items or with any other offers. Valid for one purchase per store.

Expires 12/31/99.

Obtain your discount by redeeming this ***Buying Retail Is Stupid!—Chicago*** coupon at the store listed on opposite side. Discount may not be valid on certain items or with any other offers. Valid for one purchase per store.

Expires 12/31/99.

BUYING RETAIL IS STUPID!—CHICAGO
Swatch Outlet
Gift of Swatch Guard If You Buy One or More Swatches at Any Price
Redeemed:

BUYING RETAIL IS STUPID!—CHICAGO
Threads, Etc.
15% Off Purchase
Redeemed:

BUYING RETAIL IS STUPID!—CHICAGO
Tiny Tots Turnaround
10% Off Purchase; No Minimum
Redeemed:

BUYING RETAIL IS STUPID!—CHICAGO
Trendy Tots Resale Shop
$5 Off on Purchase of $25 or More
Redeemed:

BUYING RETAIL IS STUPID!—CHICAGO
20th Century TV & Stereo Center
10% Off Purchase
Redeemed:

BUYING RETAIL IS STUPID!—CHICAGO
U.S. Toy Co./Constructive Playthings
10% Off (Excludes Sale or Closeout Merchandise)
Redeemed:

Obtain your discount by redeeming this ***Buying Retail Is Stupid!—Chicago*** coupon at the store listed on opposite side. Discount may not be valid on certain items or with any other offers. Valid for one purchase per store.

Expires 12/31/99.

Obtain your discount by redeeming this ***Buying Retail Is Stupid!—Chicago*** coupon at the store listed on opposite side. Discount may not be valid on certain items or with any other offers. Valid for one purchase per store.

Expires 12/31/99.

Obtain your discount by redeeming this ***Buying Retail Is Stupid!—Chicago*** coupon at the store listed on opposite side. Discount may not be valid on certain items or with any other offers. Valid for one purchase per store.

Expires 12/31/99.

Obtain your discount by redeeming this ***Buying Retail Is Stupid!—Chicago*** coupon at the store listed on opposite side. Discount may not be valid on certain items or with any other offers. Valid for one purchase per store.

Expires 12/31/99.

Obtain your discount by redeeming this ***Buying Retail Is Stupid!—Chicago*** coupon at the store listed on opposite side. Discount may not be valid on certain items or with any other offers. Valid for one purchase per store.

Expires 12/31/99.

Obtain your discount by redeeming this ***Buying Retail Is Stupid!—Chicago*** coupon at the store listed on opposite side. Discount may not be valid on certain items or with any other offers. Valid for one purchase per store.

Expires 12/31/99.

BUYING RETAIL IS STUPID!—CHICAGO
Valentine & Son, Inc.
10% Off on Purchase of $50 or More
Redeemed:

BUYING RETAIL IS STUPID!—CHICAGO
Vertical Blinds Factory
10% Off on Purchase of $299 or More
Redeemed:

BUYING RETAIL IS STUPID!—CHICAGO
Vitamin House, Inc.
20% Off Purchase
Redeemed:

BUYING RETAIL IS STUPID!—CHICAGO
Wholesale Carpet Designs, Inc.
$3 Off per Square Yard (1 Square Yard Minimum Purchase)
Redeemed:

BUYING RETAIL IS STUPID!—CHICAGO
Wickes Furniture Clearance & Budget Center
Gift with Every Purchase
Redeemed:

BUYING RETAIL IS STUPID!—CHICAGO
Wine Discount Center
Free Vacu Vin Vacuum Wine Server Kit with Purchase of $10 or More
(One per Family)
Redeemed:

Obtain your discount by redeeming this ***Buying Retail Is Stupid!—Chicago*** coupon at the store listed on opposite side. Discount may not be valid on certain items or with any other offers. Valid for one purchase per store.

Expires 12/31/99.

Obtain your discount by redeeming this ***Buying Retail Is Stupid!—Chicago*** coupon at the store listed on opposite side. Discount may not be valid on certain items or with any other offers. Valid for one purchase per store.

Expires 12/31/99.

Obtain your discount by redeeming this ***Buying Retail Is Stupid!—Chicago*** coupon at the store listed on opposite side. Discount may not be valid on certain items or with any other offers. Valid for one purchase per store.

Expires 12/31/99.

Obtain your discount by redeeming this ***Buying Retail Is Stupid!—Chicago*** coupon at the store listed on opposite side. Discount may not be valid on certain items or with any other offers. Valid for one purchase per store.

Expires 12/31/99.

Obtain your discount by redeeming this ***Buying Retail Is Stupid!—Chicago*** coupon at the store listed on opposite side. Discount may not be valid on certain items or with any other offers. Valid for one purchase per store.

Expires 12/31/99.

Obtain your discount by redeeming this ***Buying Retail Is Stupid!—Chicago*** coupon at the store listed on opposite side. Discount may not be valid on certain items or with any other offers. Valid for one purchase per store.

Expires 12/31/99.

Buying Retail Is Stupid!—Chicago
Worldwide Diamonds

Free Bottle of Jewelry Cleaner with Purchase

Redeemed:

Buying Retail Is Stupid!—Chicago
Wrigleyville Antique Mall

10% Off Purchase of $10 or More

Redeemed:

Obtain your discount by redeeming this ***Buying Retail Is Stupid!—Chicago*** coupon at the store listed on opposite side. Discount may not be valid on certain items or with any other offers. Valid for one purchase per store.
Expires 12/31/99.

Obtain your discount by redeeming this ***Buying Retail Is Stupid!—Chicago*** coupon at the store listed on opposite side. Discount may not be valid on certain items or with any other offers. Valid for one purchase per store.
Expires 12/31/99.

About the Authors

Trisha King and **Deborah Newmark**, two of America's leading bargain-shopping experts, are coauthors of *Buying Retail Is Stupid!—Southern California*, a bestseller since 1989, called "the shoppers bible" by *Orange Coast* magazine.

King and Newmark write a highly popular bargain column, which has appeared weekly in the *Los Angeles Daily News* since 1990. Their column has developed a wide and loyal readership. They have been frequent guests on major TV and radio shows such as *Fox News, KABC Talk Radio, KNX/CBS, Live in L.A., The Vicki Lawrence Show, The Susan Powter Show, The Wave,* and many others. Trisha was the weekly *Fox News* bargain reporter in Los Angeles for two years.

Known for their energetic, entrepreneurial, and engaging personalities, Trisha and Deborah are dedicated to providing consumers with information on where and how to buy more for less, stretch their paychecks, and get true value for every dollar spent. They are also the coauthors of *Buying Retail Is Stupid!—USA*, which allows a wider consumer public to profit from the work of these two bargain experts.

Barbara Jacobs, the coauthor of *Buying Retail Is Stupid!—Chicago*, is a professional writer, corporate and marketing communications consultant . . . and veteran bargain shopper. The daughter of a Baltimore retailer, she emigrated west over 20 years ago, worked as a journalist and public relations executive, and now counts many Fortune 500 companies as her clients. Barbara writes regularly for *Woman's Day Decorating Ideas* and other national publications. Her major leisure activity includes scouring flea markets and antique shows across the United States for best buys—from a set of '50s aluminum drinkware to an undiscovered Stickley rocking chair.